Business Valuation

Business Valuation: Real-World Applications in Emerging Markets serves as a useful guide for those who want to learn business valuation methodology from scratch, applying corporate finance theory to real-world cases. Based on the author's extensive professional and teaching experience, this text illustrates how basic corporate finance principles and theories shape decisions made by market practitioners and offers an in-depth discussion of various business valuation methods and models with a focus on emerging markets.

By adopting a step-by-step approach, it helps the reader to gain a deeper understanding of this topic, starting with an explanation of essential concepts before gradually moving on to more advanced valuation techniques. To help the reader navigate common valuation processes, brief real-world examples are woven throughout the text with the final part containing four real valuation cases on which the author served as the appraiser. Vital learning and teaching features include: key terminologies; discussion questions; boxed examples and real-world cases; mathematical appendices; and a suite of supplementary instructor's resources.

This will be a valuable textbook for students taking advanced undergraduate and postgraduate-level courses in business valuation, as well as a practical guide for appraisers.

Guillermo L. Dumrauf is a senior expert in valuation and a part-time professor at Universidad del CEMA, Argentina, where he teaches courses on valuation and econometrics at the bachelor's and master's levels of finance. He possesses more than 30 years of academic and practical experience in the field, having taught valuation at more than 50 universities and presented and discussed papers at finance conferences. He has authored several textbooks on corporate finance, fixed income, macroeconomics, investments, and applied mathematics to finance. Guillermo obtained his PhD in Economics from the University of Buenos Aires and serves as a director of a Brazilian company. Writing, teaching, and advising are his passions.

Business Valuation

Real-World Applications in Emerging Markets

Guillermo L. Dumrauf

Routledge
Taylor & Francis Group
LONDON AND NEW YORK

Designed cover image: Nikada / Getty Images

First published 2026
by Routledge
4 Park Square, Milton Park, Abingdon, Oxon OX14 4RN

and by Routledge
605 Third Avenue, New York, NY 10158

Routledge is an imprint of the Taylor & Francis Group, an informa business

British Library Cataloguing-in-Publication Data
A catalogue record for this book is available from the British Library

ISBN: 978-1-041-04494-9 (hbk)
ISBN: 978-1-041-04493-2 (pbk)
ISBN: 978-1-003-62849-1 (ebk)

DOI: 10.4324/9781003628491

Typeset in Bembo
by codeMantra

Access the Support Material: www.routledge.com/9781041044932

Contents

TABLE 2.11 Forecasted free cash flow

	Historical		Projected			
	2023	2024	2025	2026	2027	2028
EBIT	50	54	57	60	63	66
Depreciation	6	10	10	10	11	11
EBITDA (1)	56	64	67	70	74	77
Accounts receivable	6	2	2	2	2	2
Inventories	4	1	2	1	1	1
Accounts payable	5	1	2	1	1	1
Changes in working capital (2)	5	3	2	2	2	2
Income taxes (3)	20	22	23	24	25	26
Cash from operations (4) = (1)–(2)–(3)	31	40	42	44	46	48
Capital expenses (5)	10	11	11	12	13	13
Free Cash Flow (6) = (4)-(5)	21	29	31	32	34	35
Dividends	8	0	0	0	0	0
Increase (decr.) in cash	13	29	31	32	34	35

TABLE 2.12 Forecasted balance sheet

	Historical		Projected				
	2022	2023	2024	2025	2026	2027	2028
Cash and equivalents	10	23	52	82	115	148	184
Accounts receivable	30	36	38	40	42	44	46
Inventories	20	24	25	27	28	30	31
Fixed Assets	45	49	50	51	53	55	57
Total assets	105	132	165	201	238	278	318
Accounts payable	20	25	26	27	29	30	31
Total liabilities	20	25	26	27	29	30	31
Shareholder's equity	85	107	139	174	210	247	287
Tot. liab. + S. Equity	105	132	165	201	238	278	318
Control	0	0	0	0	0	0	0

Sanity checks

It is convenient to introduce some formulas for sanity checks in the spreadsheet to ensure the consistency of the model. For example, you should include two rows at the bottom of the balance sheet and at the bottom of the cash flow statement with the following formulas:

1. Total assets – total liabilities + shareholders' equity = 0
2. Cash at the beginning + increase (decrease) in cash – cash at the end = 0

Other checks include the CAPEX/depreciation ratio and the CAPEX/Sales ratio; you must examine if the fixed assets support the forecasted sales, as an increase of sales implies more production. Sanity checks on a spreadsheet are intended to ensure the accuracy of the calculations and should not display in printed documents.

Sensitivity analysis

Once we have a preliminary forecast for our financial statements, it would be natural to wonder what would happen if the forecasted sales growth, costs, or DSO were lower or greater, respectively. *Sensitivity analysis shows how an output variable is sensitive to the change of an input, while keeping constant the other inputs.* Using Excel's "table" command, we can easily and quickly perform a sensitivity analysis of an output such as the forecasted free cash flow or EBIT, or any other output. This command is extremely useful to perform a sensitivity analysis and we recommend practicing it intensively and promptly, as it is easy to forget! We firs do a sensitivity analysis to determine how sensitive the free cash flow is to a change in sales growth, performing the following steps:

1. In cell M30, refer to the value in cell L25, which contains the free cash figure for 2024, the first year forecasted. It is required that the output cell always contain a formula!
2. Enter the sales growth rate in range L31:L33 to calculate the value of Free Cash Flow (cell 30 does not include a value. For example, –10%; 0%, 10%.
3. Select the range L30:M33, then select the tab "Data", "What-If Analysis" and "Data Table". A window will open, and in the "Column input cell" we will refer to cell D17 (the expected sales growth rate in 2024). Finally, after clicking "OK" the Free Cash Flow resulting from the selected different sales growth rates will be displayed in the range M31:M33. Remember that the cell disposition must be strictly respected to perform the correct calculations.

You can perform sensitivity analyses for different input data sets. For example, if you are interested in the sensitivity of the free cash flow to DSO, you must follow steps 1, 2, and 3, but include different DSO, for example, 30, 60, and 90 days in the range L31:L33, and in the column input cell you must reference the value in cell D23:

It is evident that the free cash flow is more sensitive to DSO than sales growth rate. To perform a sensitivity analysis for two input data at the same time, the disposition is a bit different, since you must refer to cell M25 which contains

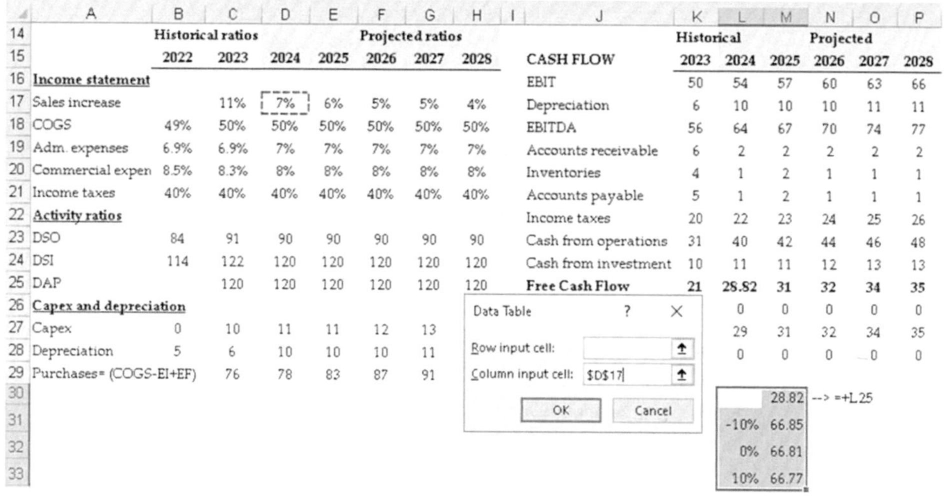

	A	B	C	D	E	F	G	H
14		Historical ratios				Projected ratios		
15		2022	2023	2024	2025	2026	2027	2028
16	**Income statement**							
17	Sales increase		11%	7%	6%	5%	5%	4%
18	COGS	49%	50%	50%	50%	50%	50%	50%
19	Adm. expenses	6.9%	6.9%	7%	7%	7%	7%	7%
20	Commercial expen	8.5%	8.3%	8%	8%	8%	8%	8%
21	Income taxes	40%	40%	40%	40%	40%	40%	40%
22	**Activity ratios**							
23	DSO	84	91	90	90	90	90	90
24	DSI	114	122	120	120	120	120	120
25	DAP		120	120	120	120	120	120
26	**Capex and depreciation**							
27	Capex	0	10	11	11	12	13	
28	Depreciation	5	6	10	10	10	11	
29	Purchases= (COGS-EI+EF)		76	78	83	87	91	

J	K	L	M	N	O	P
	Historical			Projected		
CASH FLOW	2023	2024	2025	2026	2027	2028
EBIT	50	54	57	60	63	66
Depreciation	6	10	10	10	11	11
EBITDA	56	64	67	70	74	77
Accounts receivable	6	2	2	2	2	2
Inventories	4	1	2	1	1	1
Accounts payable	5	1	2	1	1	1
Income taxes	20	22	23	24	25	26
Cash from operations	31	40	42	44	46	48
Cash from investment	10	11	11	12	13	13
Free Cash Flow	**21**	**28.82**	**31**	**32**	**34**	**35**
		0	0	0	0	0
		29	31	32	34	35
		0	0	0	0	0

	28.82	--> =+L25
-10%	66.85	
0%	66.81	
10%	66.77	

FIGURE 2.4 Sensitivity analysis of forecasted free cash flow

TABLE 2.13 Free cash flow sensitivity to DSO

+D23	**28.82**
30	54.14
60	41.48
90	28.82

TABLE 2.14 Free cash flow sensitivity to sales growth and DSO

	28.82	**60**	**90**	**120**	**-->DSO**
Sales growth -->	–10%	40.8	30.1	19.4	
	0%	41.2	29.3	17.5	
	10%	41.6	28.6	15.6	

the forecasted free cash flow for 2024 in the left superior angle, as well as inputs in the row and column. For example, put DSO in the row and sales growth rate in the column. Then you will obtain the free cash flow from each combination.

Free cash flow and equity cash flow

Greenworth is a full equity financed or unlevered company. Full equity companies are uncommon; companies generally finance their operations with a capital structure that includes both debt and equity. As we have explained, free cash flow is the cash flow of the business, after accounting for cash outflows that support operations and capital expenses, regardless of how it is financed. The term free cash flow can

EBIT	→ Operating income
+ Depreciation & amortization	
- Income tax on operations	
± Changes in working capital	
- Capital expenses	
Free Cash Flow	→ Business cash flow
- Interest payments	
± Changes in debt	
+ Tax savings	
Equity cash flow	→ Disposable cash flow
- Dividends	
- Marketable securities	
Incr/decrease in cash	

FIGURE 2.5 Free cash flow and equity cash flow

be attributed to Joel Stern et al. (2001).[6] When a company uses debt to finance its operations, we must account the cash flow from financing when calculating the equity cash flow making the following adjustments:

1. Adding/subtracting debt changes
2. Compute interest payments.
3. Income taxes on operations are calculated based on EBIT to reflect the theoretical taxes a company would pay if fully equity-financed. However, because interest payments result in a tax savings equal to interest payment x lawful tax rate, we include the tax savings in the cash flow from financing, indicating that the tax shield or tax saving goes directly to stockholders' pockets! Finally, the equity cash flow is like a residual that can be distributed as dividends or used to purchase marketable securities.

Consider what would have happened if Greenworth had issued a bond with a coupon rate of 5% and used the $20 million proceeds to buy treasury stocks in 2024.[7] The balance sheet, income statement and cash flow in 2024 would be as illustrated in tables 2.15, 2.16 and 2.17. We can see the following changes:

1. The balance sheet shows a reduction of $20 million in shareholder's equity due to debt replacement.
2. The income statement, as the company pay interest for its debt, income taxes decrease by the interest expense multiplied by the legal tax rate (1x40% = 0.40 million). Under current tax law, debt has an important advantage over equity: interest payments on debt are tax deductible, which means fewer income taxes.
3. The cash flow statement calculates potential income taxes as EBIT x t, as if the company is entirely financed with equity. It is worth noting that this method of computing income tax still allows for the display of free cash flow. The cash flow from financing is then calculated by adding the interest expense and the tax savings of $0.40 million.

The last row of Table 2.17 shows the capital cash flow, which is the sum of interest payments and dividends to shareholders (we assume that all equity cash flow is distributed as dividends). Taking on debt generates a tax shield or tax saving since interest on debt is a tax-deductible expense. A tax saving is the reduction in income taxes that results from taking an allowable deduction from taxable income. Notice that getting a tax shield is a way to save cash, since the cash flow to distribute among all capital providers is higher than when the company was full equity financed. The capital cash flow exceeds the free cash flow by exactly $0.4 million, which represents the periodic tax saving. An increase in cash flow means an increase in the value of the business; thus, the tax shield is an important factor in business valuation. This topic will be discussed in further detail in subsequent chapters.

TABLE 2.15 Balance sheet

	2023
Cash and equivalents	23
Accounts receivable	36
Inventories	24
Fixed assets	49
Total assets	132
Accounts payable	25
LT debt	20
Total liabilities	45
Shareholder's equity	87
Tot. liab. + S. equity	132

TABLE 2.16 Income statement

	2023
Sales	144
COGS	72
Gross margin	72
Adm. expenses	10
Comm. expenses	12
EBIT	50
Interest expense	1
Earnings before taxes	49
Income taxes	19.6
Net income	30.4

TABLE 2.17 Cash flow statement

	Historical		Projected			
Cash flow	**2023**	**2024**	**2025**	**2026**	**2027**	**2028**
EBIT	50	54	57	60	63	66
Depreciation	6	10	10	10	11	11
EBITDA	56	64	67	70	74	77
Accounts receivable	6	2	2	2	2	2
Inventories	4	1	2	1	1	1
Accounts payable	5	1	2	1	1	1
Income taxes	20	22	23	24	25	26
Cash from operations	31	40	42	44	46	48
Cash from investments	10	11	11	12	13	13
Free cash flow	21	28.8	30.6	32.2	33.7	35.4
Interest	0	1	1	1	1	1
Tax savings		0.4	0.4	0.4	0.4	0.4
Dividends	8	0	0	0	0	0
Cash flow from financing	8	−0.6	−0.6	−0.6	−0.6	−0.6
Equity cash flow	13	28.2	30.0	31.6	33.1	34.8
Capital cash flow	21	29.2	31.0	32.6	34.1	35.8

Concluding thoughts

A professional cash flow model must connect the balance sheet, the income statement, and the statement of shareholder's equity. The construction of the cash flow statement relies on the double entry principle, which guarantees the consistency of the model. After creating a cash flow model, you will have gained a thorough understanding of the company's activities.

The historical cash flow is a fact, unaffected by accounting conventions. An accounting convention can affect earnings but not cash flow, because the double-entry bookkeeping system, using simple rules guarantees that every entry to an account require an opposite entry to a different account.

While the free cash flow represents the cash flow generated by the business, without considering financial effects (interest payments, change in debt, and tax savings), the cash flow to equity represents the residual, the cash flow disposable to shareholders. Once we have analyzed and understood the historical performance, we'll have some ratios to help us create the assumptions needed to forecast the free cash flow.

Questions and short problems

1. A purchase of inventories means (you have to choose the correct option):

   a) An inflow, if the company purchases inventories on credit.
   b) An inflow, if the company purchases inventories in cash.
   c) An outflow, if the company pays in cash.

2. An increase in accounts payable means (you have to choose the correct option):

   a. There is no cash effect, if the company pays the bill in cash.
   b. A neutral effect on cash flow, if the increase in accounts payable is a consequence of an inventory's purchase on credit.
   c. An inflow, if the increase is a consequence of an inventory's purchase in cash.

3. An increase in fixed asset means (you have to choose the correct option):

   a) An outflow, if the company purchases fixed assets on credit
   b) There is no cash effect if the company purchases fixed assets on cash
   c) An outflow, if the company purchases fixed assets on cash

4. A decrease in accounts receivable always means (you have to choose the correct option):

   a) An outflow
   b) There is no cash effect
   c) An inflow, since a decrease in accounts receivable means that the company collected its sales

5. Suppose a company, for tax purposes, uses the accelerated depreciation of its fixed assets. Explain the effects on the balance sheet and the cash flow, if any.
6. Elmo's bar sales in 2021 were 130 million and grew to 150 million in 2022. As a consequence, the company had to invest in working capital (accounts receivable, inventories, and accounts payable).

TABLE 2.18 Elmo's bar sales	Dec 2022
Expected increase in sales	**20**
Changes in accounts receivable	6
Changes in inventories	4
Changes in accounts payable	5

   a) How much was the net investment in working capital in 2022?
   b) How much did the company have to invest in working capital per unit of increase in sales?

   Questions 7, 8, and 9 require the use of the file "Forecasting cash flow".

7. Suppose Greenworth's sales growth assumption for the year 2024 is 70% instead of 7%, as we assumed in our first projection. Assuming the sales growth is the only change in our original assumptions, answer:

   a) How much did the free cash flow change? (you could use the Excel function "table" with one entry for a rapid answer to this question)
   b) Is the free cash flow sensitive to the sales change? What is the reason?

8. Greenworth's senior management wishes to estimate the free cash flow would in 2024 based on certain assumptions: DSO: 60, 90, and 120 days; sales growth: 7%, 10%, and 20%. Establish combinations for the free cash flow in 2024 using the function "table" with double entry to respond to this question. Is the free cash flow more sensitive to changes in DSO or sales growth? What is the reason?
9. Imagine that these operations occurred on the last working day of December 2024:

   a) Greenworth got a bank loan of $50 million.
   b) Greenworth paid $15 million on accounts payable
   c) San Temo collected $10 million in receivable.

   Show how these operations would modify the original balance sheet. Is the cash flow affected?
10. Suppose a company that in the year 2023 had:

   - An EBITDA of $100
   - An increase in accounts receivable of $30
   - A decrease in inventories of $10
   - A decrease in accounts payable of $20
   - Income taxes were of $20

   Capital expenditures were of $50

   a) How much is the cash from operations?
   b) How much is the free cash flow?

11. Suppose a company that in the year 2020 had:

   - An EBIT of $90
   - A depreciation of $10
   - An increase in accounts receivable of $30
   - A decrease in inventories of $10
   - A decrease in accounts payable of $20
   - Income taxes were $20
   - Capital expenditures were of $40

   The free cash flow was (true or false)

   a) –10
   b) 0
   c) 10

12. Write one suitable word in each space:
   Cash flow from operations equals to EBIT plus........................, minus.......................in accounts receivable, minus............................ in inventories, plus.................................in accounts payable

minus income........... The company's free cash flow equals the cash flow from........................minus cash from.....................Finally, the cash balance at the end equals the cash balance at the.. plus the............................in cash.

13. Greenworth's forecasted balance sheet is expected to have $184 million in cash and cash equivalents by 2028. Does it make any sense for a company to hold this much cash and cash equivalents?
14. When projecting a company's cash flow, an analyst fails to account for annual depreciation, resulting in inaccurate CAPEX and EBITDA. However, the cash flow is entirely consistent with the balance sheet.

    a) Why do the cash flow and balance sheet cash balance match?
    b) Has the cash flow been affected?
    c) How does not accounting for annual amortization affect cash flow?

15. IDEAYA is a clinical-stage precision medicine oncology company traded on NASDAQ. Using its financial statements, calculate the cash flow from operations and the free cash flow for years 2022 and 2023.

TABLE 2.19 Financial statements for IDEAYA

	Dec 21	Dec 22	Dec 23
Cash and cash equivalents	246,770	364,829	525,114
Accounts receivable	1,103	211	18
Other assets	3,123	5,414	7,500
Current assets	250,996	370,454	532,632
Property, plant and equipment	4,763	6,509	6,164
Operating lease right-of-use assets	3,898	2,484	2,246
Other	121,690	8,522	108,274
Non-current assets	130,351	17,515	116,684
Total assets	381,347	387,969	649,316
Accounts payable	2,100	4,280	6,598
Operating lease liabilities	30,739	10,439	20,503
Accrued expenses	12,320	16,999	0
Current liabilities	45,159	31,718	27,101
Long-term operating lease liabilities	34,674	6,796	1,125
Non-current liabilities	34,674	6,796	1,125
Total liabilities	79,833	38,514	28,226
Shareholders' equity	301,514	349,455	621,090
Total liabilities and shareholders' equity	381,347	387,969	649,316

(Continued)

TABLE 2.19 (Continued)

	Dec 21	Dec 22	Dec 23
Shareholder's equity at the beginning	198,274	301,514	349,455
Net income	–49,762	–58,655	–112,961
Net issuance of stock under LT incentive plans	144,763	96,371	361,461
Other comprehensive income/loss	–719	–2,159	3,433
Dividends declared	8,958	12,384	19,702
Shareholder's equity at the end	301,514	349,455	621,090
	Dec 21	**Dec 22**	**Dec 23**
Total revenue	27,941	50,931	23,385
Cost of goods sold	58,158	89,536	129,508
Gross margin	–30,217	–38,605	–106,123
Selling and adm. expenses	20,051	23,897	28,306
EBIT	–50,268	–62,502	–134,429
Interest income	506	3,847	21,468
Income before taxes	–49,762	–58,655	–112,961
Tax expense			
Net income	–49,762	–58,655	–112,961
Depreciation & amortization	0.01	0.03	–0.02

16. Calculate cash flow from financing and net cash increase/decrease for 2022 and 2023 using the information from exercise 15.

Notes

1 If the company stopped purchasing fixed assets, their value would reduce year by year by the amount of depreciation until it reached zero. As a result, a building's book value could be zero, but its market value could have climbed if the property market value has increased.

2 There are additional changes in assets and liabilities, such as tax credit and tax and social liabilities, but accounts receivables, account payables and inventories are the more significant.

3 We often argue that ending inventories may be overvalued in some small companies seeking a loan, but may be undervalued if the business is highly profitable.

4 We valued a biotechnology firm, that used an equipment called "freeze dryer" to produce erythropoietin. When we asked the responsible for the production when would be necessary to acquire an additional freeze dryer, according with our sales and production forecasts, he made a forecast where new equipment had to be acquired every three years.

5 This 90-day cycle usually needs to be funded through a bank operating line, and the interest on this financing is a carrying cost that reduces the company's profitability.

6 According to the book *The EVA Challenge*, the term *free cash flow* was coined by Stern et al. in 1972, in a work titled *Analytical Methods in Financial Planning*.

7 Treasury stock lowers shareholders' equity by the amount paid for the stock since it represents the quantity of shares repurchased from the open market.

8 The example is intended to facilitate the reasoning. Usually, it is better to use percentage variations instead of levels, to avoid problems of autocorrelation.

References

Grupo Exxel (2023). Retrieved from https://es.wikipedia.org/wiki/Grupo_Exxel

La Nacion (2006, June 21). Retrieved from www.lanacion.com.ar: www.lanacion.com.ar/economia/carrefour-y-exxel-entran-en-guerra-por-us-120-millones-nid816608/

Stern, J., Shiely, J., & Ross, I. (2001). *The EVA Challenge, Implementing Value-Added Change in an Organization*. New York: John Wiley and Sons.

Supermercados Norte (2018). Retrieved from https://es.wikipedia.org/wiki/Supermercados_Norte

Appendix A Sales forecast using regression analysis

Under certain conditions and with adequate long data series, sales can be projected using the linear regression analysis. Table 2.18 reports the Greenworth growth sales, and the GDP historical growth rate from 2005 to 2023. Growth rates were calculated using current prices for the GDP, as sales are likewise expressed in current prices.

TABLE 2.20 Greenworth's sales and GDP growth rates

Year	GDP	Sales
2005	7.1%	10.3%
2006	5.8%	7.0%
2007	–1.0%	–4.7%
2008	4.3%	5.5%
2009	3.0%	3.9%
2010	6.0%	7.0%
2011	6.0%	5.3%
2012	7.2%	8.0%
2013	6.0%	7.0%
2014	7.1%	8.0%
2015	–2.0%	–2.9%
2016	6.7%	7.8%
2017	–1.2%	0.5%
2018	7.4%	6.0%
2019	8.5%	9.0%

(Continued)

TABLE 2.20 (Continued)

Year	GDP	Sales
2020	7.0%	7.2%
2021	5.2%	8.0%
2022	6.4%	7.0%
2023	7.5%	10.77%

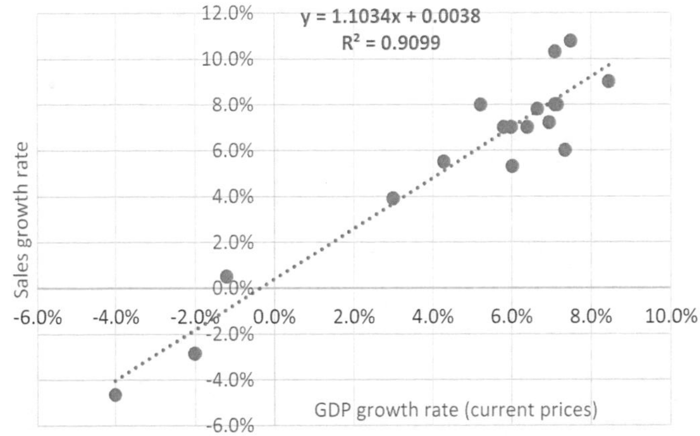

FIGURE 2.6 Sales growth rate forecasting

Simple regression analysis usually begins by plotting the set of XY values on a scatter diagram and determining by inspection whether an approximate linear relationship exists:

Figure 2.6 shows that the relationship between GDP growth rate and sales growth rate is approximately linear (the points would fall on or near a straight line). We can use an excel tool to make a simple regression analysis[8] which entails fitting a straight line to the data using the ordinary least-squared method (OLS). The OLS method is a technique for fitting the "best" straight line to the sample of XY observations (GDP growth rate is the explanatory variable X and sales growth rate represents the explained variable Y). It involves minimizing the sum of squared (vertical) deviations of points from the line:

$$\text{Min} \sum (Yi - \hat{Y}i)^2$$

Yi refers to the actual observations, $\hat{Y}i$ refers to the corresponding fitted values, and $(Yi - \hat{Y}i) = e_i$, the residual. The deviations are calculated by taking the squared differences between each value and the corresponding fitted value, which is the mean value. We cannot take the sum of the deviations from the line because deviations that are equal in size but opposite in sign cancel out, hence the sum of the deviations equals 0. Squaring makes each term positive, ensuring that values above the mean do not cancel values below the mean.

Year	GDP	Sales			
2024	5.5%	7.0%	=+$E$25+$F$25*B22		
2025	4.0%	5.4%			
2026	4.0%	5.4%		Interception	Slope
2027	4.0%	5.4%		0.0095	1.1036
2028	4.0%	5.4%			

FIGURE 2.7 Sales growth rate forecasting

Although Excel has more than one way to perform a regression analysis, a simple approach is described in three steps:

1. Select the independent and dependent variable ranges in Table 2.25; then click in "insert" and choose "dispersion" in the graph menu.
2. We left-click in one point of the graph and then right-click and choose "Adding trend line".
3. Mark "linear", "show the equation in the graph" and "show the R^2 in the graph".

Once the linear regression equation was obtained, we can use the equation of Figure 2.5 to project the next year's sales. Remember that linear regression equation establishes a relationship between GDP and sales, thus, we must first provide a GDP growth rate estimate.

The linear regression equation is: $Y = b_0 + b_1X$. It provides us two values: b_0 and b_1, where b_0 is the Y interception and b_1 is the slope of the straight line. Applying this equation, the sales growth rate forecast for 2012 is:

$$Sales_{GR} = 0.0038 + 1.1034GDP_{GR}$$

To forecast the sales growth rate for each year, simply multiply the expected GDP growth rate by the slope for every year and add the interception. Using the World Bank's forecast value is one method for obtaining a GDP growth rate forecast.

The interception is the expected mean value of Y when X = 0. In the case of Greenworth growth rate, an interception value of 0.0038 means that for a GDP growth rate = 0, Greenworth growth rate is 0.38%. The slope of a regression line represents the percent change in the Y-value for a percent change in the X-value. Because Y is dependent on X, the slope describes the predicted values of Y given X. A slope of 1.1036 means that for a one percentual point of change in GDP growth rate, the sales growth rate will change approximately 1.10%.

CHAPTER

3

Valuing streams of cash flows

Introduction

The goal of this chapter is to provide an overview of the financial mathematics required for business appraisal. Because we will need to calculate present values, we will go over the main formulas for calculating the present value of a stream of cash flow payments.

DOI: 10.4324/9781003628491-4

After reading this chapter, you will be able to:

- Compute geometric and arithmetic means;
- Calculate the present value cash flow streams with different patterns (annuities, uneven, growing perpetuity).

The time value of money

Most of us have heard the phrase "a dollar today is worth more than a dollar tomorrow". So how do we interpret this phrase? It is quite simple. Let us consider two scenarios:

1. You have $0.98 today.
2. You have the right to get $1 in one year

Having $0.98 today, allows us the opportunity to make some use of that money during one year, and earning a profit. Let's assume that a local bank pays an annual rate of 2% on the deposits and it is the best alternative available to us. Thus, we can deposit our money in this bank and receive $1.00 ($0.98 initial amount + $0.02 in interest) a year from now.

$$FV = P(1+i). \quad [3.1]$$

$$FV = 0.98(1+0.02) = 1.00$$

The interest earned represents the time value of money compensation; we sacrifice consumption today to consume more tomorrow. If you have the right to get $1 in one year, you already know the future value; however, as one dollar today is worth more than one dollar in a year, the present value of one dollar to be received in a year must be less than one dollar. So, we have to calculate the present value of one dollar a year from now. To find it, we can just reverse the formula that we used for calculating the future value. If the annual interest rate is 2%, the present value will be equal to:

$$PV = \frac{FV}{(1+i)}. \quad [3.2]$$

$$PV = \frac{1}{(1+0.02)} = 0.98$$

The discount factor is defined as 1/(1 + 0.02), and 2% interest rate is referred in finance as the "discount rate". The present value of 0.98 is equivalent to $1 in a year; again, the difference is due to the time value of money.

Compounded interest

Previous examples assumed no compounded interest and when there is no compounded interest, the nominal and effective interest rates are equal; so, the 2%

interest rate was both nominal and effective. Compounded interest is interest that is applied not only to the principal of an investment but also to the accumulated interest from previous periods. When interest is compounded, you earn interest on your interest. For instance, the future value of a sum compounded over n periods is

$$FV = P(1+i)^n. \quad [3.3]$$

The future value of a PV = 0.98 compounded over ten periods at a 2% interest rate is

$$FV = 0.98(1+0.02)^{10} = 1.1946$$

Nominal, proportional, and effective interest rates

The nominal interest rate is a contractual rate that refers to the stated interest rate on a bank deposit, bond[1] or loan before compounding or inflation. For example, if you invest \$100 at a nominal interest rate j = 10% for a year, this is the rate that will be applied to the capital or principal amount, regardless of how the interest is compounded. The annual interest amount will be

$$I = P \times j. \quad [3.4]$$
$$I = 100 \times 10\% = 10$$

On the other hand, the effective interest rate takes into account compounding interest; for example, if interest is compounded semiannually, the effective annual interest rate will be higher than the nominal annual interest rate. To calculate the effective rate, first calculate the semiannually interest rate dividing the nominal rate j by the number of compounding periods m to get the effective semiannually interest rate j/m. Assuming principal = 1 and j = 10%, the effective semiannually rate is 10%/2 = 5% and the future value in a semester is \$1.05. If 1.05 are capitalized for an additional semester, the end-of-year value will be $(1.05)^2$ = 1.1025. Notice that the annual effective rate is 10.25%, and it can be defined as the interest rate that yields the same future value in only one capitalization as the semiannually interest rate j/m, compounded over m periods:

$$(1+i)^1 = \left(1+\frac{j}{m}\right)^m,$$

Finally, subtracting 1 from the right member

$$i = \left(1+\frac{j}{m}\right)^m - 1. \quad [3.5]$$

Formula 3.5 calculates the effective interest rate from the nominal interest rate j. Therefore, the annual effective rate, if the nominal interest rate is 10% and compounded semiannually, is

$$i = \left(1+\frac{0.10}{2}\right)^2 - 1 = 10.25\%$$

Equivalent interest rates

Equivalent interest rates are effective interest rates with different compounding frequency that produce the same future value for the same given present value and period. For example, suppose you want to calculate the equivalent semiannually rate i_m given a 10% annual effective rate.

$$(1+i_m)^m = (1+i),$$

$$i_m = (1+i)^{\frac{1}{m}} - 1. \qquad [3.6]$$

$$i_m = (1+0.10)^{\frac{1}{2}} - 1 = 4.88\%$$

For example, it is indifferent to invest $1 for one year at 10% than investing 1 for one semester at 4.88% and reinvesting for another semester. Frequently you will wish to calculate the equivalent compounded return of an investment over a specific time (monthly, annual), where you now the principal, number of periods, and the future value. For this case, the calculation is very similar. Suppose you invested $100 and the capital increased to $125 after five years. The annual equivalent return is

$$FV = P(1+i)^n,$$

$$\frac{FV}{P} = (1+i)^n,$$

$$i = \left(\frac{FV}{P}\right)^{\frac{1}{n}} - 1. \qquad [3.7]$$

$$i = \left(\frac{125}{100}\right)^{\frac{1}{5}} - 1 = 4.56\%$$

Notice that formulas 3.6 and 3.7 are similar because the quotient FV/P in formula 3.7 equals (1 + i) in formula 3.6.

Real interest rate

Because the inflation rate is not zero, the effective interest rate does not represent the true return. To calculate the real interest rate, we must remove the effects of inflation. The real interest rate is calculated as follows:[2]

$$i_R = \frac{(1+i)}{(1+\pi)} - 1. \qquad [3.8]$$

i = effective interest rate
π = inflation rate

Suppose you earn a 3% annual interest rate and inflation is 2%. The real interest rate is a positive 0.98%.

$$i_R = \frac{(1+0.03)}{(1+0.02)} - 1 = 0.98\%$$

If inflation rate exceeds the effective rate, the real interest rate is negative. For example, if the inflation rate would have been 4%, the real interest rate would be a negative 0.96%.

$$i_R = \frac{(1+0.03)}{(1+0.04)} - 1 = -0.96\%$$

Arithmetic and geometric mean

When we purchase an asset and hold it for an extended length of time, we often wish to know the corresponding annual or monthly return. When calculating the cost of capital, you want to calculate the arithmetic or geometric mean return of a stock index or asset, such as treasury bonds. Table 3.1 displays the annual return on a hypothetical asset over a period of six years.

The arithmetic mean (AM) or arithmetic average, is simply the total of returns divided by the number of returns:

$$AM = \frac{1}{n}\sum_{i=1}^{n} r_i = \frac{r_1 + r_2 + \ldots + r_n}{n}. \quad [3.9]$$

$$AM = \frac{8.82\% + 11.43\% + 10.07\% + 18.64\% + (-2.29\%) + 7.60\%}{6} = 9.05\%$$

The geometric mean (GM) is calculated using formula 3.7 by dividing the latest price by the initial price and raising it to the inverse of the number of periods:

$$GM = \left(\frac{3.68}{2.21}\right)^{\frac{1}{6}} - 1 = 8.87\%$$

Notice that the geometric mean is lower than arithmetic because it takes into account the compounding that occurs from year to year, whereas the latter does not.[3] The geometric mean can also be calculated adding one to each periodic return, multiplying all capitalization factors and raising their product to the power of one divided by number of periods. Then, we subtract one from the result.

TABLE 3.1 Annual returns

Data	Price	Return
Dec 2013	2.21	–
Dec 2014	2.41	8.82%
Dec 2015	2.68	11.43%
Dec 2016	2.95	10.07%
Dec 2017	3.50	18.64%
Dec 2018	3.42	–2.29%
Dec 2019	3.68	7.60%

$$GM = \left[(1+r_1)\times(1+r_2)\times\ldots\times(1+r_n)\right]^{\frac{1}{n}} - 1. \qquad [3.10]$$

$$GM = [(1+0.0882)\times 1+0.1143)\times(1+0.1007)\times(1+0.1864)\times(1-0.0229)$$

$$\times(1+0.076)]^{\frac{1}{n}} - 1 = 8.87\%$$

The geometric mean takes into account the effect of compounding growth from different periods of return, and in that sense, can provide a better picture of return than the picture provided by the arithmetic mean for investors who wish to analyze their portfolio performance over a number of periods. However, since in Valuation we always value expectations, it is pertinent to inquire about the statistical properties of both means. We address this issue in Chapter 7, since the election of the arithmetic or geometric mean to estimate the market risk premium in capital asset pricing models has been motive of debate.

The value of a stream of cash flows

In finance, there are typically three types of cash flow streams, such as:

1. Finite-term cash flows (e.g., bank loans).
2. Perpetual cash flows.
3. Uneven cash flows.

Types 2 and 3 are common in valuation. The next sections explain how to calculate the present value in each case.

The present value of constant cash flow payments

Suppose we have a stream of cash flow payments where C represents the cash flow payment to be paid at the end of each year, during n years. To calculate its present value, we must calculate the present value of each cash flow:

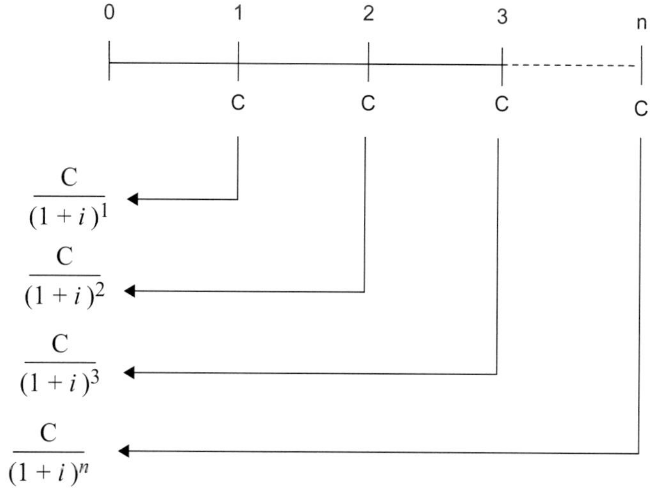

FIGURE 3.1 Present value of a stream of cash flows

Each present value is equal to the cash flow of each period divided by (1 + i), raised to the number of periods considered. For example, the present value of the second cash flow is equal to the cash flow over (1 + i) raised to the second power; the present value of the third cash flow is equal to the cash flow over (1 + i) raised to third power, and so on:

$$PV = \frac{C}{(1+i)} + \frac{C}{(1+i)^2} + \frac{C}{(1+i)^3} + \frac{C}{(1+i)^4} + \ldots + \frac{C}{(1+i)^n}.$$

If we look at this expression, we notice a regularity since each term is equal to the previous term multiplied by a common ratio of 1/(1 + i). Because the ratio is less than one, we can conclude that this stream represents a *decreasing geometric progression*, with the last cash flows experiencing an exponential decrease towards zero. The sum of the first *n* terms of a decreasing geometric progression is given by the formula:

$$S = a_1 \frac{1-q^n}{1-q}. \qquad [3.11]$$

Where:

a_1 = first term of the progression

q = common ratio

Replacing a_1 and q in [3.11] we get:

$$S = \frac{C}{(1+i)} \frac{1 - \frac{1}{(1+i)^n}}{1 - \frac{1}{(1+i)}},$$

Simplifying we get:

$$PV = C \frac{(1+i)^n - 1}{(1+i)^n i}. \qquad [3.12]$$

Formula 3.12 is largely used in financial contracts, like loan payments, lease payments, annual equivalent cost when valuing investment projects, and present values of other constant cash flow streams.

Example: calculate the present value of a stream of ten cash flow payments, if the annual interest rate is 10% and the cash flow is $1,000.

$$PV = 1{,}000 \frac{(1+0.10)^{10} - 1}{(1+0.10)^{10} 0.10} = 6{,}144.57$$

Present value of a cash flow stream for payment made at the beginning of the period

Former formulas are for payments at the end of the period; when the payments are at the beginning of the period, the cash flows stream appear as

$$PV = C + \frac{C}{(1+i)} + \frac{C}{(1+i)^2} + \frac{C}{(1+i)^3} + \ldots + \frac{C}{(1+i)^{n-1}}.$$

Since this expression is also a decreasing geometric progression, substituting the first term and the common ratio 1/1 + i:

$$S = C \frac{1 - \frac{1}{(1+i)^n}}{1 - \frac{1}{(1+i)^n}},$$

$$PV = C(1+i)\frac{(1+i)^n - 1}{(1+i)^n i}. \qquad [3.13]$$

The value of a stream of cash flow with payments at the beginning of the period is always equal to the value of a stream of cash flows with payments at the end of the period *multiplied by (1 + i)*. This formula will be useful in understanding the duration of a perpetuity, which we address in an appendix to Chapter 10.

The future value of a stream of cash flows

Although is not common to calculate a future value in a valuation process, it is important to know the relation between the present value and future value of a stream of cash flow. Suppose we have a stream of cash flow payments where C represents the amount of cash flow to be paid at the end of each year, during n periods:

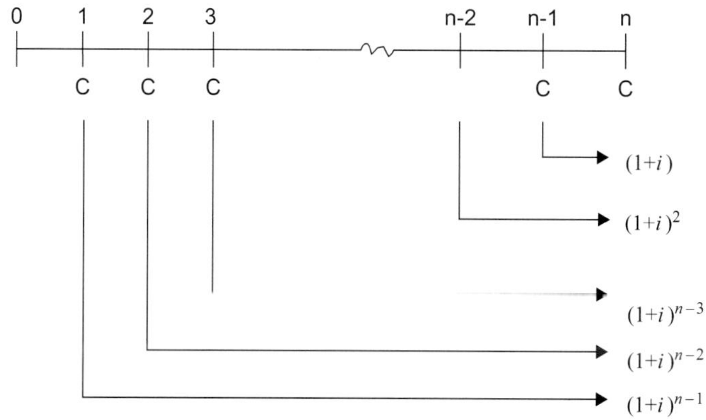

FIGURE 3.2 Future value of a stream of cash flows

The future value of a cash flow stream is the sum of the future values of each cash flow, which must be calculated to the same point in the future, known as the "n" period. The future value of each cash flow is equal to the corresponding cash flow multiplied by the factor (1 + i), raised to the n period minus the corresponding period's number. For example, the future value of the first cash flow is equal to C multiplied by $(1 + i)^{n-1}$, the future value of the second cash flow is equal to C multiplied by $(1 + i)^{n-2}$, and so on. Notice that the last payment earns no interest, because it is collected at the end of year n. Applying the commutative property of a sum, we have

$$FV = C + C(1+i) + C(1+i)^2 + \ldots + C(1+i)^{n-2} + C(1+i)^{n-1}.$$

Notice that each term is equivalent to the previous one multiplied by the ratio (1 + i). Because the interest rate is positive, (1 + i)>1, hence the cash flow stream follows an *increasing geometric progression*. The sum of *n* terms of an increasing geometric progression is given by the formula:

$$S = a_1 \frac{q^n - 1}{q - 1}. \qquad [3.14]$$

Where:

a_1 = first term of the progression

q = common ratio

Substituting a_1 and q in [3.14] we get:

$$S = C\frac{(1+i)^n - 1}{(1+i) - 1},$$

Simplifying we have:

$$FV = C\frac{(1+i)^n - 1}{i}. \tag{3.15}$$

Formula 3.15 could be used to calculate the amount of money required to achieve certain financial goals such as vacation plans, emergency savings, college plans, and retirement savings.

Example: calculate the future value of a stream of ten cash flow payments, if the annual interest rate is 10% and the cash flow is \$1,000.

$$FV = 1{,}000\frac{(1+0.10)^{10} - 1}{0.10} = 15{,}937.42$$

Example: supposing you want to accumulate \$100,000 in 60 months, calculate the cash payment if the monthly interest rate is 0.2%.

Solving from C in [3.15]:

$$C = FV\frac{i}{(1+i)^n - 1} = 100{,}000\frac{0.004}{(1+0.004)^{60} - 1} = 1{,}477.97$$

Equivalence of present and future values

When evaluating the time value of money, the present and future values of a finite stream of constant cash flows are equal; the difference is that the former is expressed today, whereas the latter is expressed at the last period. Therefore, the present value is equal to the future value discounted by n periods:

$$C\frac{(1+i)^n - 1}{i}\frac{1}{(1+i)^n} = C\frac{(1+i)^n - 1}{(1+i)^n i}.$$

And the future value is equal to the present value capitalized over n periods:

$$FV = C\frac{(1+i)^n - 1}{(1+i)^n i}(1+i)^n,$$

$$FV = C\frac{(1+i)^n - 1}{i}.$$

The present value of a perpetuity

Perpetuity is a stream of payments that will continue indefinitely. The Nobel Prize and Consol Bonds[4] are two real-world examples of perpetuities. Suppose we have an endless stream of cash flow payments since it continues forever:

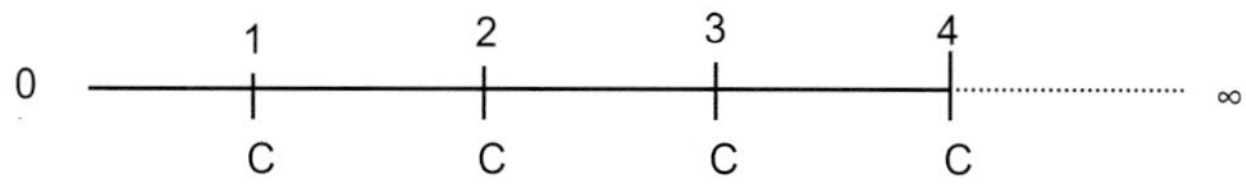

FIGURE 3.3 Cash flows in perpetuity

To calculate its present value, we have to calculate the present value of each cash flow.

$$PV = \frac{C}{(1+i)} + \frac{C}{(1+i)^2} + \frac{C}{(1+i)^3} + \frac{C}{(1+i)^4} + \ldots \infty$$

However, because the stream's life span is endless, it seems to never end...

However, there is a mathematical regularity in this stream, as each term is equal to the previous term multiplied by a common ratio equal to 1/(1 + i). Because the ratio is less than 1 (one), this stream represents a *decreasing geometric progression*. The sum of n terms of a decreasing geometric progression is given by the formula 3.11:

$$S = a_1 \frac{1-q^n}{1-q}. \qquad [3.11]$$

Where:

a_1 = first term of the progression

q = common ratio

Replacing a_1 and q in [3.11] we get:

$$S = \frac{C}{(1+i)} \frac{1 - \frac{1}{(1+i)^n}}{1 - \frac{1}{(1+i)}},$$

Because $1/(1 + i)^n$ tends to zero as n approaches infinity, we have:

$$PV(\infty) = \frac{C}{(1+i)} \frac{1}{\frac{(1+i)-1}{(1+i)}},$$

Simplifying, we get:

$$PV(\infty) = \frac{C}{i}. \qquad [3.16]$$

Formula 3.16 provides a shortcut to calculate the present value of a constant cash flow stream. It is beneficial to facilitate the reasoning and teaching of various finance theories, such as Modigliani & Miller (1958) and Modigliani & Miller (1961), because they employed perpetuities to explain their famous propositions.

Example: calculate the present value of a \$1,000 annual cash flow in perpetuity at a 10% annual interest rate.

$$\frac{1,000}{0.10} = 10,000$$

A \$1,000 perpetuity has a present value of \$10,000 today. Doesn't seem too low? We have a \$1,000 cash flow stream that continues indefinitely; nevertheless, its present value is $10,000. This is because the present value of the distant cash flows approaches zero. Table 3.2 shows how the present value decreases with time; it is evident that beyond year 100, the following cash flows add essentially nothing to the present value, and therefore the total of present values converges to $10,000 (some rows were hidden for space reasons).

Figure 3.4 and Figure 3.5 depict the present value of $1,000 and the accumulated present value. Notice that the present value of a future cash flow approaches zero in year 100, but the accumulated present value approaches $10,000.

TABLE 3.2 Sum of present value of cash flows

Year	PV
1	909.09
5	620.92
10	385.54
50	8.52
100	0.07
Total	9,999.27

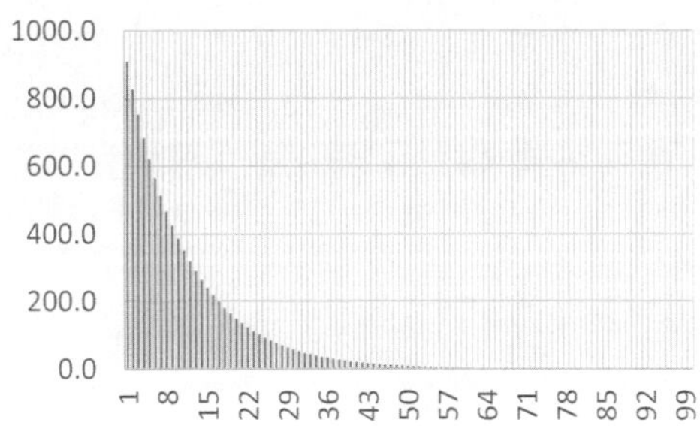

FIGURE 3.4 Present value of cash flows

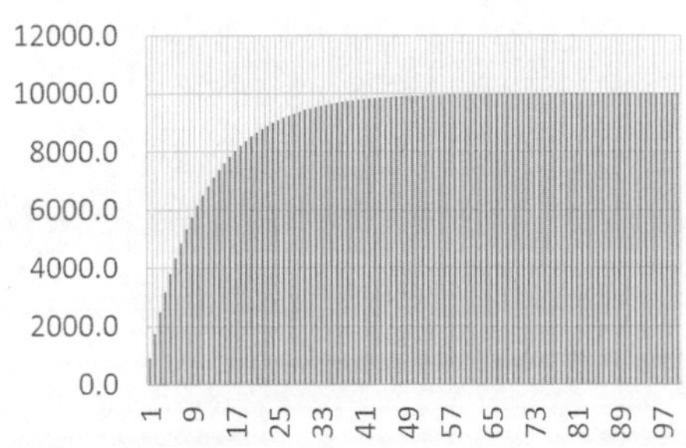

FIGURE 3.5 Accumulated present value of cash flows

Box 3.1 Case study: The fund that provides perpetual financing for the Nobel Prize

In 1895, Alfred Nobel, the inventor of dynamite, puy his fortune in a fund that provides perpetual financing for the Nobel Prize to individuals making exceptional contributions to Medicine or Physiology, Physics, Peace, Literature and Chemistry. If a fund generates an interest earning every year and only the interest is taken, we will have an infinite stream of interest payments because the original capital is kept as a deposit. The Nobel Prize in Economics is another perpetuity, an endowment "in perpetuity" established in 1968 from Sweden's central bank, Sveriges Riksbank, to award the Nobel prize in economics to individuals making exceptional contributions to economics.

We can also find perpetuities in financial instruments. For instance, during the Napoleonic Wars, the Bank of England sold a large bond issue with no maturity date an used the proceeds to repay a number of smaller issues that had financed past wars. Because the bonds were used to consolidate past debts, they were called *consols*. Consol bonds were perpetual bonds, redeemable at the option of the government. The first British Consols were issued in 1751. 100-years bonds are sometimes referred as perpetuities, since their present value is similar to the present value of a perpetuity.

The growing perpetuity formula

When we value a company, we forecast the free cash flow for an explicit period. The value of the company's continuity, beyond the explicit forecast period is referred to as the "terminal value". Terminal value is calculated using the growing perpetuity formula, which assumes that the company's free cash flow will grow at a constant rate over time. As we shall see, the formula is as follows:

$$TV = \frac{FCF_T(1+g)}{(i-g)}. \quad [3.17]$$

Figure 3.6 shows the explicit forecasted cash flow over T periods, where FCF_T corresponds to the last forecasted free cash flow, multiplied by the factor (1+g), where "g" is the nominal (constant) growth rate at which the free cash flow is expected to grow over time.

The PV of the stream of cash flow, after the explicit forecast period, would be:

$$PV = \frac{FCF_T(1+g)}{(1+i)} + \frac{FCF_T(1+g)^2}{(1+i)^2} + \frac{FCF_T(1+g)^3}{(1+i)^3} + \ldots \infty$$

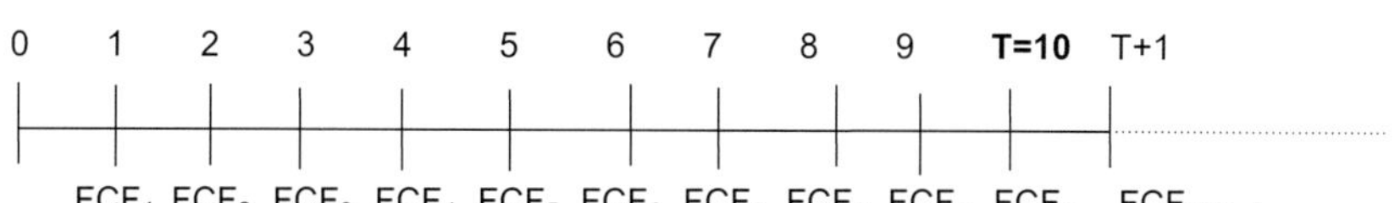

FIGURE 3.6 Explicit forecasted cash flow and perpetuity

This stream also has a mathematical regularity, as each term is equal to the previous term multiplied by a common ratio of (1 + g)/(1 + i). Because the ratio is less than one (in valuation, the cost of capital is always higher than the growth rate) we can conclude that this stream represents a *decreasing geometric progression* with an exponential decrease towards zero. The sum of *n* terms of a decreasing geometric progression is given by the formula 3.11:

$$S = a_1 \frac{1-q^n}{1-q}. \qquad [3.11]$$

Where:

a_1 = first term of the progression
q = common ratio

Replacing a_1 and q in [3.11] we have:

$$S = \frac{C}{(1+i)} \frac{1-\frac{1}{(1+i)^n}}{1-\frac{1}{(1+i)}},$$

Because the term $(1 + g)^n/(1 + i)^n$ tends to zero when n tends to infinite, we have:

$$PV = \frac{FCF_T(1+g)}{(1+i)} \frac{1}{\frac{(1+i)-(1+g)}{(1+i)}},$$

Simplifying and rearranging we have:

$$PV = \frac{FCF_T(1+g)}{i-g}. \qquad [3.17]$$

Formula 3.17 is equal to the famous dividend growth formula (Gordon, 1959). It´s important to note some details in the formula:

- If the growth rate is 0%, the formula becomes constant perpetuity.
- If g>i, the denominator turns negative, and the formula cannot be applied. As we will explain later, g is always less than the cost of capital for valuation purposes.
- Including an expected growth rate in the formula has the same effect as a reduction in the discount rate.

Example: The last forecasted free cash flow over a ten-year period was $1,000. We want to know the Terminal Value of the business, taking into account that the free cash flow is expected to grow at a 3% rate in perpetuity and the interest rate is 10% per year:

$$TV = \frac{1{,}000\,(1+0.03)}{0.10-0.03} = 14{,}714.29$$

Disentangling the dividend growth formula

The growing perpetuity or terminal value formula is similar to the famous Gordon dividend formula. When investors purchase shares, they expect to receive two sort of returns: dividends and capital gains. To estimate the current stock price, we should discount the expected dividend (D_1) and the stock price one year from now:

$$P_0 = \frac{D_1 + P_1}{(1+ke)},$$

In turn, D_1 will be equal to the expected dividend of year two plus the expected price at the end of the second year, discounted by one year:

$$P_1 = \frac{D_2 + P_2}{(1+ke)} = \frac{D_1(1+g) + P_2}{(1+ke)},$$

P_2 is equal to the expected dividend of year three plus the expected price at the end of the third year, discounted by one year:

$$P_2 = \frac{D_3 + P_3}{(1+ke)} = \frac{D_2(1+g) + P_3}{(1+ke)^2},$$

Replacing successively P_1, P_2, P_3,..., in [3.6], P_0 is the present value of an infinite stream of dividends, as the present value of future stock price converges to zero as time passes.

$$P_0 = \frac{D_1}{(1+ke)} + \frac{D_1(1+g)}{(1+ke)^2} + \frac{D_1(1+g)^2}{(1+ke)^3} + \frac{D_1(1+g)^3}{(1+ke)^4} + \ldots\infty$$

This expression is identical to the terminal value formula because $D_1 = D_0(1+g)$.[5]

$$P = \frac{D_1}{ke - g}. \quad [3.18]$$

Note that when $g = 0$,

$$P = \frac{D_1}{ke}. \quad [3.19]$$

In Chapters 15 and 16, Gordon's formula will be used to determine market expectations for long-term growth rates based on price earnings multiples.

Table 3.3 shows the composition of the stock price. As we move away in time, the participation of the accumulated present value of dividends increases while the present value of the future stock price tends to zero.

TABLE 3.3 Composition of stock price

Year	PV accum. dividends	PV future price	Total
1	8.33	41.67	50
2	15.28	34.72	50
3	21.06	28.94	50
4	25.89	24.11	50
10	41.92	8.08	50
50	49.99	0.01	50

The present value of a three-stage growth rate

As we discussed in Chapter 2, most successful businesses usually grow at a vigorous rate in an initial phase, often as a result of the launch of new, innovative product. For example, the cell phone business grew at a faster rate in the beginning than it did later on. In a second phase, "the competitive advantage period", the growth rate is typically slower due to the entrance of new competitors with whom the growth must be shared. The end of this phase marks the end of the explicit forecast period. Finally, in the third phase, the company matures, and the continuing value is estimated with the growing perpetuity formula we explained earlier, assuming that the company's free cash flow is expected to grow at a constant rate over time. Therefore, the present value of a business can be expressed as:

V = PV FCF of extraordinary phase + PV FCF of CAP + Terminal Value

Since each stream of cash flows has different growth rates and the first two are finite, we need to derive the formula for the present value of a stream which grows at a constant rate over a certain number of periods. This stream starts with a forecasted free cash flow that grows at a rate g until the n period:

$$PV = \frac{FCF}{(1+i)} + \frac{FCF(1+g)}{(1+i)^2} + \frac{FCF(1+g)^2}{(1+i)^3} + \ldots + \frac{FCF(1+g)^{n-1}}{(1+i)^n}.$$

Because the explicit forecast period has n period, the growth rate is compounded by n-1 periods, therefore the last cash flow is equal to the first cash flow multiplied by $(1 + g)^{n-1}$. This stream also has a mathematical regularity, as each term is equal to the previous term multiplied by a common ratio equal to (1 + g)/(1 + i). When cash flows are finite, there is not restriction on considering a ratio less than one, as explained in the case of the growing perpetuity formula. The formula 3.11 represents the sum of the first *n* terms of a decreasing geometric progression:

$$S = a_1 \frac{1-q^n}{1-q}. \qquad [3.11]$$

Where:

a_1 = first term of the progression
q = common ratio

Replacing a_1 and q in [3.11] we have:

$$S = \frac{FCF}{(1+i)} \frac{1 - \frac{(1+g)^n}{(1+i)^n}}{1 - \frac{(1+g)}{(1+i)}},$$

Simplifying and rearranging we have

$$PV = C \frac{1 - \frac{(1+g)^n}{(1+i)^n}}{i-g}. \qquad [3.20]$$

In case i<g, the numerator and denominator are both negative, resulting in a positive quotient. The formula of the present value of three stages may be useful for:

1. Estimating a smooth version of the implied equity risk premium, as we describe in Chapter 7, since analysts could assume a high earnings growth rate for the current year.
2. Estimating expected (implicit) growth rates in earnings multiples, given the expected dividend and the cost of capital, as we describe in Chapter 16.
3. Determining the present value of a stream of an uneven cash flow using different average growth rates for each stage, assuming a high growth at the beginning and decreasing growth until achieve an organic growth at the end of the projection.

Example: Table 3.4 shows the forecasted free cash flow of Boar Electronics. The first row contains the free cash flow growth rate from 2025 to 2033.

The present value of the free cash flow with a discount rate of 7.23% is:

$$PV = \sum_{t=1}^{\infty} \frac{FCF}{(1+0.0723)^t} = 468{,}587.51$$

The average growth rate from 2025 to 2028 is 14.00%, with 8.15% from 2029 to 2033. From 2034 and beyond the free cash flow is assumed to grow at 3% per year. Figure 3.7 shows how the free cash flow would appear if we use the average growth rates for each stage.

TABLE 3.4 Forecasted free cash flow of Boar Electronics

	Growth rate	**16.63%**	**12.00%**	**14.86%**	**12.50%**	**10.97%**	**9.85%**	**6.28%**	**9.82%**	**3.83%**
	Jul 24	**Jul 25**	**Jul 26**	**Jul 27**	**Jul 28**	**Jul 29**	**Jul 30**	**Jul 31**	**Jul 32**	**Jul 33**
FCF	11,208	13,072	14,640	16,816	18,918	20,993	23,061	24,509	26,916	27,947
T. Value										680,506
FCF + T. Value	11,208	13,072	14,640	16,816	18,918	20,993	23,061	24,509	26,916	708,453

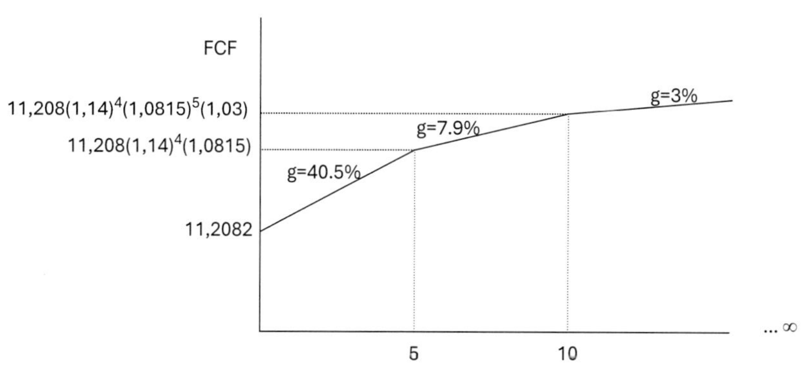

FIGURE 3.7 Three-stage free cash flow growth rate

Applying the three-stage formula:

$$PV = 11{,}208\frac{1-\dfrac{(1.14)^5}{(1.0723)^5}}{0.0723-0.14} + 11{,}208(1.14)^4(1.0815)\frac{1-\dfrac{(1+0.0815)^5}{(1+0.0723)^5}}{0.0723-0.0815}\frac{1}{(1.0723)^5}$$

$$+11{,}208\ (1.14)^4(1.0815)^5(1.03)\frac{1}{(0{,}0723-0{,}03)(1.0723)^{10}}$$

$$PV = 59{,}290.54 + 68{,}500.67 + 339{,}292.16 = 467{,}083.37$$

The three-stage formula works well when the growth rates for each stage remain relatively constant from year to year. Since the calculation involves some details that require careful, it may be more convenient to calculate the present values of each cash flow and then sum up. If the growth rates for each stage are constant, the three-stage formula gives identical result as the Excel NPV function (see exercise 15).

The present value of an uneven stream of cash flow

When performing a valuation, the general scenario is an expected stream of *uneven* cash flows. Analysts usually forecast the business cash flow for an explicit period, using a set of assumptions as we explained in Chapter 2, resulting in a different cash flow for each year. Therefore, there is no other alternative than to calculate the present value of each cash flow and sum them. Fortunately, Excel offers a formula that can quickly compute the present value of uneven cash flows.

Figure 3.8 shows the forecasted cash flow of WPS Services for a period of ten years. The last year includes the cash flow for year 10 plus the terminal value. The value of WPS is calculated with the Excel formula "NPV" in cell B5, with an interest rate of 10%.

The internal rate of return

The "internal rate of return" (IRR) is the interest rate at which the present value of the future cash flow equals the investment cash flow (I).

$$I = \frac{FCF_1}{(1+IRR)^1} + \frac{FCF_2}{(1+IRR)^2} + \frac{FCF_3}{(1+IRR)^3} + \ldots + \frac{FCF_n}{(1+IRR)^n}. \quad [3.21]$$

An alternative definition is the discount rate that causes the NPV to be zero, although this should not be confuse with the NPV calculation, which requires using the cost of capital rather than the IRR as a discount rate.

	Yr 1	Yr 2	Yr 3	Yr 4	Yr 5	Yr 6	Yr 7	Yr 8	Yr 9	Yr 10
Free cash flow	336	672	1,085	1,297	1,645	1,680	1,736	1,802	1,880	18,182
Interest rate	10%									
Present value	14,070	-> =NPV(B4;B2:K2)								

FIGURE 3.8 Present value of uneven cash flows

	Yr 0	Yr 1	Yr 2	Yr 3	Yr 4	Yr 5	Yr 6	Yr 7	Yr 8	Yr 9	Yr 10
Free Cash Flow	(14,070)	336	672	1,085	1,297	1,645	1,680	1,736	1,802	1,880	18,182
IRR	10%	=+IRR(B11:L11)									

FIGURE 3.9 IRR of an investment

From the mathematical point of view, it is the root of a polynomial, for someone, a tautology; the confusion begins when we want to interpret it as a rate of return, mainly due to the return to maturity ex-post usually differs from the IRR, which is an ex-ante measure. Because an investment will not yield the same rate of return every year, the IRR constitutes a weighted average measure. In the case of projects or bonds, reinvesting the future cash flow in other investments at an interest rate identical to IRR, the return to maturity will be equal to the IRR, another obvious. If you understand its shortcomings, you can use the IRR as a rapid metric; for example, bond investors buy bonds based on yield to maturity rather than price.

The IRR has some weaknesses, which have been largely discussed in corporate finance textbooks and are beyond the scope of this book. Nonetheless, in Chapter 12, we explain the irrational value of the EMBI+ in the case of an inverted yield curve.

Solving for the IRR requires an iterative (trial-and-error) procedure using different interest rates until the present value of cash flows equals the investment cash flow. In the context of valuation, the price paid for the company is the investment cash flow. Suppose we want to calculate the IRR for an investor that acquires WPS Services. Excel has a tool that allows you to calculate the IRR immediately using the free cash flow from Figure 3.9.

Notice that the IRR equals the cost of capital of 10%, which we used to calculate the value of a company of $14.07 in Figure 3.8.

Concluding thoughts

In valuation, we work with a stream of cash flows rather than a single cash flow. The present value is an inverse function of interest rate; therefore, the present value of the distant cash flows tends to zero, due to the compounding interest. Perpetuities formulas are widely used in finance to estimate present values of a stream of cash flows, and growing perpetuity formula is used to calculate the terminal value. There is not closed-formula to calculate the present value of an uneven stream of cash flow; however, this is not important, since the spreadsheet does it for us in an instant.

Short questions and problems

1. Calculate the present value of $100 to be received one year from now, if the interest rate is:

   a. 0.5% (the expected return of a German T-Bill)
   b. 1% (the expected return of a US T-Bill)
   c. 1.5% (the expected return of a Brazilian T-Bill)

2. Which is the largest present value if interest rates are of 10%?

   a) $600 to be received five years from now
   b) A future value of $1,000 after ten years
   c) $380 received right now
   d) $100 annuity for five years

3. Calculate the present value if the interest rate is 10%:

   a) A free cash flow of $100 in perpetuity
   b) A free cash flow of $100 for 50 years

4. Calculate the price of a five-year bond that pays an annual interest rate of 10% and the principal at maturity. Its face value is $100 and the investor requires a yield of 10%.
5. Now calculate the price of the bond if the required yield goes up to 11%.
6. Finally, calculate the price of the bond if the required yield falls to 9%.
7. Table 3.5 shows the values of three index markets at the end of 1927 and 2013. What were the average geometric returns?

TABLE 3.5 Stocks, T-Bills and T-Bonds values

Year	Stocks	T-Bills	T-Bonds
1927	100	100	100
2013	255,553.31	1,972.72	6,295.79

8. If the last forecasted free cash flow $FCF_T = 100$ and the cost of capital is of 10%, calculate the terminal value assuming the long-term growth rate is:

   a) 2%
   b) 3%
   c) 4%

9. Calculate the present value of VVV Corp.'s cash flow using an interest rate of 15%. Year ten includes the terminal value.

TABLE 3.6 Forecasted free cash flow of VVV Corp

	Yr 1	Yr 2	Yr 3	Yr 4	Yr 5	Yr 6	Yr 7	Yr 8	Yr 9	Yr 10
FCF (millions)	124	372	585	652	769	820	885	910	995	5,512

10. Supposing VVV was acquired by XXX Corp., calculate the investor's internal rate of return if the price paid was:

    a) 2,500
    b) 2,797.77
    c) 3,000

11. The estimated dividend per share of ZZ Corp. is $10. What is the stock price if it is expected to grow at 5% per year in perpetuity and the required cost of capital is 10%?

12. If ZZ Corp. distributed all of its earnings as dividends, it could pay a regular stream of dividends per share of $15. Since it only distributes a dividend of $10, how much is the market willing to pay for growth opportunities?
13. Horizon is traded at $22 and is expected to grow at 5% per year.

    a) What is the dividend yield given the expected dividend of $3?
    b) What is the capital gain yield?

14. A stream of dividends is expected to grow at 5% during ten years, and 2% from year 11 and beyond. The next year's dividend per share is $10. Calculate the equity fair value using a cost of equity capital of 20%.
15. Table 3.7 shows the forecasted free cash flow of Diamond Brews, which is expected to grow at 8% from 2025 to 2028, 4% from 2029 to 2033, and 3% from 2034 and beyond. Calculate the present value using a discount rate of 10%.

TABLE 3.7 Forecasted free cash flow of Diamond Brews

	Dec 24	Dec 25	Dec 26	Dec 27	Dec 28	Dec 29	Dec 30	Dec 31	Dec 32	Dec 33
FCF	1,000	1,080	1,166	1,260	1,360	1,415	1,472	1,530	1,592	1,655
T. Value										24,356
FCF + T. Value	1,000	1,080	1,166	1,260	1,360	1,415	1,472	1,530	1,592	26,011

16 Table 3.8 shows an unreasonable free cash flow forecast for Diamond Brews made by a potential investor. Determine the implicit cost of capital to obtain a present value equal to that found in Exercise 15.

TABLE 3.8 Potential acquirer's forecasted free cash flow of Diamond Brews

	Dec 24	Dec 25	Dec 26	Dec 27	Dec 28	Dec 29	Dec 30	Dec 31	Dec 32	Dec 33
FCF	3,000	3,240	3,499	3,779	4,081	4,245	4,415	4,591	4,775	4,966
T. Value										73,067
FCF + T. Value	3,000	3,240	3,499	3,779	4,081	4,245	4,415	4,591	4,775	78,033

Notes

1 For the case of bonds, the nominal rate is called "coupon rate".
2 If we assume that interest rates are continuously compounded, the real interest rate is the difference between the effective interest rate and the inflation rate.
3 Only for the unlikely event that all periodic returns are equal, the arithmetic and geometric mean would be identical.
4 Consols Bonds were perpetual bonds, redeemable at the option of the government.
5 The first term of the terminal value formula is FCF_T (1+g); because D_1 is equal to the last dividend payment multiplied by 1+g: D_0 (1+g), both formulas are identical.

References

Gordon, M. (1959). Dividends, Earnings, and Stock Prices. *The Review of Economics and Statistics, 41*(2), 99–105.

Modigliani, F., & Miller, M. (1958). The Cost of Capital, Corporation Finance, and the Theory of the Firm. *The American Economic Review, 48*(3), 261–297.

Modigliani, F., & Miller, M. (1961). Dividend Policy, Growth and the Valuation of Shares. *The Journal of Business, 34*(4), 411–433.

CHAPTER

4

The cost of capital

Introduction

The aim of this chapter is to provide an overview of cost of capital calculations, including their components and how the weighted average cost of capital (WACC) is estimated. The risk-return relationship is addressed with a brief introduction of the famous Capital Asset Pricing Model (CAPM), which is the most commonly employed model by appraisers to assess the cost of equity. Chapter 7 provides a more thorough explanation of the CAPM and other capital asset pricing models.

After reading this chapter, you will be able to:

- Understand the risk-return relationship for an investor who is fully diversified;

DOI: 10.4324/9781003628491-5

- Estimate the beta coefficient and calculate the cost of equity capital;
- Calculate the cost of debt and the weighted average cost of capital.

The risk-free rate

The risk-free rate is the return on a security that has no default risk. Government bonds, such as the US Treasury bond or the Treasury bill, are considered risk free securities. For example, we would get an annual return of 1% investing in a T-Bill which matures in one year. Treasury bills are zero coupon bonds, which do not pay interest to investors and are therefore offered at a discount. "At discount" indicates that the price is always less than its face value. When the bond reaches maturity, investors receive its face value. Suppose that we purchase a treasury bill today with one year to maturity for \$99 with a face value of \$100; we can calculate the annual return or yield with the following formula:

$$Yield = \frac{Face\ value}{Purchase\ price} - 1 \qquad [4.1]$$

$$Yield = \frac{1000}{990} - 1 = 0{,}0101 = 1.01\%$$

- If the annual inflation rate is around 0.2%, the pure interest rate is approximately 0.8%. The risk-free rate varies with maturity. For example:
- Treasury bills, with maturities ranging from three months to one year, have low interest rate risk and smaller returns.
- Treasury Notes and T-Bonds are bullet bonds, which pay interest semiannually and the principal at maturity. Their maturities range from five to 30 years. They are also considered as risk-free securities; they yield more than T-Bills but carry a higher interest rate risk.

What is the difference between T-Bills and T-Bonds? The difference is the interest rate risk, which refers to the change in bond price caused by an interest rate change. Bond prices fall when interest rates rise, while bond prices rise when interest rates fall.

Buy-and-hold investors don't worry about the interest rate risk because they intend to hold the bond until it matures. So, they will receive periodic interest

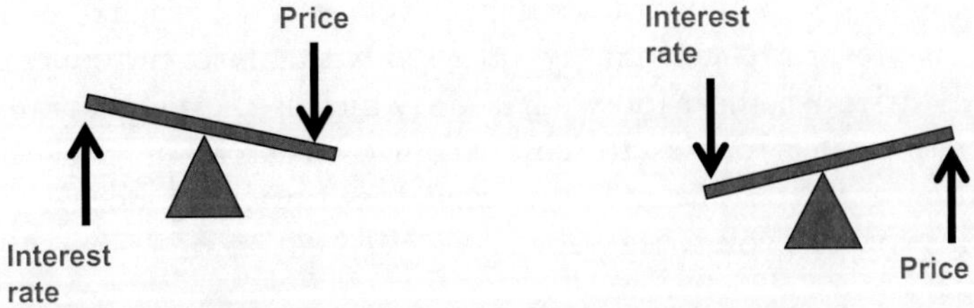

FIGURE 4.1 Bond price and interest rate relationship

payments until the bond's face value is repaid to them. The bond's price is equal to the present value of the promised cash flow, which is discounted by the required yield y:

$$P = \frac{CF}{(1+y)} + \frac{CF}{(1+y)^2} + \frac{CF}{(1+y)^3} + ... + \frac{CF + PR}{(1+y)^n}. \quad [4.2]$$

The required yield is estimated investigating the bond yields with similar credit risk, liquidity and maturity. Bonds[1] have a higher interest rate risk than treasury bills because of the compounding interest rate. Suppose the required return on a one-year T-Bill is 1%, and the required return for a bond with a coupon rate of 4% and interest paid annually, is 4%. The prices are:

$$P = \frac{100}{(1+0.01)} = 99.00$$

$$P = \frac{4}{(1+0.04)} + \frac{4}{(1+0.04)} + \frac{4}{(1+0.04)} + \frac{4}{(1+0.04)} + \frac{104}{(1+0.04)^5} = 100$$

Suddenly, the interest rate increases by 0.5% for all maturities, so the new required returns are 1.5% and 4.5%. Both prices fall, but the T-Bill falls by 0.48% [(98.52/99.00) – 1], and the T-Bond falls by about 2.2% [(97.8/100) – 1].

$$P = \frac{100}{(1+0.015)} = 98.52$$

$$P = \frac{4}{(1+0.045)} + \frac{4}{(1+0.045)} + \frac{4}{(1+0.045)} + \frac{4}{(1+0.045)} + \frac{104}{(1+0.045)^5} = 97.8$$

Although investors can pay less or more for bonds than the face value, the issuer must pay the bondholder the face value when the bonds mature. Remember that a bond is a commitment to pay; purchasing a T-Bill or a T-Bond means lending money to the government. The government must pay both interest and principal; if it does not, it will be on default.

But what happens when we move to the stock market?

The inverted casino and the trade-off between risk and return

Figure 4.2 shows the evolution of one dollar from December 1925 to December 2023 when invested in four alternatives (inflation rate, T-Bills, T-Bond, and S&P500). We construct the series using the data of the Nobel Prize Robert Shiller's website, assuming reinvesting in the same asset. Notice that the geometric market risk premium calculated as the difference between the S&P return and the T-Bonds return was 5.57% (10.46% – 4.89). If you believe that the future will be similar to the past, then 5.57% might be regarded as the expected market risk premium. Figure 4.2 reveals a lot about the risk-return trade-off. It is worth noting that treasury securities outperform the inflation rate by 1.12% for T-Bills and by nearly 3% for T-Bonds. The difference represents a positive, real return. Was the investor rewarded for taking the risk of investing in stocks? The evidence is clear: if you invested in a portfolio that mimicked the S&P500, were patient, and still had years ahead of you,[2] you would have won 10.46%. The stock market is similar to an

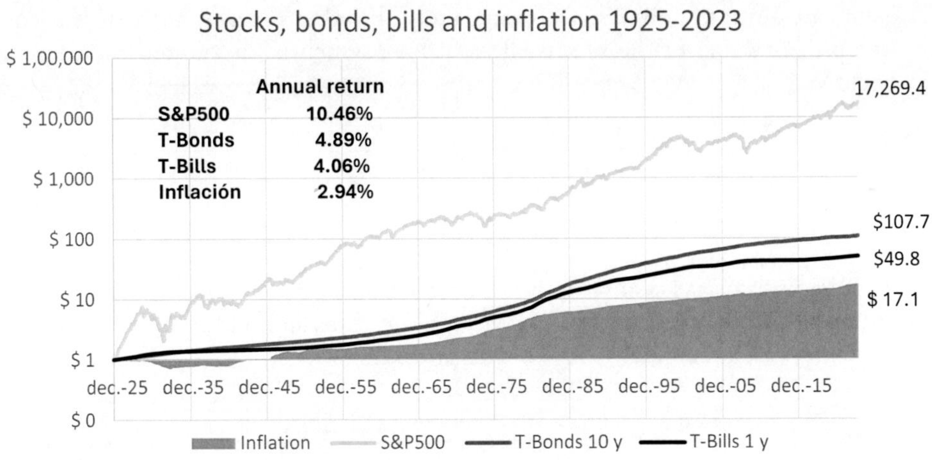

FIGURE 4.2 Stocks, bonds, bills and inflation
Source: Robert Shiller online data and Federal Reserve

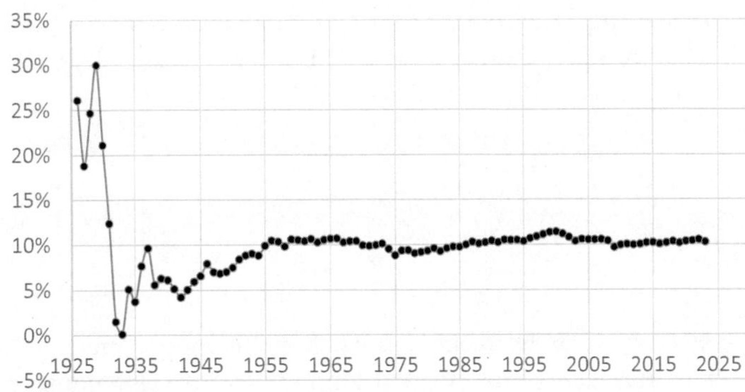

FIGURE 4.3 S&P500 geometric return 1925–2023

inverted casino in that the chances are always stacked against you, but patient investors are rewarded in the long run. You may lose money in a given year or period, but if you stick with it long enough, you may turn one dollar into a hundred, or a hundred dollars into a thousand.

A risk-free rate in the range of 4/5% and a market risk premium around 5/5.5% are recurrently mentioned and used in valuation. The fact that stocks outperformed bonds in the long run indicates that those who took risks were rewarded. As we will explain later, there is another measure of the market risk premium known as the implied equity risk premium.

Stocks and treasury returns are typically assessed from 1925. Figure 4.3 shows the cumulative geometric average return of S&P500 from 1925 to 2023. It was calculated using data from the Robert Shiller's website. Notice how became stable around 10% from 1960.

As previously stated, the market risk premium is the difference between the stock index return (for example, the S&P500) and the risk-free rate. Sometimes you will hear the terms "expected return" or "required return". The market does not reward you for investing in stocks, because this type of investment is risky; simply, when we talk about expectations, these are based on data; for the case of the market risk premium, these are based on data; in the case of market risk premium, it is usually calculated as the difference of geometric or arithmetic average return of the S&P500 over the geometric or arithmetic average rate of T-Bonds over a long time series.

Introducing the risk-return relationship

Stocks are considered risky securities as returns are not guaranteed. While stocks have historically performed well over the long run, there is no assurance that you will profit from them at any given time. Nobody can predict a stock's future performance. There is no certainty that prices will rise or the company will pay dividends. Or that a company will remain in business. High-risk investments should be compensated with a greater premium to encourage investors to take on riskier investment.

A basic principle of risk in finance is that it can be eliminated through diversification. Diversification works because there is no perfect positive correlation between stock's return (they don´t move perfectly in phase with one another), thus, some volatility cancel out. Some stocks move up, others move down and others don´t move at all. This relationship leads to a very crucial truth:

> *The variability of the portfolio returns is always less than the weighted average variability of the asset returns included in the portfolio.*

This fact is simple to illustrate. Suppose you have two stocks, denoted A and B for lack of imagination. A's expected return is 10%, whereas B's is 20%. If you invest half of your money in A and the other half in B, the expected portfolio return is equal to the average of its component stocks.

$$\text{Expected portfolio return} = 0.50 \times 10\% + 0.50 \times 20\% = 15\%$$

Supposing the variability of A´s return is 10% and the variability of B´s return is 20%. What is the variability of portfolio return? It will always be less than 20%, since there is no perfect positive correlation between two assets, as some movements in A cancel out some movements in B (for example, one day A goes up 1% while B goes down –0.5%, etc.)

Systematic versus unsystematic risk

Unsystematic risk, also known as "specific risk", "diversifiable risk", is the risk that is specific to a company or industry. This type of risk could include:

- Sudden labor strikes
- A natural disaster such as a fire
- Slumping sales
- An unfavorable litigation

Two common sources of unsystematic risk are business risk and financial risk. Unsystematic risk can be reduced through diversification, buying stocks of different companies. For example, if you buy stocks of an oil company it may drill little or no oil in a given year. Instead, you may mitigate this risk by investing in several different oil companies as well as in companies having nothing to do with the oil industry.

Systematic risk, also known as "market risk", is the uncertainty inherent to the entire market. Systematic risk is associated with macroeconomic events such as:

- Changes in interest rate
- Recession
- Wars
- Devaluation

All of them are sources of systematic risk because they affect the market as a whole and cannot be mitigated through diversification. Systematic risk is the day-to-day fluctuation in a stock's price. Because market movement is the reason why people can make money from stocks, volatility is essential for returns, and the more unstable the investment, the higher the chance of having a dramatic change in either direction. How can we calculate the systematic risk of a stock?

The stock market's beta

Beta is a measure of how sensitive stock return are to the market return. In other words, beta gives a sense of a stock's market risk compared to the greater market. Beta is calculated using regression analysis, and can be defined as the tendency of a security's return to respond to swings in the market. For example, a stock with a beta of 1.2, is theoretically 20% more volatile than the market. So, historically, the stock return has changed 1.2 times more than the market return. Many utility stocks have betas below one. Conversely, most high-tech Nasdaq-based stocks have a beta greater than one, offering the possibility of a higher rate of return, but also posing more risk.

Beta is a key component for the capital asset pricing model, which is used to calculate the cost of equity capital. Recall that the cost of capital represents the discount rate used to arrive at the present value of a company's future cash flow. All things being equal, the higher a company's beta is, the higher its cost of capital.

The CAPM equation

The capital asset pricing model or CAPM (Sharpe, 1964) has had a large influence both in academics and practitioners as a method to estimate the cost of equity capital. William Sharpe shared the Nobel Prize in 1990 for his contribution to financial economics. In essence, the CAPM postulates that the opportunity cost of equity is equal to the return on risk free securities (rf) plus an expected market risk premium (E(rm)–rf) multiplied by the company's systematic risk measured by the asset's beta coefficient.[3] The market risk premium is the difference between the expected rate of return on a market portfolio and the risk-free rate, estimated using the stock market return series, usually using a very long-time frame to eliminate the effects of short-term anomalies in the measurement. The equation for the cost of equity is as follows:

$$ke = rf + \left[E(rm) - rf\right]\beta. \quad [4.3]$$

Estimating the beta when the company's equity is traded

The approach required for estimating the Beta coefficient depends on whether the company's equity is traded or not. If we are dealing with a public company, its beta surely is published and if it is not, it can be calculated using regression analysis. Stock betas are usually estimated from historical data fitting a straight line through the points representing past combinations of returns on the market and the stock as illustrated in Figure 4.4 for Schlumberger, the world's largest offshore drilling company. Beta is the slope of the characteristic line and is the regression coefficient (1.83 in the regression equation) on the market returns. Historically, when the market rises 1%, Schlumberger rises an average of 1.83%.

Technically, the beta of a risky asset j is the covariance of returns on that asset with the market returns divided by the variance of the market return:

$$\beta_j = \frac{\sigma_{R_j,R_M}}{\sigma^2_{R_M}}. \quad [4.4]$$

The covariance is the correlation coefficient multiplied by the standard deviations of the company's and market returns, $\rho_{jM}\sigma_j\sigma_M$. Making the substitution yields

$$\beta_j = \frac{\rho_{R_j,R_j}\sigma_{R_j}\sigma_{R_M}}{\sigma^2_{R_M}},$$

$$\beta_j = \rho_{R_j,R_j}\frac{\sigma_{R_j}}{\sigma_{R_M}}. \quad [4.5]$$

Betas are also provided by many websites. We will address the market beta calculations in further detail in Chapter 7.

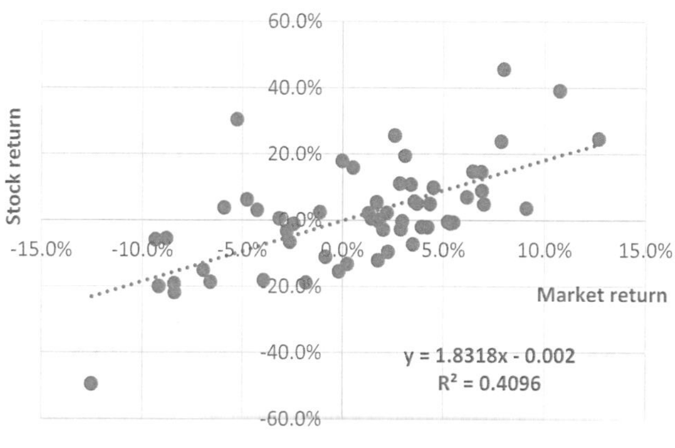

FIGURE 4.4 Beta calculated using regression analysis

TABLE 4.1 Betas in the American Industry (Containers & Packaging)

Company	Country	Market beta	D/E	Effective tax rate
Sound	US	1.1	30%	34%
Pacman	US	1.1	35%	32%
Bemis	US	1.0	25%	36%
Greif	US	1.5	40%	34%
Sealed Air	US	1.4	32%	34%
Mean		1.22	32%	34%

Estimating the beta when the company's equity is not traded

Because Greenworth, the company we analyzed in Chapter 2, is a private company, no betas are available. We use the "bottom-up beta approach" that consists in identifying the publicly traded competitors most similar to the company in developed capital markets. Industry's average is more stable than company betas and measurement errors tend to cancel out. The levered beta for the industry "Containers & Packaging" was found to be 1.22.

The unlevered beta

Because the industry beta is an average beta that reflects the effect of the financial debt, we must unlever it. We do this using the Hamada's formula (Hamada, 1972) that takes into account the levered beta (1.22), the industry average capital structure D/E = 32%, and the industry marginal tax rate (34%):

$$\beta_U = \frac{\beta_L}{\left[1 + \frac{D}{E}(1-t)\right]}. \quad [4.6]$$

$$\beta_U = \frac{1.22}{[1 + 0.32\,(1 - 0.34)]} = 1.01$$

Hamada's formula will be discussed in further detail in Chapter 8.

The levered beta and the expected capital structure

The industry has unlevered beta of 1.01, which represents simply its business risk. If Greenworth would remain full-equity financed, the unlevered beta should be used to calculate its cost of equity capital. However, to take advantage of the tax savings that debt provides, the senior management seriously considered modifying the current capital structure, leveraging it to achieve a D/V ratio of 20% (20/100), which corresponds to a D/E ratio of 20/80 = 25%. Therefore, we should estimate a levered beta for Greenworth, relevering the unlevered beta according to its expected capital structure and marginal tax rate of 40%. The formula for calculating the unlevered beta is:

$$\beta_L = \beta_U \left[1 + \frac{D}{E}(1-t)\right]. \tag{4.7}$$

$$\beta_L = 1.01\left[1 + \frac{20}{80}(1-0.40)\right] = 1.16$$

The cost of equity capital

The risk-free rate has been considered as the 10 years T-Bond current yield of 4% and the market risk premium is estimated to be 5.5%. If Greenworth remains unlevered, the unlevered cost of equity would be, using formula [4.3]

$$k_U = 4\% + [5.5\%]1.01 = 9.54\%$$

Taking into account that Greenworth's senior management believes that the capital structure that will prevail throughout the company's life suggests a D/V ratio of 20/80, the cost of equity would be higher, indicating the greater dispersion that debt would create in the shareholder return. The cost of equity is estimated using the levered beta of 1.16 we calculate earlier.

$$ke = 4\% + [5.5\%]1.16 = 10.37\%$$

Cost of debt after taxes

We assume that, if Greenworth decides to modify its capital structure, it can issue a bond with a coupon rate of 7% and sell it at par value. Because interest charges are tax deductible, the cost of debt must be expressed on an after-tax base. Therefore, the cost of debt after tax is:

$$kd(1-t). \tag{4.8}$$
$$kd(1-t) = 7\%(1-0.40) = 4.2\%$$

Remember that the cost of capital is always the marginal cost adjusted for taxes; the interest rate of 7% represents the cost of borrow one additional dollar.

Weighted average cost of capital (WACC)

In order to estimate the weighted average cost of capital (WACC) for an expected D/V = 20%, we must consider the cost of debt after taxes, the levered cost of equity capital and fair values weights for the capital structure. The WACC equation is as follows:

$$WACC = kd(1-t)\frac{D}{E+D} + ke\frac{E}{E+D} \tag{4.9}$$

Where:

kd: pretax cost of debt

t: marginal tax rate

D: financial debt
ke: cost of equity
E: fair value of equity
V: fair value of the assets (V = E+D)

$$WACC = 7\%(1-0.40)\times 0.20 + 10.37\% \times 0.80 = 9.14\%$$

Remember that if Greenworth would remain as an unlevered company, its cost of capital would be 9.5%, thus, there would be room to reduce the cost of capital through debt financing. In the next chapter, we will use the WACC of 9.14% to estimate the fair value of Greenworth's operations. The WACC method assumes a constant D/V ratio along the lifetime of the business, therefore, implying that the capital structure is periodically rebalanced.

It's important to clarify that Greenworth cannot use the WACC of 9.14% as the cost of capital for acquiring a new business or project unless the following two conditions are met:

1. the target's D/V ratio must be the same as the company;
2. the target must have a similar risk to Greenworth.

Why is the cost of equity considered "higher" than the cost of debt?

Typically, the cost of equity exceeds the cost of debt. It is due that equity holders support more risk than the lenders. Bondholders support less risk because they are always paid before the stockholders. If we look at the income statement of any company, we can understand why it is argued that equity holders support more risk than lenders. Employees, suppliers, and banks get paid before the equity holders. While every company supports the *business risk* (measured by EBIT dispersion), a levered company also supports *financial risk* (measured by net income dispersion). Payment on a debt is required by law, regardless of a business´s profit. Fixed interest charges introduce more dispersion on the stockholder´s return (if EBIT by 50%, net income will vary by more than 50%). Suppose a company with an EBIT of $100 million and a standard deviation of 50%. If the EBIT is normally distributed, EBT will vary between $150 million and 50 million with a 68% probability. Assuming the company has to pay $50 million in interest charges. Then, its net income would vary from 0 to $100 million, a 100% dispersion!

Finally, there is no certainty that the net income will be distributed as dividends. Therefore, considering the net income as a shareholder´s return is misleading.

TABLE 4.2 Business risk and financial risk

EBIT	50	100	150
Interest	50	50	50
EBT	0	50	100
Income taxes (40%)	0	20	40
Net income	0	30	60

Although the part of net income not distributed today can be considered as "potential dividends" to distribute in the future, it is clear that interest payments are paid before and represents a more secure stream, which explains why debt is "cheaper" than equity. The order in which the firm's stakeholders are paid is reflected in the income statement. For instance, salaries – a crucial business responsibility – and supplier payments are included in the cost of goods sold as well as administrative and commercial expenses. If the business has debt, it must pay interest to banks; after calculating its pre-tax earnings, it must pay taxes to the government; and lastly, it must pay shareholders. Nonetheless, as we mentioned, it does not mean that the net income will be distributed all or in part as dividends, since it must be approved by the board of directors. More fixed charges imply more variability in the shareholder's return, which is often reflected in a higher stock beta and a higher cost of equity capital.

Concluding thoughts

This chapter discusses the cost of capital and its components. The CAPM assumes that for a fully-diversified investor the only risk that commands premium is the systematic risk, which is measured by beta. When betas cannot be observed, we can use the bottom-up beta approach to estimate the cost of equity capital.

When the business is financed with debt and equity, we must calculate the weighted average of the cost of capital, where the best estimation for the cost of debt is the target company's bond yield adjusted by tax effects and the best estimation for the cost of equity is obtained with the CAPM model.

Questions and short problems

1. Mark these affirmations as true or false:

   a. The WACC method assumes a constant leverage, implying that the company's capital structure is rebalanced periodically.
   b. The cost of capital is always a marginal cost.
   c. Debt is cheaper than equity.
   d. The cost of capital depends on what it is used for, not on the origin of the resources.
   e. Internal funds have the same cost that a new issue of common shares.

2. Bavarian Corp. is considering to issue a bond to finance an investment of \$10 million. The marginal cost of debt for a bbb-rated bond is around 9%. After consulting with an investment bank, the senior management decided to issue a bullet bond with a coupon rate of 9%, interest paid annually, and five-year maturity. The statutory tax rate is 30%.

   a) Calculate the effective cost of debt, taking into account that floating cost are estimated being 1.5% of the issue and the bond will issue at par value.
   b) Calculate the present value of tax shield considering the bond's maturity and a discount rate equal to the cost of debt.

3. A company has a beta of 0.6, the arithmetic and geometric market risk premium are 6% and 5.5%, respectively, and the risk-free rate is 5%. Calculate the cost of equity using both arithmetic and geometric market risk premiums.
4. Calculate the cost of equity for exercise 3 with a beta coefficient ranging from 0.60 to 1.60. What about using arithmetic or geometric market risk premium when beta varies?
5. La Lucila Garden has a beta of 1.4; the market risk premium is 6% and the risk-free rate is 5%. D/V = 50%; kd = 10%; t = 35%. Calculate the WACC.
6. Sweet Valley has a target D/V = 45%. The cost of equity capital is estimated as 15%, the cost of debt is 8%, and t = 35%. Estimate the WACC.
7. ZZZ is considering to acquire a small unlevered company YYY which has a beta of 1.5. The risk-free rate is 4.5%, the market risk premium is 6%, and the WACC of ZZZ is 10%. Could the WACC of ZZZ be used as a discount rate to estimate the value of YYY?
8. In which case the WACC of a company can be used as the discount rate to calculate the present value of an investment project or business?
9. CCC has 50 million in long-term loans contracted at different interest rates: 40% was contracted at 10% while the remaining 60% was contracted at 9%. Today, the company may issue an 8% coupon bond with a ten-year maturity and par value. Which of the following is the marginal cost of debt?

   a) The weighted average of the different interest rates
   b) 8%

10. XXX is a private company involved in the real estate industry. To estimate its beta, we´ll use the comparable beta approach. The levered beta of the peer group is $\beta_L = 1.2$; D/E = 20% and t = 30%. The target D/E of XXX is 33% and the statutory tax rate = 35%. Calculate the levered beta of XXX.
11. Why the risk-free rate is considered as having a zero beta since bond returns are also volatile, but lower than stock returns?
12. Supposing the market risk premium rm-rf = 6%, calculate the cost of equity capital for each of the following companies using the CAPM model and draw a scatter diagram with the required return on the y-axis and beta on the x-axis, starting with rf = 3% and beta = 0. Is there a linear relationship between beta and required return? Why?

TABLE 4.3 Data for use in scatter diagram

Asset	Beta
T-Bonds	0.00
AstraZeneca PLC	0.38
Linde India Ltd	1.08
Shell PLC	1.13
Diageo PLC	0.52
Prudential PLC	1.46
HSBC Holdings PLC	0.96

(Continued)

TABLE 4.3 (Continued)

Asset	Beta
Unilever PLC	0.41
GSK plc	0.59
Rolls-Royce Holdings PLC	1.90
Compass Group PLC	1.18

Notes

1 Bonds can be issued by governments, states or local governments, municipalities or corporations.

2 If you were 90 years old in 1928 and invested in stocks, you would hardly have been able to see your money back.

3 When the company has financial debt in its capital structure, the beta coefficient is a "levered beta".

References

Hamada, R. (1972). The Effect of the Firm's Capital Structure on the Systematic Risk of Common Stocks. *The Journal of Finance*, *27*(*2*), 435–452.

Sharpe, W. (1964, September). Capital Asset Prices: A Theory of Market Equilibrium Under Condition of Risk. *Journal of Finance*, 277–293.

Shiller, R. (2022). *Online Data Robert Shiller.* Retrieved from www.econ.yale.edu/~shiller/data.htm

CHAPTER

5

Introduction to the DCF and relative valuation

Introduction

This chapter uses the DCF model to estimate the fair value of Greenworth by integrating its expected free cash flow and cost of capital, which we calculated in Chapters 2 and 4, respectively. We also introduce some important concepts as the business cycle and the terminal value, as well an introduction to relative valuation.

After reading this chapter, you will be able to:

- Understand the economics of the business cycle and estimate the company's terminal value;
- Estimate the company's fair value using the WACC or free cash flow method;
- Compare values from DCF and relative valuation approach.

Estimating the company value with the DCF Model

In order to estimate the fair value of Greenworth, we use the discounted cash flow (DCF) model that consists in calculating the present value (PV) of forecasted free cash flow (FCF) using a risk adjusted cost of capital. In finance, we call this method as "free cash flow method". Free cash flow reflects the cash flow that is generated

DOI: 10.4324/9781003628491-6

$$\underbrace{V=\frac{FCF_1}{(1+WACC)^1}+\frac{FCF_2}{(1+WACC)^2}+\frac{FCF_3}{(1+WACC)^3}+\ldots+\frac{FCF_T}{(1+WACC)^T}}_{\text{PV of forecasted free cash flow}}+\underbrace{\underbrace{\frac{FCF_T(1+g)}{(WACC-g)}}_{\text{Terminal value}}\times\frac{1}{(1+WACC)^T}}_{\text{PV terminal value}} \quad [5.1]$$

FIGURE 5.1 Present value of forecasted free cash flow

TABLE 5.1 Forecasted free cash flow of Greenworth operations

	2024	2025	2026	2027	2028
Free cash flow	29	31	32	34	35
Terminal value					594
FCF + Terminal value	29	31	32	34	629

by the business, excluding effects (debt changes, interest payments, and tax savings) and available to all the company's capital providers, both debt and equity. To avoid double counting of financial effects, the discount rate must be the weighted average cost of capital (WACC) since it computes the debt's tax shield. This manner, the financial effect is only counted once.

We compute the company fair value by separating the value of the business into two time periods: during and after an explicit forecast period. The explicit forecast period is projected until the company reaches a steady-state, after which the free cash flow is assumed to grow at a constant rate "g" over time:

We will now complete the valuation of Greenworth. Table 5.1 reproduces the free cash flow forecast from Chapter 2. The terminal value is estimated assuming a long-term growth rate of 3%, which includes both an expected inflation rate of 2% and an expected real growth rate of 1%.

The WACC was estimated in Chapter 4 as 9.14%, assuming a D/V ratio of 20%. Terminal Value is calculated using formula [3.17]:

$$TV=\frac{35(1+0.03)}{(0.0914-0.03)}=594.00$$

The fair value of operations is the present value of the forecasted free cash flow from 2024 to 2028 plus the present value of the terminal value:

$$V=\sum_{t=1}^{5}\frac{FCF}{(1+WACC)^1}+\frac{TV}{(1+WACC)^T}. \quad [5.2]$$

$$V=123.56+383.65=507.21$$

Notice that the present value of terminal value represents almost 76% of the firm value (390.93/511.79–1 = 75.64%). This occurs when the free cash flow is forecasted for a short period of five years. We use five years in the Greenworth example for learning purposes, but in practice, we choose a long period of time, usually ten years, which we believe has some advantages that we will discuss later.

Firm value and equity fair value

Equity fair value is calculated by subtracting the long-term debt from the firm's value:

$$E = V - D$$

Because other non-financial liabilities were already factored into working capital, we simply need to subtract financial debt. In practice, D is always the debt book value which coincides only by chance with the debt considered in the expected capital structure. Given the expected D/V ratio of 20%, the debt should be 507.21 x 20% = 101.44 to be consistent.

Is the target (expected) capital structure the best approach?

In practice, the debt book value rarely coincides with the expected value of debt, as implied by the target capital structure. If we use an expected D/V ratio, we are assuming that Greenworth will instantly modify its capital structure immediately. This change, and capital structure rebalancing rarely happen in the real-world, as we will see in Chapter 11. Although we use this approach to facilitate reasoning, we will later discuss other approaches including their pros and cons.

Length of the forecast period and stages of the industry life cycle

In our analysis of Greenworth, we have forecast the free cash flow for five years, assuming Greenworth is a mature company. Masters of Finance students frequently asked me about how long the explicit forecast period should be. While it is common in Valuation to assume a ten-year timeframe, the rule should be that *it be long enough for the company to reach a steady-state by the end of this period.* Figure 5.2 depicts how the business performance along its life is logically related to the three industry growth stages. We briefly comment the characteristics of each stage, which will be discussed in further detail in Chapter 10.

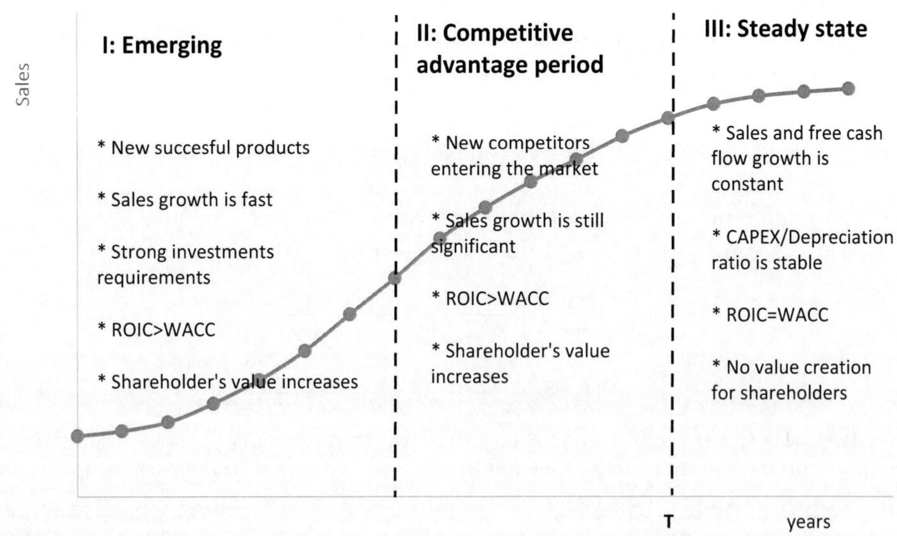

FIGURE 5.2 Industry growth stages

First stage: Vigorous growth, extra-profitability

The first stage or emerging stage is typically characterized by vigorous growth. When a new business is launched, if it is successful, sales grow fast, there are extra-profits, and the return on invested capital (ROIC) exceeds the cost of capital, allowing the company to create value for its shareholders. The end of this period coincides with the beginning of the competitive advantage period (CAP).

Second stage: Competitive advantage period

Attracted by the profits, many competitors enter the market, reducing growth rates and profit margins. By that time, the firm must have been exhausted its competitive advantage, disappearing the possibility of extra-profits in the long run. At the end of this period, the business grows theoretically at a rate similar to the GDP growth rate plus the internal inflation rate, and the return on capital (ROIC) converges to the cost of capital.

Third stage: The steady-state and the terminal value

The steady-state assumes that cash flows grow at a constant perpetual growth rate from period "T" and beyond, where "T" represents the last year of the explicit forecast period. The value after the explicit forecast period is referred to as the "terminal value" or "continuing value" which is calculated using the growing perpetuity formula [3.17]:

$$TV = \frac{FCF_T(1+g)}{(WACC - g)}.$$

No company can grow at a rate higher than the economy because it will eventually outgrow the economy; the company cannot create value for its stockholder forever, just as trees don´t grow up to the sky. It implies that as the company matures, the return on capital converges to the cost of capital. We will save Chapter 10 for a more in-depth discussion of these assumptions; for the time being, we will note that, empirically, Clendenin and Cleave (1954) found that growth rates greater than 5% per year were difficult to find for large companies. Chan, Karceski, and Lakonishok (1993) discovered that the median growth rate was between 3 and 3.5% when dividends were not reinvested.

Some practitioners use an EBITDA exit multiple to estimate the Terminal Value, avoiding assuming a long-term growth rate. If you like this procedure, we recommend finding out what the implicit LT growth rate is in this multiple. For example, if they use an EV/EBITDA of 5, for a company with a $EBITDA_T$ of \$300, a FCF_T of \$100, and a WACC of 10%, the implicit g of 3.13% is calculated by solving the equation 200 x 5 = 100(1 + g)/(0.10 – g). Terminal values that incorporate implicitly a nominal, higher LT growth must be carefully scrutinized, especially if the inflation rate is not very different from the international inflation rate, since it would imply the maintenance of competitive advantage for an indefinite period.[1]

The length of the explicit forecasted period

In practice, we usually forecast the explicit free cash flow for ten years. Although mature companies have already reached a steady state, the launch of a new product can extend a growth rate above the long, organic growth rate. There are three additional reasons:

1. Duration: the free cash flow duration is usually 7/8 years, similar to the US T-Bond ten-year maturity, and similar to the stock index duration. Hence, the matching between cash flow and securities duration is more closely aligned.
2. Even for the case of mature companies, a period of recession followed by an economic re-emergence may justify a lengthy period until the company recovers and returns to a steady condition.
3. For growing companies, a ten-year forecast permits for a slower convergence to the LT growth rate compared to a five-year forecast.
4. Compared to a five-year forecast, the present value of terminal value accounts for a small percentage of the firm value.

We'll back on the long-term growth rate in Chapter 10, which is dedicated to the terminal value. There are further challenges to address with terminal value, which typically accounts for a significant percentage of the company's fair value.

Introduction to the relative valuation approach

Another method to value a company is relative valuation, using multiples observed for similar companies. A multiple is a ratio that relates a company's market value to its earnings. There are also some multiples that relates market values with sales, cash flow, and book value.

The process consists of identifying comparable companies (known as the peer group) and calculating, for example, their EBITDA multiples, such as price/EBITDA (P/EBITDA) or enterprise value/EBITDA (EV/EBITDA). Once the multiples were obtained, the sample mean (or the median, if there are any outlier) is calculated and applied to the current company´s EBITDA to estimate the fair value. The P/EBITDA is calculated as follows:

$$\text{P/EBITDA} = \frac{\text{Market capitalization}}{\text{EBITDA}}. \tag{5.3}$$

The Price/EBITDA indicates how much investors are willing to pay per dollar of EBITDA. If a company is currently trading at a multiple P/EBITDA of 7, this suggests that an investor is willing to pay $7 per one dollar of current EBITDA.

In mergers, acquisitions, and transactions involving non-financial companies, another EBITDA multiple known as enterprise value/EBITDA is employed. It is based on enterprise value (the market value of equity plus the value of financial debt). EV/EBITDA is calculated as follows

$$\text{P/EBITDA} = \frac{\text{Market capitalization} + \text{D}}{\text{EBITDA}}. \tag{5.4}$$

AN advantage of this multiple is that it is capital structure neutral, and, therefore, this multiple can be used to directly compare companies with different levels of debt, as we will address in a later chapter.

TABLE 5.2 Greenworth fair value using DCF and relative valuation

	DCF Method	EV/EBITDA approach
Company fair value	507.21	487.20

Applying the relative valuation approach to Greenworth

Suppose the average EV/EBITDA multiple for the peer group was 8.7. Once the multiple is determined, we can apply to Greenworth by multiplying it by the current EBITDA of $56 (recall that the EBITDA in 2012 was 56 million). Therefore, the estimated equity fair value is

$$E = 8.7 \times 56 = 487.20$$

Usually, discounted free cash flow is used in tandem with the relative valuation approach. The DCF value is compared to a multiple of EBITDA to determine whether the former yields a value that is consistent with market prices. In our example, the value using EV/EBITDA is around 4% lower than the DCF value.

DCF and relative valuation approaches do not always give similar values, and sometimes can be quite different. Remember that DCF method is based on expectations about earnings and cash flows and relative valuation is accounting based since it uses an earning measure in the denominator. Furthermore, a normalized EBITDA is frequently used in place of the last fiscal year's EBITDA. EBITDA, as an accounting measure, could be affected by accounting conventions, like different depreciation or amortization methods. The market values also could be stressed by events such financial crise, recession or political crise, giving illogical multiples. All of these drawbacks obligate analysts to make some adjustments to establish a better comparison, that we'll address on Chapter 16. Greenworth is an unlevered company, hence P/EBITDA and EV/EBITDA give the same value. When the target company is levered, if we used EV/EBITDA instead of P/EBITDA, which gives the total company value, we would have to deduct the debt to get the equity fair value.

Concluding thoughts

In this chapter we outline the discounted cash flow method, using the forecasted free cash flow we discussed in Chapter 2 and the cost of capital estimated in Chapter 4. Free cash flow method and WACC method are synonymous; if we value the firm using the free cash flow, we must use the WACC to avoid tax shield duplications. In addition, we make an introduction to relative valuation and then we compare the values provided by the two methodologies.

Questions and short problems

1. Suppose Greenworth's free cash flow is forecasted for ten years, with a 4% growth rate in years six and beyond. Would there be any difference with the firm value of $511.28 estimated in this chapter?

2. Assume Greenworth's terminal value is calculated using a long-term growth rate of 3% rather than 4%. How sensitive is the DCF value to a change in the long-term growth rate?
3. Is there any difference between the present value of terminal value in 2 and the present value of TV in this chapter, which is $390.93?
4. Why is it said that once the business achieves a steady state, all fundamentals (sales, costs, earnings, capex/depreciation ratio, and cash flows) grow at the long-term growth rate?
5. Does the firm's value grow at the long-term growth rate, as mentioned in question 4?
6. Regarding question 4, is it true that fundamentals grow at a constant growth rate?
7. Suppose you are valuing a company in an emerging country where the inflation rate is 10% per year, while the international inflation rate is 2%. How the different inflation rates affect the cost of capital, long-term growth rate, and cash flows?
8. Assume Garden Inc.'s free cash flow will increase by 45% in the first year and decrease to 15% by year five. Is it reasonable to estimate a long-term growth rate of 3% for years six and beyond when calculating the terminal value in year five?
9. The terminal value of Greenworth is $594 million, calculate with the growing perpetuity formula. Suppose the terminal value is calculated using an EBITDA multiple of six. The five-year EBITDA is $76.55 Is it similar to the terminal value calculated using the growing perpetuity formula?
10. What should be the long-term growth rate in the terminal value formula to achieve the same result as 6xEBITDA?
11. Suppose the forecasted capex/depreciation ratio for the implicit forecasted period is 0.80; does it have any implication on the terminal value?
12. Suppose the free cash flow of a mature company is $100M, growing 3% at perpetuity. The cost of capital is 12%. If the current conditions hold, the DCF value should be:

    a. 100(1.03)/0.12
    b. 100(1.12)/(0.12–0.03)
    c. 100(1.03)/(0.12–0.03)
    d. 100(1.03)/(0.12–0.03) x 1.03

Note

1 The situation is different in emerging markets, where the inflation rate is usually higher than the international inflation rate. In this case, the inflation rate must be computed both in the long-term growth rate and in the cost of capital.

References

Chan, L., Karceski, J., & Lakonishok, J. (2003). The Level and Persistence of Growth Rates. *Journal of Finance*, 643–684.

Clendenin, J., & Cleave, M. V. (1954). Growth and Common Stock Values. *The Journal of Finance*, *9*(4), 365–376.

PART

2 Theoretical cornerstones in valuation

The goal of Part 2 is to provide the theoretical framework necessary to better address the valuation issues that appear in real life. Finance theory has contributed many works to economic science. We should mention the modern portfolio theory (Markowitz, 1952), the theorem about the firm value and cost of capital (Modigliani & Miller, 1958), the capital asset pricing model (Sharpe, 1964), the theory of efficient capital markets (Fama, 1970) and Black & Scholes (1973) for the formula of option pricing as the cornerstones in valuation. All these contributions were laureates with the Nobel Prize in Economics and are a source of pride in economics.

In valuation, the MM theorem and the CAPM model have had an enormous impact since they both provide theoretically sound tools for practitioners. We are in debt to MM as they have taught us much we know about valuation, and, in some ways, the MM theorem should be considered today as a "center of gravity" for finance theory. The CAPM model is taught throughout academia and continues to be the gold standard for estimating the equity cost of capital.

Chapter 6 describes the Modigliani-Miller theorem without and with corporate taxes. It was the origin of corporate finance.

Chapter 7 describes three capital asset pricing models: the capital asset pricing model (CAPM), the arbitrage pricing theory model (APT), and the Fama-French three-factor model (FFM). The emphasis is on the CAPM since it is the model widely used in practice. We start by explaining the CAPM model from Markowitz's work. Although in practice the corresponding formulas are used directly, we encourage the study of underlying mathematics to acquire a comprehensive understanding of it. The reader uninterested in the mathematical derivation of the CAPM can skip this part since we include an intuitive example.

Chapter 8 demonstrates the equivalence of discounted cash flow methods: free cash flow, equity cash flow, capital cash flow, and adjusted present value using perpetuities, including a simple derivation of Hamada's formulas to unlever and relever the beta coefficient. Because the WACC valuation assumes the company periodically rebalances its capital structure, we could not fail to include the explanation of the Miles-Ezzel formula and the different approaches proposed to compute the present

DOI: 10.4324/9781003628491-7

value of tax shields and the corresponding formulas to calculate betas and cost of capital.

Chapter 9 describes a bond rating trade-off model to estimate the optimal capital structure and the main theories that have tried to explain the capital structures as the trade-off theory and the pecking order theory, and the factors affecting the capital structure such the agency costs, asymmetric information, size, debt rating, creditworthiness, and strategy.

CHAPTER

6

The Modigliani-Miller theorem

Introduction

The Modigliani-Miller theorem (Modigliani & Miller, 1958) can be considered the birth of corporate finance since before Modigliani-Miller (MM) entered the scene, there was nothing like corporate finance theory. Merton Miller was awarded the Nobel Prize in Economics for their contributions to financial economics in 1990.

Given that Modigliani and Miller are largely responsible for what we know about valuation, appraisers must possess a thorough understanding of the Modigliani-Miller theorem (Modigliani & Miller, 1958) and Modigliani & Miller (1963) because it provides a foundation for understanding how the company's leverage affects the cost of equity capital and WACC. Furthermore, Chapter 8 demonstrates how well it integrates with the CAPM model.

DOI: 10.4324/9781003628491-8

Even though MM's work is today recognized as a crucial part of capital structure theory, the major objective was to provide a rule for the cost of capital for investment decisions, which was the principal area of research at the time.

After reading this chapter, you will be able to:

- Understand how the company value and the cost of capital are not affected by the capital structure in a world without taxes and perfect capital markets;
- Avoid confusion about the right cost of capital, according to the Proposition III's rule for investment decisions;
- Recognize how taxes can affect the company's value and its cost of capital.

Modigliani-Miller without taxes (1958)

Modigliani-Miller framework is supported by the fulfillment of five assumptions:

1. Capital markets are perfect
2. Individuals are rational and seek to maximize profit and market value
3. Firms can be divided into equivalent return classes
4. There are no taxes, neither corporate nor personal
5. There are no bankruptcy costs

As in other economic theories, the assumptions describe the framework in which the theory is supposed to work, so it is convenient to make some comments. We assume that all the information about the firm has already been included in the stock price and there are no transaction costs when we say capital markets are "perfect". Individuals acting rationally, will prefer to maximize the returns. The third assumption is the most important and requires clarification. According to the law of one price, if two securities have the same return and perfectly correlated into all nature states, they should have the same price when are traded in a free market. Any differences between asset prices should be immediately eliminated due to the opportunity for a profitable arbitrage. Thus, "equivalent returns" is associated with the law of one price.

MM initially assumes a tax-free world before examining the impact of taxes on the company's value. If there are no bankruptcy fees, the business will file for bankruptcy and its ownership will be transferred without incurring further expenses for accountants and attorneys.

As MM used propositions to develop their theorem, remember that a proposition deals with the connection between two existing concepts. The main difference between proposition and hypothesis is that a hypothesis must be testable and measurable, while a proposition deals with pure concepts for which no laboratory test is currently available. As a result, propositions rely on reasonable assumptions.

Proposition I

The market value of an unlevered firm in equilibrium is the present value of the expected operative income X in perpetuity, divided by the cost of capital corresponding to its class.

$$V = \frac{X}{ku}. \qquad [6.1]$$

Alternatively, the cost of capital can be expressed as:

$$ku = \frac{X}{V}. \qquad [6.2]$$

Therefore, the average cost of capital to any firm is independent of its capital structure and is equal to the cost of capital of a pure equity stream of its class. Since the operative income stream is produced by the firm's assets and nothing in Proposition I refers to the debt-equity mixture, the conclusion is that the capital structure is irrelevant, it cannot create or destroy value.

This statement is immediately counterintuitive for everyone who hears this assessment; neither academics nor practitioners accepted this conclusion at this moment, however, MM offered the arbitrage proof.

The arbitrage proof

As long as the relations [8.1] or [8.2] do not hold between any pair of firms in a class, arbitrage will occur and restore the stated equilibrium. Let's suppose two firms in the same class and assume for simplicity that the expected operative income is the same for both firms. Let company A be an all-equity firm and B a levered firm. In the event that Proposition I does not hold, we will assume the value of the levered firm exceeds the value of the unlevered firm ($112.5 vs. $100).

MM state that this situation cannot hold in a perfect capital market, because the arbitrage would immediately correct the discrepancy. By buying shares of B, we get 24%, a higher return than investing in stocks of A, which yields 20%. However, we

TABLE 6.1 Firms in the same equivalent return class in a world without taxes

	Firm A	Firm B
Operative income	20	20
Interest payment	0	5
Earnings before taxes	20	15
Income taxes	0	0
Return on equity capital	20%	24%
Equity market value	100	62.5
Debt market value	0	50
Firm market value	100	112.5
Cost of capital	20%	17.70%
D/E	0%	80%

can do something better. Suppose we have ten million in shares of B. We can do the following to create a profitable arbitrage:

1. Selling our holding on B, getting $10 million
2. Borrowing $8 million at a rate of 10%. In this way, we would replicate the capital structure of B (now we have $18 million, which is made up of $10 million in equity and $8 million borrowed)
3. Purchase $18 million of A, getting 18 x 20% = $3.6 million. After interest is paid, we will have 3.6–8 x 10% = $2.8 million

Because we get 28% (2.8/100), which is better than getting 24% in B, all investors would sell the stocks of B to buy stocks of A, exploiting these arbitrage opportunities, so the value of the overpriced shares will fall and the underpriced shares will rise, eliminating the discrepancy between the market values of A and B.

Formally, suppose you hold initially a fraction α of the total outstanding stock of B. Your return is equal to α multiplied by the net income (the operative income minus interest payment):

$$Y_B = \alpha(X - k_d D_B). \quad [6.3]$$

Now suppose you exchange the initial holding for another portolio. You sell your holding of B and implement a homemade leverage, borrowing yourself in a percentage equal to αD_B and using the total amount of money $\alpha(E_B+D_B)$ to buy shares of A, giving these shares as collateral. Your new holding is $\alpha(E_B+D_B)/E_A$. The return of the new portfolio is equal to α multiplied by X less the interest payment:

$$Y_A = \frac{\alpha(E_B + D_B)}{E_A} X - k_d \alpha D_B. \quad [6.4]$$

It also can be expressed as:

$$Y_A = \alpha \frac{V_V}{V_A} X - k_D \alpha D_B. \quad [6.5]$$

If $V_B > V_A$, then $Y_A > Y_B$. Hence, investors in B will sell their holdings decreasing E_B and also decreasing V_B, and will buy shares of A, increasing EA and also increasing V_A. In equilibrium we must have $V_B = V_A$, as stated in Proposition I:

Proposition II

For companies that are debt financed, MM derive a second proposition concerning the rate of return on common stock. According to Proposition I, the equity fair value of a levered company would be:

$$E = \frac{X - Interest}{ke}. \quad [6.6]$$

X can be expressed as Vku and the interest payment as Dkd:

$$E = \frac{Vku - Dkd}{ke},$$

Because V = D+E

$$ke = \frac{(E + D)ku - Dkd}{E},$$

Dividing each term of the numerator by E

$$ke = \frac{E}{E}ku + ku\frac{D}{E} - kd\frac{D}{E},$$

Eliminating terms and taking D/E as a common factor, we have:

$$ke = ku + (ku - kd)\frac{D}{E}. \quad [6.7]$$

The equity cost of capital of Firm B is:

$$ke = 20\% + (20\% - 10\%)\frac{50}{50} = 30\%$$

Since Proposition II is derived from Proposition I, and it has been proved that under arbitrage conditions, the company value is not modified by the capital structure choice. Thus, if the Proposition I hold, the equity value must be 50 million. And if the company B's debt increases to 60 million, the equity value must be $40 million and so forth. The hole is always the sum of the parts. This situation can be plotted as the "pizza story" a funny anecdote[1] told by Miller (1997) that had Yogi Berra as the protagonist:

> I have a simple explanation (for the first Modigliani – Miller proposition). It's after the ball game, and the pizza man comes up to Yogi Berra and he says, "Yogi, how do you want me to cut this pizza, into quarters?" Yogi says, "No cut it into eight pieces, I'm feeling hungry tonight". Now when I tell that story the usual reaction is, "And you mean to say that they gave you a (Nobel) prize for that?"

The weighted average cost of capital before taxes

The expected rate of return ke, on the stock of any company belonging to an equivalent return class is a linear function of leverage. That is, the expected yield of a share of stock is equal to the appropriate cost of capital ku for a pure equity stream in the class, plus a premium related to financial risk, which is the debt-to-equity ratio times the spread between ku and kd. Or equivalently, the market price of any share of stock is given by discounting its expected return (Operative Income-Interest) at the rate ke. Notice that the average weighted cost of capital (before taxes) remains constant:

$$WACC_{BT} = kd\frac{D}{V} + ke\frac{E}{V}. \quad [6.8]$$

$$WACC_{BT} = 10\%\frac{50}{100} + 30\%\frac{50}{100} = 20\%$$

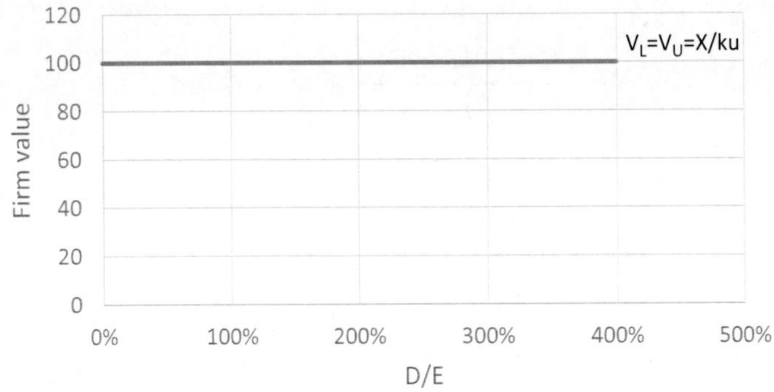

FIGURE 6.1 Firm value in a world without corporate taxes

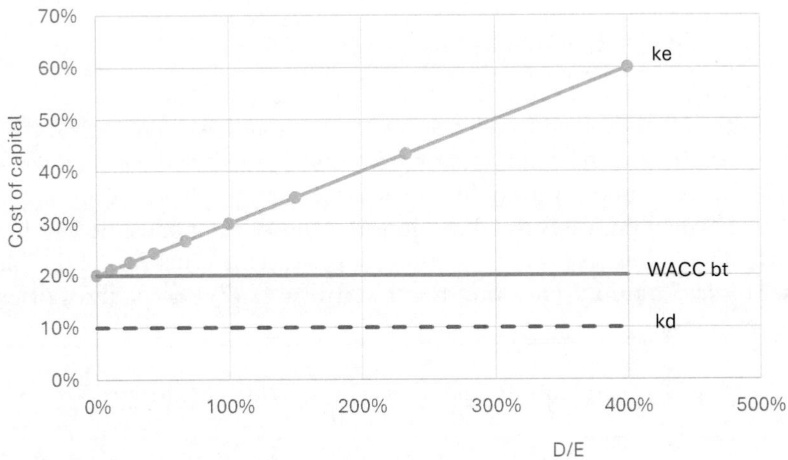

FIGURE 6.2 Cost of capital in a world without corporate taxes

Propositions I and II can be summarized graphically in Figures 6.1 and 6.2. Notice that under MM propositions without taxes, $V_L = V_U$, and the unlevered cost of capital is ku = 20%. Since debt is currently "cheaper" than equity, many practitioners believed that leverage can reduce the cost of capital. However, MM told us that there is no free lunch; as the company increases its leverage, the cost of equity capital also increases due to the financial risk, exactly offsetting the economy's debt financing. Lastly, the cost of capital (a weighted cost of capital without taxes or before taxes) remains constant.

Proposition III

Proposition III states (see pages 288–296 of the MM 1958 paper):

> If a firm in class k is acting in the best interest of the stockholders at the time of the decision, it will exploit an investment opportunity if and only if the rate of return on the investment, is as large as or larger than its cost of capital.

After over seven decades, one could ask "Who doesn't know that? There wasn't anything new in this statement". However, in this assertion, there is a significant misunderstanding on the relevant cost of capital. Suppose you are the CEO and a manager comes to you saying "We have an excellent project; if we invest one million now, it is expected a return of 1.1 million one year from now or a return of 10%. It makes sense to invest in such a project for two reasons: first, it can be entirely financed by a bank loan, which has an interest rate of 5%, lower than the project's return; second, we will have earned 0.5 million in a year without investing a single dollar. Therefore, the return is infinite". Figure 6.3 illustrates the cash flows associated with this reasoning:

Today	**One year from now**
Investment = 1M	Expected cash flow: 1.10M
Loan = 1M	Loan repayment: −1.05M
Net investment: 0	Expected net cash flow: 0.05M

FIGURE 6.3 Expected cash flow of an investment financed with debt

At first sight, the investment appears to be a profitable opportunity since the expected return doubles the interest rate. Should we undertake this business? Would you put money into it? First, you should be aware that the 1.10 million payoff is an expectation; however, the 1 million cash flow investment, the loan received from the bank, and the cash flow payment of 1.05 million to the bank are all certain cash flows. Nothing guarantees that the investment will yield 1.10 million in a year, even though the investor is still responsible for repaying the bank loan or suffer legal consequences. But have to make a choice and you are not sure about the future, you do not have the "Monday's newspaper".[2]

Therefore, how can we determine whether the business is convenient or not? The obvious response is to calculate the net present value, but what is the appropriate cost of capital? The 5% interest rate on bank loan? No! The 5% rate represents the bank's cost of capital, which reflects the loan's risk, which the borrower must pay punctually or suffer penalties. For this reason, because of the certainty of the payment, the bank charges a rate of 5%. The decision depends on the appropriate cost of capital; supposing we can get another investment opportunity of similar risk with a 15% return, the project's net present value will be negative by 0.4 million:

$$NPV = -1 + \frac{1.10}{1.15} = -0.04$$

I typically ask my Master's students if they would be willing to invest in the project. Answers range from "of course" to more sophisticated "depends on the cost of capital". All of them, nevertheless, seem to have a free lunch in mind – getting 0.5 million in a year. After explaining the convenience of not undertaking this business, they "accept" my explanation, but I think they would do the opposite in a real situation. If you are still not convinced, consider selling the business rather than investing in it. Nobody would pay more than its fair value since a bad investment cannot be turned into a good investment by financing. Someone might think that in the real world, they would undertake the business, and get 0.5 million one year from now without investing a single dollar. The appropriate cost of capital is irrelevant, they may believe, once the project is finished in a year. Not true! In this case, they would be acting as if they knew the future beforehand; however, the business is being evaluated now, not in a year. It is not possible to know beforehand what will happen. Therefore, the goodness of the investment depends on whether the risk-adjusted (marginal) cost of capital.

Misinterpretation of Proposition III can be avoided by remembering that it states that the minimum expected rate of return required for a project to be just worth doing, is a property of the project and its risk, and not of the particular securities that happen to be used to finance it.

Modigliani-Miller with taxes

In 1958, MM told us that the capital structure is irrelevant in a world without taxes. However, the original work contained an error that was later corrected in Modigliani & Miller (1963). In the presence of income taxes, capital structure matters due to the interest payments reducing income tax, and propositions I and II need to be revised. We reproduce our example of Firms A and B, including income taxes, this time using a 40% legal income tax.

TABLE 6.2 Firms in the same equivalent return class in a world with corporate taxes

	Firm A	Firm B
Operative income	20	20
Interest payment	0	5
Earnings before taxes	20	15
Income taxes (40%)	8	6
Earnings after taxes	12	9
Return on equity capital	20%	30%
Equity market value	60	30
Debt market value	0	50
Firm market value	60	80

Take note of two crucial things:

1. Firm A distribute $12 in dividends to shareholders, while Firm B distribute $14 in cash flow to stakeholders (interest of $5 and dividends of $9). The tax saving of $2 represents the difference (interest x t = 5 x 40%).

2. B's firm market value is \$80, while A's firm market value is \$60; the present value of the tax is \$20, which accounts for the difference:

$$PVTS = \frac{Dkdt}{kd} = Dt. \qquad [6.9]$$

$$PVTS = 50 \times 40\% = 20$$

Therefore, the value of the levered company is equal to the unlevered company plus the present value of the tax shield:

$$V_L = V_U + Dt = 60 + 20 = 80$$

Just one thing to clarify. Suppose firm A issues \$50 in debt to acquire its outstanding shares. Some people may get confused at this point since when they compare the equity value of \$60 at the start with the equity value of \$30 following the change in capital structure. The equity market value drops from \$60 to \$30 instead of \$10 (60 – 50) because the shareholders keep the tax shield's present value. Therefore, capital structure decisions can raise shareholder value.

Proposition I

Now we must consider the operative income after taxes. Therefore, the operating income after taxes is X(1 – t).

$$V = \frac{X(1-t)}{ku}. \qquad [6.10]$$

Proposition II and WACC

Proposition II under taxes is derived from Proposition I under taxes:

$$E = \frac{(X - Int)(1-t)}{ke},$$

$$ke = \frac{[E + D)ku - Int](1-t)}{E},$$

$$ke = ku + (ku - kd)\frac{D}{E}(1-t). \qquad [6.11]$$

The weighted average cost of capital is calculated using the formula [4.9] which we discussed in Chapter 4.

$$WACC = kd(1-t)\frac{D}{V} + ke\frac{E}{V}. \qquad [4.9]$$

Figures 6.4 and 6.5 show the firm value and cost of capital.

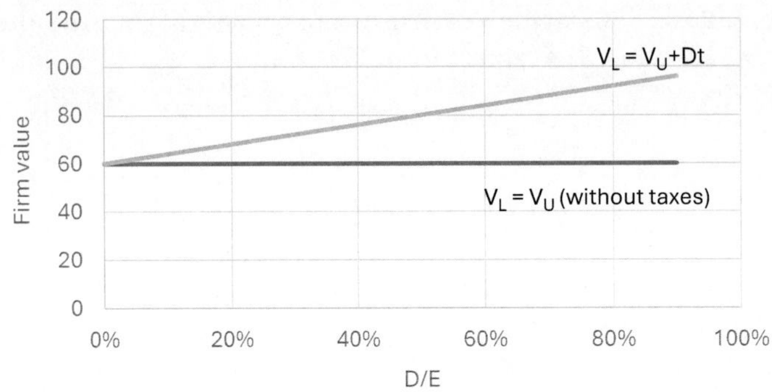

FIGURE 6.4 Firm value under MM propositions with and without taxes

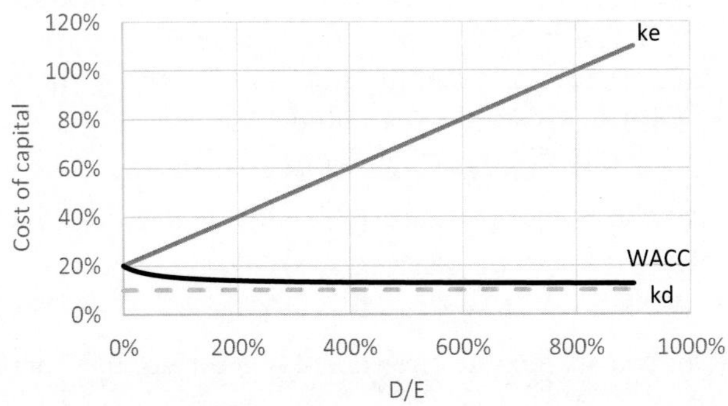

FIGURE 6.5 Cost of capital under MM propositions with taxes

Proposition II with taxes implies that for a higher leverage ratio, the WACC would converge to the cost of debt. The asymptotic form of the WACC can be demonstrated by taking the first and second derivatives of the WACC with respect to the cost of debt. Let's d the after- tax cost of debt, e the cost of equity, and W the WACC:

$$W = d\frac{D}{D+E} + e\frac{E}{D+E},$$

$$W = (dD + eE)(D+E)^{-1},$$

Deriving W with respect to d

$$W' = (dD + eE)(-1)(D+E)^{-2} + (D+E)^{-1}e,$$

The first derivative is negative, indicating that the function is decreasing:

$$W' = -(dD + eE)(D+E)^{-2} + (D+E)^{-1}e.$$

The second derivative is positive, indicating that the function is concave:

$$W'' = (dD + eE)2(D+E)^{-3} + (D+E)^{-2}e + (D+E)^{-1}(0) - e(D+E)^{-2}.$$

Several works on MM propositions were published after the seminal paper to analyze different frameworks. For example, Miller (1977) introduced the effect of personal taxes on capital structure decisions. Other memorable papers are Miller (1988) and Modigliani (1988). For an analysis of the concepts of risk class, arbitrage, and taxation, see Ross (1988).

How MM helps us in practice

Up to here, many skeptics would agree that the MM is a sound theory but they believe that it belongs to the realm of "blackboard economics", where there is little correspondence between theory and practice. However, there is not something more practical than a good theory. By the way, do you think practitioners know that the extensively used in practice Hamada's formulas require all the assumptions of the CAPM and the MM model with taxes? Thinking that "the sum of the parts is equal to the whole", is very useful in finance. In Chapter 17, we will discuss on a crossroad we faced when valuing Sofora's holding and how MM theory helped us in resolving it. According to Ross (1988), economists owe Miller and Modigliani at least as much as mathematicians and philosophers owe Godel.

The optimal capital structure

According to the MM model with taxes "more debt, more value". However, in practice, no financial manager is extreme. With moderate leverage, one may assume that the tax shield goes to the shareholder, allowing the company to increase shareholder value. Nonetheless, at any point of leverage, due to financial risk, investors would require a higher cost of capital, and the share prices would start to decline, offsetting the benefits of debt, suggesting an optimal capital structure. Therefore, there would be a tradeoff between the fiscal benefits and the expected financial distress cost. While the trade-off is appealing in theory, in practice, the election of

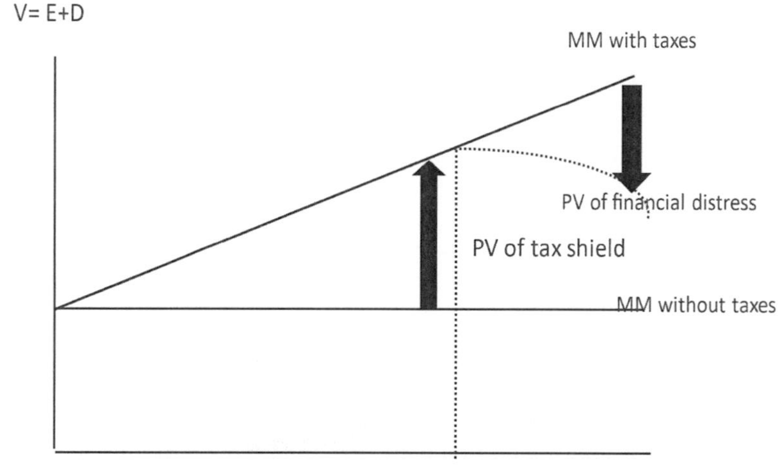

FIGURE 6.6 Optimal debt/equity ratio

the optimal D/V ratio involves more than one tradeoff and other considerations, as we will explain in Chapter 9.

About the realism of MM propositions

Regarding the truth of MM propositions, I would prefer to reproduce a dialogue that took place during a deposition in a lawsuit between Merton Miller and the attorney of the other side, which appear on Miller (1997):

Attorney: Professor, do you or do you not believe that the M&M Propositions are true?

Merton Miller: Those Propositions were conditional propositions. They say that if you accept the specific assumptions we made about the nature of the capital markets, then you must accept the conclusions. The M&M Propositions follow logically from the assumptions and in that sense, they are certainly true.

Attorney: But what if the assumptions underlying the derivatives are false? Doesn't that mean that the M&M Propositions are false?

Merton Miller: You still do not seem to understand the principles of scientific inquiry. The minute you are questioning the assumptions underlying the model you leave the world of pure logic behind. You have gone from deduction to induction, from an ideal world to the empirical world where terms like true and false no longer apply. On empirical matters, you cannot speak of anything as simple as right or wrong, but only of the degree of accuracy of the predictions of the model. And for judging the accuracy of the predictions, the literal accuracy of the assumptions is beside the point. It all comes down to the question of "goodness of fit" and that alas cannot be given any simple, one-word, or even one-line answer. How good a fit is, depends on the specific context and on the specific purpose in asking the question.

Concluding thoughts

In 1958, MM told us that, in a world without taxes, the firm value comes from its expected operative income, and the capital structure was irrelevant; modify the capital structure cannot increase the firm value in a perfect capital market, since the arbitrage operates to correct any difference between firms in the same class.

In 1963, they corrected a mistake from the 1958 paper and concluded that a leveraged firm is equal to the value of the unleveraged firm plus the present value of tax savings. Since more debt means tax savings but on the other hand could mean financial distress, it would suggest an optimal capital structure defined as a trade-off between the present value of tax savings and the present value of financial distress costs. However, the optimal capital structure does not depend on unique tradeoffs. In Chapter 9, we will discuss an optimal capital structure model as the factors that can affect the capital structure decision.

Short questions and problems

1. Mark true or false:

   a) Financial risk is represented by the dispersion of shareholder's returns when the firm is leveraged.
   b) The expected return on equity increases as the firm leverages, due to the probability of bankruptcy rises.
   c) For an unlevered firm that does not grow and does not pay income taxes, EBIT = EBT = Net income = Dividends.
   d) Under MM propositions without taxes, if the firm uses leverage, the earnings per share (EPS) increases while the price/earnings decreases.
   e) If the firm leverages, the shareholder's return increases, although their wealth remains invariant under MM propositions without taxes.

2. Mark true or false:

   a) Only accounting values of debt and equity must be considered in the capital structure rather than market values.
   b) The accounting values are historical and do not reflect the marginal cost of capital.
   c) The cost of capital is always marginal.

3. Comment on this phrase: "in the world of Modigliani-Miller without taxes, debt financing reduces the weighted average cost of capital".
4. Comment on this phrase: "MM ignore the fact that when the leverage increases, the interest rate on debt increases".
5. Complete the following table, explain a possible arbitrage strategy that would yield the same return as investing in Firm B but investing less money, and

TABLE 6.3 Exercise about MM in a world without taxes

	Firm A	Firm B
EBIT	20	20
Interest	0	4
EBT	20	16
Income taxes	0	0
ke = ku + (ku-kd)D/E	20%	?
Equity market value (E)	100	70
Debt market value (D)	0	40
Firm market value (V)	100	110
WACC before taxes	20%	?
D/E	0%	?

demonstrate that the WACC before taxes is of 20% after the arbitrage process, in a world without taxes (Hint: remember "the pizza story" when calculating ke using Proposition II).

6. ku = 20%; kd = 10%, t = 0%. Draw the ke function and the WACC before taxes according to proposition II without taxes for the following D/E ratios (the first is done for you):

   a) D/E = 0%: ke = 20% + (20%–10%)0 = 20%; WACCbt = 10% x 0 + 20% x 1,00 = 20%
   b) 30%
   c) 60%

7. For the following D/V ratios, what is the equivalent D/E ratio (the first was done for you):

   a) D/V = 20% answer: (20%/80% = 25%)
   b) D/V = 50%
   c) D/V = 60%
   d) D/V = 90%

8. Suppose you are the CEO of a company and the CFO approaches you with the following statement: "We have an excellent investment opportunity since we have to invest $10 million today in a project that has an expected return of 10% after taxes, and can be financed with a bank subsidized loan of 6%". As a CEO, do you agree with the financial manager's opinion? Consider the scenario in which you accept the investment and try to sell it to someone else right away, when the cost of capital with a similar level of risk is 12%. What is the NPV of the investment?
9. The following table shows the free cash flow of a project whose internal rate of return is 9% and its cost of capital is 12%; thus, the project must be rejected. However, the CFO thinks that the project should be accepted if it is fully financed by a 6% a bank-subsidized loan, because the tax savings would make the project profitable. The capital is redeemed in five installments of two million. What do you think?

TABLE 6.4 Exercise about an investment finance with debt

	Yr 0	Yr 1	Yr 2	Yr 3	Yr 4	Yr 5
EBIT		4.3	4.3	4.3	4.3	4.3
Taxes (40%)		1.72	1.72	1.72	1.72	1.72
Free Cash Flow	–10	2.58	2.58	2.58	2.58	2.58

10. Under MM propositions with taxes the firm market value of an unlevered firm is V_U = 500 million. Assume Firm A decides to issue bonds for $400 million, modifying its capital structure. Assume kd = 7%, ku = 12%, t = 40%

    a) What is the new firm value, the WACC, and the EBIT?
    b) If the firm issues debt for $400 million and uses the money to repurchase shares, why the new equity value does not reduce by $400 million?

11. Suppose that an unlevered firm, with a cost of capital ku = 20%, decides to modify its capital structure to a D/V ratio of 99%. If the company goes into bankruptcy, the bondholders would be the new shareholders. What is the new shareholders' required return?
12. ZZ Corp. is a leveraged firm. Its operative income is $50 million. The unleveraged cost of equity is ku = 10%, D = 100 million, and kd = 6%. Calculate the unlevered and levered firm value under each of the following conditions:

    a) MM without taxes, verifying that the WACC before taxes is 10%.
    b) MM with taxes, t = 40%, In addition, demonstrate that VL = FCF/WACC and E = CFE/ke

Notes

1 When we explain this point to students in a Master's finance course, we ask them whether they can understand the 1958 paper's analogy, where MM describe the firm value as the price of whole milk. The farmer can intend to increase its wealth by transforming the pure milk into butter; however, the benefit of skimming the milk rather than selling whole milk would be purely illusory since the earnings gained from selling the high-priced butter fat would be lost in selling the low-priced residue of thinned milk. In this scenario, the stream of whole milk corresponds to free cash flow, the stream of butter corresponds to the interest, and the residue of thinned milk corresponds to the cash flow to equity.

2 In some countries, horse races are run on weekends. You would have a money machine if you had the Monday newspaper on Friday, as you would be aware of the outcomes in the future. You are unsure, nevertheless, about the project's 1.10 million payback.

References

Miller, M. (1977, May). Debt and Taxes. *Journal of Finance*, *32*, 261–276.

Miller, M. (1988). The Modigliani-Miller Propositions After Thirty Years. *Journal of Economic Perspectives*, 2(4), 99–120.

Miller, M. (1997, December). Testimony in Glendale Federal Bank's lawsuit against the U.S. government.

Miller, M. (1998). The M&M Propositions 40 Years Later. *European Financial Management*, 4(2), 113–120.

Modigliani, F. (1988). MM, Past, Present, Future. *Journal of Economic Perspectives*, 2, 149–158.

Modigliani, F., & Miller, M. (1958, June). The Cost of Capital, Corporation Finance, and the theory of the Firm. *The American Economic Review*, *48*(3), 261–297.

Modigliani, F., & Miller, M. (1963, June). Corporate Income, Taxes and the Cost of Capital: A Correction. *The American Economic Review*, *53*(3), 433–443.

Ross, S. (1988). Comment on the Modigliani-Miller Propositions. The Journal of Economic Perspectives, 2(4), 127–133.

CHAPTER

7

From the modern portfolio theory to capital asset pricing models

Introduction

This chapter focuses on the famous capital asset pricing model, which is a fundamental piece of corporate finance and the model used by most appraisers use to estimate the cost of equity capital (including situations of absence of market values). We will describe the CAPM from its connection with the modern portfolio theory as it is a development of Markowitz's work.

DOI: 10.4324/9781003628491-9

As empirical tests of the CAPM revealed that it cannot fully explain assets return using the market beta factor, multifactor models such as the Fama-French three-factor model and the arbitrage pricing theory (APT) were proposed.

After reading this chapter, you will be able to:

- Understand the connection between modern portfolio theory and the CAPM;
- Calculate the beta coefficient using a spreadsheet;
- Perform the Fama-French model using multiple regression.

The modern portfolio theory

The modern portfolio theory (MPT), was developed by Markowitz (1952), who shared the Nobel Prize in Economics in 1990 for his contribution to financial economics. According to Markowitz, it is possible to design an "efficient frontier" of optimal portfolios, which are the portfolios that offer the maximum possible expected return for a given level of risk or the minimum level of risk for an expected return. MPT relies on the following assumptions:

- Investors are risk-averse and rational in nature (they seek to maximize returns while minimizing risk)
- The portfolio's risk is defined by the variability of returns
- Investors receive all pertinent information regarding their investment decisions promptly.
- Investors can borrow or lend at a risk-free rate of interest.
- Investors prefer to increase consumption and are risk averse, so their utility function is concave and increasing

We start by explaining how to calculate the risk of a portfolio and its expected return. Suppose we have two assets; asset 1 has an expected annual return of 10% and a risk of 30%; asset 2 has an expected annual return of 20% and a risk of 40%. While asset 2 offers an expected higher return, asset 1 has carries less risk. A conservative investor would invest in asset 1, whereas an aggressive investor would invest in asset 2. Which is the best choice? We can't say because it will depend on the subjective risk-return preferences of each investor. However, we are not obligated to invest in only one asset since we can invest in a combination of two or more, and as we will see, diversification pays off!

The expected portfolio return is the weighted average return on the assets included in the portfolio, where X represents the weight of each asset and r its expected return:

$$E(r_p) = X_1E(r_1) + X_2E(r_2) + \ldots + X_NE(r_N). \qquad [7.1]$$

$$E(r_p) = 0.6 \times 10\% + 0.4 \times 20\% = 14\%$$

The portfolio's risk is represented by the variance of the portfolio's return. In the case of two assets, it is equal to:

$$\sigma_p^2 = X_1^2\sigma_1^2 + X_2^2\sigma_2^2 + 2X_1X_2\sigma_{12}. \qquad [7.2]$$

Since the last expression is the variance of a weighted sum of random variables[1], each weight X is squared first and then multiplied by the corresponding variance. Now let's analyze the last term: notice that the covariance between asset 1 and asset 2 (σ_{12}) is multiplied by the weights of each asset and also multiplied by 2; this is because when we have two assets in the portfolio, we have two covariances: the covariance between asset 1 and asset 2, and the covariance between asset 2 and asset 1:

$$\sigma_p^2 = 0.6^2 \times 30\%^2 + 0.4^2 \times 40\%^2 + 2 \times 0.6 \times 0.4 \times 0.5 = 0.0868$$

A variance of 0.0868 is an unreliable squared measure that cannot interpret directly.[2] For this reason, the risk of a portfolio is calculated as the standard deviation, which is the square root of the variance. Note that standard deviation is a percentage of 29.46%, and since the expected return is also measured as a percentage, it now has a meaningful interpretation: "portfolio's expected return is 14% with a standard deviation of 29.46%".

$$\sigma_p = \sqrt{\sigma_p^2} = 29.46\% \tag{7.3}$$

In Markowitz's model, expected return and variance estimations are made using historical returns, based on the statistical argument that the sample mean is an unbiased estimator of the population mean.

The only free lunch in finance: Diversification pays

It is worth noting that the standard deviation of 29.46% *is lower than the weighted average of the standard deviations of the assets included in the portfolio,* which would be:

$$\sigma_p = 0.6 \times 30\% + 0.4 \times 40\% = 34\%$$

However, the portfolio's risk can only be calculated in this way if the correlation coefficient between asset 1 and asset 2 is 1, indicating that they are perfectly correlated. Any correlation coefficient less than one lowers the risk below 34%. If we add one more asset to the portfolio (asset 3), we'd have one more variance and six covariances: cov(1,2), cov(2,1), cov(1,3), cov(3,1), cov(2,3), and cov(3,2)

$$\sigma_p^2 = X_1^2\sigma_1 + X_2^2\sigma_2 + X_3^2\sigma_3 + 2X_1X_2\sigma_{12} + 2X_1X_3\sigma_{13} + 2X_2X_3\sigma_{23}. \tag{7.4}$$

In a well-diversified portfolio, we have n assets and a spider of covariances. Since the individual weights (X_i^2) are 1/n and tend to zero, the portfolio risk is defined by the sum of covariances:

$$\sigma_p^2 = X_1^2\sigma_1^2 + X_2^2\sigma_2^2 + \ldots + X_N^2\sigma_N^2 + 2X_1X_2\sigma_{12} + 2X_1X_3\sigma_{13} + \ldots + 2X_NX_N\sigma_{NN.}$$

$$\sigma_p^2 = \sum_{i=1}^{N} X_i^2\sigma_i^2 + \sum_{i \neq j} X_iX_j\sigma_{ij} = \sum_i\sum_j X_iX_j\sigma_{ij}. \tag{7.5}$$

Figure 7.1 depicts the covariance matrix, which is used to structure the portfolio's covariances. To calculate the total covariances, first sum the covariances in the first row above the diagonal dashed line using only values of i ≠ j until you reach the of columns. Then, repeat the process for the remaining rows until you reach the final row.

$$\begin{bmatrix} \sigma_{11} & \sigma_{12} & \sigma_{13} \cdots & \sigma_{1N} \\ \sigma_{21} & \sigma_{22} & \sigma_{23} \cdots & \sigma_{2N} \\ \cdot & \cdot & \cdot & \cdot \\ \cdot & \cdot & \cdot & \\ \sigma_{N1} & \sigma_{N2} & \sigma_{N3} \cdots & \sigma_{NN} \end{bmatrix}$$

FIGURE 7.1 Covariance matrix

The variance of a well-diversified portfolio is the average covariance. The number of covariances that we have to estimate are those that remain above the diagonal represented by a dotted line, which can be counted like this: N-1 covariances in the first row, N-2 in the second row, and one covariance in the penultimate row, forming an arithmetic progression. Therefore, we have a sum of terms of an arithmetic progression whose formula is

$$S = \frac{First\ term + last\ term}{2} Number\ of\ terms,$$

$$S = \frac{(N-1)+1}{2}(N-1) - \frac{N^2 - N}{2}. \quad [7.6]$$

The portfolio has N variances (one for each stock) and $N^2 - N$ covariances, hence, its variance is:

$$\sigma_p^2 = N\left(\frac{1}{N}\right)^2 \text{Average variance} + (N^2 - N)\left(\frac{1}{N}\right)^2 \text{Average covariance}. \quad [7.7]$$

As n increases, the variance of the portfolio continuously approximates the average covariance.

Efficient portfolios

All portfolios are not equal since some portfolios have a better risk-return relationship. These portfolios are known as "efficient portfolios" since they provide the greatest expected return for a given level of risk or the lowest risk for a given return. Supposing that we have to find the combination that maximizes the portfolio's expected return:

$$E(r_p) - X_1E(r_1) + X_2E(r_2) + \ldots + X_NE(r_N). \quad [7.8]$$

At the same time, three restrictions must be verified:

1. The proportions invested in each asset must be positive[3]
2. The sum of the proportions must be equal to 1
3. The variance of a particular combination is V★:

$$X_1, X_2 ..., X_N \geq 0$$

$$X_1 + X_2 + ... + X_N = 1$$

$$\sigma_p^2 = \sum_i \sum_j X_i X_j \sigma_{ij} = V\star$$

Figure 7.2 shows the possible combinations that can be achieved in the risk-expected return space, and the collection of all such portfolios defines a region in this

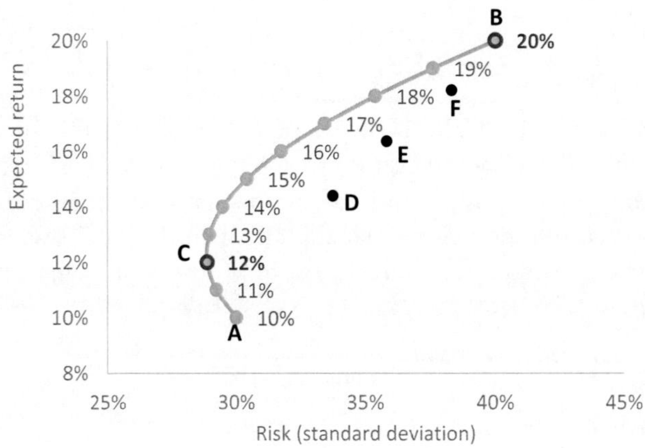

FIGURE 7.2 The efficient frontier

	Asset A	Asset B
Return	10%	20%
Risk	30%	40%
Corr. Coeff.	0.5	

=SQRT(+A8^2*$B$3^2+B8^2*$C$3^2 + 2*$B$4*$B$3*$C$3*A8*B8)

Weight in A	Weight in B	Risk	Return	
0%	100%	40%	20%	=+A9*$B$2+B9*$C$2
10%	90%	38%	19%	
20%	80%	35%	18%	
30%	70%	33%	17%	
40%	60%	32%	16%	
50%	50%	30%	15%	
60%	40%	29%	14%	
70%	30%	29%	13%	
80%	20%	29%	12%	
90%	10%	29%	11%	
100%	0%	30%	10%	

FIGURE 7.3 The efficient frontier calculated with Excel

space. Substituting V⋆ in the first quadratic parametric problem and optimizing, we will obtain the combination of values X_1, X_2,..., X_N, which indicates how we should assign the money among the different assets to achieve the optimum portfolios. Combinations from point C to point B constitute the efficient frontier represented by portfolios with the lowest risk for a given level of expected return or the highest expected return for a given level of risk. Nobody would invest in combinations outside the C-B function since these combinations offer less return with more risk.

The capital market line

Tobin (1958) expanded the efficient frontier to include risk-free securities in the efficient portfolio. The investment process can be separated from its owner's investment preferences into two steps:

1. The construction of an efficient portfolio, as described by Markowitz
2. The decision to combine this efficient portfolio with a riskless investment

Tobin demonstrated that in a perfect capital market where stocks are traded with the option to lend or borrow at a risk-free rate, investors do not need to calculate a multiplicity of covariance terms. The expected return of a portfolio composed of a stock portfolio and a risk-free security is:

$$E(r_p) - X_1 rf + (1 - X_1)E(r). \quad [7.9]$$

Since the risk-free security has no risk[4], the variance of the expected portfolio's return is:

$$\sigma_{rp}^2 = (1 - X_1)^2 \sigma_r^2. \quad [7.10]$$

The standard deviation of such a portfolio is:

$$\sigma_{rp} = (1 - X_1)\sigma_r. \quad [7.11]$$

Deriving expressions [7.9] and [7.11] for changes in X, we have:

$$\frac{dE(r_p)}{dX_1} = rf - E(r). \quad [7.12]$$

$$\frac{d\sigma_{rp}}{dX_1} = -\sigma_{rp}. \quad [7.13]$$

Dividing expression [7.12] by σ_{rp} and multiplying by -1 we obtain a functional expression for the risk-return relationship:

$$\frac{dE(r_p)}{dX_1} = \frac{E(r_p) - rf}{\sigma_{rp}}. \quad [7.14]$$

The new capital market line (CML) can be represented as the tangent line connecting the risk-free rate and the efficient frontier. Although combinations like C are available, there are no better combinations like M, also known as the market portfolio, because the M portfolio is the best risk-return combination that all investors would hold. CML represents the best linear combinations between risk-free securities and efficient portfolios and expresses the expected return as the risk-free rate plus the market risk premium multiplied by $\frac{\sigma_r}{\sigma_{r_M}}$.

$$E(r) = r_f + (r_M - r_f)\frac{\sigma_r}{\sigma_{r_M}}. \quad [7.15]$$

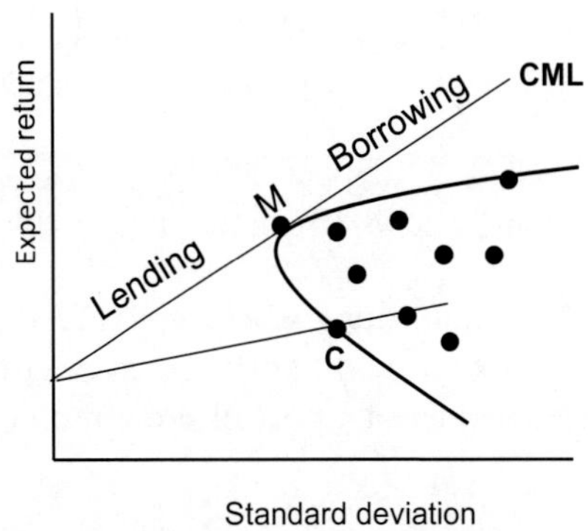

FIGURE 7.4 The capital market line

Equation 7.8 has a crucial implication: the market risk premium of an efficient portfolio varies in proportion to its standard deviation. Including risk-free securities in the portfolio expanded the investment alternatives in comparison to the efficient frontier proposed by the modern portfolio theory. In equilibrium, all investors will be placed along the CML according to their preferences of risk-return, for example:

- Conservative investors could invest in some combination of risk-free assets and the market portfolio. Therefore, lending money to the government and buying the portfolio M.
- An aggressive investor could borrow money at a risk-free rate and invest in the market portfolio. The principle of leveraged investing is that if the stock market goes up, higher profit could be realized, coming from the difference between the investment return on the borrowed capital and the cost of the associated interest. However, if the stock market goes down, losses amplify. Therefore, this strategy involves more risk.

The CML assumes that investors can lend and borrow at risk-free interest, and the expectations about returns, standard deviations, and correlation coefficients are homogeneous.

The capital asset pricing model

In 1964, William Sharpe, John Lintner, Jack Treynor, and Jan Mossin developed a model that would have an enormous influence among practitioners and academics. Sharpe was the only one who published his work and won the Nobel Prize in Economics in 1990.

The CAPM assumes the perspective of a fully diversified investor, and because the individual risk is eliminated by diversification, in such a world, the only risk that commands a risk premium is the market risk, which is measured by the market asset beta. The CAPM relies on the following assumptions:

1. Investors are risk-averse, and have the same holding period.
2. All investors have homogenous subjective expectations on returns, variances, and covariances for all assets in the portfolio.
3. Risk and reward are correlated linearly.
4. There are no taxes or transaction costs.
5. Investors have free access to all available information at no cost.
6. There is no restriction on borrowing and lending at risk-free.

Friedman (1962) claimed that economic theories are to be judged by their predictions and not by the realism of their assumptions. Of course, assumptions come from the world of logic and deduction; in the empirical world, there is not a simple answer as "true" or "false" where econometric tests are required to respond if "the hypothesis is significant at 5%".

Assumptions 1 and 2 are frequently founded in finance theories, although it is impossible to know whether investors have homogeneous expectations or not.

Assumption 3 is necessary to support the linear relationship between risk (measured by beta) and return, as derived from formula 7.9. In favor of assumption 4, we must say that there are transactions costs in the real-world, however they are not significant enough to inhibit a purchase or sale of assets. Assumption 5 relies on Fama's sense that capital markets are efficient. Although you probably don't have access to all available information, your broker can help you to fill the gap, and on the other hand, there are not too many cases where someone can benefit from insight information. Assumption 6 is realistic since you can lend money to the US treasury at a risk-free rate, and borrow money at an interest rate similar to the risk-free rate, giving your shares as collateral.

Market (systematic) risk and unique risk

The specific or unique risk of an asset is that affects one asset or a small group of assets. Examples of specific risks are the loss of a patent, a major natural disaster, a new competitor in the marketplace, or a regulatory change affecting the company's operation. The good news is that it can be eliminated by diversification. Figure 7.5 shows that if we add more stocks in the portfolio, the unique risk reduces fast at first and then gradually until reaches a plateau, or limit[5], leaving a portion of risk known as market risk or systematic risk.

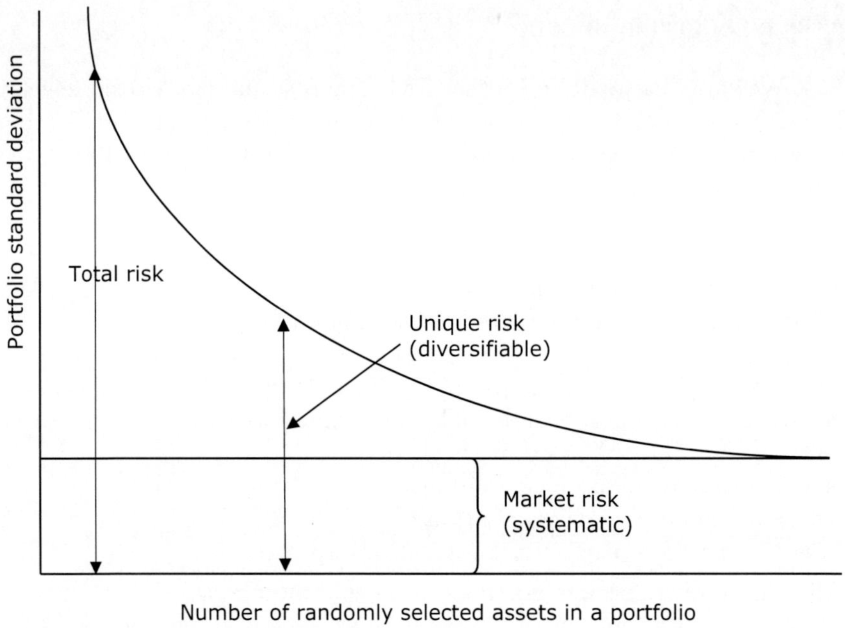

FIGURE 7.5 Unique risk and market risk

The market risk cannot be diversified away because it affects the overall market performance. Examples of market risk include interest rate moves, inflation rate change, financial crises, exchange rate fluctuations, recessions or geopolitical events. These changes usually have a "surprise effect" since the market cannot anticipate this effect.

The beta portfolio

When an investor adds a new asset to a portfolio, the relevant risk of the asset is represented by its marginal contribution to the portfolio's risk, which is measured by the beta portfolio and the weight of asset j in the portfolio.

$$\beta_P = \frac{Cov(R_j, R_P)}{\sigma^2_{R_P}}. \quad [7.16]$$

How does beta help portfolio managers?

High-beta stocks go up more than the index when the markets are bullish and go down when the markets are bearish. Adding an asset with a beta greater than one will increase the risk of a portfolio; if a stock has a beta lower than one, it will reduce the risk of a portfolio. Therefore, the criteria to include a new asset in the portfolio and thus improve the risk-return relation is not the isolated correlation of the stock with any stock or a group of stocks of the portfolio, but the covariance of the asset with the portfolio as a whole, represented by the beta portfolio. Instead of analyzing the stock return matrix correlation, we must consider the interaction between the stock return with the portfolio return. Any reader interested in learning how the interception and beta coefficients are derived can refer to any econometrics textbook.

The market beta

When the portfolio is the market portfolio M, we discuss the market beta, which is a measure that indicates how sensitive is the stock return to a change in the stock index return. Beta can also be expressed as the correlation coefficient between the stock return and the market return times $\frac{\sigma_r}{\sigma_{r_M}}$.

$$\beta = \frac{\rho_{r,r_M}\sigma_r\sigma_{r_M}}{\sigma^2_{r_M}} = \rho_{r,r_M}\frac{\sigma_r}{\sigma_{r_M}}. \qquad [7.17]$$

Notice that adding the correlation coefficient between the asset return and the stock market return to the formula 7.15, the CML formula becomes the CAPM formula.

$$E(r_j) = r_f + (r_M - r_f)\beta_j. \qquad [7.18]$$

The intuition behind the formula tells us that an investor should claim a risk-free rate (which it is supposed compensate the time value of money) plus a market risk premium, adjusted by the beta coefficient. The risk-free asset is generally estimated using the US ten-year T-Bond yield that accounts for the time value of money (inflation plus a real interest rate). The market risk premium is the expected return from the market over the risk-free rate, which is estimated using a historical market risk premium. Therefore, r_M-r_f is an "expectation" based on historical data (approximately 5/6% per year using the S&P500 index from 1925).[6]

Because CAPM assumes the perspective of a fully diversified investor, the portfolio is the market portfolio. As the market portfolio return is unobserved since no portfolio includes every available asset in the investment universe, a diversified portfolio, like S&P500 or MSCI EAFE, is used as a proxy. The beta of the stock market return is 1 (one) because the correlation between the stock market return and itself is 1:

$$\beta = \rho_{r_M,r_M}\frac{\sigma_{r_M}}{\sigma_{r_M}} = 1. \qquad [7.19]$$

The security market line and the market equilibrium

The CAPM states that in an efficient market, buyers and sellers will trade the asset so that its price will reflect its market risk, which is represented by beta. What happens if an asset fails to line up on the SML? Suppose asset A offers an expected return higher than the CAPM predicts; since stock A is underpriced, the arbitrage takes place, and investors will buy this asset, the price goes up, and the returns fall to achieve the SML. The opposite happens if the return is less than the SML prediction, which is the case for stock B. Therefore, prices adjust to inform a consensus expected return along the Security Market Line. As William Sharpe stated, as cited by Bernstein (2007):

> Yes, I still think it is good to assume that you have to take higher risks if you are seeking higher returns. If you take risks other than the risk of being in the market itself, you probably will not be rewarded, because stock picking seldom pays off. So why do it?

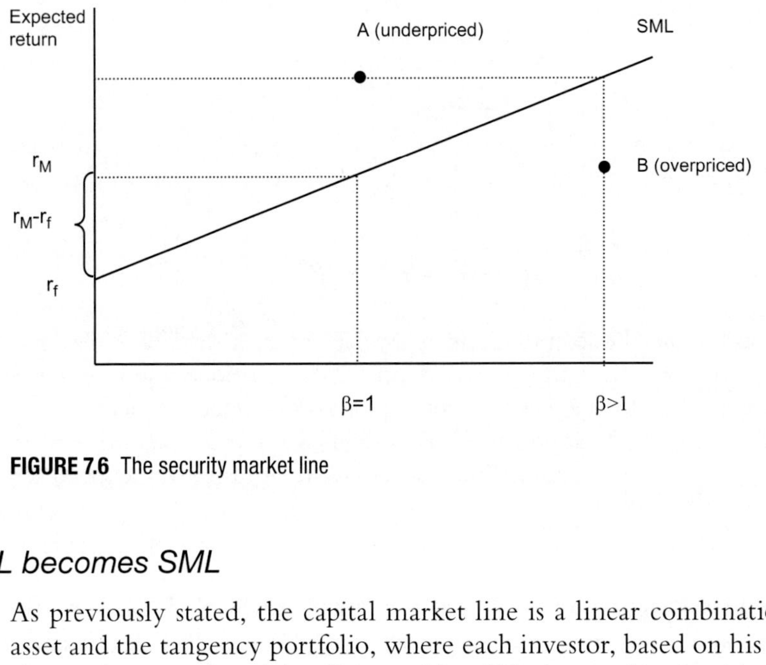

FIGURE 7.6 The security market line

CML becomes SML

As previously stated, the capital market line is a linear combination of a risk-free asset and the tangency portfolio, where each investor, based on his risk preferences, chooses how much weight of his wealth will be invested in the risk-free asset and the tangency portfolio M. While CML states the return-risk relationship as a trade-off between the expected return of a portfolio and its standard deviation, SML defines the risk-return relationship as a trade-off between an asset or portfolio's expected return and its beta. While the CML only deals with portfolio risk, the SML deals with market risk and can be used to both portfolios and individual assets.

Instead of calculating all pairwise covariances and resulting portfolio risk, the market risk of a well-diversified portfolio is determined via securities' weighted covariances with the stock market index. In equilibrium, any portfolios and assets that do not reflect the expected return predicted by the SML vanish, and CML transforms into SML.

Box 7.1 Summary

From the individual risk-return relationship to the security market line, Figures 7.7 to 7.12 summarize the evolution of the risk-return relationship across the time, describing how pieces were added to the puzzle. Initially, the choice was between investing in an asset with a higher return as B, and an asset with a lower return and risk, such as A. The decision depends on subjective risk-return preferences. Asset A, which has a lower return but carries less risk, is preferred by conservative or lower risk investors over high-risk investors, who choose asset B. Because diversification pays by reducing risk, it was better investing in a portfolio A+B rather than individual assets. Markowitz discovered the efficient frontier, which states that only portfolios located along the efficient frontier will be accepted. Years later, Tobin adds risk-free assets to the portfolio bringing it to the CML. All investors would have the market portfolio M, which could include risk-free bonds to form a lending portfolio or borrow money at risk-free rate to form a borrowing portfolio. Until now, the only measure of risk was standard deviation, but Sharpe introduces the CAPM and revealed that the only outstanding risk that commands premium is beta.

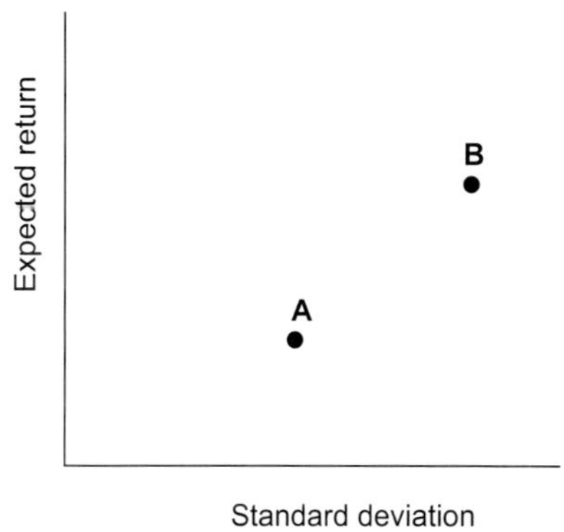

FIGURE 7.7 Relationship between risk and return

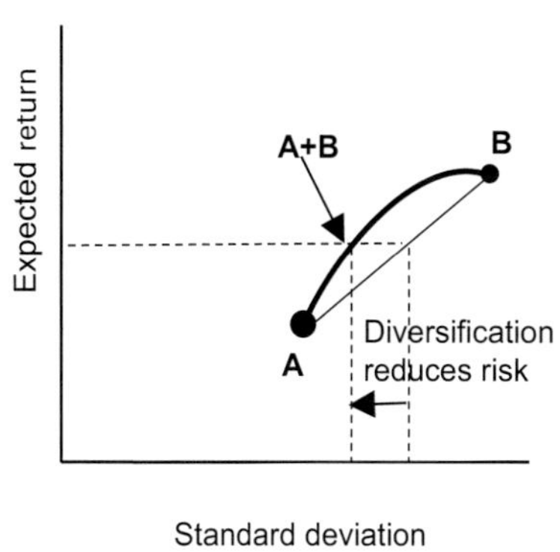

FIGURE 7.8 Diversification reduces risk for individual assets

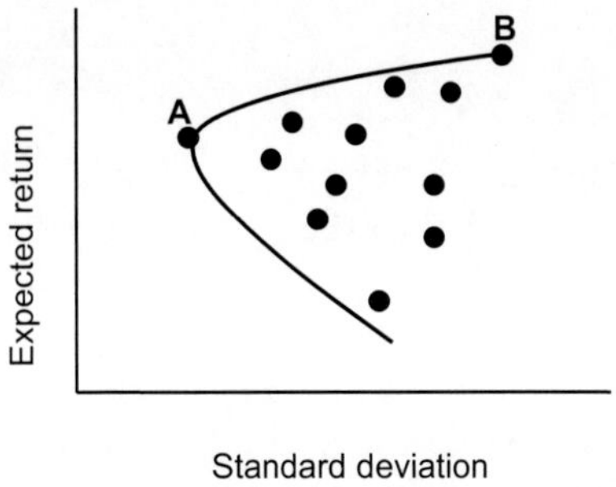

FIGURE 7.9 The efficient frontier: only portfolios

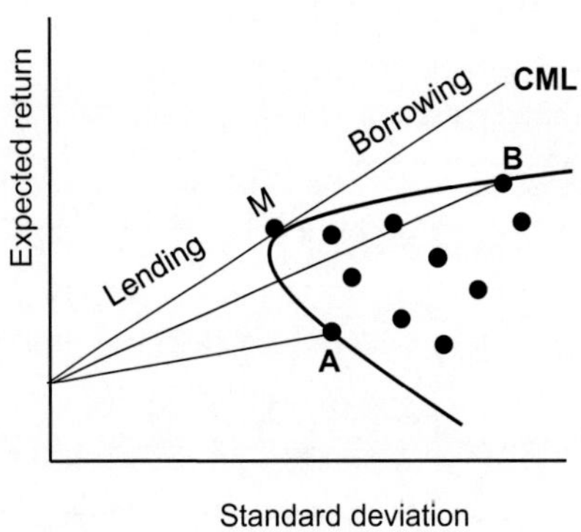

FIGURE 7.10 The new efficient frontier

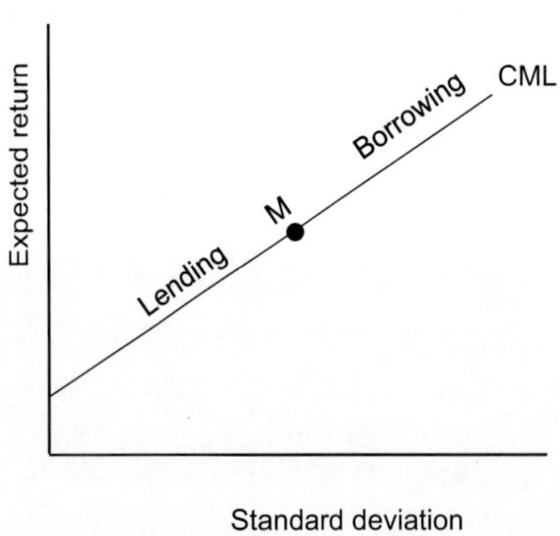

FIGURE 7.11 CML

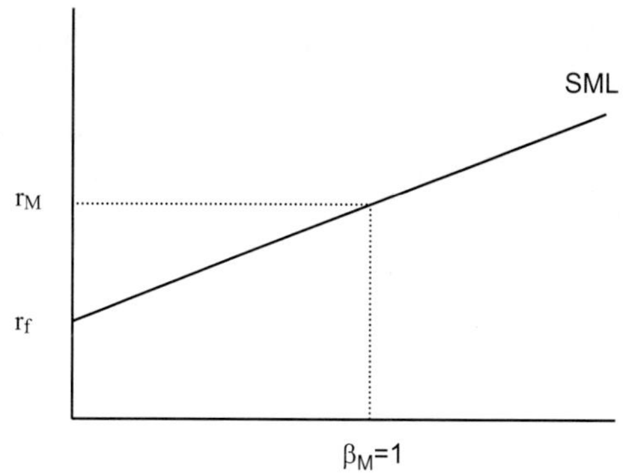

FIGURE 7.12 Security market line

How to calculate beta using a spreadsheet

We calculate the beta of a stock by one of three methods:

1. Scatter graph
2. Ratio covariance/variance
3. Regression Analysis

The scatter graph provides an immediate intuition of the asset return sensitivity to respond to swings in the market.

Example

Before using a method to calculate the beta, you must do two steps:

1. Download the historical prices for the stock and the benchmark index. We will use the Schlumberger Limited (SLB) stock prices and the S&P500 as the benchmark index. We can go to Yahoo! Finance, then Historical Data, and select "5 Y" as the timeframe and monthly as the frequency[7]. Then we download the time series "Adj Close"[8] for the S&P500 and Schlumberger and reduce the table data to three columns: the date, the S&P500 price, and Schlumberger price. Data ranges from September 2018 to August 2023, or 60 monthly observations.
2. Calculate the percentage returns[9] for the stock and the index using the formula in cell F3 of Figure 7.13 (=+C3/C2–1), where cell C2 refers to the previous period price of SLB, and C3 refers to the current price.

Date	S&P500	SLB	S&P500 return	SLB return	
Sep-18	2,913.98	52.42			
Oct-18	2,711.74	44.51	-6.9%	-15.1%	**=+C3/C2-1**
Nov-18	2,760.17	39.12	1.8%	-12.1%	
Dec-18	2,506.85	31.30	-9.2%	-20.0%	
Jan 19	2,704.10	38.77	7.9%	23.9%	

FIGURE 7.13 S&P500 and Schlumberger Limited returns

1. Select the sample of XY observations, then choose "dispersion" from the graph Excel menu. It suggests a linear relationship. We left-click on one point of the graph, then right-click and choose "Add Trendline". We must check "Linear", "Display equation on the chart" and "Display the R-squared value on chart". In the equation "Y = 1.8318 + 0.002", 1.8318 represents the beta of Schlumberger, and 0.002 represents the interception.

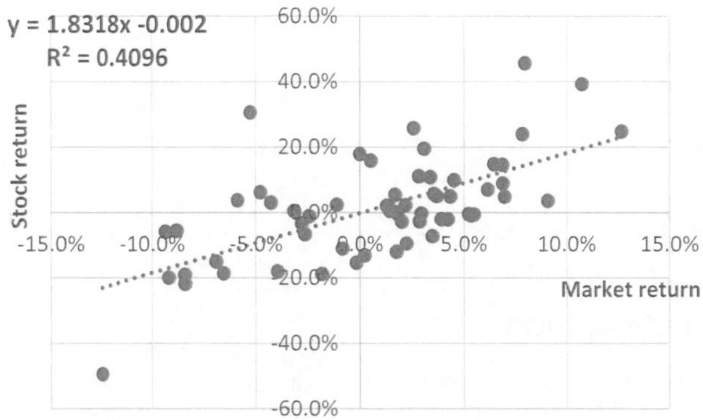

FIGURE 7.14 Beta calculated with trendline Excel function

Notice that almost all observations lie in quadrants one and three, showing a positive relationship between the stock market and asset returns, as expected, while quadrants two and four contain some observations indicating a negative relationship.

Excel uses the OLS method which is a technique for fitting the "best" straight line to the sample of XY observations. It involves minimizing the sum of the squared (vertical) deviations of points from the fitted value.

Second method

With the "analysis tool pack" installed, go to the "Data" tab and click on "Data analysis". From the menu that comes up, click on "Regression" and then "OK". Click the "Input Y-range" box and select the range of cells containing your target stock's returns. Next, click on the box for the "Input X-range" box and select the range of cells containing the market's returns. Once you fill out both boxes with your data, hit "OK" to see a summary output spreadsheet. There are a lot of numbers here that you can use for different analysis, but the one for beta calculation is in the "X variable" row and the "Coefficient" column. It is 1.8318, the same number we obtained with the first method.

Third method

Beta can also be calculated as the covariance between the expected return on an asset Rj, and the expected market return Rm, divided by the variance of the market return. To calculate the sample's covariance with Excel, we must select the ranges for the SLB and S&P returns, and only the range for the S&P return must be used to calculate the sample variance.

S&P500 return	SLB return		
-6.9%	-15.1%	=+C3/C2-1	
1.8%	-12.1%		
-9.2%	-20.0%	2.1378	=COVARIANCE.S(D3:D61;E3:E61)/VAR.S(D3:D61)
7.9%	23.9%		
3.0%	-0.3%		
1.8%	0.0%		

FIGURE 7.15 Covariance between SLB and S&P500 returns

Market risk premium: Geometric or arithmetic mean?

When the market risk premium is considered to estimate the cost of equity capital using the CAPM formula, the question of whether to use arithmetic or geometric average arise. The arithmetic mean is the simple average of percentage returns for each period, while the geometric mean reflects the compound rate of return over the investment horizon. Suppose you buy a stock for $1. Its continuous annual volatility is 30%, calculated using the last 60 monthly returns. Using the exponential formula to convert continuous volatility in upside and downside discrete factors we obtain:

$$e^{U} = e^{0.30} = 1.35$$

$$e^{D} = e^{-0.30} = 0.74$$

Using the upside and downside factors, we can construct the binomial tree with the possible trajectories of the stock price over a two-year horizon. The odds of rising or falling are 50/50.

1. In the up scenario, the price can rise to $1.35 in the first year, and reach $1.82 after two years.
2. In the down scenario, the price can fall to $0.74 (–26%) in the first year, and $0.52 after two years.
3. In the up-down scenario, the price can rise to $1.35 in the first year before dropping back to $1 after two years.

The gross line of Figure 7.16 depicts the observed trajectory after two years: the price grew to $1.35 in the first year before falling to $1 in the second. The average geometric (observed) return is zero.

$$(1/1)^{1/2} - 1 = 0.00\%$$

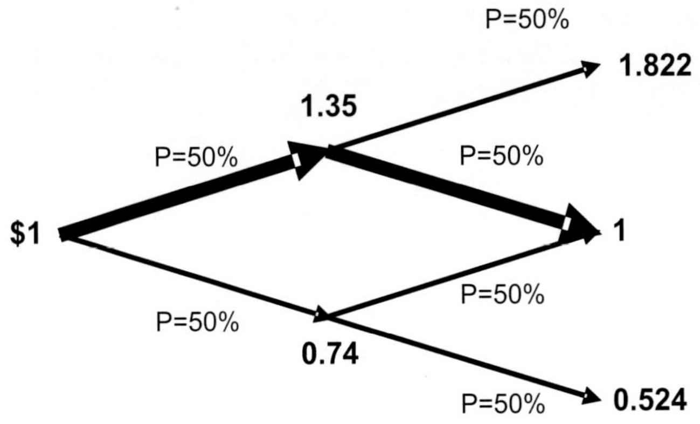

FIGURE 7.16 Stock returns during the investment horizon

The arithmetic mean is the simple average of the single period rates of return: (34.98% – 26%)/2 = 4.53%, and if we calculate the mean expected return at the beginning, based on a probability 50/50 of up and down, we have four equally likely paths: 35%t followed by 35%, –26% followed by –26%, and two equivalent paths since 35% followed by –26% give identical result as –26% followed by 35%:

$$r = 0.5 \times 0.5 \times 1.3498 + 0.5 \times 0.5 \times 0.5488 + 2 \times 0.5 \times 0.5 \times 1 = 1.0927$$

The annual equivalent return is $(1.0927)^{1/2} - 1 = 4.53\%$, which is identical to the average arithmetic mean. While the geometric mean is an ex-post measure since uses historical returns, the arithmetic mean has better statistical properties since infers expected returns by assuming independence, is expected-oriented, and is an ex-ante measure. When we value an asset, we value expectations and we do not know the future movements of the price; the only information we have at this moment is the historical volatility. The dilemma of using the arithmetic or geometric mean for an investment horizon longer than one period has received considerable attention in academia. Blume (1974) and Indro & Lee (1997) demonstrated that even if returns are independent and normally distributed, the arithmetic mean return of past returns will overestimate the expected return, whereas the geometric will underestimate it. As a result, both measures produce biased estimates when the investment horizon exceeds the unit time, and the biases increase with the length of the investment horizon. Cooper (1996) stated that the arithmetic mean of historical returns is less biased than the geometric mean. Blume explains that when the number of future periods of the time horizon, n, is larger than the number of historical observations (T), the geometric mean will be downward biased. When the number of periods is longer than one, the arithmetic mean will be upward biased. He therefore suggests that the weighted average of the arithmetic mean and geometric mean should be used to not overstate and understate the true return:

$$r = (wa^n + (1 - w)g^n. \qquad [7.20]$$

a = arithmetic mean
G = geometric mean
w = weight
r = weighted mean

$$d = \frac{T - n}{T - 1}. \qquad [7.21]$$

In valuation practice, T is usually greater than n, so the arithmetic mean will have a higher weight (If T = n, r = a).

Fama & French (1999) stated that as the expected returns estimates enter the present value expressions in a nonlinear way, estimates of the cost of capital that produce unbiased estimates of present values are weighted averages of average simple and compound returns, with weights that depend on the maturity of the cash flow to be valued.

Among the defendants of the geometric mean, Damodaran (1999) stated that the arithmetic mean return is likely to overstate the premium due to stock returns on stocks being negatively correlated over time.

Missiakoulis, Vasiliou, & Eriotis (2010) investigated the arithmetic mean within different periods to produce unbiased estimates for long-term investment horizons. They made an experiment assuming they were in December 1996 and forecast the terminal value of the S&P500 and the Dow Jones Industrial index for December 2006. First, they use the various mean values (arithmetic, geometric, logarithmic, Blume and Cooper methods) and show that all estimated terminal values of December 2006 are biased. Then, they select only five annual observations for each of five decades, 1956, 1966, 1976, 1986, and 1996, one for every ten years, and calculate their arithmetic means, denoted by Arithmetic-10. Finally, they compare the different terminal values using the different mean values and conclude that all estimates overestimate the true value being Arithmetic-10 closest to the actual.

There is no such thing as a final word when it comes to expected returns. If you believe that a period of high returns tends to be followed by period of low returns, implying that the returns are negatively correlated, the geometric mean could be a better approach. If you believe the returns are unpredictable, the arithmetic mean could be the better indicator.

Table 7.1 shows the geometric and arithmetic returns of the S&P500 from 1925 to 2022 and their corresponding market risk premiums. The mean of averages is 5.81%. If you are not sure about which mean to use, a mean of averages could constitute a compromise solution.

TABLE 7.1 Geometric and arithmetic means 1925–2022

Mean	SP500	T-Bonds 10Y	Market risk premium
Geometric	10.36%	4.90%	5.47%
Arithmetic	11.10%	4.94%	6.16%
Mean of averages	10.73%	4.92%	5.81%

Source: Shiller online data using monthly returns

The implied equity risk premium

Botosan (1997) proposed a new approach to estimate the equity risk premium that does not require historical data. The implied equity risk premium (IERP) represents a prediction of how much the stock market would outperform the risk-free return. The calculation of IERP starts with the calculation of the implicit cost of equity in the dividend Gordon formula:

$$ke = \frac{D_1}{P} + g, \qquad [7.22]$$

$$ke = Dividend\ yield + g. \qquad [7.23]$$

D_1 = Dividend per share for the next year
g = dividend growth rate

Subtracting the risk-free rate from ke, we get the implied equity risk premium (IERP).

$$IERP = ke - rf. \qquad [7.24]$$

Rather than using the geometric or arithmetic average equity risk premium, the implied cost of equity and the implied equity risk premium are based on the current price, short and long-term earnings and dividends forecasts, and long-term growth rate.

Example

On October 1, 2023, the S&P500 was 4,280.88, the expected dividend yield ($Dividend_1/P$) was 4.14% and the forecasted dividend growth rate was 1.64% (source: Refinitiv Eikon). Dividend yield reported by Robert Shiller online data or Nasdaq data link were similar, ranging between 1.6% and 1.7%. The implied cost of equity was

$$ke = 4.14\% + 1.64\% = 5.78\%$$

Given that UST10y was 4.57%, the implied equity risk premium was

$$IERP = 5.78\% - 4.57\% = 1.21\%$$

Because the stock index changes every day, the IERP reported by databases does as well. Other way to estimate the growth in dividends is assuming that it will track the economic growth. For example, if the estimated GDP growth rate for 2024 is 3/4%, the cost of equity and the IERP will be greater. However, history shows that the real GDP growth rate rarely will translate in a similar dividend growth rate. Sometimes, the short-term dividend growth rate exceeds the real GDP growth rate. As it is impossible to sustain a higher growth rate in the long run, we can use the three-stage model we explained in Chapter 3, considering a high growth rate, a lower growth rate of 8% for the first five years, a 5% growth from year 6 to year 10, and an organic growth rate of 4% from year 11 and beyond. Considering that the S&P is 4,280.88, the consensus estimate for the EPS is 217, the payout is 80.85%, the dividend for next year would be 217 x 80.85% = 175.44.

$$4,280.88 = 175.44\frac{1-\frac{(1+0.08)^5}{(1+ke)^5}}{ke-0.08} + 175.44\,(1+0.08)^4(1+0.05)\frac{1-\frac{(1+0.05)^5}{(1+ke)^5}}{ke-0.05}\frac{1}{(1+ke)^5}$$

$$+\frac{175.44(1+0.08)^4(1+0.05)^5(1+0.04)}{(ke-0.04)(1+ke)^{10}}$$

Solving by iteration, ke = 8.86327%, and the implied equity risk premium is

$$IERP = 8.86\% - 4.57\% = 4.29\%$$

The three-stage formula requires to be careful with the calculations. Perhaps you feel safer using a spreadsheet to calculate the stream of dividends, their present value, and the terminal value. Figure 7.17 shows the inputs in column B and the necessary calculations.

S&P500	4280.9				
		Year	Dividends	PV	
Dividends	175.44	1.00	175.44	161.16	=+E5/(1+$B$17)^D5
EPS mean estimate	217	2.00	189.48	159.88	
FY1 earnings yield	5.07%	3.00	204.64	158.61	
Payout ratio	80.85%	4.00	221.01	157.36	
Dividend yield	4.098%	5.00	238.69	156.11	
g1	8%	6.00	250.62	150.57	
g2	5%	7.00	263.16	145.22	
g3	4%	8.00	276.31	140.07	
ke	8.86%	9.00	290.13	135.10	
Risk-free rate	4.57%	10.00	304.64	130.31	
IERP	4.29%		T. Value -->	2,786.49	=+D14*(1+B12)/((B13-B12)*(1+B13)^10)
				4,280.88	=SUM(E5:E15)

FIGURE 7.17 Implied equity risk premium

The implied cost of equity and implied equity risk premium fluctuate over time in response to changes in stock price, forecasted earnings per share, interest rates, and growth, and are very sensitive to these inputs. For example, some analysts use the US T-Bill rate as the risk-free rate, while others use the five years treasury note. We must be cautious since the analysts' forecasting data tend to be optimistic and slowly updated (Dechow & Sloan, 1997). For methods to mitigate the influence of sluggish forecasts and improve the ability of the implied cost of equity estimates see Guay, Kothari, & Shu (2011). Remember the IERP is a forward-looking number that represents a prediction of how much the stock market would outperform the risk-free return; some years it has been above the mean while some year has been under the mean; therefore, we can figure out that the IERP tends to reverts to the mean.

The equity premium puzzle

Some appraisers or MSc. finance students may be surprised that the equity risk premium constitutes one of the unsolved puzzles in financial economics. Even though investing in stocks is thought to be riskier than bond investment, this is not adequately account for the 5/6% equity risk premium of that has been observed for over a century because it implies an aversion risk that is so big that is incompatible with other branches of the economy.

Mehra & Prescott (1985) found that for appropriate risk aversion levels, a standard general equilibrium model calibrated to display key US business cycle fluctuations, generated an equity premium of less than 1%. This result contradicts the average equity premium of 5/6% observed from 1925 to 2023. A range of explanations have been presented, including rare events hypothesis, modifications to the assumed preferences of investors, imperfections in the model of risk aversion, until consider the possibility that the equity premium does not exist and is a statistical illusion. Kocherlakota (1996) present a detailed analysis of these explanations in financial markets and conclude that the puzzle exists and remains unexplained. Mehra (2003) after analyzing the research effort to enhance the discrepancy between model prediction and empirical data concludes that the proposed resolutions fail along crucial dimension. The bottom line is that the equity premium continues to be a puzzle.

Empirical evidence of CAPM

From this time, the CAPM has been under attack. There have been a myriad of valuable, famous empirical tests that have helped to understand the CAPM implications and limitations. We mentioned briefly the main characteristics of the most famous tests since the idea is to understand why multifactor models, rather than a single factor like market beta, have been proposed presented as superior than CAPM based on empirical results. The empirical tests of the CAPM have been focused on whether the intercept was equal to zero when the regression is running using excess returns,[10] whether the market risk premium was similar to the observed in the time period considered to perform the test, and whether beta was able to explain the cross-sectional variation of expected returns.

Using monthly returns, Black, Jensen, & Scholes (1972) estimated a beta for each stock on the New York Stock Exchange over the period 1931–1965. They then ranked order all of the betas and formed ten portfolios. The intercept of the SML was greater than the return of risk-free bonds, and they found a significant and positive linear relationship between the beta and the average excess portfolio return. The results of the study appeared to be consistent with the zero-beta version of the CAPM proposed by Black (1972) that postulates that a risk-free portfolio with zero beta can be designed and then combined with the market portfolio in a linear relationship, where the intercept is allowed to change in each period.

Fama & MacBeth (1973), in a seminal paper, performed a famous test on CAPM that involved a two-step regression. The first step is to regress the return of every asset against the stock market index and obtain the beta coefficient. In a subsequent step, they used a cross-section regression to regress the observed returns over a specified time period against the asset betas acquired in the previous stage. They reported a larger intercept term than the risk-free rate and that the linear relationship holds when the data covers a long period. However, Fama & French (1992), in a subsequent study, found weak evidence on these relationships.

Roll (1977) argued that the global market portfolio was unobservable and that using a proxy in its place can lead to false inferences as to the validity of the CAPM: (i) the beta computed for alternative portfolios would be wrong because the market portfolio is inappropriate, (ii) the SML derived would be wrong because it goes from the risk-free rate through the improperly specified market portfolio. Due to the impossibility of observing the global market portfolio, the existence of the CAPM equilibrium hypothesis might not be empirically testable unless the exact composition of the market portfolio is known.

Basu (1977) and Banz (1981) found that small cap returns overperformed large cap returns. Thus, using beta alone to explain stock returns leads to biased results. The size effect has been thoroughly researched and is well documented and persistent (Fama and French, 1992; 1993; 1995; 1996). Stattman (1980) and Rosenberg, Reid, & Lanstein (1985) reported that firms with high book value/market value (BM) ratios tend to experience high average returns compared to those predicted by the CAPM model. These results are also supported by Fama and French (1992; 1996), who even suggest that the B/M ratio is stronger than the size effect in explaining cross sectional average returns.

In a review of the evidence on the CAPM, Fama & French (2004) claimed that the model's empirical record is poor enough to invalidate the way it is used in applications. They argue that even in studies that validate the model, the observed relationship between beta risk and return is too flat. The model's empirical problems may reflect failings due to shortcomings of the empirical test, using poor proxies for the market portfolio, which plays a central role in the model's predictions. They conclude that these shortcomings pose challenges to be explained by more complicated models.

While the CAPM states that high-beta stocks should outperform low-beta stocks, the superior performance of low-beta and low-volatility stocks has been documented in the literature since the 1970s by Black, Jensen, & Scholes (1972). This phenomenon, known as the "beta anomaly" has been observed in various markets around the globe, and constitutes a significant deviation from traditional financial theories. Some researchers attribute this to behavioral factors such investor desire for low-risk stocks, resulting in higher performance and a demand for "lottery-like" stocks, which are often high-beta.

Multifactor models

Due to the inability of the CAPM beta to explain the assets returns, a number of multifactor models appeared to defeat the throne of the CAPM. We will discuss the two most well-known in the following sections.

Fama-French three-factor model

The Fama and French three-factor model (1992) expands on the capital asset pricing model (CAPM) by adding a size premium and a value risk factor to the market risk premium factor in CAPM. This model considers the fact that value and small-cap stocks outperform markets on a regular basis and the outperformance of high book-to-market value companies versus low book-to-market value companies. By including these two additional factors, the model adjusts for this outperforming tendency, which is thought to make it a better tool for evaluating manager performance. The model is as follows:

$$r = rf + \beta_1(rm - rf) + \beta_2 SMB + \beta_3 HML. \qquad [7.25]$$

$(rm - rf)$ = Market risk premium

SMB (small minus big) = Historic excess returns of small-cap companies over large-cap companies

HML (high minus low) = Historic excess returns of value stocks (high book-to-price ratio) over growth stocks (low book-to-price ratio)

The factor SMB measures the difference in returns of portfolios composed by small-cap companies and big companies and pretends to measure the "size effect" since in the long-term, small-cap companies tend to see higher returns than big-cap companies.[11] A possible explanation for the size effect is that small-cap companies are nimbler and move faster than big-cap companies. Size beta can take positive values as well as negative ones. In practice, some practitioners include a size premium to the cost of capital.

HML (high minus low)

HML measures the historic difference returns between value stocks (companies with a high book-to-market value relative) and growth stocks (companies with a low book-to-market value ratio). The explanation is that growth companies have a low BV/MV ratio because the market is willing to pay a premium for the expectations of higher future earnings, even if they are not reflected today on the book value. Companies in industries that have few physical assets, like technology companies, tend to have a low BV/MV ratio. Like the SMB factor, the HML beta coefficient can also take positive or negative values. According to Fama-French, in the long term, small companies overperform large companies, and value companies beat growth companies.

Example

Using the file "10 industry portfolios" available on French's website, we run the Fama-French Three-Factor Model for four industries: durables, high tech, utilities, and manufactures. The dependent variable was the excess return over the risk-free rate and the explanatory variables were the market risk premium, SMB, and HML. The analysis was performed on 2022/10/23, using monthly returns from July 1926 to August 2022 (1,154 observations). It is expected that the SMB factor has a positive sign and is significant. Supposedly, "value" companies should have a higher BV/MV ratio, since they had more time to accumulate earnings. Conversely, "growth" companies should have a lower BV/MV ratio, since they are in the "emerging" phase of the business cycle and have yet to generate earnings, but have a higher market value because the market anticipates a promising future. Table 7.2 shows that the interception was not significant, market risk premium and HML were significant at 1% level, and SMB was significant for high tech and utilities. A positive coefficient means that a portfolio has a positive relationship with the value premium; notice that the SMB is negative for utilities and manufacturing industries, indicating a negative premium, which would be the case of industries that are composed of large companies. The HML was positive and significant at 1% level, but it was negative for the high-tech industry, as it is expected for this industry since it is composed of growth companies.

TABLE 7.2 Size and HML factors in different industries

	Durables	High tech	Utilities	Manufactures
Interception	−0.0008	0.1071	0.0507	−0.0394
MRP	1.2416***	1.2568***	0.7554***	1.0956***
SMB	0.0604	0.0857**	−0.1669***	−0.0019
HML	0.1470***	−0.3099***	0.2597***	0.1390***
Adj. R2	0.73	0.85	0.59	0.93

, and* denotes significance at the 5%, and 1% level, respectively.

Fama-French five-factor model

Fama & French (2015) adapted their model to include two more factors: "profitability", which refers to the concept that companies reporting higher future earnings have higher returns in the stock market; and the fifth factor, referred to as "investment patterns", which relates to internal investment and returns, suggesting that companies allocate their profits towards major growth projects are likely to experience losses in the stock market. RMW is the difference between the returns on high-profitability and low-profitability diversified portfolios. CMA represents the difference between the returns on diversified portfolios of conservative and aggressive investment firms, where low/high investment indicate a low/high reinvestment ratio.

$$r = rf + \beta_1(rm - rf) + \beta_2 SMB + \beta_3 HML + \beta_4 RMW + \beta_5 CMA. \qquad [7.26]$$

Although the results show the model explains between 71% and 94% of the cross-section variance of expected returns, its weakness is its failure to capture the low average returns on small companies whose returns perform like those of firms that invest a lot despite low profitability.

The arbitrage pricing model

Arbitrage pricing theory (APT) is a multi-factor asset pricing model proposed by Ross (1976) which, unlike the CAPM and its variants, uses certain macroeconomic variables linearly related that capture systematic risk. The main characteristic of the APT model is the absence of arbitrage opportunities and the requirement for a partial equilibrium between asset returns rather than a general equilibrium, like the one proposed by the CAPM with the SML. APT assumes markets sometimes misprice securities before the market eventually corrects and securities move back to fair value. Once the arbitrage opportunities become exhausted and the market is in equilibrium, the expected return on an asset is a linear function of various macroeconomic factors.

$$r = rf + \beta_1 X_1 + \beta_2 X_2 + \beta_3 X_3 + \ldots + \beta_n X_n. \quad [7.27]$$

In practice, APT users typically employ less than five factors and a variety of criteria, so the results vary depending on their choice. Chen, Roll, & Ross (1986) found empirical evidence consistent with APT using US return data from 1958 through 1984, based on five factors:

1. Change in expected inflation rate
2. Unexpected change in inflation rate
3. Unexpected change in yield curve
4. Unexpected change in risky bond premium
5. Monthly industrial growth.

While APT is more flexible than the CAPM since it does not require a market portfolio nor a general particular distribution of returns, it is much more complex. The CAPM only takes into account one factor – market risk – while the APT formula considers multiple factors, including unexpected changes in the inflation rate, gross national product (GNP), corporate bond spreads, and shifts in the yield curve. However, analysts commonly use other factors such as commodity prices, market indices, and exchange rates. It is important to note that finding proxies for risk factors takes a considerable time of research. Brooks (2008) provides an example of the spirit of APT utilizing Microsoft's results. For an interesting application of the APT to estimate the international cost of capital of a private manufacturer of jet aircraft components based in Brazil, see McLelland (2019).

Concluding thoughts

Nearly 60 decades after its appearance, the CAPM is still widely used by practitioners, for tasks including estimating the cost of equity capital and assessing the performance of managed portfolios. Additionally, it may be the only asset pricing model taught at the MBA-level investment courses and the one that is largely taught in Master of Finance courses. The attraction of the CAPM relies on its powerfully simple logic about the risk and return relationship. However, due to its simplicity and reduced benefit/cost relationship, it does not need to be replaced by any other capital asset pricing model, at least at the practitioner level, despite the model's poor empirical record.

Various multifactor models seem to overtake the CAPM since the market beta is unable to account for the asset returns. Multifactor models are empirical, whereas the CAPM model is theoretical; multifactor models are complex, whereas CAPM is straightforward.

The APT model requires considerable research time to find good risk proxies; on the other hand, the size effect of the Fama-French model, although well documented in the American market, is uncertain in emerging markets. Since the CAPM is also used in emerging markets, we go over some adaptations to the model in Chapter 11 capture other risk factors than market risk.

Questions and short problems

1. Classify these events between unsystematic (U) and systematic risk (S)

   a) An increase of the interest rate
   b) A devaluation
   c) A prohibition to imports
   d) The entrance of a new competitor in the industry of cellular phones
   e) A regulatory change that has an impact in the telecommunication companies' revenue
   f) A decrease of the oil price
   g) A lawsuit lost by a utility company
   h) An international financial crisis

2. A well-diversified portfolio (mark true or false)

   a) Increases systematic risk
   b) Reduces systematic risk
   c) Increases unsystematic risk
   d) Reduces unsystematic risk

3. A beta coefficient of 1.2 implies (mark true or false)

   a) On average, the stock's return was 1.2 times the market return
   b) The stock is less risky than the market
   c) The market's return will be 1.2 times the stock's return

4. An investor may reduce the risk of a portfolio by selecting (mark true or false)

   a) The stock's return having a lower beta with the portfolio's return
   b) The stock's return that is least correlated with the portfolio's return
   c) The stock with lower standard deviation

5. Mark true or false:

   a) The CAPM assumes the perspective of a fully diversified investor, and the only risk that need to be compensated is the systematic risk
   b) A stock with a negative beta, may reduce drastically the risk of a portfolio
   c) A stock with a volatility of 40% will have a higher beta than a stock with a volatility of 30%.

6. Complete each sentence with a suitable word or words. The first one has already been done for you.
   The *expected* portfolio's return is equal to the ....average of the assets 'return included in the portfolio. The risk of a portfolio is lower than the...................... standard deviation of the individual assets included in a portfolio, due to the fact that changes in the assets' return are always imperfectly......................................The risk of a well-diversified portfolio is always.......................than the risk of investing in an individual stock. Investors can eliminate the unsystematic risk through.............................but they cannot eliminate the ....risk.
7. Mark TRUE/FALSE:
   a) A portfolio composed 50% market portfolio and 50% US T-Bonds, has a beta higher than 1.
   b) If a stock has a negative beta, then its correlation coefficient with the portfolio is positive
8. Why is the stock market beta 1?
9. Complete each sentence with a suitable word or words. The first one has already been completed for you.
   The beta coefficient represents the *slope* of the ....line and is also equal to the...between the stock return and market return over the ....of the market return.
10. If the current risk-free rate is 5%, the historical market risk premium is 5.5%, the geometric average return of the SP500 from December 1925 to December 2022 is 10%, and the beta of ZZ Corporation is 1.5, assuming that the CAPM's hypothesis holds, the expected return is:
    a) 12.5%
    b) 13.25%
    c) 10.5%
11. The S&P500 on December 3, 2023, was 4,845.60, the expected dividend yield was 1.47%, the analysts projected a dividend growth rate of 9%, and the UST10y is 4%. Calculate the implied equity risk premium.

Notes

1 If $\sigma_1$and $\sigma_2$are random variables, and X_1 and X_2 are constant, $[X_1\sigma_1 + X_2\sigma_2]^2 = X_1^2\sigma_1^2 + X_2^2\sigma_2^2 + 2X_1X_2\,\text{cov}_{12}$

2 You can say that a variance of 0.20 is higher than a variance of 0.1, but it would be an indirect interpretation and not meaningful.

3 It is possible to have an asset in the case of a short sale. It occurs when you sell an asset you don't have, and the market value of the short security comes into the portfolio as a negative amount.

4 Assuming a buy and hold investor will keep the risk-free security until maturity, there is no risk, so the variance is zero.

5 The law of diminishing marginal returns apply here.

6 We comment later about the use of geometric or arithmetic average.
7 In Valuation, it is common to use 60 monthly observations, although some use different periods.
8 Adjusted close price adjusted for splits, dividends, and capital gain distributions.
9 The CAPM is tested using an excess return econometric model, as (r-rf) = (rm-rf) + u. If the CAPM works, the intercept should be zero, and the market risk premium should be similar to the observed market risk premium for the period considered.
10 The corresponding regression model is (r-rf) = (rm-rf)β + ε
11 The famous graph of Ibbotson, which can be viewed instantly by searching for "Ibbotson chart", provides a quick overview of the excess returns.

References

Banz, R. (1981). The relationship between return and market value of common stocks. *Journal of Financial Economics, 9*, 3–18.

Basu, S. (1977). The investment performance of common stocks in relation to their price earnings ratios: A test of the efficient market hypothesis. *Journal of Finance, 32*, 663–682.

Bernstein, P. (2007). *Capital Ideas Evolving*. New Jersey: Wiley.

Black, F. (1972, July). Capital Market Equilibrium with Restricted Borrowing. *Journal of Business*, 444–455.

Black, F., Jensen, M., & Scholes, M. (1972). The Capital Asset Pricing Model: Some Empirical Tests. In Jensen, M.C. (ed.), *Studies in the Theory of Capital Markets* (pp. 79–121). New York: Praeger.

Blume, M. (1974, September). Unbiased Estimators of Long Run Expected Rates of Return. *Journal of the American Statistical Association, 69(347)*, 634–638.

Botosan, C. (1997). Disclosure Level and the Cost of Equity Capital. *The Accounting Review, 72*, 323–349.

Brooks, C. (2008). *Introductory Econometrics for Finance*, 2nd edition. New York: Cambridge University Press.

Chen, N.-f., Roll, R., & Ross, S. (1986, July). Economic Forces and the Stock Market. *Journal of Business*, 383–403.

Cooper, I. (1996). Arithmetic vs geometric mean estimators: setting discount rates for capital budgeting. *European Financial Management, 2*, 157–167.

Damodaran, A. (1999). *Estimating equity risk premiums, Working Paper Series 99-021,Leonard N. Stern School Finance Department, New York University*. Available at www.aragon-gil.com/pdfs/paper_24.pdf

Damodaran, A. (2012). *Investment Valuation*. New York: John Wiley and Sons.

Dechow, P., & Sloan, R. (1997). Returns to contrarian investment strategies: Tests of naive expectations hypotheses. *Journal of Financial Economics, 43(1)*, 3–27.

Fama, E. (1970). Efficient Capital Markets: A Review of Theory and Empirical Work. *The Journal of Finance, 25(2)*, 383–417.

Fama, E. (1996). Multifactor Portfolio Efficiency and Multifactor Asset Pricing. *Journal of Financial and Quantitative Analysis, 31(4)*, 441–465.

Fama, E., & French, K. (1992). The Cross-Section of Expected Stock Returns. *Journal of Finance, 47(2)*, 427–465.

Fama, E., & French, K. (1993). Common Risk Factors in the Returns on Stocks and Bonds. *Journal of Financial Economics, 33(1)*, 3–56.

Fama, E., & French, K. (1995). Size and Book-to-Market Factors in Earnings and Returns. *Journal of Financial Economics, 50(1)*, 131–155.

Fama, E., & French, K. (1999). The corporate cost of capital and the return on corporate investment. *The Journal of Finance, 54*, 1939–1967.

Fama, E., & French, K. (2004). The Capital Asset Pricing Model: Theory and Evidence. *Journal of Economic Perspectives, 18(3)*, 25–46.

Fama, E., & French, K. (2015). A five-factor asset pricing model. *Journal of Financial Economics, 116(1)*, 1–22.

Fama, E., & MacBeth, J. (1973, May). Risk, Return, and Equilibrium: Empirical Tests. *Journal of Political Economy*, 607–636.

Friedman, M. (1962). *Essays in Positive Economics*. Chicago and London: The University of Chicago Press.

Guay, W., Kothari, S. P., & Shu, S. (2011). Properties of Implied Cost of Capital Using Analysts' Forecasts. *Australian Journal of Management 36*, 125–149.

Indro, D., & Lee, W. (1997). Biases in arithmetic and geometric averages as estimates of longrun expected returns and risk premia. *Financial Management, 26*, 81–90.

Kocherlakota, N. (1996). The Equity Premium: It's Still a Puzzle. *Journal of Economic Literature, 34(1)*, 42–71.

Markowitz, H. (1952, March). Portfolio Selection. *Journal of Finance*, 77–91.

McLelland, M. J. (2019). *International cost of capital estimation: Methods based on modern asset pricing theory*. Independently published.

Mehra, R. (2003). The Equity Premium: Why Is It a Puzzle? *Financial Analysts Journal, 59(1)*, 54–69.

Mehra, R., & Prescott, E. C. (1985). The equity premium: A puzzle. *Journal of Monetary Economics, 15(2)*, 145–161.

Missiakoulis, S., Vasiliou, D., & Eriotis, N. (2010). Arithmetic mean: a bellwether for unbiased forecasting of portfolio performance. *Managerial Finance*, 36(11), 958–968.

Roll, R. (1977, March). A Critique of Asset Pricing Theory's Tests: Part I: On Past and Potential Testability of the Theory. *Journal of Financial Economics*, 129–176.

Rosenberg, B., Reid, K., & Lanstein, R. (1985, Spring). Persuasive Evidence of Market Inefficiency. *Journal of Portfolio Management, 11*, 341–360.

Ross, S. (1976, May). The Arbitrage Theory of Capital Asset Pricing. *en Journal of Economic Theory*, 13, 341–360.

Sharpe, W. (1964, September). Capital Asset Prices: A Theory of Market Equilibrium Under Condition of Risk. *Journal of Finance*, 277–293.

Stattman, D. (1980). Book Values and Stock Returns. *Journal of Financial Economics, 10(3)*, 237–268.

Tobin, J. (1958). Liquidity Preference as Behavior Towards Risk. *Review of Economic Studies, 25(1)*, 65–86.

CHAPTER

8

Discounted cash flow methods

Introduction

In this chapter, we analyze the equivalence of different cash flow methods in valuation. Knowing the equivalencies helps one to understand the different risks, tax effects, and the appropriate cost of capital. As we explain, there are circumstances where one approach may be better than another.

After reading this chapter, you will be able to:

- Know why the Hamada formulas were developed;
- Determine the equivalence between the different DCF valuation methods considering the consistency of risk with the cost of capital and tax shield effects;
- Understand the assumptions behind the Miles & Ezzel formulas and alternative formulas to unlever and relever betas.

DOI: 10.4324/9781003628491-10

Integrating MM and CAPM: Hamada formulas

Before dealing with the discounted cash flow methods, we need to integrate the MM propositions with the CAPM model. Hamada (1972) joined the CAPM (Sharpe, 1964) with the MM propositions with taxes. Any practitioner or student of finance is familiar with these two famous formulas, which were introduced in Chapter 4 and are extensively used in valuation practice, known as the formulas to calculate the unlevered beta and the levered beta.

$$\beta_L = \beta_U\left[1+\frac{D(1-t)}{E}\right]. \qquad [4.6]$$

$$\beta_U = \frac{\beta_L}{\left[1+\frac{D(1-t)}{E}\right]}. \qquad [4.7]$$

Let's demonstrate the origin of the formulas. Beta is obtained by dividing the covariance between the stock return and the stock market return by the variance of the stock market return.

$$\beta = \frac{Cov(r_i, r_M)}{\sigma^2_{r_M}}. \qquad [8.1]$$

Under MM proposition with taxes, r_U is the stock return of an unlevered company and r_L the stock return of a levered company:

$$r_U = \frac{X(1-t)-\Delta I}{E_U}. \qquad [8.2]$$

$$r_L = \frac{X(1-t)-Int+\Delta D-\Delta I}{E_L}. \qquad [8.3]$$

Int = interest payment
ΔD = debt change
I = change in working capital and net capital expenditure

Substituting [8.2] and [8.3] in equation 8.1 and supposing that the covariance between the components of equity cash flow (Int, ΔD, I) and the market return r_M is negligible:

$$\beta_U = \frac{Cov\left(\frac{X(1-t)}{E_U}, r_M\right)}{\sigma^2_{r_M}}. \qquad [8.4]$$

$$\beta_L = \frac{Cov\left(\frac{X(1-t)}{E_L}, r_M\right)}{\sigma^2_{r_M}}. \qquad [8.5]$$

Because E_U and E_L are constant values, we can express[1]:

$$\beta_U = \frac{1}{E_U}\frac{Cov[X(1-t), r_M]}{\sigma^2_{r_M}}. \quad [8.6] \qquad \beta_L = \frac{1}{E_L}\frac{Cov[X(1-t), r_M]}{\sigma^2_{r_M}}. \quad [8.7]$$

Since $E_U\beta_U = E_L\beta_L = \dfrac{Cov[X(1-t), r_M]}{\sigma^2_{r_M}}$,

$$E_L\beta_L = E_U\beta_U. \rightarrow \beta_L = \frac{E_U}{E_L}\beta_U. \quad [8.8]$$

The levered firm value V_L is equal to the unlevered value E_U plus the present value of tax shield and is also equivalent to the levered equity value E_L plus debt:

$$V_L = E_U + Dt = E_{L/T>0} + D,$$

$$E_U = E_{L/T>0} + D - Dt. \quad [8.9]$$

Replacing [8.11] in [8.10] we get the famous formula for the levered and unlevered betas we introduced in Chapter 4.

$$\beta_L = \frac{E_L + D - Dt}{E_L}\beta_U.$$

$$\beta_L = \beta_U\left[1 + \frac{D(1-t)}{E}\right]. \quad [4.6]$$

$$\beta_U = \frac{\beta_L}{\left[1 + \frac{D(1-t)}{E}\right]}. \quad [4.7]$$

Notice that Hamada's formulas are valid for the case of perpetuities and uneven cash flows since they consider all cash flow components, including changes in working capital and net capital expenditures. We used the Hamada formulas in Chapter 2 to estimate Greenworth's beta.

The equivalence of DCF methods in perpetuity

Many discounted cash flow methods give identical net present values. This equivalence has common sense: if we value cash flows, then changing the method must not alter the cash flow value. The key to demonstrating equivalence is using the corresponding cost of capital and accounting tax effects, deriving formulas using logic and deduction, one from another.

ECO Corp. is a company that produces food and beverages. Financial data and market values are:

- The expected EBIT is $20 million
- Its beta is 1.0

- Debt is $100 and kd = 5%
- The corporate tax rate t = 40%, the risk-free rate rf = 5%, and the expected market return rm = 10%

Assuming perpetuity, the free cash flow (FCF), the equity cash flow (ECF), and the capital cash flow (CCF) are:

FCF = EBIT(1–t) = 20 (1–0.40) = 12
ECF = (EBIT–Int)(1–t) = (20–5)(1–0.40) = 9
CCF = interest + dividends = 5 + 9

Note that the CCF represents all cash flows the company pays to bondholders and stockholders. CCF is also the FCF plus the tax shield period:

CCF = FCF + interest x t = 12 + 5 x 0.40 = 14

Remember that when we assume cash flow perpetuities, the business does not grow anymore and does not invest in itself. Therefore, net working capital investments are zero and capital expenses cancel out; hence, the net income equals the equity cash flow and is distributed as dividends.

Equity cash flow method

This method, sometimes called the residual method, uses the cash flow distributed to shareholders and because the equity cash flow is riskier than free cash flow, to be consistent, the risk-adjusted rate must be the cost of equity capital. Assuming a risk-free rate of 5%, a market risk premium of 5%, and a levered beta of 1.0, the cost of equity is:

$$ke = 5\% + (10\% - 5\%)1.0 = 10\%$$

Therefore, the equity fair market value is:

$$E = \frac{ECF}{ke}. \quad [8.10]$$

$$E = \frac{9}{0.10} = 90$$

Naturally, the firm value is the sum of equity value plus the debt value:

$$V = E + D = 190$$

Free cash flow method

Because the free cash flow does not count the tax shield effect, the cost of capital must be the WACC, which takes into account the tax saving effect in the cost of debt expressed on an after-taxes basis, as kd(1–t). The WACC is:

$$WACC = 5\%(1 - 0.40) \times \frac{100}{190} + 10\% \times \frac{90}{190} = 6.316\%$$

$$V = \frac{FCF}{WACC}. \qquad [8.11]$$

$$V = \frac{12}{0.06316} = 190$$

Capital cash flow method

The capital cash flow (CCF) or firm cash flow is the sum of equity cash flow and cash flow to debt, so it includes the tax shield effect on the cash flow to equity. Using perpetuities, the cash flow to debt is the interest stream, and the cash flow to equity is equivalent to the dividend stream:

$$CCF = Interest + Dividends \qquad [8.12]$$

Since tax savings were previously taken into account, the cost of capital must not take the tax effect into account to avoid duplications. Therefore, we must use the "WACC before taxes", which is equal to the WACC without considering the tax effect (1–t).

$$WACC_{BT} = 5\% \times \frac{100}{190} + 10\% \times \frac{90}{190} = 7.368\%$$

$$V = \frac{CCF}{WACC_{BT}}. \qquad [8.13]$$

$$V = \frac{14}{0.07386} = 190$$

Adjusted present value method

The adjusted present value (APV) was first introduced by Myers (1974). This method calculates the value of a company as its unlevered value plus the present value of the tax shield, which is equal to Dt in perpetuity. As the tax shield comes from the use of debt to finance the business, the present value of the tax shield is calculated using the cost of debt as the discount rate, which implies that the tax shield's risk and the risk of the debt are similar.

$$V = Vu + \frac{Dkdt}{kd} = \frac{FCF}{ku} + Dt. \qquad [8.14]$$

The unlevered value Vu is FCF/ku, where ku is the risk-adjusted rate for an unlevered business. However, since Corp. XX's beta of 1.0 is leveraged, we must first unlever its beta:

$$\beta_U = \frac{1.0}{1 + \frac{100(1 - 0.40)}{90}} = 0.60$$

Once we have the unlevered beta, ku is:

$$k_U = 5\% + (10\% - 5\%)0.60 = 8.0\%$$

$$V_U = \frac{FCF}{ku} = \frac{12}{0.08} = 150$$

$$V = V_U + Dt = 150 + 40 = 190$$

From the expression [8.14], we can derive a simple expression of WACC:

$$\text{If } V_L = \frac{FCF}{ku} + Dt,$$

$$\frac{V_L}{V_L} - \frac{Dt}{V_L} = \frac{FCF}{kuV_L},$$

$$1 - Lt = \frac{FCF}{kuV_L},$$

$$ku(1 - Lt) = \frac{FCF}{V_L} = WACC \qquad [8.15]$$

The APV allows decomposing the company value in two parts: the business value (VU) and the present value of tax savings, which comes from the capital structure decision. Although it is less used than the free cash flow method, we recommend its use for leveraged acquisitions and for some small companies that don't have a well-defined capital structure.[2] For example, for companies that use debt financing temporarily to finance investments but don't think of a stable capital structure, it is clear to value them as unlevered companies and then compute the present value of tax savings than forcing the calculation of the WACC.

Economic profit method

The economic profit method gives an identical value as the free cash flow method. In Chapter 15, economic profit is covered in full as a valuation method and as a performance metric. To value a business using perpetuities, we use the following formula, where NOPAT = EBIT (1–t):

$$V = \frac{NOPAT}{WACC}. \qquad [8.16]$$

NOPAT equals the free cash flow in perpetuities since net investment (in working capital and CAPEX) tend to be zero.

$$V = \frac{NOPAT}{WACC} = \frac{FCF}{WACC}.$$

Unlevered and levered betas assuming debt not risk-free

If the company's debt is not risk-free and you expect it will be able to fully benefit from tax savings, the unlevered and levered beta formulas are the following:

$$\beta_U = \beta_L \frac{E}{E + D(1-t)} + \beta_D \frac{D(1-t)}{E + D(1-t)}. \quad [8.17]$$

$$\beta_L = \beta_U [1 + \frac{D(1-t)}{E} - \beta_D \frac{D(1-t)}{E}. \quad [8.18]$$

Notice that these formulas require to compute an "implicit debt beta" using the CAPM formula:

$$kd = rf + (rm - rf)\beta_D,$$

$$\beta_D = \frac{kd - rf}{rm - rf}. \quad [8.19]$$

Appendix B provides an illustration of how DCF methods are equivalent when the company's debt is not risk-free.

DCF methods comparison

Figure 8.1 shows the equivalence between the different DCF methods using perpetuities.

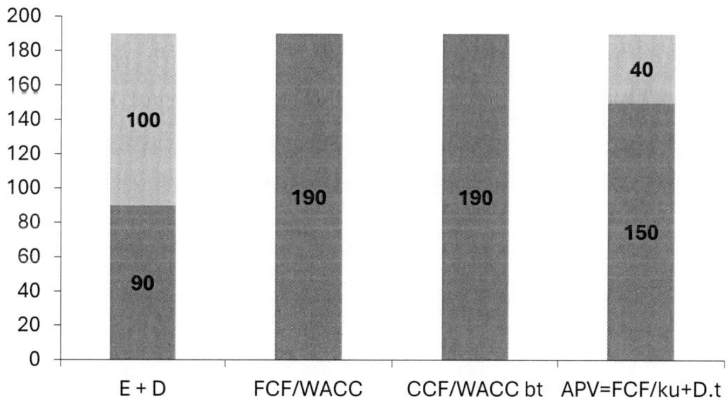

FIGURE 8.1 Company value under different DCF methods

Summarizing, there are the following differences:

- The equity cash flow method values the sum of the parts (equity and debt) separately. It is not commonly used in practice and does not directly specify a capital structure.
- Free cash flow and Capital cash flow methods state a D/V ratio, but they don't make explicit the value added by the capital structure decision.

- APV method is the only one that separates the value of the business and the value of the capital structure decision.

The free cash flow method is the most popular in practice. The APV, nevertheless, may be preferred in certain situations, such as the business has subsidized debt or when the company does not have a well-defined capital structure. We give an example later in this chapter.

MM with taxes, combined with the CAPM, only work for perpetuities when the business holds a constant debt. A business keeping its leverage constant debt is difficult or impossible to find in the real world; for this reason, researchers investigated on a formula that considers how debt varies over time.

The Miles-Ezzel formula and capital structure rebalancing

Miles & Ezzel (1980) found a formula to estimate the cost of capital that assumes a constant leverage ratio rather a constant debt. Interestingly, under certain assumptions, the ME formula is identical to the well-known WACC's formula, which is also referred as the corporate finance textbook formula. According to Miles and Ezzel, the correct interest rate to discount the tax savings with a constant D/V ratio is kd for the first-year tax saving and ku for the second year and beyond. The underlying argument is that, although the first-year tax saving is sure, the subsequent tax savings depend on the business performance, and they have a risk equal to the business' risk.

The first-year tax saving is tLV_Lkd, where L represents the D/V ratio. The tax saving for the second year and beyond is also tLV_Lkd but depends on the business' performance and its present value at the end of year one is a level perpetuity whose present value must be calculated using the unlevered cost of equity: $\frac{tLV_Lkd}{ku}$. The value of a leveraged firm equals the sum of an unlevered firm, which is equal to FCF/ku, plus the present value of tax shields. The expected value of V_L at any future point in time is the same as its current expected value: $E(V_L) = V_L$.

$$V_L = \frac{FCF}{ku} + \frac{tLV_Lkd + \frac{tLV_Lkd}{ku}}{1+kd},$$

Rearranging terms:

$$V_L = \frac{FCF}{ku} + \frac{tLV_Lkd(1+ku)}{ku(1+kd)},$$

$$V_L - \frac{tLV_Lkd(1+ku)}{ku(1+kd)} = \frac{FCF}{ku},$$

$$V_L\left[ku - tLkd\frac{(1+ku)}{(1+kd)}\right] = FCF,$$

$$V_L = \frac{FCF}{ku - tLkd\dfrac{(1+ku)}{(1+kd)}} \qquad [8.20]$$

Equation 8.20 expresses V_L as the present value of a perpetuity. The denominator provides the same number as the WACC formula. Therefore, the WACC is

$$WACC = \frac{FCF}{V_L},$$

$$WACC = ku - tLkd\frac{(1+ku)}{(1+kd)} \qquad [8.21]$$

The ME formula works for any cash flow pattern because it assumes that the increase in debt is proportional to the increase in the free cash flow in each period. Miles-Ezzel can be used with uneven cash flows since the D/V ratio is assumed to be proportional to the free cash flow.[3]

Example

Suppose the unlevered cost of equity of Southern Fire is 12%, the target leverage ratio L = 50%, t = 30%, and kd = 8%. Calculate the WACC.

Using formula [8.21]

$$WACC = 0.12 - 0.30 \times 0.50 \times 0.08\frac{(1+0.12)}{(1+0.08)} = 10.75\%.$$

Estimating the unleveraged cost of capital with the Miles-Ezzel formula

Equation 8.21 gives the WACC for a firm based on the unleveraged cost of capital ku. Then, ku can be obtained from equation 8.20 (substitutions and rearranging terms are provided in Appendix A:

$$ku = \frac{WACC + \dfrac{tLkd}{(1+kd)}}{\left[1 - \dfrac{tLkd}{(1+kd)}\right]}. \qquad [8.22]$$

$$ku = \frac{10.75\% + \dfrac{0.30 \times 0.50 \times 0.08}{(1+0.08)}}{\left[1 - \dfrac{0.30 \times 0.50 \times 0.08}{(1+0.08)}\right]} = 12\%.$$

Since the ME formula first appeared, other studies provide clarifications to the valuation of tax shields, betas, cost of capital expressions for perpetuities, and for arbitrary cash flows under constant leverage. For example, Taggart (1991) recommends using Miles & Ezzel's formulas when the company rebalances its capital structure once a year and Harris & Pringle's (1985) formulas when the target debt ratio is rebalanced continuously. As Miles & Ezzel recognize that tax savings are not risk-free, the formulas to unlever and relever betas are different from the Hamada's formulas:

$$\beta_U = \frac{E\beta_L + D\beta_D[1 - tkd / (1 + kd)]}{E + D[1 - tkd / (1 + kd)]}. \qquad [8.23]$$

$$\beta_L = \beta_U + \frac{D}{E}(\beta_U - \beta_D)\left[1 + \frac{tkd}{(1 + kd)}\right]. \qquad [8.24]$$

Notice that these formulae allow for a debt beta. The difference between Miles & Ezzel and Hamada's formulas arises from a) the discount rate used to compute the present value of tax savings from the second year and beyond and b) the debt's risk. If the target company under valuation is a public company, its beta is observed and is not necessary to perform any unlever or relever calculations, unless you prefer follow the bottom-up approach using the average industry beta.

Arzac (1996), and Ruback (1994) introduced clarifications to previous studies. They stated that the cost of capital expressions differs on the assumed tax regime and the riskiness of future interest tax shields. Ruback (2002) compares the CCF method to the APV method and provides consistent leverage adjustment formulas for both methods. Fernández (2004) proposed different formulas to calculate the betas when the company maintains a fixed book-value leverage ratio. Fernandez suggests using the following formulas, which also consider the debt is not risk-free:

$$\beta_U = \frac{E\beta_L + D(1 - t)\beta_D}{E + D(1 - t)} \qquad [8.25]$$

$$\beta_L = \beta_U \frac{D(1 - t)}{E}(\beta_U - \beta_D) \qquad [8.26]$$

These are identical to Hamada's formulas for the case of $\beta_D = 0$.

Arzac & Glosten (2005) state that in the absence of growth, constant leverage implies that the present value of the tax saving is less than Dt except for the exceptional case where the value of debt is constant as in Modigliani & Miller (1958), and Modigliani & Miller (1963) and derive formulas for the value of tax shields, betas and cost of capital for growing perpetuities.

None of these formulas work for all circumstances since they are based on different assumptions. For example, it is hard to believe that the company holds a fixed market value leverage ratio, although a book-value leverage ratio could be considered less variable than the market-value leverage ratio. Assuming that the debt is not risk-free leads to formulas considering a debt beta coefficient calculated with the CAPM formula to obtain an "implied" beta coefficient. Suppose a company has a cost of debt of 12%; the implied debt beta coefficient would be greater than the stock market beta, which is illogical. Hamada formulas assume the company is able to take full advantage of tax savings, which is consistent with a forecasted free cash flow that does not expect a loss tax shield along the projection.

In practice, you should use the formulas best aligned with your expectations. Hamada's formulas could fit if your forecasted free cash flow assumes no loss tax shield and that the company rebalances the D/V ratio periodically. If you consider the tax savings are not entirely risk-free, you can manage the issue considering a tax rate lower than the legal tax rate, say $t^\star < t$ (see next section for an example). If you have an observed levered beta of a peer group and have to calculate the unlevered beta (which is usually the case), Hamada's formulas provide a value slightly lower than Miles & Ezzel's formulas (see problem 13); if you have the unlevered beta and need to calculate the levered beta, Hamada's formulas provide a higher value (see problem14). For unlevered betas greater than one, the difference in levered betas is negligible and decreases with the size of the unlevered beta.

An example of adjusted present value

MM formulas are appropriate for investments that generate perpetual cash flows, but most investments do not generate cash flow perpetuities. Furthermore, the tax advantage derived from leverage is difficult to estimate for any particular firm. Sometimes, companies finance a new project with subsidized bank loans. These loans are conceded for five or ten years with an amortization schedule; therefore, the project does not have a well-defined capital structure since the D/V is higher in the beginning and lower in the latter years. For these cases, the APV method is recommendable since we can calculate the present value of tax savings with precision.

Suppose Nimbus Inc. is considering building a new distribution facility that would cost 10 million financed 50% with a subsidized debt and 50% equity. The expected free cash flow is $2 million per year for ten years, after which the business will be sold for a salvage value of $0.5 million. The bank loan will charge an annual interest rate of 6%, while the capital will be repaid in equal installments of $1 million over five years, starting at the end of the first year. Although the statutory tax rate is $t = 35\%$, the marginal tax rate $t^\star$ is estimated as 30% and $ku = 12\%$.

Figure 8.2 shows the project's free cash flow and tax-saving cash flow. The APV is calculated as the present value of the free cash flow using the required unlevered cost of capital plus the present value of tax savings, using $t^\star$ as the effective tax rate and the cost of debt as the discount rate. If we had used $t = 35\%$ as the tax rate and $ku = 12\%$ as the discount rate of tax savings, we would obtain very similar values: PV Tax savings = 0.49 and APV = 11.95.

	Yr 0	Yr 1	Yr 2	Yr 3	Yr 4	Yr 5	Yr 6	Yr 7	Yr 8	Yr 9	Yr 10
Free cash flow	-10	2	2	2	2	2	2	2	2	2	2.5

	Yr 0	Yr 1	Yr 2	Yr 3	Yr 4	Yr 5
Loan balance	10	8	6	4	2	0
Installments		2	2	2	2	2
Interest payments		0.6	0.48	0.36	0.24	0.12
Tax savings (t=30%)		0.21	0.168	0.126	0.084	0.042

PV FCF	$ 11.46	=+NPV(O5;C3:L3)
PV Tax savings	$ 0.49	=+NPV(K10;C9:G9)
APV	$ 11.95	=+B11+B12

Loan	5
kd	6%
t	35%
ku	12%

FIGURE 8.2 Tax savings calculations with the APV method

Concluding thoughts

Understanding the relationships between the different cash flow measures, the appropriate discount rate, and tax effects is more crucial than the DCF equivalence. However, MM formulas are valid under certain conditions: cash flow perpetuities, debt is risk-free and is a fixed amount. Companies that keep their debt constant do not exist in the real world. ME formula assumes a debt proportional to the company's free cash flow and that the company periodically rebalances its leverage ratio, which, in principle, may be considered a better argument than a constant debt. Numerous studies added clarifications to the valuation of tax shields, betas, and cost of capital expressions with corporate and personal taxes, for perpetuities and, for arbitrary cash flows under constant leverage, which lead to different formulas. Since these formulas are based on different assumptions, they work under certain conditions. The choice of the formula to estimate the cost of capital should be consistent with your expectations about the risk of tax savings.

Short questions and problems

1. Taking into account that the cash flow to equity of XX is \$9 million, calculate the free cash flow knowing that interest payments are \$5 million and the tax rate is t = 40%
2. If the Capital cash flow is \$14, what is the Free cash flow, since D = 100, kd = 5%, and t = 40%
3. If the Free cash flow is \$12, D = 100, kd = 5%, and t = 40%, what is the cash flow to equity?
4. Explain why Miles-Ezzel argued that ku, not kd, is the appropriate discount rate for calculating the present value of future tax shield from the second year and beyond when it is assumed that the firm rebalance its capital structure.
5. If we use a marginal tax rate t* lower than the legal tax rate t, which should be the discount rate to calculate the present value of tax savings, kd or ku? Why?
6. Explain the underlying assumption between the D/V ratio and the free cash flow behind the ME formula.
7. Suppose the unleveraged required return of Maples Ltd is 16%, the marginal tax rate is t = 30%, and assume that Maples rebalances its capital structure each year to maintain a target leverage ratio L = 33%. The marginal cost of debt is kd = 10%. What is the WACC?
8. What is the difference between the Miles & Ezzel formula for the cost of capital and the WACC formula of the finance textbooks?
9. Suppose GD Landscape Corp. wants to estimate its unleveraged required return. Its leverage ratio is L = 20%, kd = 7%, t = 30%, WACC = 12%. What is ku, the unlevered cost of equity?
10. Large Arrow Corp. has an unleveraged cost of capital of 18% and rebalances its D/V ratio each year to a target of L = 0.50. t = 30% and can borrow at a rate of kd = 12%. What is Large Arrow's WACC?

11. Naked Bikes Corp. is a small company whose leverage ratio L = 27% t = 35% Beta leveraged = 1.6 t = 0.20 kd = 7%%, rf = 4%, rm = 12%. Supposing that the company rebalances its leverage ratio annually:

    a) What is Naked Bike's WACC?
    b) What is ku?
    c) What is the unleveraged beta implied by ku?

12. Green Lantern Inc. is considering investing in the residential real estate industry. The initial investment would cost 10 million, financed by 40% debt and 60% equity. The expected free cash flow is 4 million per year for ten years, without salvage value. The loan will bear an interest rate of 12% payable annually. It will be repaid in equal annual installments of $400,0000, beginning at the end of year one. The corporate tax is t = 30, and the unleveraged cost of capital ku = 16%

    a) Calculate the project's APV using ku to calculate the present value of tax savings
    b) Calculate the WACC (hint: since the D/V ratio is not constant, use an iteration)

13. Determine the unlevered beta using the following peer group data and the formulas of Hamada and Miles & Ezzel: β_L = 1.00; D/E = 0.5; t = 30%; kd = 7%; rm = 10%; rf = 5%.
14. Using the data from problem 13, calculate the levered beta using the Hamada and Miles & Ezzel formulas, knowing that the peer group unlevered beta is 0.93.
15. John Mart Company has a beta coefficient of 1.15, a debt/equity ratio of D/E = 32% and its effective tax rate is 34%. Supposing Mark X modifies its capital structure, increasing the D/E ratio to 50%, the legal tax rate is 40%, what is the new beta if you use Hamada equations?

    a) 1,2733
    b) 1,2343
    c) 1,2246

16. Complete each sentence with a suitable word or words. The first one has already been completed for you. If the company is not traded, the beta can be obtained using the bottom-up or comparable approach, which consists in identified similar companies, and then calculate the.....................beta of the peer group. Since the capital structure of the target may be different to the capital structure of the peer group, we have to ....the unlevered beta of the peer group, and then adjusting it using the capital structure of the............ target and the legal ....rate.
17. Table 8.1 shows the expected income before taxes of Chief Corp. The business generates a tax-loss carryforward due to its negative taxable income. It may then be used to reduce taxable income in subsequent years. Assuming an income tax rate of 30% and a discount rate of 6%, calculate the present value

of tax savings, taking into account that tax saving only has value when it can actually be used.

TABLE 8.1 Forecasted income before taxes of Chief Corp

	Year 0	Year 1	Year 2	Year 3	Year 4
Income before taxes	–840.0	–1,152.0	–150.0	6,800.0	12,400.0

Notes

1 [X(1–t), *rm*] can be expressed as a matrix, so 1/Eu[X(1–t), *rm*] is a matrix multiplied by a scalar.

2 Some businesses use a small number of bank loans to finance investments, but they don't consider maintaining a stable D/V ratio. To value these companies, it is more straightforward to use the APV and compute the present value of tax savings rather than forcing a WACC calculation.

3 Remember that Hamada assumes zero covariance between working capital CAPEX, interest, and debt changes with the operative income, and therefore are suitable for uneven cash flows. On the other hand, Miles & Ezzel formula assumes the D/V ratio is proportional to an uneven free cash flow.

References

Arzac, E. R. (1996). Valuation of Highly Leveraged Firms. *Financial Analysts Journal, 4*, 42–50.

Arzac, E., & Glosten, L. (2005). A Reconsideration of Tax Shield Valuation. *European Financial Management, 11(4)*, 453–461.

Fernández, P. (2004). The Value of Tax Shields is NOT equal to the Present Value of Tax Shields. *Journal of Financial Economics, 73(1)*, 145–165.

Hamada, R. (1972). The Effect of the Firm's Capital Structure on the Systematic Risk of Common Stocks. *The Journal of Finance, 27(2)*, 435–452.

Harris, R., & Pringle, J. (1985). Risk-Adjusted Discount Rates: Extensions from the Average Risk Case. *Journal of Financial Research*, 237–244.

Kaplan, S., & Ruback, R. S. (1995). The valuation of cash flows: An empirical analysis. *Journal of Finance, 50(4)*, 1059–1093.

Miles, A., & Ezzel, J. (1980, September). The Weighted Average Cost of Capital, Perfect Capital Markets, and Project Life: A Clarification. *Journal of Financial and Quantitative Analysis*, 719–730.

Modigliani, F., & Miller, M. (1958, June). The Cost of Capital, Corporation Finance, and the theory of the Firm. *The American Economic Review, 48(3)*, 261–297.

Modigliani, F., & Miller, M. (1963, June). Corporate Income, Taxes and the Cost of Capital: A Correction. *The American Economic Review, 53(3)*, 433–443.

Myers, S. (1974). Interactions of Corporate Financing and Investment Decisions: Implications for Capital Budgeting. *Journal of Finance*, 1–25.

Ruback, R. (1994, November). A Note on Capital Cash Flow Valuation. *Harvard Business Review*, 9–295-069.

Ruback, R. (2002). Capital Cash Flows: A Simple Approach to Valuing Risky Cash Flows. *Financial Management, 31(2)*, 85–103.

Sharpe, W. (1964, September). Capital Asset Prices: A Theory of Market Equilibrium Under Condition of Risk. *Journal of Finance*, 277–293.

Taggart, R. A. (1991). Consistent valuation and cost of capital expressions with corporate and personal taxes. *Financial Management*, 8–20.

Appendix A Unleveraged cost of capital derivation from Miles-Ezzel formula

Miles-Ezzel formula of WACC is

$$WACC = ku - tLkd\frac{(1+ku)}{(1+kd)}.$$

$$ku = WACC + tLkd\frac{(1+ku)}{(1+kd)},$$

$$ku = WACC + \frac{tLkd + tLkdku}{(1+kd)},$$

$$ku = WACC + \frac{tLkd}{(1+kd)} + \frac{tLkdku}{(1+kd)},$$

$$ku - \frac{tLkdku}{(1+kd)} = WACC + \frac{tLkd}{(1+kd)},$$

$$ku\left[1 - \frac{tLkd}{(1+kd)}\right] = WACC + \frac{tLkd}{(1+kd)},$$

$$ku = \frac{WACC + \frac{tLkd}{(1+kd)}}{\left[1 - \frac{tLkd}{(1+kd)}\right]}.$$

Appendix B Equivalence DCF methods when the debt is not risk-free

The equivalence remains when the debt is not risk-free. Suppose kd = 8%, higher than rf = 5% and the free cash flow (FCF), the cash flow to equity (CFE), and the capital cash flow (CCF) are:

FCF = EBIT(1–t) = 20 (1–0.40) = 12
CFE = (EBIT–Interest)(1–t) = (20–8)(1–0.40) = 7.2
CCF = Interest + Dividends = 8 + 7.2 = 15.2

Notice that FCF remains invariable. Calculating the equity fair value using the CAPM we have:

$$ke = 5\% + (10\% - 5\%)1.0 = 10\%$$

$$E = \frac{7.2}{0.10} = 72$$

And the value of the business is

$$V = E + D = 72 + 100 = 172$$

For the free cash flow method, the WACC is

$$WACC = 8\%(1 - 0.40) \times \frac{100}{172} + 10\% \times \frac{72}{172} = 6.97\%$$

$$V = \frac{12}{0.0697} = 172$$

For the capital cash flow method, the WACC before taxes is

$$WACC_{BT} = 8\% \times \frac{100}{172} + 10\% \times \frac{60}{172} = 8.84\%$$

$$V = \frac{15.2}{0.0884} = 172$$

And finally, for the case of APV, since the debt is not risk-free, we proceed to calculate the unlevered beta as the weighted average of debt and equity betas:

$$\beta_U = \beta_L \frac{E}{E + D(1-t)} + \beta_D \frac{D(1-t)}{E + D(1-t)}. \quad [8.27]$$

We need to estimate an "implicit beta" using the CAPM formula:

$$kd = 5\% + (10\% - 5\%)\beta_D = 8\%$$

$$\beta_D = 0.60$$

$$\beta_U = 1.0 \frac{72}{72 + 100(1 - 0.40)} + 0.60 \frac{100(1 - 0.40)}{72 + 100(1 - 0.40)} = 0.818$$

Once we have the unlevered beta, ku is:

$$k_U = 5\% + (10\% - 5\%)0.818 = 9.09\%$$

$$V_U = \frac{FCF}{ku} + Dt$$

$$V_U = \frac{12}{0.0909} + 100 \times 0.40 = 172$$

CHAPTER

9

Optimal capital structure

Introduction

In this chapter, we explain how to create a bond-rating capital structure trade-off model from scratch, estimating the cost of equity with the CAPM model and the cost of debt on the bond rating. Since the optimal capital structure does not have a unique tradeoff, then we describe other factors affecting the decision and some real-world cases about the capital structure decision.

After reading this chapter, you will be able to:

- Recognize the many trade-offs involved in the capital structure decision;
- Consider other factors that may influence the choice of capital structure.

DOI: 10.4324/9781003628491-11

Creating a capital structure model in a spreadsheet

We will start our analysis by estimating the market value that ECO Corp., the company we used as an example in Chapter 8. When the firm has no financial debt, its beta is unlevered, it's cost of capital reflects the required return for an unlevered company, and its value would be unlevered firm's value. For estimating the unlevered cost of capital ku, we must first unlever its beta of 1.0, using the fair market values of equity and debt. Remember from Chapter 8 that ECO Corp.'s equity market value is currently \$90, and its debt market value is \$100. The market risk premium and the risk-free rate are the same as used in Chapter 8.

$$\beta_U = \frac{1.0}{1 + \frac{100(1-0.40)}{90}} = 0.60$$

$$k_U = 5\% + (10\% - 5\%)0.60 = 8.00\%$$

$$V_U = \frac{20(1-0.4)}{0.08} = 150$$

To estimate the firm value for different D/V ratios, we enter different D/V ratios as input data on a spreadsheet, from 0% to 90%. We'll start by assuming that the cost of debt remains constant for each D/V ratio; later, this assumption will be eliminated and suggest a practical way to estimate the cost of debt for different D/V ratios. Because we use perpetuities, EBIT and the free cash flow remain constant at \$12 million; however, when the D/V ratio changes, the beta changes as well, which affects the cost of equity changes and the WACC. For each D/V ratio in Table 9.1, there is an equivalent D/E ratio (for example, a 50% D/V ratio to a 100% D/E ratio). To calculate the fair value for different D/V ratios, you must follow systematically the following steps:

1. Calculate the new (levered) beta using the Hamada formula.
2. Using the beta found in step 1, calculate the cost of equity.
3. Determine the WACC.
4. Determine the firm value as V = FCF/WACC
5. Determine the amount of debt for a D/V = 10% ratio (D = V x 10%).
6. Calculate the interest payment and the EBIT/Interest ratio.

The new levered beta, cost of equity, WACC, and firm value will be:

$$\beta_L = 0.60\left[1 + 0.10(1-0.40)\right] = 0.64$$

$$k_e = 5\% + (10\% - 5\%)0.64 = 8.20\%$$

$$WACC = 5\%(1-0.40) \times 0.10 + 8.20\% \times 0.90 = 7.70\%$$

$$V = \frac{12}{0.077} = 155.8$$

A D/V ratio of 10% indicates that the debt must be the equal to the firm value V times 10%, which is D = 155.8x10% = 15.6 and the interest payment is 15.6x5% = 0.8. Table 9.1 and Figures 9.1 and 9.2 show the beta, cost of capital, and the firm value for different D/V ratios. Notice that when the firm leverages, the WACC decreases and the firm value increases.

TABLE 9.1 Leverage and firm value

					Leverage					
D/V	0%	10%	20%	30%	40%	50%	60%	70%	80%	90%
D/E	0%	11%	25%	43%	67%	100%	150%	233%	400%	900%
Debt	0	15.6	32.6	51.1	71.4	93.8	118.4	145.8	176.5	210.9
Interest payment	0	0.8	1.6	2.6	3.6	4.7	5.9	7.3	8.8	10.5
					Cash flow					
FCF	12.0	12.0	12.0	12.0	12.0	12.0	12.0	12.0	12.0	12.0
ECF	12.0	11.5	11.0	10.5	9.9	9.2	8.4	7.6	6.7	5.7
CCF	12.0	12.3	12.7	13.0	13.4	13.9	14.4	14.9	15.5	16.2
					Betas					
β_L	0.60	0.64	0.69	0.75	0.84	0.96	1.14	1.44	2.04	3.84
					Cost of capital					
ke	8.0%	8.2%	8.5%	8.8%	9.2%	9.8%	10.7%	12.2%	15.2%	24.2%
kd	5.0%	5.0%	5.0%	5.0%	5.0%	5.0%	5.0%	5.0%	5.0%	5.0%
ku	8.0%	8.0%	8.0%	8.0%	8.0%	8.0%	8.0%	8.0%	8.0%	8.0%
WACC	8.0%	7.7%	7.4%	7.0%	6.7%	6.40%	6.1%	5.8%	5.4%	5.1%
WACC bt	8.0%	7.9%	7.8%	7.6%	7.5%	7.4%	7.3%	7.2%	7.0%	6.9%
					Firm value					
V = FCF/WACC	150.00	156.3	163.0	170.5	178.6	187.50	197.4	208.3	220.6	234.4

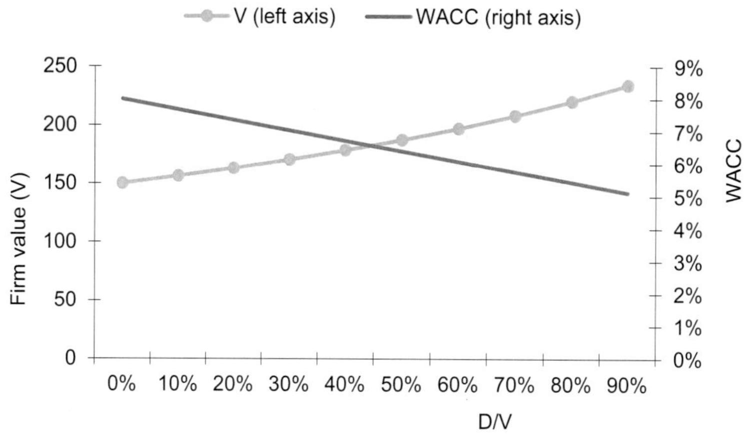

FIGURE 9.1 Firm value and WACC under MM propositions with taxes

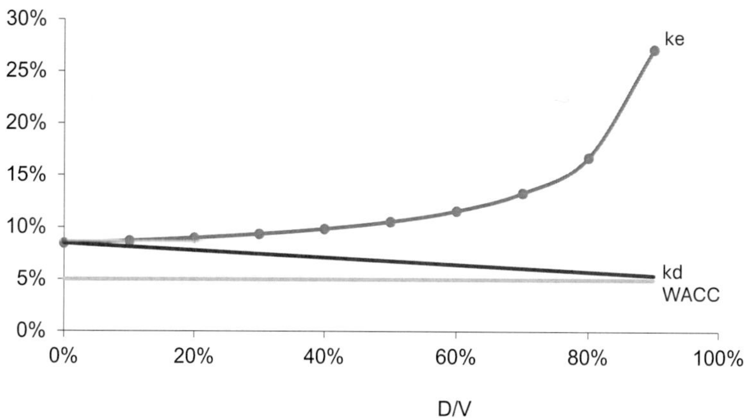

FIGURE 9.2 Cost of capital under MM propositions with taxes

As the company increases its leverage, we can see that:

- The cost of equity increases as the beta increases, reaching values rarely observed in practice.[1]
- Since kd is constant in the analysis, the WACC always decreases to reach kd when the company D/V ratio is close to 100%, and the company value always increases.

In the presence of taxes, when kd is assumed to be constant, we obtain the same results that postulate MM with taxes: more debt means more value. However, as leverage rises, the cost of debt changes, thus we need a practical method[2] of estimating kd for different leverage ratios.

The interest coverage ratio

The interest coverage ratio (ICR) represents the company's ability to pay its current interest payment on its outstanding debt using its earnings. The ICR is calculated by dividing earnings before interest and taxes (EBIT)[3] during a given period by the company's interest payments during the same period:

$$ICR = \frac{EBIT}{Interest\ payment} \qquad [9.1]$$

The ICR is a crucial metric for bondholders and shareholders because they want to know if the company will be able to meet its obligations. Agency ratings usually calculate a normalized measure of ICR based on expected operating income, which is calculated using current operating assets and an average EBIT/Op. Assets ratio over 3/4 years (normalized ICR = current operational assets x average EBIT/Op. assets). ICR is not the only measure considered when assigning a credit rating; additional considerations include its trend and volatility, the matching between debts and credits expressed in foreign currency, and the quality of senior management.[4]

The relationship between ICR and the debt cost is as follows: the more leveraged the firm, the higher the interest payments and the lower the coverage ratio; the lower the coverage ratio, the worse the bond rating and the higher will be the bond's interest rate.

More leverage→more interest payments→ICR decreases→Rating decreases→kd increases

Table 9.2 illustrates the relationship between the interest coverage ratio and the bond rating: the lower the ICR, the lower the rating. We construct the table in the following manner: First, we calculate the average yields for each related rating using a sample of corporate bonds with a modified duration more than five years (Source: Refinitiv Eikon). The margin over the ten-year Treasury note is then

TABLE 9.2 Interest coverage ratio and bond rating

Low	High	Rating	Spread	kd
1.00	1.50	CCC	8.62%	13.62%
1.50	2.00	B-	4.81%	9.81%
2.00	2.50	B	3.88%	8.88%
2.50	3.00	BBB-	1.73%	6.73%
3.00	3.50	BBB	1.26%	6.26%
3.50	4.00	A	0.46%	5.46%
4.00	4.50	A+	0.61%	5.61%
4.50	5.00	AA	0.29%	5.29%
5.00	>5	AAA	0.13%	5.13%

estimated for December 2024. The marginal cost of debt was determined by combining the observed spread and the ten-year treasury yield. Trying to define IRC intervals from a bond sample is very hard, if not impossible, because the rating contains additional aspects that can affect the theoretical rating, as we commented above. See a real-world application in Box 9.1. As a result, we apply a simple rule. High-quality and investment-grade bonds have lower spreads than speculative or highly speculative bonds. AAA-rated corporate bonds typically (but not always) have an IRC of 5 or higher, whereas CCC-rated bonds have an IRC of 1/1.5. As a result, we create a scale IRC ratio using an interval of 0.5, ranging from 5 or more for excellent quality to a minimum of 1 for very speculative.[5]

Box 9. 1 Case study: EBIT/interest ratio and credit rating relationship

Figure 9.3 shows the relationship between the interest coverage ratio and credit rating in Argentina. Using data from the Buenos Aires Stock Exchange and the Securities Commission from 1988 to 2000, the coverage ratio was computed using the financial statements that were closest to the bond issuance date. We can appreciate some interesting issues. For example, most companies with a ratio greater than four are rated AAA. A ratio of 2 to 4 is most common among AA, A+, and A ratings, while some companies have a greater ratio than 4. Most BBB grades occur at a ratio of two, whereas those near BB have a ratio of one. For a ratio less than one, there are a few C-rated companies, and for a negative ratio, three companies are in default.

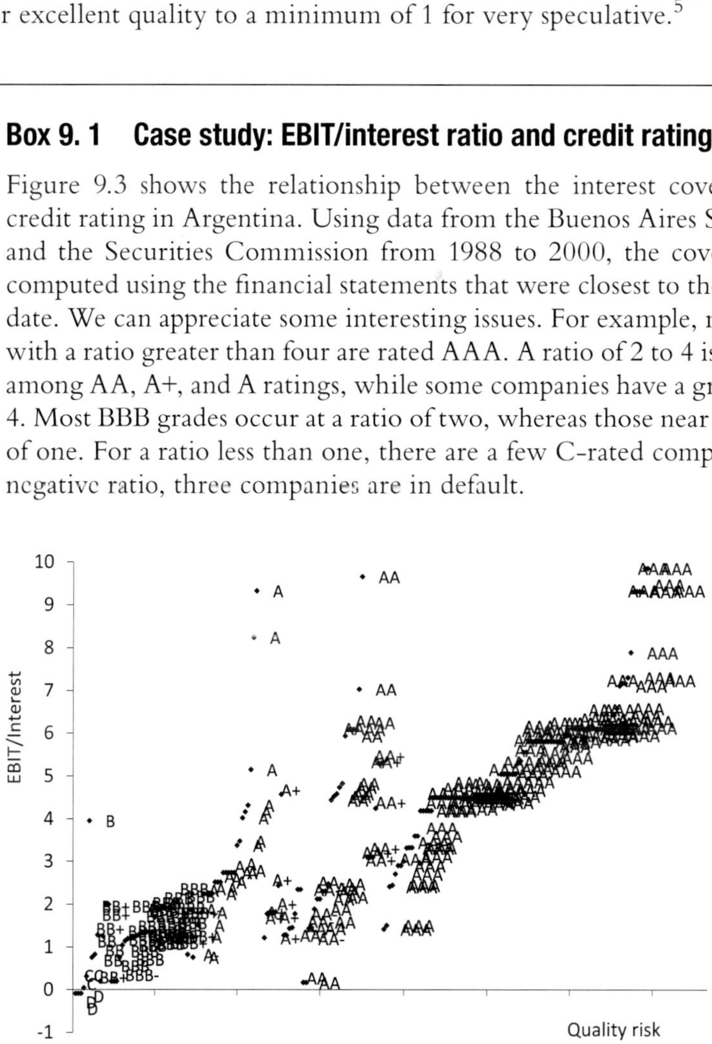

FIGURE 9.3 EBIT/interest ratio and credit rating relationship

Source: Buenos Aires Stock Exchange and the Securities Commission.

Based on the cost of debt estimated in Table 9.2 for each rating, we can seek an optimal mix of debt and equity to minimize the weighted average cost of capital. The D/V ratio that leads to the minimum WACC (and the maximum firm value) is near D/V = 40/50%. The cost of equity capital is estimated using the CAPM model following steps 1–6 described in the previous section.

TABLE 9.3 Leverage and firm value considering bond rating

					Leverage and rating					
D/V	0%	10%	20%	30%	40%	50%	60%	70%	80%	90%
D/E	0%	11%	25%	43%	67%	100%	150%	233%	400%	900%
Debt	0.0	15.6	32.5	51.0	70.7	86.7	96.3	108.0	123.9	110.5
Interest	0.0	0.8	1.7	2.6	3.7	5.8	8.6	10.6	12.2	15.0
EBIT	20	20	20	20	20	20	20	20	20	20
IRC	######	25.0	12.0	7.6	5.3	3.4	2.3	1.9	1.6	1.33
Rating	AAA	AAA	AAA	AAA	AA	BBB-	B	B-	B-	CCC
					Cash flow					
FCF	12	12	12	12	12	12	12	12	12	12
ECF	12	12	11	10	10	8	7	6	5	3
CCF	12	12	13	13	13	14	15	16	17	18
					Betas					
b_L	0.60	0.64	0.69	0.75	0.84	0.96	1.14	1.44	2.04	3.84
					Cost of capital					
ke	8.0%	8.2%	8.5%	8.8%	9.2%	9.8%	10.7%	12.2%	15.2%	24.2%
kd	5.1%	5.1%	5.1%	5.1%	5.3%	6.7%	8.9%	9.8%	9.8%	13.6%
WACC	8.0%	7.7%	7.4%	7.1%	6.8%	6.9%	7.5%	7.8%	7.7%	9.8%
					Firm value					
V = FCF/WACC	150.0	156.1	162.7	169.9	176.7	173.4	160.5	154.2	154.9	122.8

The sixth row contains the interest coverage ratio; the higher the coverage ratio, the better the ability of the company to fulfill its obligations to its lenders. When the leverage increases, fiscal savings increase, but the ICR and bond rating decrease, therefore, kd increases. For D/V ratios lower than 40%, tax savings outweigh the disadvantages of rising kd.

For a D/V = 40%, the coverage ratio is 5.3, which indicates that the company can meet its obligation; however, for a D/V ratio higher of 50%, the rating would be BBB-, so the company's bond rating could diminish and the cost of debt increases rapidly. Koller, Dobbs, & Huyett (2011) state that most large companies with investment-grade debt ratings of BBB to A have and EBITDA/interest ratio of about 4.5 to 10, and the difference in value between these times coverage ratios is less than 10%. Also, if the IRC drops below four times, the company's bond rating could be lower than the investment grade. Therefore, an optimal capital structure could lie between a 40/50% D/V ratio.

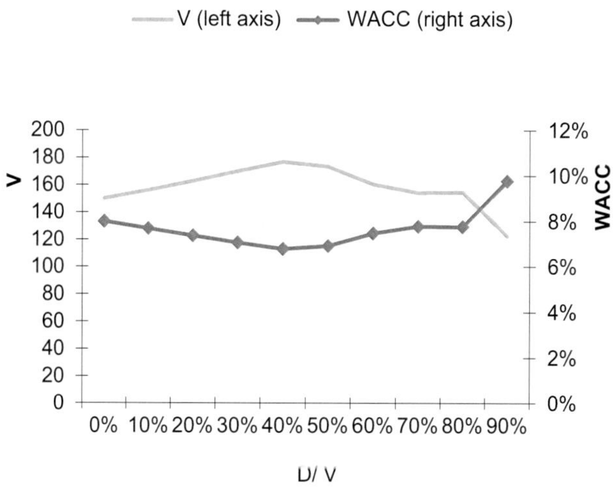

FIGURE 9.4 Firm value and WACC considering the coverage ratio

Figure 9.5 shows that when the company reaches its theoretical maximum value, the WACC hits its minimum value. Figure 9.5 depicts the cost of equity capital, the cost of debt and WACC. The kd and WACC functions are not continuous because the cost of debt is subject to the yield spread resulting from the bracket for the interest coverage ratio.

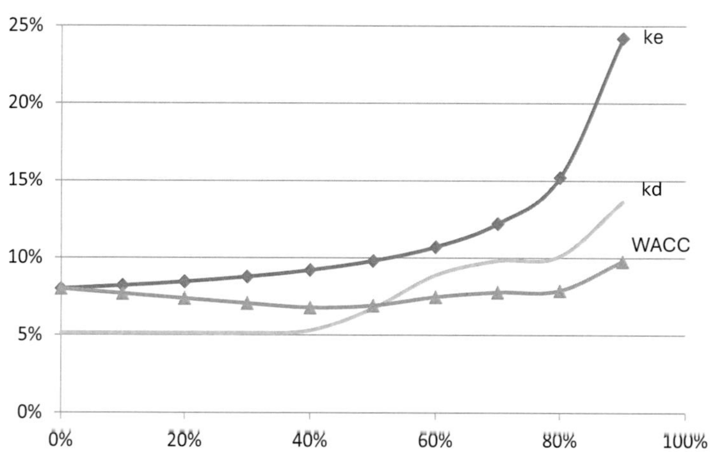

FIGURE 9.5 Cost of capital considering coverage ratio

A bond rating tradeoff model can help us start looking for an optimal capital structure but it is merely a starting point; a strict model might occasionally impose undesirable constraints, and it is always preferable to be somewhat correct rather than precisely wrong. In real life, other factors influence the capital structure decision. We should ask ourselves if we prefer flexibility or discipline. Companies that are actively involved in mergers and acquisitions may be interested in flexibility and a leverage reserve to take advantage of investment opportunities. Companies that suffer from agency costs, on the other hand, may want to increase debt in order to discipline operations and repay the debt. Control and asymmetrical information are other aspects that could arise. They are not the same for all companies nor operate in all of them. The next section discusses real-world examples of capital structure changes driven by different motivations.

Other factors affecting the capital structure choice

Although we can develop a bond rating trade-off model to identify a theoretically optimal capital structure, the choice of capital structure choice is influenced by a wide range of additional factors, including local conditions (regulations, income tax laws, local conditions) and other factors (e.g., agency, costs, unobservable management reputation that influences capital-raising abilities, company strategy, asymmetrical information).

The local company's management has been operating in the local conditions for years and is more familiar with the factors better than we, as knowledgeable but uninformed outsiders, are. For example, throughout the 1990s, two Argentine telecommunications companies, Telecom and Telefonica, operating in Argentina, exhibited a capital structure of D/V = 45/50%. However, after the strong depreciation of the peso currency in 2002 and the freezing of tariffs, the EBIT dropped, and Telecom defaulted its debt. The loss extinguished retained earnings and the legal reserve, and even though the company had surplus free cash flow, Telecom was forced to suspend dividend payment to its shareholders without first reconstituting retained earnings and the legal reserve. As we will see in Chapter 17, Telecom used the surplus cash flow to purchase marketable securities and pay the principal of its corporate bonds as they matured. Telefonica, its competitor, did the same. By the end of 2017, both companies became almost unlevered companies. Therefore, because a trade-off model does not consider this circumstance. our subject company may appear to have a non-optimal capital structure.

Many questions we should all be asking arise, for example: how do we know we're more knowledgeable than management is about all the local business, economic, and capital market conditions relevant to the company? The following sections outline a few hypotheses that explain some factors that influence the capital structure choice including real case studies. Although we used the trade-off model in some of them, the motivations for a change in the capital structure were different.

Agency costs tradeoff

The agency theory (Jensen & Meckling, 1976; Jensen, 1986; Jensen, 2001) states that an internal cost arises from an agent acting on behalf of a principal and typically generating conflicts of interest between shareholders and management. The "principal-agent relationship",[6] refers to the relationships between shareholders and management (where shareholders are principals and management personnel are agents). Since shareholders want management to make decisions that maximize shareholder value, an agency cost arises when the senior management prefers to grow the company in ways that maximize their power and wealth, prejudicing the shareholders' best interests. This conflict of interest is lessened by corporate governance mechanisms, such as boards of directors and debt increases. However, using debt could cause another agency cost.

An agency cost of debt arises when managers may want to engage in risky actions such as investing in risky business that presumably would benefit shareholders, who seek a high rate of return. Bondholders, who are typically interested in a safer investment, may want to place restrictions on the use of their money to reduce risk. Because owner, manager, and bondholders all have distinct objectives, employing debt could result in another potential conflict of interest. Management may make strategic decisions in their own best interests rather than shareholders or bondholders.

One way to protect lenders from borrowers defaulting on their obligations is implementing debt covenants. Debt covenants consist of requirements about the level of key financial ratios; for example, a maximum debt-asset ratio, a minimum interest coverage ratio, and/or liquidity ratio or working capital levels. If the company did not meet a covenant, the lender typically has the right to call back the debt obligation from the borrower.

Since lower debt ratios could imply more agency cost of debt, Jensen and Meckling (1976, p. 117) argue that an optimal capital structure can be obtained by trading off the agency cost of debt against the benefit of debt.

Box 9.2 Case study: Aluminum Manufactures

Aluminum Manufactures (AM) is a mid-size company involved with the production of aluminum pots. The firm is very profitable, and has an enviable surplus cash flow due its short cash cycle, which makes management feels excessively comfortable and gentrified.

During a meeting in 2016, the senior management explained that decisions made without a proper analysis had resulted in unfavorable outcome from this wealth of resources. For example, at the end of 2015, they bought large quantities of aluminum since they expected a local currency depreciation against the dollar, resulting in higher production costs. The currency depreciation effectively took place in 2015, and the price of aluminum rose; the decision would seem correct. But the high increase in the value of inventories reduced the Cost of Goods Sold (COGS) and therefore increased income taxes! The choice would have been made by the management without considering all potential outcomes. Senior management asked us hot to increase discipline since they understood that operations needed to be under more pressure to reduce agency costs.

In order to accomplish two goals, we proposed an "intelligent" use of debt, increasing the leverage to achieve two objectives:

1. putting pressure on the operations to reduce the agency costs;
2. reducing income taxes.

Discipline and flexibility tradeoff

More debt certainly means less income taxes and perhaps less management agency cost. However, takin on more debt may also result in less flexibility. Businesses in the growing phase of the business cycle may prefer to keep some flexibility to finance the investment requirements with their own resources and/or a leverage reserve to employ debt in the event that further new investment requirements.

Box 9.3 Case study: WPS Petroleum Services

The expansion of the oil and gas industry in Vaca Muerta, Neuquen, Argentina, in 2023 resulted in the permanent award of new contracts to WPS, a petroleum service provider, by YPF, the own state local company. This requires WPS to make new and continuous investments in equipment and tools. The company was considering a shareholder buyout at the same time, financing the acquisition with debt. However, more leverage would introduce restrictions because the obligation to pay interest and principal. Because WPS needs the cash flow to finance the expansion, it decided to delay the acquisition until later when the investment requirements decreased.

Credit rating

We explored the effect on the interest coverage ratio on the bond rating and provide an estimation of the bond yield spread based on the rating. However, a potential change in bond rating as a result of a significant change in capital structure is rarely discussed. This is what happened when we value YPF, Argentina's largest market capitalization in 2007.

Box 9.4 Case study: YPF Argentina

In 2007, we value YPF, an Argentinean public company with a market cap of US$15.3 billion at the time. We needed to work as quietly and soon as possible, therefore our fair value estimate ranged between US$13 billion and US$17 billion. The idea was to purchase 51% of the outstanding shares to achieve a controlling interest, but it would require an enormous issuance of sovereign bonds, therefore we performed an analysis to estimate the bond rating because it is likely that the rating would decline after the capital structure change. Asking about the options, the potential acquirer started consulting with a few investment banks. During one meeting, a senior executive of an American multinational investment bank and financial services company, said: "an interest coverage ratio below 2 is perceived as unhealthy, so be careful with the leverage". Since a lower credit rating would negatively impact the stock price, it would not be acceptable. There was no deal, although would have been a market transaction at the time. Years later the company was nationalized by the Argentine government.

Dividends

Box 9.5 Case study: CDS Energy

CDS Energy is a South American company that operates in the liquefied gas industry. At the beginning of 2002, it suffered government intervention, which froze electricity rates for 15 years. Because the inflation rate during that period was high, the costs increased, and its profits fell. As a result, the price of energy became relatively cheap, and consumer demand increased. The company reduced its investments, did not pay more dividends, and the system was on the brink of collapse.

But in 2016, the new Government abandoned the freeze on public service prices, seeking to align the level of international prices. As a result, the company immediately increased its earnings and cash flows. At this time, the senior management considered a change in the capital structure, whose objective was to increase the company's ability to pay dividends to shareholders. Since CDS was an unlevered company, we analyzed the capital structure to achieve three objectives: 1. pay dividends to shareholders 2. ensure debt service payments 3. reduce income taxes. Finally, we considered that a ratio of D/V = 30% would accomplish the goal while preserving the company's capacity for additional leverage.

Pecking order view and asymmetric information

The pecking order theory (Myers & Majluf, 1984) states that companies establish an order for their financing sources, using internal funds first to finance their investments, and when these run out, they prefer to issue debt and equity as a last resource:

1. Internal cash flow
2. Debt
3. Equity

Rather than introducing corporate taxes and financial distress into the MM framework, the key assumption of the pecking order theory is the asymmetric information: managers, who know more about the company´s prospects, risk, and value than outside investors, decide to issue new equity when the stock is overpriced; however, investors would be reluctant to pay a higher price to the equity issuance, since they suspect about the management intentions. Therefore, asymmetric information favors the issue of debt over equity, avoiding sending adverse signals to the stock market. Some believe that the debt issuance could be interpreted as a signal of the board´s confidence that investment is profitable, while the equity issuance signals a lack of confidence.

The pecking order could explain why profitable firms have low debt ratios: This happens not because they have low debt ratios since they do not need external financing. As always, the empirical evidence is controversial. While some authors have found evidence that the pecking order view is a good approximation of reality, others authors disagree.

Capital structure as a strategy

Matsa (2010) stated that maintaining high levels of liquidity can encourage workers to raise their wage demands, companies with external finance constraints has an incentive to use the cash flow demands of debt service to improve their bargaining position with workers. A union can demand a portion of a firm's liquidity, which the firm keeps mainly to insure against negative shocks, since it is a provider with market power. To reduce the impact of collective bargaining on profits, the firm has an incentive to undertake costly actions that reduce its appropriable liquidity. Capital structure also can play a strategic role for firms active in M&A since they prefer to maintain corporate liquidity and leverage reserves to take advantage of acquisition opportunities.

Box 9.6 Case study: Grupo Cementos de Chihuahua

Grupo Cementos de Chihuahua (GCC) is a Mexico-based public company primarily engaged in the construction materials sector. It also operates in the United States through subsidiaries, and its product portfolio includes Portland grey cement, ready-mixed concrete, gypsum, additives, and limestone aggregates, among others. Looking at its balance sheet, it is immediately striking that marketable securities represent more than 30% of total assets. On the other hand, it maintains a conservative D/V ratio of 20% as of September 2024, has a debt rating of BBB–, an interest coverage ratio of 14.5 and US$723 million in cash equivalents that could be used to pay off the US$512 million long-term debt right away. It seems that there is room to explore an alternative capital structure to reduce the cost of capital since it would be possible to issue a bond with a coupon rate below 6%. However, as the company is active in M&A, the low leverage is explained because the company prefers flexibility for acquisitions. A low D/V ratio and extra cash give GCC the flexibility to take advantage of an acquisition when it comes along.

Size, creditworthiness, profitability, and control

Size matters because small companies face difficulty in raising long-term borrowing. On the other hand, large companies with good reputations, profitability, and a long track record are usually perceived as having a reputation for paying back their loans on time, which allows them to raise funds on less stringent terms and at lower interest rates. These factors presumably lead to a more leveraged capital structure; nonetheless, the empirical evidence is puzzling. On the other hand, much leverage could mean a danger of loss of control through a leveraged buyout.

Table 9.4 summarizes some factors that affect the capital structure decision, accompanied by some comments. While the tax shield can be estimated numerically, the other factors can hardly be put into numbers.

TABLE 9.4 Capital structure factors

Factor	Debt/Equity choice
Taxes	Debt generates fiscal savings, but Equity does not. Empirical evidence suggests that tax influence is less influential than theory prompts.
Agency costs	Although more leverage reduces management agency costs, but it may also lead to disputes between shareholders and debtholders.
Flexibility/Discipline	Debt imposes discipline to manage resources and reduces management agency costs. However, leverage reduces flexibility to lead with unexpected downturns or take advantage of investment opportunities.
Debt rating	When a bond rating drops, the cost of financing rises, hence managers must be aware of the company's bond rating.
Asymmetric information	Managers can raise money by using their knowledge of the company's performance and prospects, which they possess more than investors Because there is a higher potential for conflicts of interest, investors could demand higher returns from companies with asymmetry in information.
Size	Small-sized companies face difficulty in raising long-term finance. Even if they do get these loans, usually they have to pay high-interest rates and stringent repayment conditions, which limits their ability to grow their business.
Strategy	Some companies keep a leverage reserve (and maybe a considerable number of marketable securities), in case they need to raise funds for acquisitions.
Creditworthiness	A good repayment history and credit score help to raise funds on less stringent terms and at lower interest rates.

Concluding thoughts

In this chapter we have outlined a bond rating trade-off model to estimate an optimal capital structure. While the cost of equity capital was estimated with the CAPM model, there is no scientific formula to calculate the marginal cost of debt. A practical way to look for it is to observe the default spread over treasuries and add a default spread to the US 10Y yield treasury.

Although taxes and financial distress costs suggest a logical trade-off between the advantages and disadvantages of leverage, other considerations and trade-offs are involved in the capital structure decision. Asymmetric information, strategy, agency costs and the trade-off between discipline and flexibility are some examples.

Numerous studies have attempted to explain the capital structure. However, although they have contributed to our understanding of the factors affecting capital structure choice, the empirical evidence continues to be a puzzle.

Short questions and problems

1. If the company while the cost of debt remains constant, should be the optimal D/V ratio 99.99%?
2. Assuming V = 163M, free cash flow = 12, D/V = 20%, t = 40%, and $\beta_L = 0.69$. If the leverage increases to a D/V = 40% while the cost of debt of 5% remains constant, what are the new beta, cost of equity, WACC and firm value if rf = 5% and rm = 10%?
3. Now suppose that for a D/V ratio of 40%, the marginal cost of debt increases to 6.3% because the bond rating moves from AA to A–. Calculate the corresponding WACC and firm value, verifying the results with Table 9.3.
4. Considering Table 9.3, if the cost of debt rises to 6.3% as the bond-rating predicts, is it worth modifying the leverage ratio?
5. Suppose a company has a 50% D/V ratio, the marginal cost of debt is 6%, and t = 40%. Based on the historical performance, the CFO believes that the expected tax rate should be 20% rather than 40%. What is the WACC change?
6. Now, respond to question 4 assuming that the free cash flow will increase marginally from 12 to 12.5 due to the reduction in the management agency costs.
7. Explain how the asymmetric information can influence on the capital structure decision.
8. Suppose you are the financial manager of Real Estate Group, which has a market cap of $2,700 million, estimated with a DCF model. The current WACC is 9.62%, the D/V ratio is 17%, kd = 5.6%, and ke = 10.6%. Because the company is active in acquisitions, and wants to keep a leverage reserve and marketable securities of $700 million, to finance future acquisitions. The manager believes that raising the D/V ratio from 17% to 30%, would reduce the WACC to 9.1%, without affecting kd, increasing the firm value from $2,700 to an estimated $2,850 million. This would leave $200 million in marketable securities to finance future acquisitions, and $500 million for dividend payments. What are your thoughts?
9. SSX's financial manager of SSX has identified two alternative capital structures. If the firm borrows 15% of firm value, it can borrow the money at kd = 10%, and the shareholder's required return would be ke = 15%. If the firm borrows 40% of the firm value, it can borrow the money at kd = 11%, and the shareholder's required return would be ke = 17%. The marginal tax rate is 35%. Which capital structure should SXX adopt?
10. ZZZZ is an unleveraged firm with 10 million shares of common stock outstanding, which is traded at a price of $10, thus, the total value of ZZZZ is

$100 million. The expected EBIT is $22 million, t = 40%, FCF = 13.20 million; ku = 13.20%. The senior management of ZZZZ wants to identify an optimal structure considering two different debt levels: $30 million and $40 million, which would be use to repurchase common stock. Although they are familiar with the CAPM model, they prefer to rely on the cost of equity estimations provided for investment banks. In addition, they are also concerned with the impact on the firm's earnings per share (EPS). Assuming perpetuities, fill in the values on Table 9.5 using the following calculations:

a) Cash flow to equity (CFE) = [(EBIT-Dkd)(1-t)]/ke
b) Stock price: Equity value/number of shares at the beginning
c) Number of shares = number of shares at the beginning – Debt/Stock price
d) EPS = CFE/Number of shares

TABLE 9.5 Optimal capital structure

Debt ($)	Equity	ke		Firm value	D/V	CFE	Stock price	WACC	Number of shares	EPS
0.00	100.00	13.20%		100.00	0%		10.00	13.20%	10.00	1.32
30.00		14.00%	10.00%				11.14		9.29	
40.00		16.00%	12.00%							

11. Describe some ways to minimize the following agency costs:

 a) Managers focus on short-term gains and underinvest in projects that maximize shareholder value in the long run while pursuing projects that increase their compensation.
 b) Managers of a company with surplus funds do not make the required efforts to make decisions that maximize shareholder value.
 c) Majority shareholders prioritize higher dividend payouts that benefit themselves at the expense of minority shareholders.

Notes

1 The cost of equity capital is a linear function of the D/E ratio but not of the D/V ratio. Although the CAPM considers the financial risk in the levered beta, it does not consider the expected financial distress costs derived from a highly leveraged firm.

2 To the best of my knowledge, there is no scientific formula to calculate the cost of debt.

3 Sometimes, the ICR is calculated using EBITDA or EBIAT (earnings before interest after taxes) instead of EBIT. While EBITDA increases the ICR, using EBIAT reduces it, being the most conservative.

4 Years ago, we noticed that one agency's rating method involved three steps. In the first step, if the normalized coverage ratio was greater than 8, showed a positive trend, and had low variability in the previous years, the initial letter assigned was A. In the second step, different financial ratios are analyzed alongside other firm's characteristics. The final phase involved performing a forecast under a stressful scenario.

5 In a large sample of active and comparable bonds, the intervals could be narrowed.

6 The principal-agent relationship may also refer to other pairs of connected parties with similar power characteristics, such as the relationship between students (principals) and professors (agents) and politicians (agents) and the community (principals).

References

Jensen, M. (1986, May). Agency Costs of Free Cash Flow, Corporate Finance, and Takeovers. *American Economic Review*, 323–329.

Jensen, M. (2001, 11 October). *Value Maximization, Stockholder Theory and the Corporate Objetive Function*. Available at http://papers.ssrn.com/sol3/papers.cfm?abstract_id = 220671

Jensen, M. C., & Meckling, W. (1976, October). Theory of the Firm: Managerial Behavior, Agency Costs and Ownership Structure. *Journal of Financial Economics*, 305–360.

Koller, T., Dobbs, R., & Huyett, B. (2011). *Value, The Four Cornerstones of Corporate Finance*. New Jersey: Wiley.

Matsa, D. (2010, June). Capital Structure as a Strategic Variable: Evidence from Collective Bargaining. *The Journal of Finance, 65*(3), 1197–1232.

Myers, S., & Majluf, N. (1984). Corporate financing and investment decisions when firms have information that investors do have. *Journal of Financial Economics, 13*, 187–221.

PART

3

DCF valuation in practice

We dedicated Parts 1 and 2 to explaining the discounted cash flow model and the theoretical cornerstones of valuation. These foundations are necessary to provide the necessary knowledge to address the issues that arise in the real world. When we move from the ideal world to the empirical world, there are a lot of caveats waiting for us, to complicate our work. For example, if we are going to calculate the terminal value with the growing perpetuity formula, what conditions the company should meet to be sure that it is in the steady-state? Chapter 10 discusses the issue of terminal value in further detail, because it counts an important portion of the company's fair value. How can we deal with the absence of market values? How can we use the CAPM since we cannot observe betas? Should we consider premiums for control and size and a discount for the lack of marketability? When analyst have to value a business in emerging markets, or in a foreign country, immediately face an additional set of questions. How the country risk should be considered in a valuation? Is the domestic currency appreciated or depreciated? Chapters 11, 12, 13, and 14 dig into all these caveats and propose how to deal with them.

Chapter 15 discusses economic profit, another valuation method. In a valuation, we also provide advice on how to measure the company's performance and raise its value. The economic profit has the merit of digging and calculate the true economic capital which produces the true economic profit and helps to focus on the operations that create value and distinguishing those that do not. We explain how to create value with investment and financial decisions, including divestitures, which are not often regarded as value creation by senior management.

We devote Chapter 16 to relative valuation, another valuation technique often used by analysts/evaluators and traders, which basically consists of using multiples of company earnings to calculate the theorical fair value. We will discuss the most common multiples and how they are applied in practice. Relative valuation is frequently perceived as an easier way to value a company than the DCF method.

DOI: 10.4324/9781003628491-12

However, it could take a considerable time of research and depending on what earning's measure you select, you might have to make some adjustments to reflect meaningful earnings. In addition, these are affected by accounting conventions and by the economic cycle. Therefore, multiples have the potential to be misused if we are not alert to these limitations and how to mitigate them.

CHAPTER

10

The terminal value

Introduction

When using the Discounted Cash Flow method to value a firm, because infinite cash flows are impossible to forecast with perfect accuracy, the cash flow is forecasted for an explicit period of some years until the company achieves a steady state once the business matures. From that moment, we assume that the free cash flow grows at a constant, long-term growth rate, and the perpetuity formula enters the scene to estimate the Terminal Value, which represents the present value of a cash flow that grows from the last forecasted period to perpetuity. Other times it is determined with the value driver formula, and the EBITDA exit multiple.

DOI: 10.4324/9781003628491-13

Since terminal value often comprises a large percentage of the firm value (sometimes more than 60%), its estimation deserves a detailed treatment.

In this chapter, we address the following issues:

- The calculation of the terminal value;
- How the long-term growth rate is estimated;
- The length of the explicit forecast period;
- ROIC-WACC convergence.

The business cycle and the length of the forecast period

In our introductory examples of Greenworth in Chapter 5, we forecasted the free cash flow for five years to introduce the DCF method. There is a vision that forecasting cash flows for more than five years makes no sense since the accuracy of the projections will suffer due to the impossibility of predicting more distant periods. We don't share this opinion since some industries can create value for longer periods. For example, industries like those involved in natural resource extraction can have a longer forecasted period. Conceptually, the free cash flow must be forecasted in detail until the business achieves a steady state, which requires two convergences:

1. The long-term growth rate cannot be greater than the GDP growth rate
2. The return on capital converges to the WACC.

Therefore, the length of the forecasted period must be related to the company cycle life, where the business performance along its life is related to the three industry growth stages. The three phases of the economic cycle, which were introduced in Chapter 5 and are now discussed in more detail, are shown in Figure 10.1.

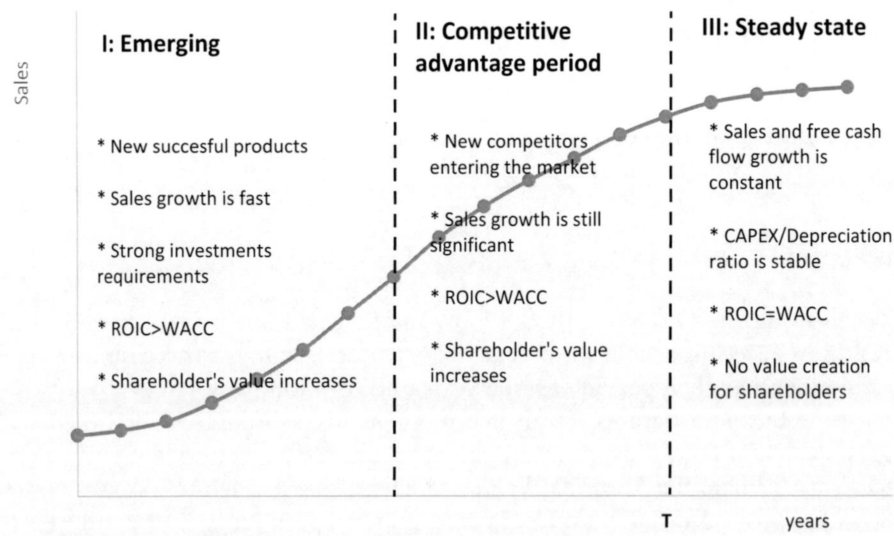

FIGURE 10.1 Industry growth stages

First stage: Vigorous growth, extra-profitability

The first stage, or emerging stage, is characterized by vigorous growth. When a new business is launched, if it is successful, the first years are usually characterized by an extra profit, sales grow fast, and the return on invested capital (ROIC) exceeds the cost of capital; thus, the company can create value for their shareholders. The end of this period coincides with the beginning of the competitive advantage period.

Second stage: Competitive advantage period and the length of the forecast period

Conceptually, the end of the first period coincides with the end of extra profitability for the firm. The second period is known as the "Competitive Advantage Period" (CAP): attracted by the extraordinary profits many competitors get into the business, and the growth rate and profit decrease since competition is expected to erode the company's advantage and eliminate abnormal returns. By that time, the firm must have exhausted its competitive advantage, leaving the possibility of extra profits in the long run, and it should mean that:

- Operative expenses and incomes are supposed to be constant as a percentage of projected sales.
- The return on capital would converge asymptotically to the WACC, and the company could not create value beyond the end of the explicit forecast period.
- The growth rate converges to the long-term growth rate of the GDP plus the inflation rate.

Table 10.1 shows the two last forecasted years of a ten-year forecast period of XX Corp. Assuming that in 2030 and 2031, sales would grow at 6% per year and that

TABLE 10.1 Last forecasted free cash flow of XX Corp

	Dec 2030	Dec 2031	Var (%)
EBITDA	486,166	509,845	4.9
Accounts receivable	12,713	13,476	6.0
Inventories	13,843	14,674	6.0
Other assets	1,237	1,312	6.1
Accounts payable	11,994	12,714	6.0
Fiscal liabilities	7,218	7,651	6.0
Other liabilities	2,062	2,186	6.0
Income tax	109,304	115,862	6.0
Cash flow from operations	370,344	387,073	4.5
CAPEX	130,000	131,000	0.8
Cash flow from investments	130,000	131,000	0.8
Free cash flow	240,344	256,073	6.5

cost/sales ratios and activity ratios would remain the same, all components of working capital and free cash flow grow at a similar rate. For this reason, using the growth perpetuity formula to calculate the terminal value is appropriate.

The length of the forecast period

Masters of Finance students frequently asked me what should be the length of the explicit forecast period. The most important is that it must be long enough so that the company reaches the conditions of a steady state by the end of this period, and the return on capital converges to the cost of capital. The ability to sustain a growth rate greater than the sum of the GDP growth rate plus the inflation rate depends on several qualitative and quantitative factors. Some companies manage to prolong the growth rate by acquisitions with positive net present value, and the success of product launches, which will depend on the quality of management. A company in an innovative industry such as information technology is more likely to grow from newly developed products. Damodaran (2012) states that the length of forecast period is conditioned by the size of the firm (small firms tend to have more room to grow and a larger potential market than large firms), the current growth rate (firms with a high return on capital are likely to sustain these returns for the next few years), barriers to entry and competitive advantages that allow the firm to maintain high growth for longer periods and the management quality.

In practice, we usually forecast the explicit free cash flow for ten years when we value companies in the competitive advantage period and also mature companies. Although mature companies have already reached a steady state, sometimes the launch of a new product or a re-emerging after a recession can extend a growth rate above the long, organic growth rate. There are four additional reasons to use a ten-year forecast:

1. Duration matching: since most practitioners use the US T-Bond ten-year's maturity as a risk-free rate, whose duration is around 7/8 years, a ten-year forecasted free cash flow has a similar duration (if the long-term rate remains constant, as we explain later). Hence, the matching between cash flow and securities included in the cost of capital is better.
2. Recession-recovering phases: even in the steady period, the company goes through periods of recession and subsequent recovery. During the recession, the company grows below the long-term growth rate; then, the company recovers, growing above the long-term growth rate until achieving an organic growth rate again. The process can take several years, and a ten-year forecast may be better to handle that situation.
3. Convergence to the long-term growth rate: while five-year forecasting can imply a sharp convergence to an organic rate of 3%, ten-year forecasting provides a more pacific convergence.
4. Terminal value as a percentage of the firm value: While five-year forecasting means a terminal value/firm value ratio frequently higher than 60%, five-year forecasting usually represents 40/45%.

Damodaran (2023) broadened his study of the corporate life cycle and classified it into six stages: Stage 1 represents the start-up, where we have an idea of the business that meets an unmet need in the market, usually financed by private equity; Stage 2 represents a young growth, when ideas become potential revenues and earnings, characterized by growth investing and maximizing value from growth; Stage 3 is a high growth phase where cash flows meet investment needs; Stage 4 is a mature growth, when the business matures, shifting from losses to profits, and investments to protect competitive advantages; Stage 5 is mature stability, with investments to defend the business from new competitors and significant excess free cash flows, and Stage 6 is when the business decline and scales down as the market shrinks.

Third stage: The steady-state and the terminal value

Once the company reaches a steady state, cash flow is expected to grow at a rate similar to the inflation rate plus a real growth rate from the period "T+1" and beyond, where "T" represents the last year of the explicit forecast.

The present value of the stream of cash flows from T+1 and beyond is calculated with the growing perpetuity formula, which is known as the terminal value formula and was discussed in further detail in Chapter 3, repeated here for ease in the explanation.

$$TV = \frac{FCF_T(1+g)}{(WACC-g)} \qquad [3.17]$$

The formula was introduced by Gordon (1959), who proposed that the price of a share could be determined assuming that dividends grow at a constant rate. FCF_T is the last forecasted free cash flow of the explicit period, multiplied by the factor (1+g), where "g" is a constant growth rate at which the free cash flow is expected to grow forever. Notice some characteristics and assumptions of the formula:

1. Terminal Value gives the present value of perpetuity cash flows on T.
2. The long-term growth rate is nominal,[1] composed of the GDP rate plus the inflation rate.
3. Terminal value denies that the company cannot create value for shareholders; the return on capital equals the cost of capital (on average).
4. The terminal value equation works if g is lower than the WACC; however, WACC is always greater than g, since g is usually 3%/4% and the WACC is always greater (actually, a growth rate greater than or equal to the cost of capital has no economic sense, since it produces a negative value on the denominator and the formula does not apply anymore).

Conditions that must be observed in the steady state

The proper application of the growing perpetuity formula requires the company to achieve the following set of conditions:

1. Revenues grow at a stable, organic rate; as a maximum, the inflation rate plus the GDP growth rate.
2. Since the operative cost is assumed to be a percentage of revenues, operating income (EBIT) also grows at a stable organic rate.

3. The gradual decline of attractive investment opportunities generates the company limits the capital expenditures to an amount for sustaining the accumulated stock of capital. Nonetheless, the CAPEX/depreciation ratio should reach a stationary point, where CAPEX equals the economic depreciation taking into account that future purchases of fixed assets will reflect current prices.[2]
4. The fulfillment of 1, 2, and 3 leads to a free cash flow that grows at a stable organic rate.
5. The return on invested capital (ROIC) is to be assumed equal to the weighted average cost of capital (WACC). The ROIC is composed by the return on current capital and the return on newly invested capital (NIC).

The stable growth phase involves both internal and external stabilization. While the internal equilibrium implies the conditions mentioned above, the external equilibrium implies a permanent repartition of the market between the participants that technically leaves the overall market growth as a unique source of additional revenue (Behr, Mielcarz, & Osiichuk, 2018)

Cornell, Gerger, Jarrel, & Canesa (2017) show that CAPEX above depreciation needs, when based on accounting data, should be calculated as a fraction of net cash flow, not as a fraction of net operating profit after taxes (NOPAT) because the net cash flow is the distributable cash flow before investment needs. Since the depreciation is calculated using historical prices and capital expenditures are made in future years, due to inflation, capex must exceed depreciation to maintain the operational capacity of fixed assets (Cornell, Gerger, Jarrell, & Canessa, 2021). On the other hand, real growth requires cash investment while inflationary growth does not; the failure to distinguish between the two sources of growth will lead to an erroneous estimate of value.

The last condition requires clarification. A company in a steady state cannot create value for its shareholders no matter the growth rate; this does not mean that the company market value cannot increase but means that it increases in an amount equal to the capital invested to sustain the growth. This assumption is supported by the vision that the return on capital converges to the WACC at the end of the competitive advantage period, where the entrance of new competitors will erode the company's advantage and eliminate abnormal returns. Later, we dedicate a separate section to discuss the ROIC-WACC convergence.

The terminal value and the growing perpetuity formula

Although the mathematics behind the growing perpetuity formula were explained in Chapter 3, we restated here its deduction to ensure clarity. Beyond the T period, once the company achieves the steady state, the free cash flow grows at a rate of g, forever:

$$FCF_T(1+g)+FCF_T(1+g)^2+FCF_T(1+g)^3+\ldots\infty$$

Then we have to calculate the present value of each cash flow, that is equal to the cash flow of each period divided by (1+i), raised to the number of periods considered:

$$TV = FCF_T\frac{(1+g)}{(1+WACC)^1}+FCF_T\frac{(1+g)^2}{(1+WACC)^2}+FCF_T\frac{(1+g)^3}{(1+WACC)^3}+\ldots\infty$$

Notice that each present value equals the previous multiplied by a common ratio equal to [1+g/1+i]. Since it is less than 1, we can say that this stream represents a decreasing geometric progression, and there will be an exponential decrease toward zero. And we can calculate the sum of n terms of a decreasing geometric progression with the formula:

$$S = a_1 \frac{1-q^n}{1-q}. \quad [10.1]$$

a_1 = first term of the progression
q = common ratio

Replacing a_1 and q in [10.1]

$$TV = FCT_T \frac{(1+g)}{(1+WACC)} \frac{1-\left[\frac{(1+g)}{(1+WACC)}\right]^n}{1-\frac{(1+g)}{(1+WACC)}},$$

Simplifying and rearranging

$$TV = FCT_T \frac{(1+g)}{(1+WACC)} \frac{1}{\frac{(1+WACC)-(1+g)}{(1+WACC)}},$$

$$TV = \frac{FCT_T(1+g)}{WACC-g}. \quad [3.17]$$

Table 10.2 shows the present value of each cash flow and the accumulated PV with a WACC of 14% and g = 3%. Note that the present value of the furthest cash flows converges to zero while the cumulative PV converges to 9.36, the same value obtained with the growing perpetuity formula.

TABLE 10.2 PV and cumulative PV of free cash flow in perpetuity

Year	FCF	PV	Cumulative PV
1	1.03	0.90	0.90
2	1.06	0.82	1.72
5	1.16	0.60	3.73
10	1.34	0.36	5.97
30	2.43	0.05	8.92
40	3.26	0.02	9.20
50	4.38	0.01	9.31
60	5.89	0.00	9.34
70	7.92	0.00	9.36
80	10.64	0.00	9.36

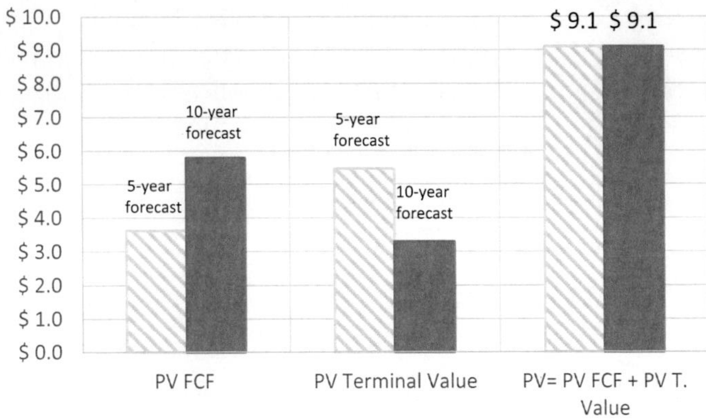

FIGURE 10.2 Composition of present value including terminal value

If we calculate the terminal value with the formula 10.1, we obtain the same cumulative value of period 80:

$$TV = \frac{1(1+0.03)}{0.10-0.03} = 9.36$$

Figure 10.2 shows the present value of a cash flow perpetuity of $1 growing at a constant rate of 3%, the corresponding present value of the terminal value, and the sum of both for explicit forecast periods of five and ten years, using a discount rate of 14.3%. Although the accumulated PV is identical, the PV of terminal value has a different weight on the company value: 60% (5.5/9.1) for the five-year forecast, and 36% (3.3/9.1) for the ten-year forecast.

An alternative to calculating the terminal value (or sometimes the firm value if it is assumed the company already is in the steady state) is the formula of "value drivers" which leads to an identical value but establishes a link between the ROIC, growth, and the net operative income after taxes. We will describe in detail this formula in Chapters 15 and 16. For now, we say that the ROIC and long-term growth rate used in the formula require distinguishing between nominal and real growth, something we already did in this chapter when explaining how to calculate the terminal value with the perpetuity formula.

The mythic long-term of 3%: Inflation rate or GDP growth rate?

Valuation practitioners in developed countries are unlikely to use a long-term growth rate greater than 3% per year on the terminal value formula. Since the international inflation rate before the pandemic was around 2% per year (Macrotrends, 2022), they implicitly assume a real growth rate of 1%, which appears conservative.

However, the inflation rate in developed countries measured over a long period (1870–2021 in the US) is closer to 3%, and the GDP growth rate has been 3% for most countries, also measured over a long period. So, why not use a nominal long-term growth rate of 6%? Using a growth rate of 6% assumes that the firm will be able to grow at a rate that includes the average GDP growth rate and the general inflation rate in its revenues and cash flows. The GDP growth rate and the inflation rate represent averages, and although some companies can grow at a high rate in their first years of life, some time will be mature companies. If an analyst uses a growth rate that exceeds the nominal growth rate of the GDP to calculate the terminal value, the company value, at some point, would be greater than the whole economy. For example, suppose we have a firm with a market cap of $5,000M, and the GDP of the country in which the company is located is $400,000. If the GDP grows at a nominal 5% rate and the market cap grows at a rate of 10%, its value would be equal to the GDP value after 94.2 years!

$$400{,}000(1.05)^{94.2} = 5{,}000(1.10)^{94.2} = 36{,}629{,}593.25$$

However, growing at a rate higher than 3% per year is not impossible. PepsiCo revenues grew at a rate of 6.7% from 1983 to 2022, while Coca-Cola revenues grew at a rate of 4.91% from 1983 to 2022 and at 7.89% from 1925 to 2022! (Source: author's calculations based on Refinitv Eikon database and Gurufocus.)

As the terminal value accounts for a large proportion of the DCF value, even assuming no manipulations and the fulfillment of the conditions that the company must meet to apply the growing perpetuity formula, the sensitivity of firm value to a change in the growth rate seems justify the selected growth rate of 3%, as we explain with an example.

Sensitivity of the firm value to the growth rate and cost of capltal

Grupo Cementos de Chihuahua (GCC) is a Mexican company having around 75% of its operations in the US. Its financial statements are presented in dollars (Investorcloud, 2022), and its market capitalization has fluctuated around US$2 billion, although a year ago, it reached US$2.4 billion (Reuters, 2022). In a theoretical valuation exercise, we have forecasted its free cash flow for 2022–2031. The WACC estimation was 9.63%, and we consider a long-term growth rate of 3% to calculate the terminal value. The inputs used to estimate the cost of capital and the projected Free Cash Flow appear in Tables 10.3 and 10.4.

Capital structure was estimated using a circularity approach that is explained in Chapter 11. The discounted cash flow has two major components:

1. the present value of the explicit forecasted period; and
2. the terminal value.

TABLE 10.3 Forecasted free cash flow of GCC 2022–2031 in millions of US$

	Dec 22	Dec 23	Dec 24	Dec 25	Dec 26	Dec 27	Dec 28	Dec 29	Dec 30	Dec 31
Free Cash Flow	179.3	162.6	166.4	178.6	181.5	194.8	208.7	214.3	230.3	247.1
Terminal Value										3,840.7
FCF + T. Value	179.3	162.6	166.4	178.6	181.5	194.8	208.7	214.3	230.3	4,087.8

TABLE 10.4 Cost of capital inputs of GCC

		Source
Country risk premium	2.4%	JP Morgan 08/30/22
Risk-free rate	3.00%	Reuters 08/31/22
Market risk premium	5.70%	Shiller Online Data 1925–2020
Beta	0.91	Reuters 08/31/22
Cost of debt	5.60%	Reuters 08/31/22
t	30%	Legal tax rate
D/V	16.7%	Estimated by iteration
E/V	83.3%	Estimated by iteration

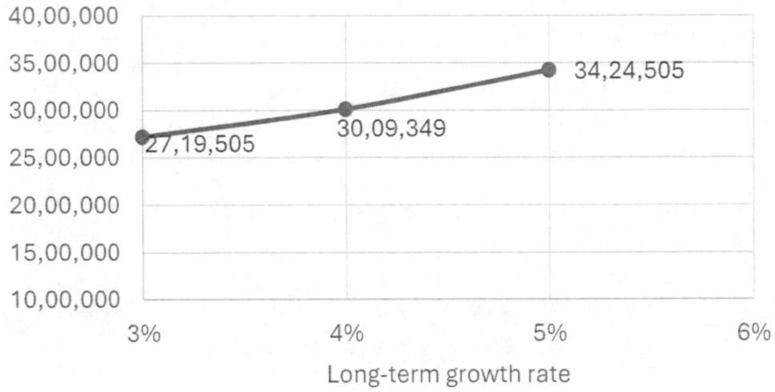

FIGURE 10.3 Firm value of GCC and growth rate

Since the terminal value is expressed at the end of year T, we still need to discount it by T periods to obtain its present value:

$$V = \sum_{t=1}^{T} \frac{FCF_t}{(1+WACC)^t} + \frac{FCF_T(1+g)}{(WACC-g)} \times \frac{1}{(1+WACC)^T} \quad [10.2]$$

$$V = 1{,}187{,}421.76 + 1{,}532{,}083.39 = 2{,}719{,}505.15$$

Notice that the present value of the terminal value represents 44% of the firm value (1,532,083.39/2,719,505.15). As a rule of thumb, for a ten-year forecast, the terminal value can represent around 40% of V, and for a five-year forecast frequently results in more than 60%, depending on the discount rate.

Since the company has a financial debt of US$539,383.00, this must be subtracted from the value of the company to obtain the equity fair value:

$$E = V - D = 2{,}180{,}122.15$$

Figure 10.3 shows the firm value for growth rates ranging from 3% to 5%. As can be seen, a percentage point increase in g means an increase of slightly more than 10% in the firm value. One percentual point of increment on the long-term growth rate is

FIGURE 10.4 Firm value of GCC and the cost of capital

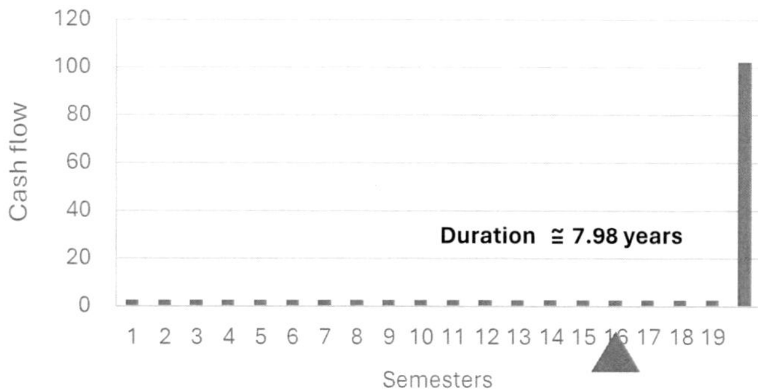

FIGURE 10.5 Cash flow UST-B ten years and duration

equivalent to a decrease of one percentual point on the cost of capital when we use the growing perpetuity formula to compute the terminal value.

Figure 10.4 shows the firm value for different levels of WACC, starting with 9.63% and increasing by one percentage point. For instance, when the WACC raises from 9.63% to 10.63%, the value decreases to 2.349 billion (–13.6%); then the impact of a WACC on firm value marginally decreases due to the convex form of the Firm value/WACC relationship.

Most practitioners use the yield on ten-year US Treasury bonds as the risk-free rate. An argument for using this security is that the Free Cash Flow of the business has a similar duration to the ten-year treasury bond (around seven to eight years), and since the price sensitivity to a change in the interest rate is a function of the cash flow duration, the argument seems correct. The concept of "duration" was developed by (Macaulay, 1938) who argued that the maturity of a bond only gave information about the date on which the last coupon payment and principal would be redeemed, but without considering the intermediate payments.

Figures 10.5 and 10.6 show the duration of an UST-B 10 years and the free cash flow of GCC. If we imagine the columns as weights placed to the left and right of a "fulcrum", duration is the point where the weights are balanced; this point is the center of gravity of the lever and is around 8 years. The duration coefficient, or more precisely, the modified duration coefficient, is a good measure of the price sensitivity to a change in the interest rate since it represents the "center of gravity" of the cash flow. See the mathematical derivation of duration and modified duration in Appendix A.

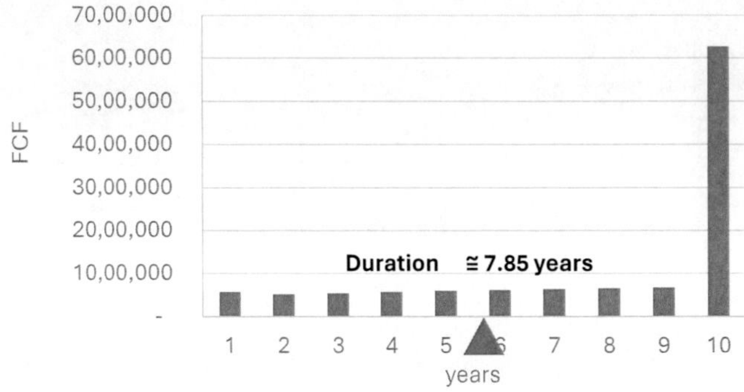

FIGURE 10.6 Forecasted FCF of GCC 2022–2031

TABLE 10.5 Firm value of GCC for different WACC and LT growth rates

WACC/g	3%	4%	5%
9.63%	2.719.520	3.009.368	3.424.530
10.63%	2.349.886	2.546.937	2.814.039
11.63%	2.066.865	2.206.452	2.388.173
12.63%	1.843.394	1.945.449	2.074.270
13.63%	1.662.605	1.739.116	1.833.367

Nonetheless, for the case of firm value, the argument is only valid if the long-term growth rate remains constant and only the interest rate changes.

Table 10.5 shows the combined effects of the cost of capital and the growth rate on the firm's value. For a simultaneous change of the growth rate and the cost of capital, both in one percentage point, the firm value can change quite more than the USTB duration indicates.

The percentage changes in the firm value, when changing both at the same time the WACC and the long-term growth rate, far exceed the percentage changes that a 10Yr US treasury bond usually changes, around 7/8% according to its duration.

When the long-term growth rate and the cost of capital change simultaneously, the coefficient duration of perpetuity provides a better approximation of the sensitivity firm value. The duration of a perpetual cash flow must be calculated with the formula:

$$D_p = \frac{(1+i)}{i}. \qquad [10.3]$$

The derivation of the formula is explained in detail in Appendix B. Figure 10.7 shows how the duration of perpetuity evolves for different interest rates.

When the interest rate or cost of capital is around 10%, the duration of the perpetuity is close to ten years. However, the change in the firm value is over 10% when the cost of capital and the long-term growth rate change simultaneously; in this case, the value change should be approximated using the bond's duration with a maturity of 30 years.[3] Therefore, up to this point, the conclusion would be that it

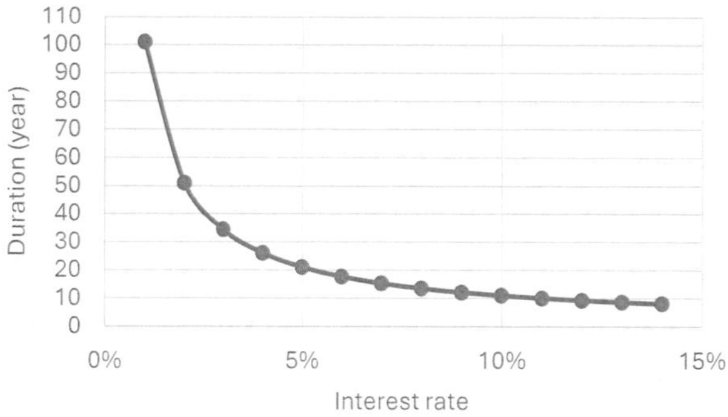

FIGURE 10.7 Duration for different interest rates

is more appropriate to use the yield of the 30-year bond as the risk-free rate rather than the ten-year one. Note that the duration of the market portfolio is also similar to the 30-year US-T bond's duration. And in the case of computing a country risk premium, the premium is calculated using bonds of 30-year maturity.

Terminal value in emerging markets and the inflation rate

In emerging countries, the inflation rate is generally higher than in developed. When the international inflation rate in the pre-pandemic period was around 2%, in Latin America and the Caribbean it was 4.26% (The World Bank, 2022). Suppose you are valuing a company in an emerging country where the inflation rate is 6% per year. Why should you use a growth rate of 3% to calculate the terminal value if only the inflation rate is higher without considering any real growth?

I remember a meeting years ago with other appraisers, and one of them was from India. When one of the consultants suggested a 3% long-term growth rate to compute the terminal value, the Indian appraiser said: "I cannot use a 3% to calculate the terminal value since the inflation rate in my country is around 7% per year".

I explained that an inflation rate higher than 3% per year was not a problem if the cost of capital expressed in Indian Rupees and the nominal long-term growth rate were adjusted by the inflation rate differential. Valuing a company in domestic currency using a long-term growth rate considerably higher than 3% gives identical value as valuing it in foreign currency, using the mythic growth rate of 3% when the simultaneous fulfillment of interest parity theory and purchasing power parity theory is assumed. We explain how to lead with these caveats in Chapter 13; but for now, we say that the WACC and the long-term growth rate used to estimate the terminal value of the business in domestic currency should be adjusted by the inflation rate differential that considers the domestic and the international inflation rate. The idea is simple: if the inflation rate is different between two countries, the cost of capital and the nominal growth rate for the higher-inflation country must add a premium for the inflation rate differential.

Evidence about GDP growth rate and long-term growth rate convergence

The GDP growth rate, over a long period and in most economies, has been approximately 3% per year.[4] Figure 10.8 shows the geometric average growth rate

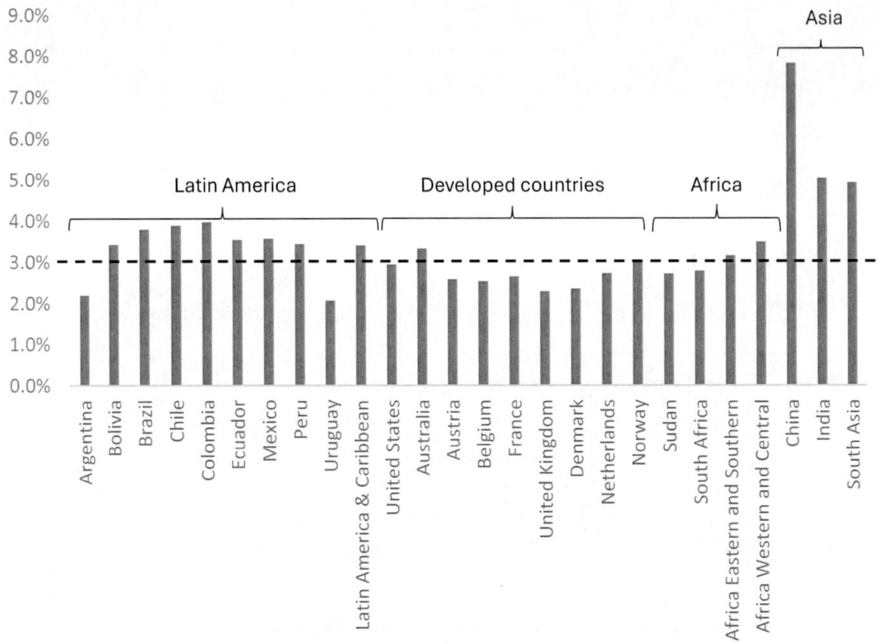

FIGURE 10.8 Growth rate of different countries

of various countries in Latin America, the United States, Europe, Africa, and Asia from 1960–2021 (The World Bank, 2022).

The empirical evidence is that a GDP growth rate of 3% prevails in most countries when considering a long period. It seems justified by the increase in productivity and the labor force increase. But what about the long-term growth rate used to estimate the terminal value?

At the company level, Clendenin & Cleave (1954) note that growth rates greater than 5% per year were difficult to find for large companies. The firm's rate of return may remain above the cost of capital, and profitable (supramarginal) investment opportunities may still arise, but this would be strictly limited in time (Schwartz, 1965). Chan, Karceski & Lakonishok (1993) analyzed historical long-term growth rates of various companies using various performance indicators. They found that the median growth rate was between 3 and 3.5% when dividends were not reinvested.

Trevino (2022) examined the accuracy of using historical industry average growth rates, historical average gross domestic product growth rates, and expected inflation as sustainable long-term growth rates using actual growth rates for 21 selected industries from 1991 to 2021 to select the most accurate forecasting method. They found that forecasts premised on expected inflation proved to be the most accurate.

Since the proportion that the terminal value represents in the DCF value and its sensitivity to the cost of capital and long-term growth rate, its use has been the target of much criticism. For example, Graham (1959) argued that combining a precise formula with highly imprecise assumptions could justify practically any value one wishes. Along the same line, Penman (2011) states that a valuation that depends on long-term growth is speculative and risky since the growth rate is like a guess and proposes using an accrual accounting method.

Damodaran (2012) recognizes that the terminal value is often manipulated, but it is due to analysts using multiples or they violate two crucial assumptions of the steady state: the long-term growth rate cannot exceed the GDP growth rate, and the firm must hold a reinvestment rate to maintain the growth rate.

Other researchers have questioned the vision of a constant growth rate along the steady state. If the cash flows are truly cyclic, the assumption of a constant perpetual growth rate after one cycle of forecasted cash flow is incorrect (Arnold & North, 2011). Since the final cash flow could be at any point within an up-trend cycle, a level period, or a down-trend, they proposed to simulate the long-run cash flow growth rate within the cycle using Monte Carlo simulation. Behr, Mielcarz, & Osiichuk (2018) worked with a sample of 970 Polish companies for a period from 1997 to 2014, checked the year-on-year fluctuations of the revenues, the capital expenditures/depreciation ratio, and free cash flow over different year observation windows, and found that the terminal value assumptions may not match the observable market dynamics. Some small companies never achieve stable growth since they cannot grow to become large or not even a middle company, although they have too many years in the industry. Their earnings and cash flows are cyclical and more vulnerable to the economic cycle.

While it is possible that the long-term growth rate changes after achieving the theoretical steady state, the terminal value does not change much if the growth rate fluctuates randomly around the average growth rate. For example, let's assume that the FCF of period T is FCFT = 100, the expected long-term growth rate is 3%, and the cost of capital is k = 10%. Then, the terminal value is

$$V = \frac{100(1+0.03)}{0.10-0.3} = 1{,}471.43$$

If the observed long-term growth rate is not the expected 3% in the steady state, how much different the terminal value would be? Could it be considerably different? One way to know is assuming that the long-term growth rate will be close to the GDP growth rate. As the average long-term growth of the US GDP was 2.96% from 1961 to 2022 and had a standard deviation of 2.17% (World Bank), we can simulate the free cash flow growth rate using the mean of the GDP growth rate and its standard deviation, and then calculate the NPV distribution. The mean of the sample distribution was 1,478.24, close to the terminal value of 1,471.43, and the standard deviation was 80.49 (see Appendix C for an explanation of the calculus).

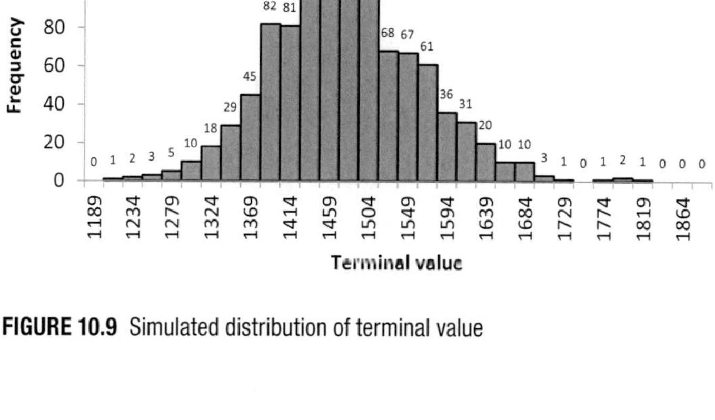

FIGURE 10.9 Simulated distribution of terminal value

We can conclude that if the long-term growth rate is normally distributed, 95% of the time the terminal value will be between 1,478.24 ± 80.49 = 1345.83/1610.64, close to 1,4741.43, and any deviation of this value would be lower in terms of present value.

The exit multiple

Some practitioners use an EBITDA multiple to estimate the Terminal Value, avoiding assuming a long-term growth rate. For this approach, we recommend you at least check the implicit LT growth rate considered in this multiple.

Example: suppose you are using an EV/EBITDA multiple = 5 to estimate the value of a company with the following fundamentals: EBITDA = \$300, FCFT = \$100, and WACC = 10%. Using the EV/EBITDA of 5, the company value would be V = 5 x 300 = 1,500; then, using the growing perpetuity formula and solving for g, we obtain an implied g = 3.125%.

$$V = \frac{100(1+g)}{0.10-g} = 1,500$$
$$100 + g100 = 150 - g1,500$$
$$g = 3.125\%$$

Sometimes the growth rate implied by the EV/EBITDA multiple may not be reasonable. For example, if the EV/EBITDA = 9, the implicit growth rate would be 6.3%. An implied growth rate higher than the inflation rate plus the GDP growth rate is not consistent since it would mean the maintenance of competitive advantage for an indefinite period.[5]

The assumption of the ROIC-WACC convergence

From a logical point of view, the company could not create value for its shareholders forever; therefore, at the steady state, the return on current capital and newly investments (NIC), should have converged to the cost of capital. In the steady-state, the company should maintain a reinvestment rate to sustain organic growth (i.e., if ROIC = 10%, a reinvestment rate = 30% leads to g = 3%).

Although in practice the long-term growth rate is defined as an input of the terminal value, some have proposed estimating it by multiplying the ROIC multiplied by the reinvestment rate RR:

$$g = ROIC \times RR \qquad [10.4]$$

RR: the fraction of ROIC plowed back into the business
Notice that this way of calculating the long-term growth rate requires using parameters that are accounting-based, such as the Capital and NOPAT, and therefore vulnerable to accounting conventions. On the other hand, cash flow is not vulnerable to accounting conventions since it uses double-entry bookkeeping that guarantees the correct way to determine cash variations.

Some studies have attempted to test the convergence indirectly. Cassia & Vismara (2009) states that an ideal constant growth rate g = ROIC x RR beyond the steady state would lead to the "ideal" target prices that should be observed according to the steady-state assumptions. Then, they compared the target prices published in equity reports to the "ideal" ones and defined a variance index between the two prices. Using a sample of 784 equity reports for European companies selected from the Investext database in 2003–2005, they stated that the accuracy index is valid as it identifies valuations.

Koller, Goedhart, & Wessels (2010) studied the sustainability of ROIC for more than 5,000 US-based nonfinancial companies from 1963 to 2008. They found that both high-ROIC companies and low-ROIC companies tend to maintain the level of their returns on invested capital, and industries that rely on sustainable competitive advantages such as patents and brands tend to have high median ROICs (15 to 20%) while companies in basic industries, such as paper, airlines, and utilities, tend to earn low ROICs (5 to 10%). The US market's median ROIC, excluding goodwill, averages nearly 10% which would seem to provide some support for the ROIC-WACC convergence.

However, the ROIC measurement is not as robust as one might imagine. A good measure of the invested capital often requires some adjustments. While accounts receivables, inventories, and other operative assets represent current values, the values of fixed assets, intangibles, and leases can distort the capital invested. Think that fixed assets reflect historical costs, generally lower than their market values; different depreciation methods also impact their reported values. In emerging countries, where the inflation rate is higher than in developed, the capital and NOPAT are still more distorted due to the inventories' values. As the beginning inventory reflects the total monetary value in stock at the start of an accounting period, while the ending inventory reflects the value at the end, the value of COGS is underestimated, leading to an overestimation of NOPAT and ROIC.

TABLE 10.6 ROIC of tech companies: September 2024

Company name	ROIC	Industry name
Apple Inc	87.4%	Technology Hardware, Storage & Peripherals
HP Inc	63.2%	Technology Hardware, Storage & Peripherals
Qualcomm Inc	77.0%	Semiconductors & Semiconductor Equipment
Motorola Solutions Inc	43.1%	Communications Equipment
Samsung Electronics Co Ltd	3.9%	Technology Hardware, Storage & Peripherals
Sony Group Corp	18.3%	Household Durables
Meta Platforms Inc	37.0%	Interactive Media & Services
NVIDIA Corp	123.9%	Semiconductors & Semiconductor Equipment
Alphabet Inc	45.3%	Interactive Media & Services
Tesla Inc	41.4%	Automobiles
PayPal Holdings Inc	30.8%	Financial Services
Microsoft Corp	36.7%	Software

Another complication to measuring the capital invested and ROIC is when a company's capital intensity is low. For example, some businesses, where assets are essentially people, like software development, IT consulting, or data processing, have lower fixed capital requirements. Due to the nature of the industry, these companies have substantial intangible assets, whose value is often influenced by subjective judgments. Table 10.6 shows the actual ROIC in September 2024 for some well-known companies involved with technology, hardware, and software, while Table 10.7 does so for companies whose income comes mostly from services.

Firms with revenues compounded by services could overstate ROIC since they don't use fixed capital for its generation. Intangible assets like goodwill are subject to impairment, which might not always be timely or accurate.

Other businesses, like supermarkets, taking advantage of a dominant position, operate with negative working capital because they collect their accounts in short terms while they can - and do- pay their suppliers in longer terms. Table 10.8 shows the actual ROIC for the industry of Supermarkets and Other Grocery Retailers (except Convenience Retailers). Notice that supermarkets with negative working capital tend to have a higher ROIC, although lower than technology or based-services companies.

When the capital invested is low, the ROIC could be large or extremely large, and the fulfillment of the ROIC-WACC convergence may require a setup that may be inconsistent with the last forecasted free cash flow, especially with companies with higher current ROIC. We show an example of this setup in Chapter 15. To the best of my knowledge, there are no econometric studies about the ROIC-WACC convergence in the steady state. Perhaps it is because the difficulties in measuring ROIC may appear in the sample of companies designed for the test.

TABLE 10.7 ROIC of service-based companies: September 2024

Company name	ROIC	Industry
Microsoft Corp	36.7%	Software Publishers
Accenture PLC	56.2%	Computer Systems Design Services
Salesforce Inc	14.6%	Computer Programming Services
Visa Inc	79.9%	Financial Transactions Processing
Spotify Technology	–21.6%	Web Search Portals and Information Services
Netflix Inc	22.0%	Web Search Portals and Information Services
Uber Technologies Inc	21.4%	Web Search Portals and Information Services
DocuSign Inc	659.3%	Software Publishers
PayPal Holdings Inc	30.8%	Software Publishers
ServiceNow Inc	46.4%	Custom Computer Programming Services
Equifax Inc	7.5%	Credit Bureaus
Adobe Inc	58.9%	Software Publishers

TABLE 10.8 ROIC of supermarkets: September 2024

Company name	ROIC	Working capital
Target Corp	17.7%	–1,806,000,000
Walmart Inc	16.9%	–15,538,000,000
Kroger Co	19.2%	–3,109,000,000
Koninklijke Ahold Delhaize NV	12.4%	–4,147,000,000
Albertsons Companies Inc	20.0%	–1,170,200,000
Carrefour SA	8.3%	–1,878,000,000
Companhia Brasileira de Distribuicao	10.4%	–
Cencosud	11.3%	–
Village Super Market Inc	0.1%	–
Sprouts Farmers Market Inc	12.3%	56,903,000
Ingles Markets Inc	11.4%	–

Concluding thoughts

Because infinite cash flows are impossible to forecast with perfect accuracy, we assume that the free cash flow grows at a constant, long-term growth rate once the business has reached a steady state, and the perpetuity formula enters the scene to calculate the terminal value. Although there is no magic number for the length of the explicit forecasted period, conceptually, it should be long enough so that the company should meet two convergences before considering that it reaches a steady state by the end of this period: the long-term (nominal) growth rate cannot be higher than the GDP growth rate plus the inflation rate (although for prudence almost always this growth rate rarely is higher than 3%) and it is assumed the ROIC converges asymptotically to WACC because the company cannot create value (on average) for its shareholders beyond the steady-state. The fulfillment of the two convergence constitutes an IDEAL state that possibly a few companies achieve.

As the terminal value often represents a large portion of the firm value and is very sensitive to the long-term growth rate, analysts must be careful to make a consistent estimation, avoiding illogical values and verifying that the company meets the conditions to achieve a steady state. No company can grow at a rate higher than the growth rate of the economy since it will exceed the size of the economy itself. Remember that the long-term growth rate represents an expected average since the company will go through periods of recession and recovery, and cash flow deviations from the expected value are lower when expressed in present value.

In the case of emerging countries, where the inflation rate is higher than in developed countries, the long-term growth rate and the cost of capital used in developed countries must reflect the different inflation rates.

The claimed ROIC-WACC convergence has strong argumentative logic but not an empirical one. Maybe the difficulties in measuring adequately the invested capital have not allowed the existence of conclusive tests. First, the return on capital is based on accounting values, while the market values do not depend entirely on ROIC, and WACC has not allowed the existence of conclusive tests. Second, the ROIC-WACC relationship varies according to industry characteristics; while in high-competition industries the convergence could be rapid, cyclical industries may not exhibit convergence. Industries with competitive advantages (e.g., patents, strong brand) or industries with high barriers to entry or competitive advantages (e.g., patents) may sustain ROIC above WACC for long periods. Third, for industries with low capital intensity, the ROIC could be extremely large (positive or negative) and nonsensical as an indicator of performance.

Perhaps we haven't seen a long enough time horizon to see the convergence occur in an empirical time series. And a final piece of advice: do not use the ROIC provided by the databases since the necessary adjustments were probably not made.

Short questions and problems

1. Suppose you are in a meeting with other appraisers, discussing the long-term growth rate to calculate the terminal value. The target is a company based in India. One of the appraisers says that the growth rate to calculate the terminal value should be 3%. Immediately, another appraiser says that he cannot use a growth rate of 3% since the inflation rate in his country is 10%. What do you recommend?
2. Suppose you make a five-year forecast for the free cash flow of Columbus Company and another forecast for ten years. Mark true or false:

   a) Both values are identical if, from year six, the growth of the free cash flow is the same as the expected long-term growth rate.
   b) Value for a ten-year projection is larger than the five-year projection if the free cash flow's growth rate from year six and beyond is higher than the expected long-term growth rate.

3. The length of the explicit forecast period should be:

   a) Five years
   b) Ten years
   c) The time to achieve a steady state

4. A company achieves the steady state when:

   a) The growth rate approximates the GDP growth rate and the return on capital equals the cost of capital
   b) The growth rate approximates 3%
   c) The growth rate approximates the GDP growth rate plus the domestic inflation rate, and the return on capital equals the cost of capital

5. Given an exit EBITDA multiple of 6, EBITDA = 1,000; FCF = 400; WACC = 10%, which is the implicit long-term growth rate?
6. Suppose you make a mistake projection of one dollar in the year 10. Calculate the present value of the mistake for these interest rates:

   a) 10%
   b) 15%
   c) 20%

7. If the last forecasted free cash flow is $FCF_T = 100$, the long-term growth rate is 3%, and the cost of capital is 10%, the terminal value is:

   a) 1,657.56
   b) 1,471.42
   c) 1,423.90

8. The forecasted free cash flow of Golden Inc. at the year 10 is $FCF_T = 100$, when the company achieves the steady state. The expected long-term growth rate is 3% from period T and beyond. The WACC is 15%. Calculate the present value of the terminal value with the growing perpetuity formula.
9. Although the terminal value of Golden Inc. was calculated assuming a constant long-term growth rate of 3%, after ten years, the observed free cash flow to calculate the terminal value does not grow at a constant rate, but at 1% from period 11 to 13, at 5% from period 14 to 16, and at 2% from 17 and beyond. Is the present value of the terminal value, very different to the value calculated with the terminal value formula assuming a constant growth rate of 3%?
10. Now suppose the WACC of Golden is 11% and calculate the present value of the terminal value. Is it very different from the value calculated in 7.?
11. After achieving the steady state, it is assumed that the ROIC converges asymptotically to the cost of capital. How confident are you with this assumption? What conditions should verify?
12. Calculate the terminal value of a company´s free cash flow if the last forecasted free cash flow $FCF_T = 100$ and the cost of capital is 10% when:

    a) The long-term growth rate is of 2%
    b) The long-term growth rate is of 3%
    c) The long-term growth rate is of 4%

13. Calculate the present value of the terminal values calculated in 4.
14. Suppose an appraiser who, instead of using the growing perpetuity formula to calculate the terminal value, considers an exit EV/EBITDA = 10. EBITDA = 250, FCF = 100, and WACC = 10%. What is the implicit long-term real growth rate if the expected inflation rate is 2.5%?

Notes

1 As the long-term growth rate is nominal since it contains inflation, cash flow and cost of capital must be expressed in nominal terms (remember that the US Treasury Bond yield is also a nominal rate).

2 The CAPEX/depreciation ratio is not constant during the steady state since CAPEX is not linearly related to the company's sales; however, if it is possible, assuming CAPEX as a percentage of sales recognizes the effect of the inflation since the depreciation is calculated using historical prices and capital expenditures are made in future years, and due to inflation, capex must exceed depreciation to maintain the operational capacity of fixed assets

3 Approximately 20 years with a coupon rate of 3%.

4 Although some countries have exceeded 3%, the rate tends to decrease over a long period (for example, Argentina, in a period of 121 years, has grown at a rate very close to 3% (Ministery of Economics, 2022) and the same has happened with Mexico (Banco de México, 2022).

5 The inflation rate and the GDP growth rate in the US have been both around 3% measured over a long period. In principle, a nominal growth rate of around 6% would be a maximum

limit. The situation is different in emerging markets, where the inflation rate is usually higher than the international. For this case, the difference between the domestic and the international inflation rate must be added to the long-term growth rate and the cost of capital.

6 A callable bond gives the issuer the option to redeem it at some point before maturity.

References

Arnold, T., & North, D. S. (2011). Firm Valuation with Long-Run Business Cycles. *The Journal of Private Equity, 14(3)*, 86–95.

Behr, A., Mielcarz, P., & Osiichuk, D. (2018). Terminal value calculation in dcf valuation models: An empirical verification. *e-Finanse: Financial Internet Quarterly, 14(1)*, 27–38.

Cassia, L., & Vismara, S. (2009). Valuation Accuracy and Infinity Horizon Forecast: Empirical Evidence from Europe. *Journal of International Financial Management and Accounting, 20(2)*, 135–166.

Chan, L., Karceski, J., & Lakonishok, J. (2003). The Level and Persistence of Growth Rates. *Journal of Finance*, 643–684.

Clendenin, J., & Cleave, M. V. (1954). Growth and Common Stock Values. *The Journal of Finance, 9(4)*, 365–376.

Cornell, B., Gerger, R., Jarrel, G., & Canesa, J. L. (2017). A note on estimating constant growth terminal values with inflation. *Business Valuation Review, 36(3)*, 102–105.

Cornell, B., Gerger, R., Jarrell, G., & Canessa, J. L. (2021). Inflation, Investment and Valuation. *Journal of Business Valuation and Economic Loss Analysis, 16(1)*, 1–13.

Damodaran, A. (2012). *Investment Valuation*. New York: John Wiley and Sons.

Damodaran, A. (2023, August 30). *The Corporate Life Cycle: Growing Up Is Hard To Do, Growing Old Is Even Harder!* Available at https://pages.stern.nyu.edu: https://pages.stern.nyu.edu/~adamodar/pdfiles/country/CorpLifeCycleReallyShort2020.pdf

Dumrauf, G. (2024, January 3). Duration of a Perpetual Cash Flow. Available at www.ssrn.com: https://papers.ssrn.com/sol3/papers.cfm?abstract_id = 4646948

Graham, B. (1959). *The Intelligent Investor: A Book of Practical Counsel*. New York: Harper.

Investorcloud (2022). Available at https://investorcloud.s3.amazonaws.com/gcc/Gobierno-Corporativo/Asambleas/estados-financieros-consolidados-2021.pdf

Koller, T., Goedhart, M., & Wessels, D. (2010). *Valuation: Measuring and Managing the Value of Companies*. Hoboken, New Jersey: JohnWiley & Sons, Inc.

Macaulay, F. R. (1938). *Some Theoretical Problems Suggested by the Movements of Interest Rates, Bond Yields, and Stock Prices in the United States since 1856*. New York: Columbia University Press for the National Bureau of Economics Research.

Macrotrends (2022). World Inflation Rate 1981–2022. Available at www.macrotrends.net/countries/WLD/world/inflation-rate-cpi#:~:text = World%20inflation%20rate%20for%202019,a%200.25%25%20increase%20from%202017.

Penman, S. (2011). *Accounting for Value*. New York: Columbia University Press.

Reuters (2022). Base de datos Refinitiv.

Shiller, R. (2022). Online Data Robert Shiller. Available at www.econ.yale.edu/~shiller/data.htm

The World Bank (September de 2022). Available at https://data.worldbank.org/indicator/NY.GDP.MKTP.KD

Trevino, G. (2022). Is Expected Inflation the Best Long-term Sustainable Growth Rate? *Business Valuation Review, 41(3)*, 84–90.

Appendix A Duration and modified duration

One of the fundamental properties of the bonds free of options[6] is that their prices change inversely with the changes in the market interest rate. So, the natural question is: How sensitive is the bond price to the interest rate change? To measure this sensitivity, we need the coefficient of modified duration, which is the sister of duration. The concept of duration is attributed to Frederick Macaulay (1938), who argued that the bond maturity does not consider the intermediate payments. Figure 10.10 shows the cash flow of a bullet bond that matures in five years and pays an annual coupon rate of 10%. If we imagine the columns as weights placed to the left and right of a "fulcrum", duration is the point where the weights are balanced; this point is the center of gravity of the lever and is 4.17 years.

Duration calculation

To calculate its duration, we use the yield to maturity of 10% to calculate the present value of cash flows, and then each cash flow is divided by the bond price. Notice that the weighting factor is the percentage that represents the present value of each cash flow over the bond price. For example, year one cash flow represents 9.09% of the bond price, year two cash flow represents 8.26%, and so on. Finally, duration is calculated by multiplying each weighted cash flow by the time to maturity and adding them.

$$D = \frac{\frac{10}{(1,10)^1}}{100} \times 1 + \frac{\frac{10}{(1,10)^2}}{100} \times 2 + \frac{\frac{10}{(1,10)^3}}{100} \times 3 + \frac{\frac{10}{(1,10)^4}}{100} \times 4 + \frac{\frac{110}{(1,10)^5}}{100} \times 5 = 4,17$$

$$D = 0.0909 \times 1 + 0.0826 \times 2 + 0.0751 \times 3 + 0.0683 \times 4 + 0.683 \times 5 = 4,17$$

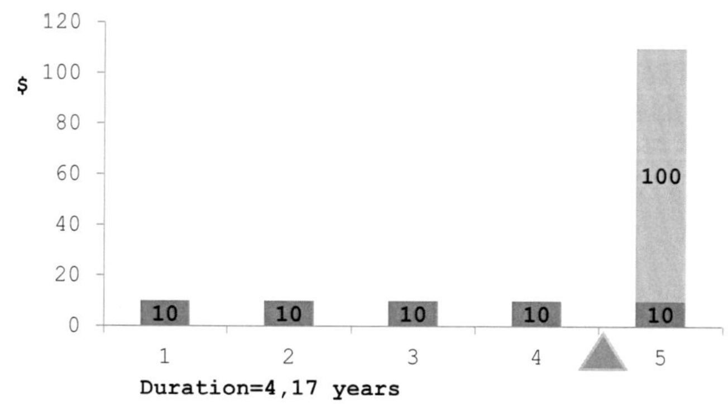

FIGURE 10.10 Duration of a bond bullet

The duration formula tells us that the numerator is a sum of discounted cash flows, each of them multiplied by the time in which it is paid, and divided by the bond price:

$$D = \sum_{t=1}^{n} \frac{tC_t}{(1+y)^t} \frac{1}{P} \qquad [10.5]$$

Although duration can be used as a rough estimation of the change in price for a unit change in yield, modified duration, which is described in the next section, is a better approximation of the price sensitivity to the changes in the yield.

Mathematical derivation of modified duration

Modified duration is related to the first derivative of the bond price concerning the interest rate in question. As we know, the bond price is the present value of the stream of its expected cash flow:

$$P = \sum_{t=1}^{n} \frac{C_t}{(1+y)^t} = C_1(1+y)^{-1} + C_2(1+y)^{-2} + \ldots + C_n(1+y)^{-n},$$

If we derive the bond price with respect to a change in the required yield, we have

$$\frac{dP}{dy} = -C_1(1+y)^{-2} + (-2)C_2(1+y)^{-3} + \ldots. + (-n)C_n(1+y)^{-n-1},$$

$$\frac{dP}{dy} = \sum_{t=1}^{n} \frac{-tC_t}{(1+y)^t} \frac{1}{(1+y)}.$$

As we note, the first derivative is negative; this indicates that when the interest rate increases, the price decreases.

Duration and modified duration relationship

You may have noted that the second member of the last equation is very similar to the duration expression; the only difference is that it is divided by (1+y) and not by the bond price. If we divide both members of the last equation by the bond price, we have

$$\frac{dP}{dy}\frac{1}{P} = \sum_{t=1}^{N} \frac{-tC_t}{(1+y)^t} \frac{1}{P} \frac{1}{(1+y)},$$

After this algebraic manipulation, we have in the second member the duration expression divided by (1 + y) which is the expression known as "modified duration" (MD):

$$\frac{dP}{dy}\frac{1}{P} = -\frac{D}{(1+y)} = -MD \qquad [10.6]$$

$$MD = -\frac{4.17}{(1+0.10)} = -3.79$$

Modified duration always carries a negative sign since the first derivative of the bond price with respect to the interest rate is negative. What –3.79 does mean? We can say that if a bond has a modified duration of 3.79, a change of one percentage point in its required yield will produce an approximate change in price of 3.79%. Therefore, if we want to know what will be the percentage change in the bond price (dP/P) for any change in the yield (dy), we must multiply the MD measure by dy:

$$\frac{dP}{P} = -MD \times dy. \qquad [10.7]$$

$$\frac{dP}{P} = -3.79 \times 0.01 = 3.79\%$$

If we want to know what will be the absolute change in the bond price for a change in yield, we calculate the dollar duration:

$$dP = -MD \times P \times dy. \quad [10.8]$$
$$dP = -3.79 \times 0.01 \times 100 = 3.79$$

		WACC	9.63%	PV FCF	2,719.51
Year	FCF	PV FCF	t x PVCF		
1	179.30	163.55	163.55	→ =+P3/(1+$R$1)^O3	
2	162.60	135.29	270.58	=+O4*Q4	
3	166.40	126.29	378.87		
4	178.60	123.64	494.57		
5	181.50	114.61	573.06		
6	194.80	112.21	673.23		
7	208.70	109.65	767.56		
8	214.30	102.70	821.63		
9	230.30	100.68	906.09		
10	4,087.80	1,630.03	16,300.30		
			21,349.43	=SUM(R3:R12)	
		Duration	7.85	=+R13/T1	

FIGURE 10.11 Company's free cash flow duration

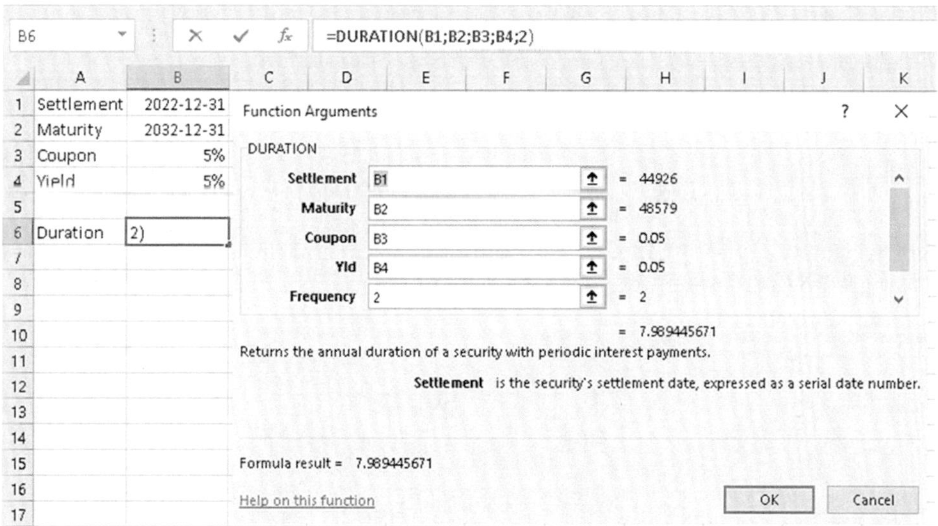

FIGURE 10.12 Duration of a UST-B10

GCC free cash flow duration and USTB10 duration

We can calculate the duration of the company's free cash flow and the duration of a UST-B10 with a spreadsheet. While the former requires making a few calculations, the duration of a bullet bond can be calculated using a specific Excel function called "duration" which requires some inputs such as the purchase, maturity dates, coupon rate, and yield.

Appendix B Duration of a perpetual cash flow

To calculate the duration of a perpetual cash flow, we proceed the same way as that of a finite cash flow. We divide the present value of each cash flow C by the bond price (which is a perpetuity C/i), and duration is calculated by multiplying each weighted cash flow by the time to maturity and adding them.

$$D_P = \frac{C\left[1\frac{1}{(1+i)} + 2\frac{1}{(1+i)^2} + 3\frac{1}{(1+i)^3} + \ldots\infty\right]}{\frac{C}{i}}. \qquad [A-1]$$

To solve [A-1], we can resort to a mathematical trick by expressing on a time axis different flow with the number 1 (one) and that read in the form of columns add up to 1, 2, 3, representing the number of each period. In this way, we have different streams of cash flow perpetuities (1), (2), (3), (4), and so on.

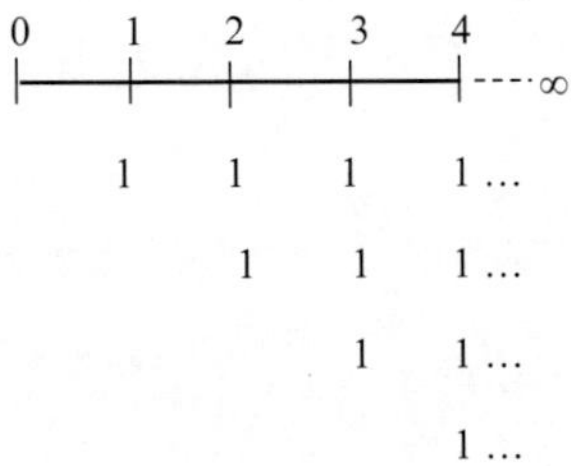

FIGURE 10.13 Present value of a series of cash flow perpetuities

The present value of the first row is 1/i; the present value of the second row is 1/i x (1/(1+i), and so on. As in all cases, the present value of each row is multiplied by 1/i we can take this expression as a common factor, and then, the values that appear in parenthesis represent the present value of a perpetual income of advance payments of value (1+i)/i.

$$\frac{1}{i} + \frac{1}{i}\frac{1}{(1+i)^1} + \frac{1}{i}\frac{1}{(1+i)^2} + \frac{1}{i}\frac{1}{(1+i)^3} + \ldots,$$

$$\frac{1}{i}\left(1 + \frac{1}{(1+i)^1} + \frac{1}{(1+i)^2} + \frac{1}{(1+i)^3} + \ldots\infty\right) = \frac{1}{i}\frac{1}{i}(1+i) \qquad [A-2]$$

Replacing [A-2] in [A-1]:

$$D_P = \frac{C\frac{1}{i}\frac{(1+i)}{i}}{\frac{C}{i}},$$

$$D_p = \frac{(1+i)}{i},$$

The last expression can be expressed as:

$$D_p = (1+i)i^{-1}.$$

Taking the first and second derivatives of Dp, we notice that the first derivative is negative and the second is positive, which means that as interest rate increases, duration decreases quickly at first and then slowly, so the function is decreasing and convex as we showed in Figure 10.7.

$$\frac{dD_P}{di} = \frac{d[(1+i)i^{-1}]}{di} = -(1+i)i^{-2} + i^{-1}.$$

$$\frac{d[2(1+i)i^{-1} + i^{-1}]}{di^2} = 2(1+i)i^{-3} - 2i^{-2}.$$

Appendix C Simulation of terminal value

Since the growth rates after the business achieved the steady state could be non-constant, one way to see how different the terminal value resulting from using a constant growth rate consists in simulating it.

The first step is generating random growth rates for many years. For this, we have to use the Excel function NORM.INV, and we write RAND() in the first window, the average GDP growth rate in the second, and its standard deviation in the third. Row 9 shows the resulting random free cash flow from year 11 to year 135, and cell B11 shows the terminal value. To generate terminal value samples, we select What-If-Analysis, and then we choose the option Table where the first column has the number of each sample from 1 to 1,000 (for space reasons, we only show thirteen values of the series).

It is important to note that in the Data Table command, we must point to an empty cell in the "Row input cell" (Figure 10.15 shows the cell H12) so that the values are generated randomly. Finally, select Data Analysis and choose "histogram".

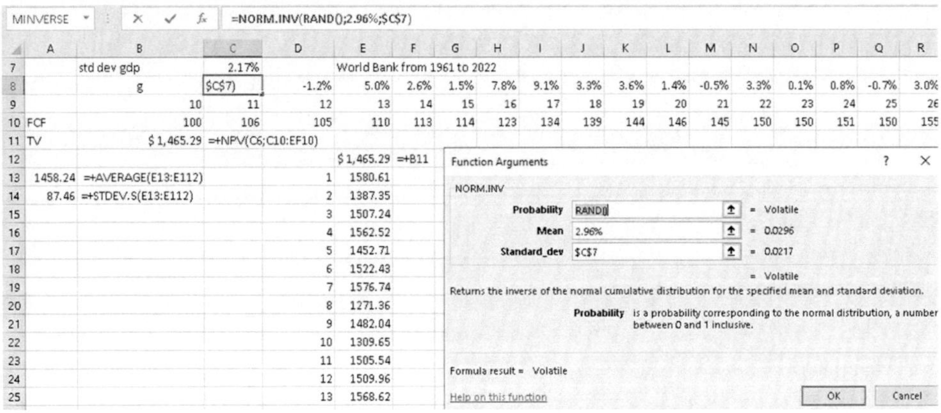

FIGURE 10.14 Growth rates generated randomly

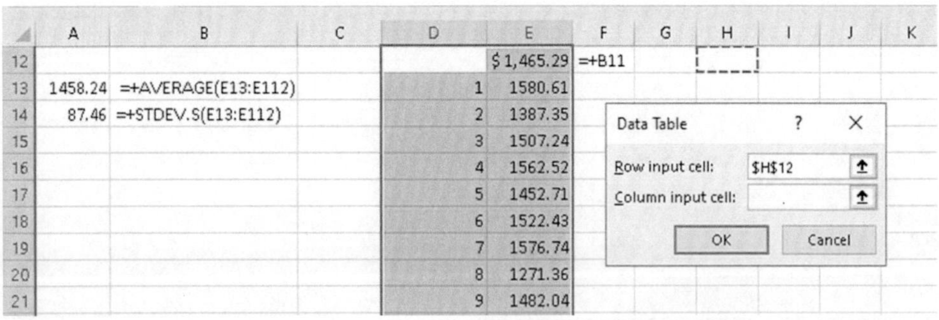

FIGURE 10.15 Terminal value sampling performing with Excel's Data Table function

CHAPTER

11 Dealing with the lack of market values

Introduction

Private companies, as opposed to publicly traded ones, are the subject of most valuations. In addition, valuing a publicly traded company is less frequent. When there are no market values, we immediately faced with a list of questions, such as how to apply the CAPM model since we are unable to calculate betas. What is the best way to estimate the capital structure, given that it should reflect fair market values? Since a representative market risk premium might not exist in emerging markets, how can we fill the gap?

DOI: 10.4324/9781003628491-14

After reading this chapter, you will be able to:

- Estimate the beta coefficient using the bottom-up approach;
- Estimate the cost of capital in the absence of market values;
- Estimate the capital structure considering different approaches.

Cost of capital inputs

There is no well-defined risk-free rate in emerging markets

The US T-Bond yield is considered risk-free since the government never defaulted on its debt. For this reason, most analysts use the US T-Bond yield with a maturity of ten years as a risk-free rate in the CAPM formula. Emerging countries issue bonds nominated in dollars, which pay a higher yield over a US T-Bond; the difference is considered the "country risk premium". Emerging countries also issue bonds in domestic currency, which have higher interest rates than those issued by developed countries due to the devaluation risk and the higher inflation rate. For all these reasons, there is no well-defined risk-free rate.

Market risk premium in emerging market is not representative

The stock index series in emerging markets are short, composed of a few companies, and much of them started in the nineties. Due to the short of the series, the average return would be seriously affected if a crash or a boom takes place in a year. Additionally, you can find some anomalies in emerging markets. For example, from January 1995 to December 2018, the Argentinean stock market index (MERVAL), had a compounded annual growth return (CAGR) of 2.2% in dollars with a volatility of 40.5%, while the Bond Market Index (IBIAMC) had a CAGR of 6.0% with a volatility of 28.9% (Dumrauf, 2019). Therefore, due to the lack of representativeness of the stock index, most analysts use the American market risk premium as a proxy.

The bottom-up beta approach

The bottom-up beta (in opposition to the regression beta, which constitutes a top-down approach) can be applied especially for private companies, but also for listed public companies with lack of marketability, and occasionally to public companies as well. Since there are no betas for private companies or non-public companies, appraisers typically employ the bottom-up approach, which involves four steps to address the problem:

1. Identify the publicly traded competitors most similar to the company in developed capital markets and take a representative sample. It constitutes the "peer group".
2. Calculate the mean of the sample (or the median if there are outliers that affect the average).
3. Since beta is affected by financial leverage, to eliminate this effect, we have to calculate the unlevered beta with the Hamada formula, using the average of the D/E ratio and the average of the legal tax rate of the sample.

4. Re-lever the unlevered beta with the Hamada Formula using the D/E ratio and the legal tax rate of the country where the company operates. The result is the levered beta of the target.

"Comparable companies" are usually firms in the same business. You can start by searching a database that provides a list of peers, and then you can look into them to see whether they are similar businesses. Concerning the size of the sample, the more firms you have in the sample, the lower the standard error of beta, which is usually higher. Suppose you have the following sample of industry betas with their respective standard error and 95% confidence interval limits:

According to the central limit theory, the standard deviation of a sampling distribution equals the standard deviation of the population divided by the square of the number of elements included in the sample.

$$\sigma_{\overline{X}} = \frac{\sigma}{\sqrt{n}}. \quad [11.1]$$

Being the average standard deviation = 0.223 and n = 4:

$$\sigma_{\overline{X}} = \frac{0.223}{\sqrt{4}} = 0.111.$$

Notice that for a sample of four companies, the standard error will be approximately half of the average standard deviation of the sample. As the sample size gets larger, the dispersion decreases, and the mean of the distribution is closer to the population mean. For example, if the sample has ten companies, the standard deviation will be reduced by more than 68%. Of course, there is a trade-off between comparability and size; in order to increase sample quality, some companies must be removed, losing precision but gaining comparability. Although a public company's beta is always available, some appraisers use the bottom-up approach even for the case of public companies due to its greater precision.

In emerging markets, when practitioners have to value a private company, sometimes there is no industry to look for comps. To deal with this issue, appraisers usually bypass the problem by using US betas as surrogates of emerging market betas. Pereiro (2010) calculated domestic industry betas for a list of emerging markets comparing the industry beta with the US industry, and performed a test of medians, finding that close to 80% of industry betas are not equivalent across classes. He finally recognized that the decision to use the industry beta of another emerging

TABLE 11.1 Betas and their standard error

Company	Beta	Standard error	Inferior limit	Superior limit
A	1.58	0.218	1.144	2.016
B	0.59	0.271	0.048	1.132
C	1.28	0.181	0.918	1.642
D	1.35	0.223	0.904	1.796
Mean	1.20	0.223	0.754	1.647

market or the US industry beta relies on the appraiser's beliefs about the plausibility of using one or another.

Finally, if you don't like to use beta based on historical data, maybe because it does not recognize a change in the company's operations, an alternative is looking for a beta provider that calculates a "forecasted beta", based on fundamental risk factors, instead of the historical beta calculated by regression analysis.

Country risk premium

Although there is no scientific methodology to include a country risk premium, there is a professional consensus that certain risks are not captured in beta when valuing in emerging markets. The probability-weighted scenario analysis, which takes into account how the business may be affected by politics and economic risk, is an alternative to adding a premium to the cost of equity capital. We will not go into depth here because the methods to count the country risk premium are covered in the next chapter.

The marginal cost of debt

The marginal cost of debt is determined by the riskless rate plus a risk premium, adjusted by the tax advantage. It is always marginal since it is the cost that the company should pay today to borrow money. There are numerous options because some firms have long-term bonds outstanding while others may not have issue any bonds at all.

Firms with long-term bonds outstanding

Corporate bonds traded every day are the simplest case to analyze since the yield undoubtedly represents the marginal cost of debt. This reasoning is valid for business in developed and emerging countries. For example, a bond issued by PesiCo maturing in February 2033 has a coupon of 4.45% and a yield of 5.15% on October 4, 2023. The bond has a rating of A+ by S&P. Another company, Atkore, which is in the industry of capital goods, issued a bond maturing in June 2031 with a coupon of 4.25%, yield of 7.22%, and a rating of BB by S&P.

Firms with long-term bonds not trading regularly

For firms with rated long-term bonds but not frequently traded, we must consider the associated default spread and liquidity! The marginal cost of debt must be estimated as

$$kd = riskless\ rate + associated\ default\ spread + liquidity\ premium$$

Suppose Dandy&Suit issued a bond that has a rating of BB and matures in June 2031. The default spread is usually calculated as the difference between the bond yield corresponding to the current bond rating over the US10Y treasury bond. For example, the US10Y was 4.73% on October 3, 2023, and taking into account that Atkore's bonds have a rating of BB and a yield of 7.22%, the associated default spread is 7.22% – 4.73& = 2.49%.

The liquidity has value. When you buy an illiquid bond, and later you decide to sell it, you may have to wait some minutes (or hours) for someone to agree to pay the offer price (likely after it has been lowered once or twice).[1] According to Jong & Driessen (2012) the estimated liquidity risk premium is around 0.6% per annum for US long-term investment grade bonds and 1.5% per year for speculative-grade bonds. Considering a liquidity premium of 0.6%/1.5%, the marginal cost of debt should be

$$kd = 4.73\% + 2.49\% + 0.6\%/1.5\% = 7.82\%/8.72\%$$

Firms in emerging markets with long-term bonds outstanding

Mid-size or large companies in emerging markets had the following cost of debt on October 2023:

- Grupo Cementos de Chihuahua, a Mexican company: Maturity: 20–4–2032; yield = 6.75%; S&P rating: BBB–
- Mercado libre, a multinational company originally settled in Argentina: maturity: 14-1-2031; yield 7.2487%; S&P rating: BB+
- Petrobras, a petroleum Brazilian company: Maturity: 3/7/2033; yield 7.44%; S&P rating: BB–

While it is sometimes argued that companies in emerging markets cannot borrow at a rate lower than the country itself, this is not totally accurate. For instance, large multinational companies with good credit ratings only include a portion of the country's risk premium or default spread (see an example in Chapter 12).

Firms in emerging markets with long-term bonds not trading regularly

We need to estimate the associated default spread by looking for other firms bonds the same rating, ideally in the local market. For example, in September 2023, CAPEX, an Argentinean company involved in the oil and energy industry, issued a bond with a coupon of 9.25%, maturing on 25/8/28, and an S&P rating of CCC–. When compared to other bonds rated as speculative, as Tenet Healthcare Corp, with a S&P rating of B- maturing on 1-1-26 and yield 7.39%, we can estimate the associated default spread as 7.39% – 4.73% = 2.66%. Therefore, the estimated marginal cost of debt is[2]

$$kd = 4.73\% + 2.66\% + 1.5\% = 8.89\%$$

Capex bond was not liquidity in September 2023, although there would be a few transactions, paying over par value, meaning that the estimated marginal cost of debt was near the true marginal cost.

Firms in emerging markets with long-term bonds issued in domestic currency

El Puerto de Liverpool SAB de CV, a Mexican Company, issued a bond with a coupon of 8.03%, maturing on 6/8/2030, rated BBB by S&P and a yield of 11.20%.

TABLE 11.2 Emerging market bond yields

Company	Coupon (%)	Maturity	Yield (%)	Rating S&P	Industry
PepsiCo	4.45	February 2033	5.15%	A+	Beverages
Atkore	4.25	June 2031	7.22	BB	Capital goods
Tenet Healthcare	4.875	January 2026	7.39	B–	Healthcare
Mercado Libre	3.13	January 2032	7.25	BB+	e-commerce
Petrobras	6.50	July 2033	7.44	BB–	Energy
Grupo Cementos de Chihuahua	3.61	April 2032	6.75	BB+	Construction
CAPEX	9.25	August 2028	8.89 (*)	CCC-	Energy
El Puerto de Liverpool	8.03	August 2030	11.20 (**)	BBB	Retail

(*) Estimation based on associated default spread and liquidity premium
(**) Expressed in Mexican pesos

Considering that Mercado Libre's dollar-denominated bonds, rated BB+, has a yield of 7.25%, the yield spread of 395bps (11.2% – 7.25%) is explained by the currency risk.

Firms in emerging markets with unrated domestic rate

It is the case an appraiser faces when valuing a small company in an emerging market. Although the firm doesn't issue any bonds, it does have loans in domestic currency, loans nominated in dollars, and possibly subsidized rate loans. These businesses occasionally obtain a five-year loan to finance investments, but when the principal is paid back, the leverage decreases, and eventually, they will get another loan to finance another investment opportunity. In Addition, since it is unclear whether the company will hold a constant leverage ratio, there is no well-defined capital structure, and it does not permit a significant estimation of the WACC. Another issue is the private premium for bonds issued by private companies. Kovner & Wei (2014) found that spreads for private companies are 30 basis points higher than those for bonds of public companies, even after controlling for observable differences, including rating, financial performance, industry, bond characteristics, and issuance timing. The premium increased to 40–56 basis points after controlling for fixed issuer effects.

Table 11.2 shows the estimated cost of debt for the bond examples we previously discussed. All the bonds are plain vanilla and expressed in dollars, with the exception of the El Puerto de Liverpool, which is nominated in Mexican pesos and its yield reflects a currency risk premium.

Capital structure on valuation

The lack of market values constitutes a problem for practitioners since two problems arise immediately:

1. There are no stock market values
2. The capital structure estimation, which must rely on *fair* market values[3]

The absence of market values prevents the beta calculation and thus the use of capital asset pricing models such as CAPM and Fama's three-factor model. If the capital structure should rely on market values, as corporate finance textbooks have postulated, how to estimate it?

Private companies are not the exception but the general case in valuation practice. For instance, in 2010, according to Forbes, of 27 million companies in the United States, less than 1% were publicly traded. And even among large firms, private owners abound, contradicting the misconception that private companies are all small. In emerging markets, where the development of capital markets is poor and the owners are generally non-diversified (Kartashova, 2014), the percentage of public companies over the total companies would be lower.

The participation of private companies in the total companies in the United States has increased in the last years since public companies have become closely held companies. According to the Center for Research in Security Prices, the number of publicly listed companies has fallen substantially from 8,000 companies at its peak in 1996 to 3,700 in 2023.

Even though the textbooks recommend market values for estimating the capital structure, practitioners and academics have different takes on this matter. Three approaches have been proposed:

1. Market values (MV): this approach is suggested in finance textbooks. The argument is straightforward: market values reflect the cost of getting capital today.
2. Book values (BV): it is based on historical values and is affected by accounting conventions.
3. Target capital structure (TCS): this is the favorite approach of practitioners and relies on the argument that the current capital structure may differ from the capital structure that will prevail along the company's life.

How often are these approaches used in practice? Bruner, Eades, Harris, & Higgins (1998) performed a survey of 27 highly regarded corporations, ten leading financial advisers, and seven best-selling textbooks and trade books. The results showed that, in the case of debt value, 52% of respondents used target weights, 15% used current values, and 26% were uncertain about what weights they used. For the equity value, 59% used target weights, 15% used book value weights, and 19% were uncertain about their weights. Bancel and Mittoo (2014) surveyed 356 valuation experts across ten European countries and found that 46% of respondents use market value weights, 34% use book value weights, and about 31% sector value weights.

Market value approach

The argument for using market values is straightforward: they reflect the marginal cost of capital. Although finance textbooks are categorical about using market values to estimate the capital structure, this approach is rarely used in practice since market values are too volatile. Figure 11.1 shows the D/V ratio of Microsoft 2001–2020.

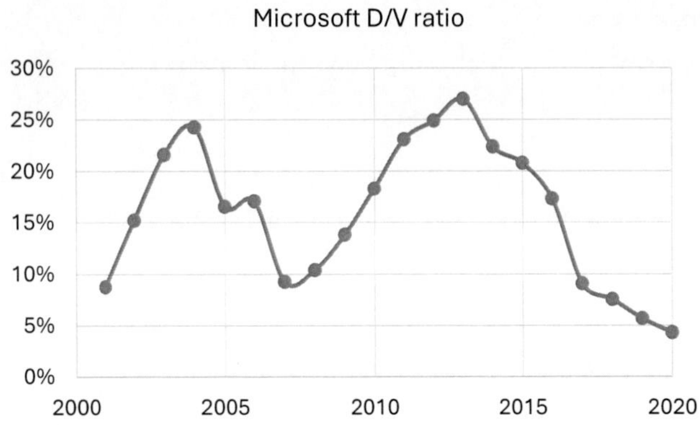

FIGURE 11.1 Microsoft D/V ratio 2001–2020

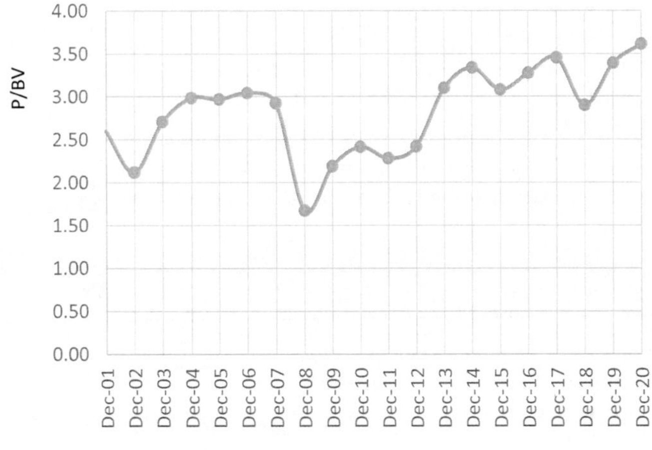

FIGURE 11.2 Median P/BV of S&P500

Book value approach

This approach has been proposed in the case of private companies and consists of using the book values of debt and common equity in the WACC formula:

$$WACC^{BVA} = ke \frac{E^{BV}}{E^{BV} + D^{BV}} + kd\,(1-t)\,\frac{D^{BV}}{E^{BV} + D^{BV}}. \tag{11.2}$$

Notice that the equity book value is used instead of equity market value. However, book values should not be used to determine the capital structure for at least three reasons.

1. Book values are historical and do not consider the future potential earnings and cash flows.
2. Firms usually create shareholder value over book value.

The empirical evidence shows that companies can create value above their book values. The easiest way to verify this assertion is by looking for the price/book value

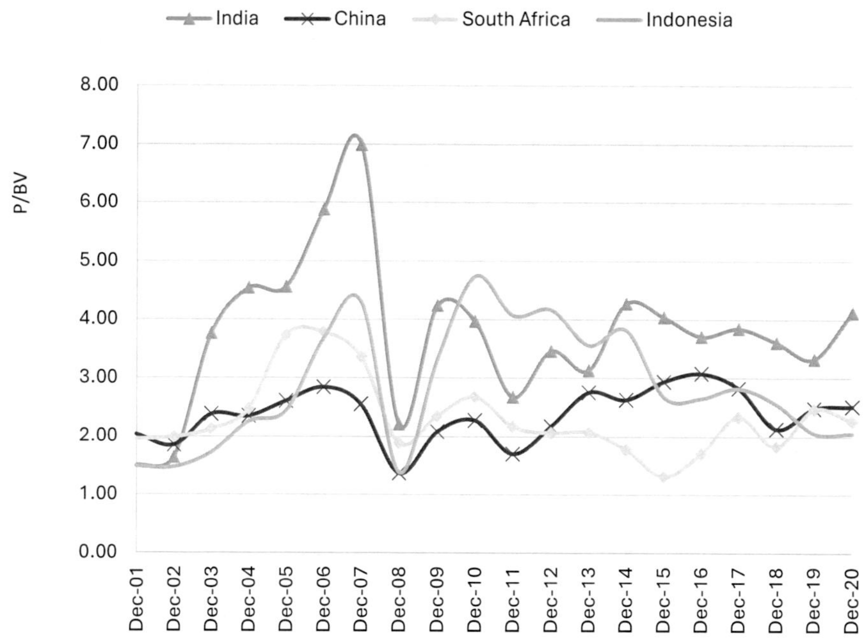

FIGURE 11.3 P/BV of China, India, Indonesia, and South Africa

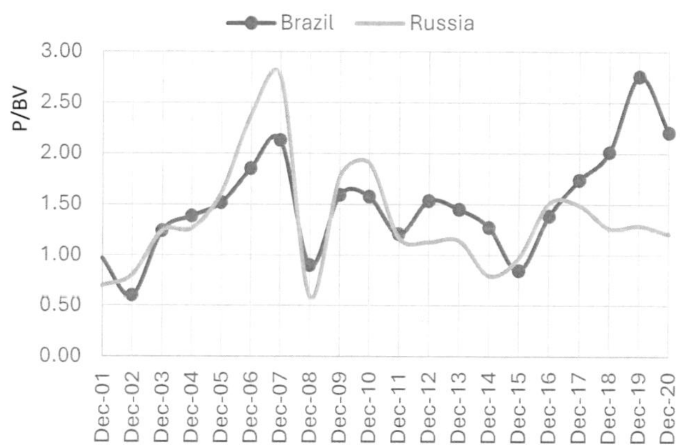

FIGURE 11.4 P/BV of BRICSI

ratio: if the price of a stock is higher than its book value, the price/book value ratio will be greater than one.

Figures 11.2 to 11.4 depict the median price/book value ratio for the constituents of S&P500 and a sample of the six emerging stock market indexes (Bovespa, RTS, BSESN, SSEC, JTOPI, and IDX 30), which correspond to Brazil, Russia, India, China, South Africa and Indonesia calculated for each calendar year, for the 2001–2020 period (Source: Reuters at 8–22-21). The empirical evidence about whether the equity market value is higher than the equity book value is forceful. In the United States, most companies observed a P/BV>1. In emerging markets, the results are similar except for Brazil and Russia in some years, perhaps reflecting the market-friendly policies prevailing in each country.

The mathematical inconsistency

Many CFOs argue that using book values is a more conservative approach than using market values, because the market value of equity is usually much higher than book value (Damodaran, 2012).

The problem with this approach is that it leads to an underestimation of the WACC since the equity's weight is artificially reduced since the equity book value is almost always lower than the fair equity market value, leading to an overestimation of the firm value. This underestimation comes from the debt/equity book value ratio; the higher the ratio, the higher the underestimation. Under this method, the fair value of the business is obtained using an accounting WACC:

$$V = \sum_{t=1}^{\infty} \frac{FCF_t}{(1 + WACC^{BVA})^t}. \qquad [11.3]$$

Then, subtracting the debt book value from the firm value, the equity fair value is:

$$V - D^{BV} = E. \qquad [11.4]$$

However, the equity fair value is different from the equity book value:

$$E^{BV} \neq E.$$

They would match only by chance, perhaps for companies that do not create value for their shareholders. Notice that when the debt is subtracted from the firm value to obtain the equity value, there is compensation since because the WACC is underestimated, the firm value is overestimated, increasing the equity value. Maybe this loop leads to convergence to an equity fair value more reasonable than the equity book value used to estimate the WACC. The opposite happens when the equity book value is higher than the equity market value, though this situation is uncommon.

Target approach

The target approach (TA) represents the most extended practice to estimate the capital structure weights. It assumes a target capital structure the company will hold throughout its life, established independently of forecasted free cash flow. This method is supposedly related to the optimal capital structure since it is expected that the target weights will optimize the share price.

However, what are the target weights? The TA has defendants both in academia and among practitioners. The argument is that the cost of capital should rely on target rather than current weights because, at any point, a company's current capital structure may not reflect the level expected to prevail over the business's life (Koller, Goedhart & Wessels, 2010).

A constant cost of capital supposes that the company periodically rebalances its capital structure; from a strictly mathematical point of view, this argument is supported by the work of Harris & Pringle (1985) which we explained in Chapter 8.

The mathematical inconsistency

The use of the TA generates a mathematical inconsistency. Once the target weights D/V and 1-D/V are defined, the target weighted cost of capital, $WACC^{TA}$ is:

$$WACC^{TA} = kd(1-t)\,\frac{D}{V} + ke\,(1-\frac{D}{V}). \qquad [11.5]$$

And the value of the operations is:

$$V = \sum_{t=1}^{\infty} \frac{FCF_t}{(1+WACC^{TA})^t}. \qquad [11.6]$$

Then, subtracting the debt book value, the fair value of equity is obtained:

$$V - D^{BV} = E. \qquad [11.7]$$

The problem with this approach is that the book value of debt never coincides with the target value of debt assumed in the capital structure. Suppose a company establishes a leverage ratio of α; then the expected debt value is different from the debt book value:

$$\alpha V \neq D^{BV}.$$

The resulting debt value in the capital structure (αV) differs from the debt book value and would match only by chance. The expected D/V ratio generally leads to a value of debt higher than the debt book value, leading to a lower WACC and a higher value of V.

From an empirical standpoint, what matters is whether companies adjust their leverage to the target ratio and, if true, the speed of adjustment since the TA assumes that this process is immediate.

Circularity approach

Analysts do not have market values when valuing private companies. To fill the gap, they use the bottom up or comparable beta approach, which consists of identifying the publicly traded competitors most similar to the company in developed capital markets and calculating the average beta of a sample; the average beta is more stable than the company beta and measurement errors tend to cancel out. Because the industry beta represents an average beta that reflects the industry leverage ratio, separating the financial risk of a levered firm from its business risk is required. Hamada (1972) integrated the Modigliani-Miller propositions with taxes (Modigliani & Miller, 1958; Modigliani & Miller, 1963) and the Capital asset pricing model to obtain the equations to unlever and relever betas. The first step is unlevering the industry beta using Hamada's formula, taking into account the industry leverage ratio and the industry marginal tax rate:

$$\beta_U = \frac{\beta_L}{\left[1+\frac{D}{E}(1-t)\right]}. \qquad [4.6]$$

β_L = industry beta (levered)
t = industry marginal tax rate
D/E = industry leverage ratio

The second step is to relever the unlevered beta considering the D/E ratio and the marginal tax rate of the target company.

$$\beta_L = \beta_U\left[1+\frac{D}{E}(1-t)\right]. \quad [4.7]$$

Then, the beta is introduced in the CAPM formula to obtain the expected return on equity ke, and then we calculate the WACC:

$$ke = rf + [E(rm) - rf]\beta_L. \quad [11.8]$$

$$WACC = ke\ \frac{E}{E+D} + kd\,(1-t)\ \frac{D}{E+D}. \quad [4.9]$$

The fair value of operations, V, is:

$$V = \sum_{t=1}^{\infty}\frac{FCF_t}{(1+WACC)^t}. \quad [11.9]$$

Finally, by subtracting the book value of debt, the equity fair value is obtained:

$$E = V - D. \quad [11.10]$$

Notice that we use market values to obtain "fair market values", generating a "*chicken and egg*" relationship. This relationship also happens when valuing a public company since the beta of a public company is calculated using market returns, which in turn is calculated using market values. The equity fair market value is obtained by an iterative process, which uses an initial seed value of equity to generate successive approximations of a solution. One possibility is using linear polynomials to construct new data points within the range of discrete known data points. Using

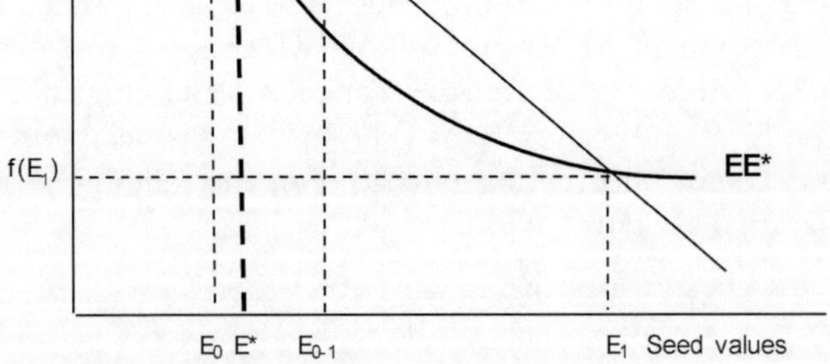

FIGURE 11.5 Equity value obtained by iteration

E_0 and E_1 as seed equity values, the two known points are given by the coordinates (E_0, f(E_0)) and (E_1, f(E_1)).

If the two known points are given by the coordinates (E_0, f(E_0)) and (E_1, f(E_1)), the linear interpolant is the straight line between these points. For a value E_{0-1} in the interval (E_0, E_1), the value E′ along the straight line is given from the equation of slopes:

$$\frac{E'-f(E_1)}{E_{0-1}-E_0}=\frac{f(E_1)-f(E_0)}{E_1-E_0}. \quad [11.11]$$

Solving equation [11.11] for E′, there is this equation:

$$E'=(E_{0-1}-E_0)\frac{f(E_1)-f(E_0)}{E_1-E_0}+f(E_1). \quad [11.12]$$

However, the function EE★ is not linear. Since the cost of equity capital is higher than the cost of debt when E increases its weight in the capital structure, the WACC also increases, and thus, the equity value decreases. Since the first derivative is positive and the second derivative is negative, the function f(E) is decreasing and convex with respect to seed value. Therefore, the first interpolated value E' contains a mistake that is eliminated by performing successive iterations until the seed value converges to the "true" equity value E★ in the function E★E★. The last value of E must satisfy the following equations we discussed and used in previous chapters:

$$\beta_L=\beta u\left[1+\frac{D}{E}(1-t)\right]. \quad [4.7]$$

$$ke=rf+[E(rm)-rf]\beta_L. \quad [4.3]$$

$$V=\sum_{t=1}^{\infty}\frac{FCF_t}{(1+WACC)^t}. \quad [11.9]$$

$$WACC=ke\,\frac{E}{E+D}+kd\,(1-t)\,\frac{D}{E+D}. \quad [4.9]$$

$$E=V-D. \quad [11.10]$$

In practice, we will not need to make these calculations since the iteration is performed instantaneously with spreadsheets, using a seed equity value and imposing the restriction that it must be equal to E = V-D.

By estimating the capital structure and the equity fair value using this process, there is no mathematical inconsistency since the equity fair value is endogenously determined. Notice that the CA also can be used to value public companies, saving the step of using the comparable beta approach to obtain the "fair beta". The iteration has been proposed by other authors (Mohanty, 2007; Koller, Goedhart, & Wessels, 2010). The next section establishes a comparison between the target and book value approaches.

An example of a private company

In this section, we apply the BVA, TA, and CA approaches to obtain the equity fair market value of "TELCO", a private company that provides telecommunication

TABLE 11.3 Forecasted free cash flow of TELCO in millions of US dollars

	Dec 21	Dec 22	Dec 23	Dec 24	Dec 25	Dec 26	Dec 27	Dec 28	Dec 29	Dec 30
FCF (US$)	123.0	104.0	111.0	122.0	131.0	142.0	149.0	152.0	155.0	158.0
Terminal Value										T. Value
FCF + T. Value	123.0	104.0	111.0	122.0	131.0	142.0	149.0	152.0	155.0	FCF + T. Value

services in an emerging country. Table 11.3 shows the forecasted free cash flow for the 2021–2030 period. It was forecasted considering the historical performance, mainly the EBITDA margin and the cash cycle observed in the last ten years. The last column contains the Terminal Value, calculated using the growing perpetuity formula, assuming a long-term growth rate of 3%. Since the Terminal Value is also affected by the weighted average cost of capital, which in turn varies with the approach applied to estimate it, there is no value in the last column.

Bottom-up beta calculations

Since TELCO is a private company, there is no beta. To fill the gap, we look for companies that provide the same telecommunication services (fixed lines, cell phones, and internet) and take the average five-year beta of a peer group. The peer group has a beta of 0.85, its leverage ratio is D/E = 82%, and has a marginal tax rate of 24%.

Using equation [11.7] to unlever the beta of the peer group:

$$\beta_U = \frac{0.85}{1+0.82\,(1-0.24)} = 0.526.$$

To estimate the beta of each approach, the D/E ratio is determined according to each model:

- BBA approach: TELCO has a debt book value of $556 million and an equity book value of $371 million in December 2020, which implies a D/E ratio of 149.9%.
- TA approach: we suppose target ratio of D/V = 50%, which implies a D/E ratio of 100%.
- The CA approach yields a D/E ratio of 31.34% by using the book value of debt and performs an iteration to obtain the equity market value that simultaneously satisfies equations 4.3, 4.7, 4.9, 11.9, and 11.10.

We compute the levered betas for the three approaches using formula [4.7] and a marginal tax rate of 35%.

$$\beta_L^{BV} = 0.526\left[1+150\%(1-0.35)\right] = 1.04.$$
$$\beta_L^{TA} = 0.526\left[1+100\%(1-0.35)\right] = 0.87.$$
$$\beta_L^{CA} = 0.526\left[1+31.34\%(1-0.35)\right] = 0.63.$$

TABLE 11.4 Peer group and financial data

Company name	D/E (%)	Tax rate (%)	Beta 5 year monthly
Telecom Argentina SA	39.3	49.0	0.60
America Movil SAB de CV	137.5	24.3	0.74
Level 3 Parent LLC	80.2	25.30	1.15
Netflix Inc	137.0	16.40	0.75
Turk Telekomunikasyon AS	84.8	16.4	1.06
Itissalat Al Maghrib Ste SA	14.7	34.9	0.87
True Corporation PCL	167.7	2.0	1.20
Emirates Integrated Telecommunications	18.5	NA	0.44
Mean	85.0	24.0	0.85

Source: Refinitiv Eikon, April 2021

To calculate the cost of equity capital we consider a risk-free rate of 3%, a market risk premium of 5.5%, and a country risk premium of 500 bps.

The marginal cost of debt

Since the target approach considers an expected D/V ratio, appraisers should consider the marginal cost of debt for the target value weights. One way followed in practice is to assume the cost of debt will increase according to the interest coverage ratio EBIT/Interest as we describe in Chapter 9. TELCO has a current coverage ratio EBIT/Interest = 4.38, and an 8% bond yield. For an expected D/V ratio of 50%, the coverage ratio would decrease to 2.06, which may cause bondholders to demand a higher yield. Looking for a reference, we found a private company, Telefonos de Mexico SAB de CV, with interest coverage of 2.01, Baa1 rating, and a bond yield of 9.23% in April 2021. Being cautious and pessimistic, we estimate a marginal cost of debt of 10% for an expected D/V ratio of 50%.

Table 11.5 and Figure 11.6 show the firm and equity values obtained by the BVA, CA, and TA, considering the same debt level and the marginal cost of debt according to the corresponding rating. When the Company is unlevered, the three approaches give the same result. Considering different D/V ratios or their equivalent debt amount, and adjusting kd to reflect the coverage ratio rating, CA and TA approaches give identical firm values. These findings may seem surprising at first, but if we consider a debt amount that implies the same D/V ratio, then both approaches must give identical results. As the D/V ratio increases, all three approaches suggest an optimal capital structure but at different levels. The BVA predicts a firm value higher than those predicted by the CA and TA for all D/V ratios.

Tables 11.6 and 11.7, and Figure 11.7 show the firm value, equity value, cost of capital and betas change as leverage increases for the three approaches. Ke and WACC functions appear perfectly overlapped because both the TA and CA approaches produce the same results.

TABLE 11.5 Firm value for different leverage

D/V (%)	Debt	kd (%)	BVA	CA	TA
0	0	8	1,501.08	1,501.08	1,501.08
31	556.00	8	2,125.14	1,773.92	1,773.91
50	895.29	10	1,945.36	1,790.58	1,790.58
60	993.81	12	1,693.71	1,656.35	1,656.35

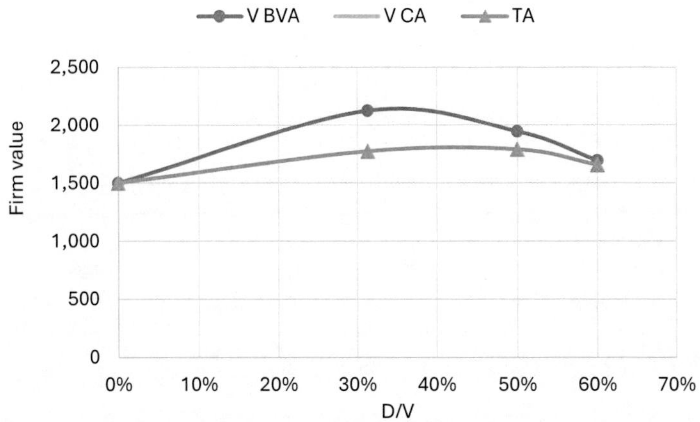

FIGURE 11.6 Firm value

TABLE 11.6 Cost of capital: Book value approach

D	D/V (%)	kd (%)	βL	ke (%)	WACC (%)	V	E = V–D
0	0.00	8.00	0.53	10.89	10.89	1,501.08	1,501.08
556	59.98	8.00	1.04	13.71	8.61	2,125.14	1,569.14
895	70.70	10.00	1.35	15.43	9.12	1,945.36	1,050.07
994	72.82	12.00	1.44	15.93	10.01	1,693.71	699.90

TABLE 11.7 Cost of capital: Target approach and circularity approach

D	D/V (%)	kd (%)	βL	ke (%)	WACC (%)	V	E = V-D
0	0.00	8	0.53	10.89	10.89	1,501.08	1,501.08
556.0	31.34	8	0.68	11.75	9.70	1,773.91	1,217.92
895.3	50.00	10	0.87	12.77	9.64	1,790.58	895.29
993.8	60.00	12	1.04	13.72	10.17	1,656.35	662.54

Do the companies rebalance their capital structures?

Regarding empirical issues, the tests about the capital structure rebalancing hypothesis and the speed of adjustment towards target leverage have provided poor

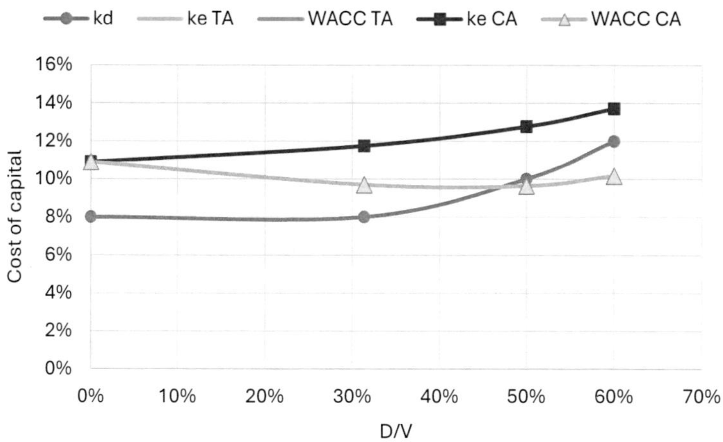

FIGURE 11.7 Cost of capital: CA and TA

evidence. Fama & French (2002) reported an adjustment speed of 7 to 18% per year. Flannery & Rangan (2006) estimated a 35.5% per year adjustment for market leverage and a 34.2% value for book leverage. Lemmon, Roberts, & Zender (2008) found that capital structures are stable over a long time and tend to remain as such for over 20 years, while Huang & Ritter (2009) reported that firms adjust toward target leverage at a moderate speed, with a half-life of 3.7 years for book leverage, and estimated a speed adjustment of 23.2% per year for market leverage and 17% per year for book leverage. DeAngelo, DeAngelo, & Whited (2011) found that firms deliberately but temporarily deviate from permanent leverage targets by issuing transitory debt to fund investment, explaining why empirical studies find slow leverage speeds of adjustment to target and argue that the model replicates industry leverage better than extant tradeoff models of capital. DeAngelo & Roll (2015) stated that capital-structure stability is the exception, not the rule, with leverage cross sections differing markedly, with similarities evaporating as the time between cross section lengthens. Industry-median leverage varies widely over time. Myers (2015) states that for mature firms, while the trade-off theory states that the change in debt will bring its debt ratio back toward a target, the pecking-order theory states that the change in debt will equal the firm's net requirement for external finance. Eckbo & Kisser (2020) tested whether high-frequency net-debt issuers with relatively low issuance costs and high debt benefits manage leverage toward long-run targets, as the trade-off theory predicts. They found that they do not and that this prediction is rejected by the negative leverage–profitability correlation, even when firms issue debt and distribute the proceeds to shareholders, precisely the case where the theory predicts it should be positive.

The timing of security issues also would play a role; however, it is confusing under the tradeoff and pecking order theory framework. Firms are more likely to issue stocks when their prices are "high". An early study by Myers (1984) pointed out that this fact is embarrassing to static tradeoff advocates since if firm value rises, the debt-to-value ratio falls, and firms ought to issue debt, not equity, to rebalance their capital structures. For the pecking order theory, the fact is equally embarrassing since there is no way firms can systematically take advantage of new stock investors in a rational expectations equilibrium, where investors would have learned it by now and would interpret the firm's issue decision accordingly.

Concluding thoughts

The lack of market values poses several challenges to appraisers: they must estimate not only the cost of capital but also the expected capital structure. We provide three approaches to circumvent these questions relative to the capital structure. The book value approach has not theoretical foundation, is mathematically inconsistent, and does not provide empirical evidence consistent with the valuation theory. The target approach relies on an expected capital structure assuming an immediate adjustment to the target ratio. Assuming a constant leverage ratio is a better assumption than assuming a constant debt, as has been derived numerous times in the literature (Modigliani and Miller, 1963; Rubinstein, 1973; Harris and Pringle, 1982). However, the expected target weights could be very different from the current ones.

The TA and CA approaches give identical results when they use the same debt level. Both are suitable for public and private companies and are computationally convenient. The weakness of the TA approach is that it assumes an immediate convergence to the target D/V ratio, which leads to a mathematical inconsistency since the implied debt considered in the WACC only coincides with the debt book value by chance. If you believe that the current capital structure is far from the expected capital structure that will prevail in the future, it would be preferable to consider a gradual adjustment to the target rather than instantaneous.

The CA approach calculate the equity fair value and beta by iteration, considering the current conditions, supporting the vision that the company has already adjusted the optimal debt ratio. There are no mathematical inconsistencies since the equity and debt values used in the cost of capital match the debt and the equity fair values.

Short questions and problems

1. Suppose the data of an industry is as follows: beta = 1.15; average D/E = 32%, t = 34%. If the target capital structure of a company is D/V = 50%, and the marginal tax rate is 35%, its beta would be:

   a) 1.258
   b) 1.566
   c) 1.466

2. If you want to estimate the beta of a company using the bottom-up approach, you must unlever first the average beta of the industry instead of adjusting the current beta due to:

   a) The Hamada formula is a linear function, and if you adjust the current beta, you compound the leverage, which makes the function nonlinear.
   b) It is indifferent since both adjustments lead to an identical estimation.

3. Is the WACC formula proposed by Miles and Ezzel compatible with the Hamada formulas for unlever/relever betas?
4. Mark P. Corp's long-term bonds are rated BB, but is not traded frequently, rated BB. Considering a risk-free rate of 4.5%, an associated default spread of 2.5%, and a liquidity premium of 0.6%, estimate the marginal cost of debt.
5. Suppose Dot Corp. has a D/V ratio of 20%. The current bond yield is 6%, rated AA, t = 40%, rf = 4%, rm-rf = 5.5%, Beta = 0.90, and the estimated Free Cash

Flow is \$100 million, which is expected to grow 3% at perpetuity. Because the senior management believe that the current capital structure does not reflect the capital structure that will prevail along the company's life, they estimate the WACC assuming a target ratio D/V = 50%, considering the new cost of equity capital using the Hamada formula, but ignoring any change in the marginal cost of debt. Calculate the firm value using the WACC with a D/V ratio of 20% and 50%.

6. Now re-calculate the WACC of Dot Corp. assuming the marginal cost of debt with a D/V ratio rises to 7% due to a decrease in the coverage ratio. In comparison to the last exercise, how much has the firm value changed?
7. A corporate bond rated B is not traded frequently. The associated spread over ust10 is 3.5%, and the liquidity premium is 1.5%. The US ten-year treasury yield is 4.7%. What is the marginal cost of debt? (Mark the correct answer)

   a) 8.9%
   b) 9.7%
   b) 9.8%

8. El Puerto de Liverpool SAB de CV, a Mexican Company, issued a bond in Mexican pesos with a coupon of 8.03%, maturing on 6/8/2030, rated BBB by S&P, and a yield of 11.20%. The yield looks higher given the BBB grade; however, this is because of the currency and country risk. Mercado Libre, a company with diversified operations across several countries, issued a dollar-denominated bond with a similar rating and a 7.25% yield. What is the currency risk premium?

   a) 2.95%
   b) 3.95%
   c) 3.68%

9. Suppose XX LTD, a small private company that has never issued a bond, is seeking for an estimation of the yield for a bond's five-year maturity. As the financial advisor, what strategy would you recommend?

   a) Search for corporate bond yields from small companies that have similar fundamentals to XX LTD (e.g., the coverage ratio) plus a liquidity premium, because the bond might not be frequently traded.
   b) Estimate the expected yield as the risk-free rate + associated default spread + liquidity premium.

10. Using the free cash flow of Table 11.4, assume that TELCO never reached the expected D/V ratio of 50%, holding a D/V ratio of 10% for the first five years of the projection and a D/V ratio of 20% from the sixth year and beyond. How much does the firm value differ from the 1,790.58 achieved in Table 11.5 with the target capital approach? Assumed kd remains constant at 8% and $\beta u = 0.526$
11. Mark true or false:

    a) The cost of debt must always be expressed on an after-tax basis.
    b) To estimate the cost of debt for valuation purposes, you must divide total interest by total debt to get the effective cost of debt.
    c) Both the cost of equity and the cost of debt are always marginal costs.

Notes

1 The author of this book once bought two identical bonds issued by two different states of an emerging country. The yield was higher for the less liquid. I had to accept a discount of 5% when I tried to sell it.
2 CAPEX was trading at $100.50 on September 28, 2023.
3 Fair value is the price at which the property would change hands between a willing buyer and a willing seller when both parties are under any compulsion to buy or sell, and the buyer has complete or at least reasonable information about the financial situation of the target company.

References

Bancel, F., & Mittoo, U. R. (2013). The Gap between Theory and Practice of Firm Valuation: Survey of European Valuation Experts. *Journal of Applied Corporate Finance 26*, 106–117.

Bruner, R., Eades, K., Harris, R., & Higgins, R. (1998), Best Practices in Estimating the Cost of Capital: Survey and Synthesis. *Financial Management 27*, 13–28.

Copeland, T., Koller, T., & Murrin, J. (2000). *Valuation: Measuring and Managing the Value of Companies*, 3rd edition. New York: Wiley.

Damodaran, A. (2012). *Investment Valuation*. New York: John Wiley and Sons.

DeAngelo, H., & Roll, R. (2015). How Stable Are Corporate Capital Structures? *Journal of Finance*.

DeAngelo, H., DeAngelo, L., & Whited, T. (2011). Capital Structure Dynamics and Transitory Debt. *Journal of Financial Economics, 99*, 235–261.

Dumrauf, G. L. (2019). Puzzles in the Argentinean Capital Market: Bonds beat Stocks. Discussion paper. *World Finance Conference*. Santiago de Chile.

Dumrauf, G. L. (July 2016). Capital Structure on Valuation. Discussion paper. *World Finance Conference*. New York.

Eckbo, B. E., & Kisser, M. (2020, November). The Leverage–Profitability Puzzle Resurrected. *Review of Finance*.

Fama, E., & French, K. (2002). Testing Tradeoff and Pecking Order Predictions about Dividends and Debt. *The Review of Financial Studies, 15*, 1–33.

Flannery, M., & Rangan, K. (2006). Partial Adjustment toward Target Capital Structures. *Journal of Financial Economics, 79(3)*, 469–506.

Harris, R., & Pringle, J. (1985). Risk-Adjusted Discount Rates: Extensions from the Average Risk Case. *Journal of Financial Research*, 237–244.

Huang, R., & Ritter, J. R. (2009). Testing Theories of Capital Structure and Estimating the Speed of Adjustment. *The Journal of Financial and Quantitative Analysis, 44*, 237–271.

Jong, F. d., & Driessen, J. (2012). Liquidity Risk Premia in Corporate Bond Markets. *The Quarterly Journal of Finance, 2(2)*.

Kartashova, K. (2014). Private Equity Premium Puzzle Revisited. *American Economic Review, 104*, 3297–3334.

Koller, T., Goedhart, M., & Wessels, D. (2010). *Valuation: Measuring and Managing the Value of Companies*. Hoboken, New Jersey: JohnWiley & Sons, Inc.

Kovner, A., & Wei, C. (2014). The Private Premium in Public Bonds. *Federal Reserve Bank of New York, No. 553*.

Lemmon, M. L., Roberts, M. R., & Zender, J. F. (2008). Back to the Beginning: Persistence and the Cross-Section of Corporate Capital Structure. *The Journal of Finance, 63(4)*, 1575–1608.

Mohanty, P. (2007). Solving the Circularity Problem in Estimating the Cost of Capital: A Practical Approach. *Icfai Journal of Applied Finance*, 29–38.

Myers, S. (2015). Finance, Theoretical and Applied. *Annual Review of Financial Economics*, 1–34.

Myers, S. C. (1984). Capital Structure Puzzle. *Journal of Finance, 39(3)*, 575–592.

Pereiro, L. (2010). The Beta Dilemma in Emerging Markets. *Journal of Applied Corporate Finance, 22(4)*, 110–122.

Ross, S. (1976, May). The Arbitrage Theory of Capital Asset Pricing. *Journal of Economic Theory, 13*, 341–360.

Rubinstein, M. E. (1973, March). A Mean-Variance Synthesis of Corporate Financial Theory. *Journal of Finance 28*, 167–182.

CHAPTER

12

The country risk premium

Introduction

Although in the CAPM's world the only risk that commands a premium is the systematic risk, there is a professional consensus that not all risks can be eliminated through diversification when valuing in emerging markets. In other words, getting the free cash flow is riskier in an emerging country than in a developed country for a similar business.

From the perspective of a foreign investor planning to invest in an emerging country, risks are frequently associated with changes in laws, failure to enforce contracts governing an investment, regulations, currency risk, and civil disturbances in a way that reduces the return on the investment. The country risk is not fiction, even though the country risk premium in valuation is debatable.

We start by reviewing the arguments to include a country risk premium. Then, we will consider some alternatives to compute it in a valuation, and finally, we will provide some evidence about how it affects the market value.

DOI: 10.4324/9781003628491-15

After reading this chapter, you will know:

- What are the political, economic, and financial components of a country's risk.
- How to compute the country risk premium in the cost of capital or/and using scenario analysis;
- How the market value of a business is affected by the country risk.

Arguments for considering a country risk premium

Stulz (1999) found that the key element was the marginal investor that led to the segmented and integrated investor perspectives.

- Segmented investor: In a segmented market, the marginal investor cannot diversify across different countries; therefore, they cannot eliminate the country's risk.
- Integrated investor: In an open market, the marginal investor can diversify and invest across different countries, reducing the country's risk. However, a portion of country's risk would still be non-diversifiable because stock markets correlation is not zero. This argument is also supported by Damodaran (2012).

For these reasons, there is a professional consensus about the convenience of counting the country's risk exposure at the level of every company. Although from a scientific point of view, it is impossible to justify the inclusion of a country risk premium, practitioners in emerging markets most commonly add a country risk premium in the cost of equity capital and less frequently, asses it using probability-weighted scenario analysis.

Mapping and measuring the country's risk

Figure 12.1 shows how Allianz Trade classified the country risk in its rating of Q2 2024 as low, medium, sensitive, and high risk. Countries classified as "sensitive" and "high risk" are mainly in Russia, the Middle East, Africa, and Latin America.

To describe the country risk as political, economic, and financial risk, we can use the information of a country risk provider. For instance, the RS Group's International Country Risk Guide rating converts political, financial, and economic data into "risk points" for each variable. ICRG ratings are calculated annually, 1984 to the present. Table 12.1 shows the several components of political, economic, and financial risks.

The political risk rating contributes 50% of the composite rating, while the financial and economic risk ratings each contribute 25%. Political risk assessments are based on subjective analysis, and financial and economic risk assessments are based on objective data. We briefly comment on the three main risks; details can be found on the ICGR webpage.

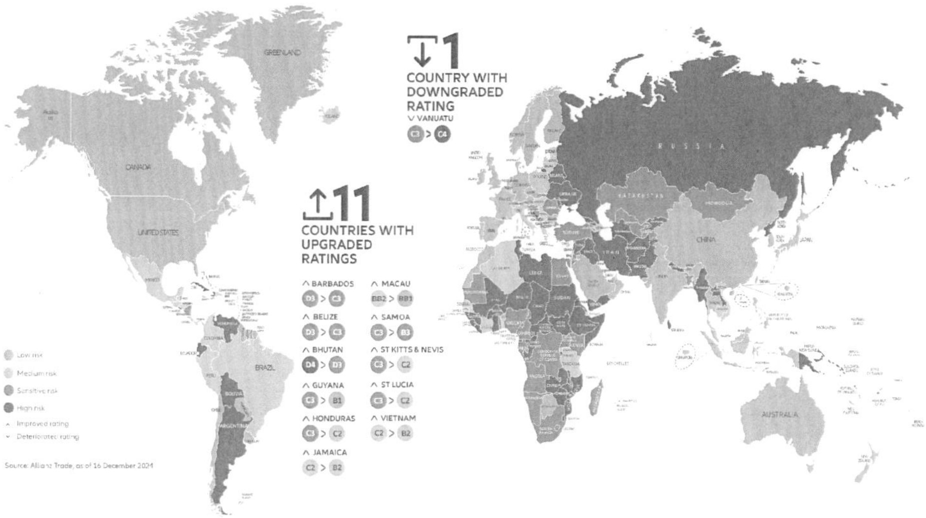

FIGURE 12.1 Country risk ratings

TABLE 12.1 Risk factors and points

	Risk factors	Maximum risk point
Political risk	Government stability	12
	Internal conflict	12
	Military in politics	12
	Ethnic tensions	12
	Socioeconomic conditions	12
	External conflict	6
	Religion in politics	6
	Democratic accountability	6
	Investment profile	6
	Corruption	6
	Law and order	6
	Bureaucracy quality	4
	Total	100
Financial risk	Foreign debt services as a percentage of exports of goods and services	10
	Foreign debt as a percentage of GDP	10
	Current account as a percentage of exports of goods and services	15
	Exchange rate stability	10

(Continued)

TABLE 12.1 (Continued)

	Risk factors	Maximum risk point
	net international liquidity as months of import cover	5
	Total	50
Economic risk	GDP per head	5
	Real GDP growth	10
	Annual inflation rate	10
	Budget balance as a percentage of GDP	10
	Current account of the balance of payment as a percentage of GDP	15
	Total	50

Source: www.allianz-trade.com/en_global/economic-research/country-reports.html

- Political risk: Each risk component is assigned a risk point; the minimum number is zero, while the maximum number of points depends on the weight assigned in the overall political risk assessment. In every case, the lower the risk point, the higher the risk. Government Stability, Socioeconomic Conditions, Investment profile, Internal Conflict, and External Conflict have a maximum risk point of 12, while the other factors have a lower risk point.
- Financial risk: The current account as a percentage of exports has a maximum of 15, foreign debt as a percentage of GDP, foreign debt as a percentage of exports, and exchange rate stability has a maximum of 10, and net international liquidity has a maximum of 5.
- Economic risk: The economic perspective refers to the ability of a country to service its external debt; if the emerging country does not meet its obligations, the default changes the business environment in a manner that could adversely affect the profit and asset value of the equity and foreign direct investments.

Each risk component considers a scale from zero to a pre-set maximum. Current account as a percentage of GDP has the maximum risk point of 15.

The individual country risk is estimated using the following categories of composite risk, where the highest rating (theoretically 100) indicates the lowest risk and the lowest rating (theoretically 0) represents the highest risk.

TABLE 12.2 Rating scale

Very high risk	00.0 to 49.9 points
High risk	50.0 to 59.9 points
Moderate risk	60.0 to 69.9 points
Low risk	70.0 to 79.9 points
Very low risk	80.0 to 89.9 points

Ratings on country risk help us to map the different risks we could find in an emerging country and act as a checklist. However, it does not give a clear-cut number to perform a valuation.

Sovereign credit rating

The sovereign credit rating is an independent assessment of the government's ability to repay its obligations, provided by a rating agency like Moody's, Fitch, or Standard & Poor's. Both sovereign and corporate ratings range from AAA to D in Standard & Poor's scale. While AAA means the maximum rating (a country or a company that can demonstrate exceptional ability to pay its obligations), a rating D is assigned to the country or company that defaulted its debts. Rating agencies evaluate the economic and political environment to assign a rating, which is essential for emerging countries that want to access the international bond market. The "investment grade" ranges from AAA to BBB, and grades of BB+ or lower are considered speculative. Ten countries have the highest or nearly-perfect credit rating: Australia, Canada, Denmark, Germany, Luxembourg, the Netherlands, Switzerland, Norway, Sweden, Singapore, and the United States. Figure 12.2 shows the sovereign ratings according to Moody's Investor Services in November 2022 (Source: Sovereign Wikirating Index). The red and orange parts of the world represent Russia, Africa, the Middle East, and Latin America. Although the rating is an ordinal measure and not a number, it gives investors insights into the level of risk for an investment in a particular country.

Credit default swap

A credit default swap (CDS) is a financial derivative that allows an investor to offset the credit exposure with another investor. For instance, suppose an investor thinks that the government of the emerging country will default on their bonds; to swap

FIGURE 12.2 Sovereign ratings by country

TABLE 12.3 CDS and S&P rating

Country	S&P Rating	5Y CDS	Default probability (*)
United States	AA+	35.98	0.60%
Germany	AAA	10.64	0.18%
Greece	BBB-	75.196	1.25%
China	A+	67.04	1.12%
India	BBB-	84.08	1.40%
Indonesia	BBB	77.11	1.29%
Italy	BBB	73.24	1.22%
Mexico	BBB	106.91	1.78%
Brazil	BB	158.15	2.64%
Turkey	B+	265.32	4.42%
Egypt	B-	618.03	10.30%
Russia	NR	13,775.17	100.00%

(*) Calculated on the hypothesis of a 40% recovery rate
Source: World Government Bonds

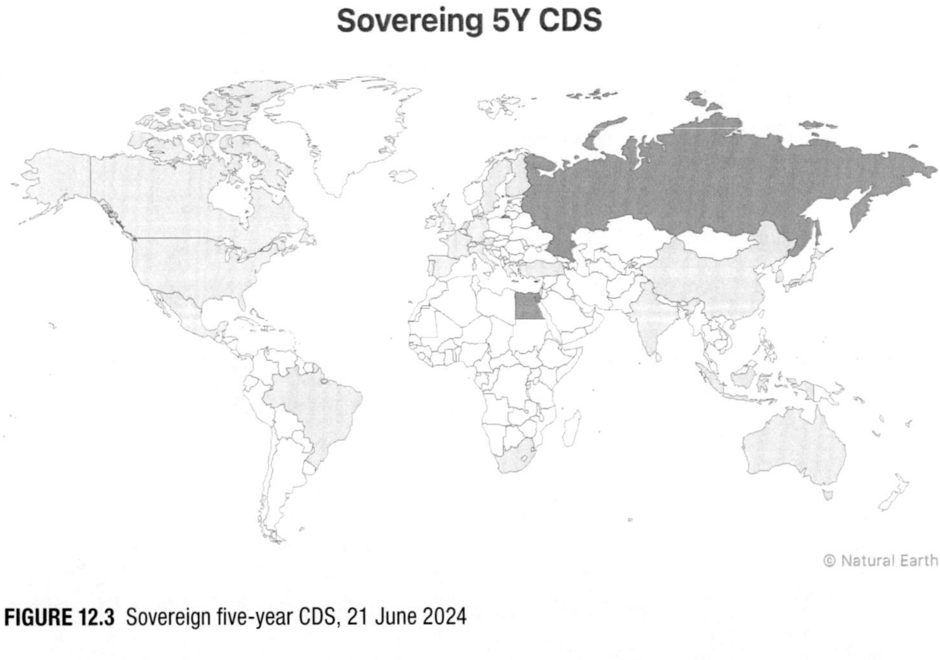

FIGURE 12.3 Sovereign five-year CDS, 21 June 2024

the risk of default, the investor buys a CDS from another investor who agrees to reimburse the lender in case the borrower defaults. In the case of default, the seller will pay the buyer the security value and all interest payments that would have been paid between that time and the maturity date. Table 12.3 shows the sovereign five-year CDS and S&P rating for countries rated B or lower on June 21th, 2024.

Figure 12.3 shows a map of the world that shows the Sovereign Five Year CDS using Highcharts by Highsoft created Natural Earth. The lower spread corresponds to countries like China, Indonesia, and Italy; medium spread corresponds to Mexico, Brazil, and Turkey. The higher spread is for Egypt and Russia. The data is summarized in Table 12.3.

CDS spread is a forward-looking measure and less costly to compile than macroeconomic data. Rodriguez, Dandapani, & Lawrence (2019) examined the relationship between sovereign debt ratings and CDS spreads and found that three-month CDS spread changes can predict sovereign crises within the next seven months, while ratings have no predictive ability. Although CDS spread is considered a measure of country risk, it is not frequently used as an input in the cost of capital.

EMBI+ spread

The EMBI+ spread represents an indicator of the risk premium for emerging market bonds, which reflects the different between the yields paid by US dollar-denominated emerging market sovereign bonds to those paid by US government bonds. It is measured in basis points and diffused by JP Morgan, which publishes the EMBI spread for several emerging countries The calculation is a little bit cumbersome since it takes the weighted averages of bond yield spreads considering the corresponding point on the yield curve of US Treasury securities (similar duration); however, it is diffused by JP Morgan every day. A low rating generally means a high sovereign spread. Sy (2001) estimated this relationship using a panel data estimation to analyze statistically significant deviations from the estimated relationship and found that when spreads are abnormally high, rating agencies tend to decline country ratings and vice versa. There are other versions of the EMBI. The regular EMBI index covers US dollar-denominated Brady bonds, loans, and Eurobonds. The Emerging Markets Bond Index Plus (EMBI+) tracks total returns for traded external debt instruments (external meaning foreign currency denominated fixed income) in the emerging markets. The JPMorgan Emerging Markets Bond Index Global (EMBI Global) tracks total returns for traded external debt instruments

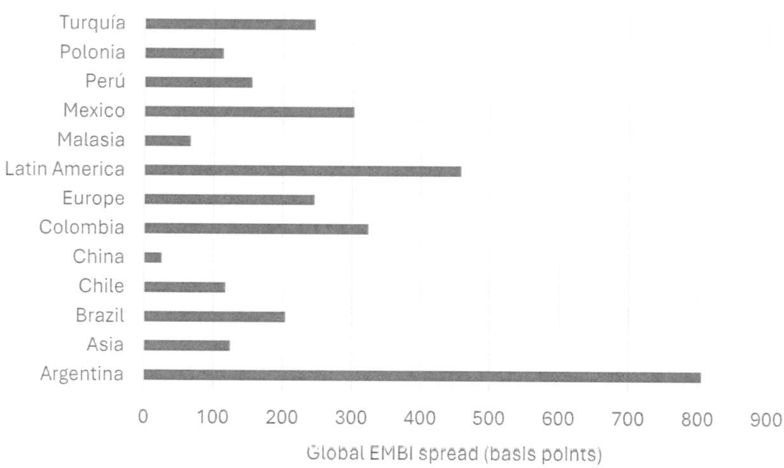

FIGURE 12.4 EMBI Global in November 2023

in the emerging markets and is an expanded version of the JPMorgan EMBI+. It covers more eligible instruments than the EMBI+ by relaxing somewhat the strict EMBI+ limits on secondary market trading liquidity.

The EMBI+ provides a single number, a measure that analysts usually add to the cost of equity capital when valuing a potential target in an emerging country. However, we must be careful when bonds are priced with a probability of default since yields are fictitious in these circumstances, as we explain later. Figure 12.4 shows The EMBI Global for some countries of Latin America, Europe, and Asia.

Country risk premium in the cost of capital

Some models have been proposed to count the country risk premium when valuing a company in emerging countries. We will discuss the most popular in valuation practice.

CAPM adjusted models

Some CAPM-adjusted models include a country risk premium, while others consider company-specific risk factors. We start with the Global CAPM since it does not count any specific factor or country risk premium, to follow by describing the characteristics of other models with their pros and cons.

Global CAPM

The Global CAPM (O'Brien, 1999; Schramm & Wang, 1999; Stulz, 1999) assumes that investors are integrated into the global capital markets: an investor in any country could acquire and sell securities in any market with minimum transactional cost, eliminating the unsystematic risk through geographic diversification. The Global CAPM uses a global market index such as the Morgan Stanley World Index, and global or international beta measures the systematic risk of a stock or portfolio about the global market index. The global risk-free rate is represented by the ten-year US Treasury Bond yield.

$$r = rf_G + (rm_G - rf_G)\beta_G. \tag{12.1}$$

A Global CAPM would be the best approach to adopt when global market integration reaches its limit (Bruner, Conroy, Estrada, Kritzman, & Li, 2002). However, segmentation requires adaptations to consider unique risks faced by investors in emerging markets. Large multinational companies with worldwide operations whose share prices more closely correlated with a proxy of the global equity index than the local equity index may find it helpful.

International CAPM (ICAPM)

The ICAPM expands the Global CAPM to incorporate a foreign currency risk premium to the systematic risk and also assumes that global markets are integrated and efficient.

$$r = rf_G + (rm_G - rf_G)\beta_G + (FCRP)\beta_{CR}. \tag{12.2}$$

The foreign currency risk premium (FCRP) is an attempt to account for the sensitivity to changes in foreign currency that can affect profitability and returns. Suppose an American company acquires a Brazilian company, the cash flow of the acquired company will be lower in dollars if the Brazilian real depreciates against the US dollar, which will impact the investment return. One possibility to count these effects is to take an FCRP adjusted by the beta of the domestic currency returns to changes in foreign currency. The beta can be calculated using this econometric model attributed to Fama (1984), where FCRP is the difference between the forward rate in t–1 and the spot rate in t–1:

$$FCRP = f_{t-1} - s_{t-1}. \qquad [12.3]$$

The null hypothesis is that if the difference between the forward rate in t-1 and the spot rate in t-1 does not influence the difference between the expected future spot rate and the forward rate in t-1, the beta is near zero and there is no currency risk premium. If the beta is not zero, there is a foreign currency risk premium due to depreciation risk. As explained in Chapter 12, we prefer to count the currency risk explicitly on the cash flow, since we believe it provides a clearer indication of what the market expects.

The local CAPM

Unlike the Global CAPM, the local CAPM, described by Pereiro (2001) and Pereiro (2006), uses the local risk free rate, beta is measured relative to the country's market index, and the equity premium is the local market premium. It adds a country risk premium (CRP) which is typically the EMBI spread measured by JP Morgan.

$$r = rf_l + (rm_l - rf_l)\beta + CRP. \qquad [12.4]$$

rf_L = local risk-free rate
rmL-rfL = local market risk premium
CRP = country risk premium expressed in percentual points

Since the EMBI spread is expressed in dollars, the risk-free rate and the market risk premium must also be expressed in the same currency. Furthermore, as we explained in Chapter 11, the lack of inputs makes its use challenging or impossible because emerging markets lack a well-defined risk-free rate, and local stock market series have few constituents, are short, and its composition has changed in relatively short periods. In addition, adding a country risk premium to the cost of capital creates a double count because the country risk also affects the market risk premium. There is another version of this model that adjusts the market risk premium by the volatility explained by the country risk premium.

The practitioner model

This model avoids duplicating the country risk premium, and all inputs are clearly understood. It uses the US T-Bond yield as the risk-free rate, the global market risk premium as a proxy of the local market risk premium, the beta is obtained by regressing the asset returns against the local stock market returns and adds a separate country risk premium to the cost of capital (usually the corresponding EMBI calculated and published by JPMorgan).

$$r = rf_G + (rm_G - rf_G)\beta_L + CRP. \quad [12.5]$$

Since the global market risk premium is usually the American market risk premium, which has no country risk, there is no duplication risk. Besides, since the free cash flow is frequently forecasted in US dollars, there is a currency matching between cash flow and cost of capital.

The Godfrey & Espinosa model

Godfrey & Espinosa (1996) state that because the country's risk has an impact on the stock market index, the political and business risks are incorporated into the CAPM through an adjusted beta to avoid duplication of the country's risk premium.

$$r = rf + (rm_{US} - rf)\beta_{adj.} + CRP. \quad [12.6]$$

The adjusted beta is defined as:

$$\beta_{adj.} = \frac{\sigma_{r_L}}{\sigma_{r_{US}}}(1 - R^2). \quad [12.7]$$

σ_L = standard deviation of returns in the local market
σUS = standard deviation of returns in the US equity market
rmUS = return of the US stock market index
R2 = coefficient of determination, which measures the percentage of the stock market volatility explained by the country risk spread

According to Erb, Harvey, & Viskanta (1995), 40% of the stock market volatility can be explained by the country's risk spread[1], while 60% is related to changes in business conditions. If the country risk spread explains 40% of the stock market return, to avoid double-counting of country risk, they proposed a corrective adjustment on the market risk premium equal to (1–R^2) = 0.6. Therefore, the adjusted beta is:

$$\beta_{ADJ} = \frac{\sigma_L}{\sigma_{US}}(1 - 0.4)$$

$$r = rf + (rm_{US} - rf)\frac{\sigma_L}{\sigma_{US}}0.60 + CRP.$$

It is assumed that the (1 – R^2) factor is constant and equal to 0.60, and that the correlation of returns between markets is constant and equal to 1. The factor $(1 - R^2)$ represents the unexplained part of the stock market return[2] to debug the market risk premium from the effects of country risk. However, the correlation between the stock market and country risk is not stable when a country defaults its obligations. For example, once a default occurred the EMBI+ typically reaches levels of 2,000bps or more, and the stock market return becomes independent from the country risk (hoping for an agreement to restructure their obligations). For example, the R^2 calculated for Argentina from January 1995 to August 2023 is 0.17.

The Goldman Sachs model

Mariscal and Hargis (1999) also use the ratio of standard deviations rather than the beta arguing that local-market volatility plays a greater role than betas in determining risk in a world market portfolio. The global equity risk premium then is multiplied by and adjusted beta and adding a country risk premium

$$r = rf + (rm_G - rf)\beta_{ADJ} + CRP. \quad [12.8]$$

To avoid the problem of double counting of country risk, replaced the 60% fixed adjustment of the Godfrey and Espinosa model by subtracting the correlation of dollar returns between the stock market and the bond return used to calculate the country risk premium. Therefore, the adjusted beta is:

$$\beta_{ADJ} = \frac{\sigma_L}{\sigma_{US}}(1 - \rho_{SB}). \quad [12.9]$$

ρ_{SB} = correlation coefficient between the local country's stock market and bond returns
σ_L = standard deviation of returns in the local stock market
σ_{US} = standard deviation of returns in the US stock market
CRP = country risk premium

They conclude by saying that the model allows for the decomposition of the discount rates into bond market variables and stock market variables, and that this feature permits to simulate the stock market sensitivity to changes in sovereign spreads, US interest rates and stock market volatility.

The Damodaran model

This model seeks to adjust country risk to firm-level, where the lambda coefficient γ is a firm-specific exposure to country risk ranging from zero to one, and B_L is the local company beta computed against a local market index. He says that a simplistic solution would be to estimate lambda as:

$$\gamma = \frac{\%\ of\ domestic\ revenues_{firm}}{\%\ of\ domestic\ revenues_{average}}. \quad [12.10]$$

The exposure factor γ is the percentage of revenues the firm gets in the emerging country related to the percentage of revenues the average firm gets in the emerging country. The higher the lambda, the higher the adjusted country risk premium:

$$r = rf_G + (rm_G - rf_G)\beta_L + CRP \times \gamma. \quad [12.11]$$

The Salomon Smith Barney model

Zenner & Akaydin (2002) proposed a model that considers how a firm is affected by specific factors that adjust the country's risk premium:

$$r = rf_G + CRP\left(\frac{\gamma_1 + \gamma_2 + \gamma_3}{30}\right) + \beta_G(rm_G - rf_G). \qquad [12.12]$$

γ_1 = firm-related score from 0 to 10, with 0 indicating the best access to capital markets
γ_2 = industry score from 0 to 10, with 0 indicating the least susceptibility of the industry to political intervention
γ_3 is a home country firm score from 0 to 10, with 0 indicating that the investment at the local level constitutes only a small portion of the firm's total assets

The global beta is leveraged for the target's capital structure and the country risk premium is assumed null for most developed markets. The sum of γ_{1+} $\gamma_{2,+}$ γ_3 will be between 0 and 30 and then divided by 30 indicating the adjustment to the country risk premium.

Models that consider specific factors can work well for particular cases, but naturally, when the specificity of a model increases, its capacity for a general application decrease. Table 12.4 summarizes the main characteristics of the CAPM adjusted versions. Except for local CAPM, all models use the ten-year USTB as a global risk-free rate. Differences are in the treatment of the market risk and country risk premium.

Despite being logical and econometrically correct, some of the models that were suggested for use in emerging economies in the 2000s resulted in irrational and high capital costs. We had the opportunity to see discussions in which the target's appraiser's estimations were extremely optimistic, and the potential buyer accepted the figures but, presumably because of a lack of business knowledge, used an unreasonable cost of capital of 30% to seemingly offset the optimistic forecast. The approach of "running the calefaction and the air conditioning at the same time" is inconvenient, inconducive, and disrupts the negotiation.

Dealing with illogical values of the EMBI+

Sometimes, in any emerging country, when investors doubt the capacity of a country to pay their obligations, bond prices start to fall, and the yield increases. While the emerging country has its public finance in equilibrium and international reserves present acceptable levels, the yield curve is upward-sloping, which is its most common shape in normal circumstances. The EMBI+ spread usually fluctuates under 200/500bps under this scenario.

Table 12.5 shows the bond prices of an emerging country under different scenarios. Maturities go from one to 30 years and interest rates go from 2% (treasury bills 1-year maturity) to 6% for the 30-years bond maturity.

Low default risk scenario: Suppose an emerging country has enough international reserves to pay its obligations and can finance a lower fiscal imbalance. The yield curve is upward-sloping and indicates a good fit, as seen in Figure 12.5. The probability of default is too low. Supposing the US 30-year bond yield is 4%, the EMBI+ spread is 200 basis points, calculated by subtracting the risk-free rate from the emerging country's 30-year bond yield (6%–4%).

TABLE 12.4 Alternative capital asset pricing models

Model	Risk free rate	Market risk premium	Country risk premium	Main characteristics
Global CAPM	rf_G	$(rm_G - rf_G)\beta_G$	-	Global Index and global beta. The investor is integrated
ICAPM	rf_G	$(rm_G - rf_G)\beta_G + (FCRP)\beta$	-	Add to the Global CAPM a foreign currency risk premium.
Local CAPM	rf_L	$(rm_L - rf_L)\beta_L$	CRP	Use domestic inputs; it is proposed for segmented investors.
Practitioner CAPM	rf_G	$(rm_G - rf_G)\beta_L$	CRP	The country risk premium is considered separately avoiding duplication of risks.
Godfrey-Espinosa	rf_G	$(rm_{US} - rf)\frac{\sigma_L}{\sigma_{US}}(1 - R^2)$	CRP	Adjusted beta to avoid country risk double-counting
Goldman Sachs	rf_G	$(rm_G - rf)\beta_G \frac{\sigma_L}{\sigma_{US}}(1 - \rho_{SB})$	$CRP + r_{id}$	Replace the adjusted beta of Godfrey & Espinosa adjusting by correlation between local bond and T-Bond yields plus a premium due to the idiosyncratic risk of the target company.
Damodaran	rf_G	$(rm_G - rf_G)\beta_L$	$CRP \times \gamma$	Proposes a firm-specific factor to country risk ranging from zero to one.
Salomon Smith Barney	rf_G	$(rm_G - rf_G)\beta_G$	$CRP(\frac{\gamma_1 + \gamma_2 + \gamma_3}{30})$	The exposure to country risk is adjusted by three factors (access to capital market, political risk, and the proportion that local investments have on the firm total assets.

TABLE 12.5 Theoretical bond prices for different default risk scenarios

Maturity (years)	Coupon (%)	Low	Moderate	High	Default
1	0	−98	−94	−90	−25
2	2.75	−100	−91	−85	−25
3	3.25	−100	−88	−80	−25
4	3.75	−100	−85	−78	−25
5	4.10	−100	−83	−74	−25
7	4.75	−100	−79	−71	−25
9	5.00	−100	−77	−66	−25
10	5.25	−100	−75	−67	−25
12	5.40	−100	−73	−64	−25
15	5.60	−100	−71	−59	−25
18	5.70	−100	−69	−58	−25
20	5.80	−100	−67	−57	−25
25	5.90	−100	−65	−56	−25
30	6.00	−100	−64	−55	−25

Moderate default risk scenario: Our emerging country is suddenly showing signs of concerns as its fiscal imbalance is increasing, and international reserves are decreasing. Figure 12.6 shows that the yield curve initiates a parallel shift, and all interest rates on all bonds increase by a similar number of basis points; although it continues showing an upward slope form, now the EMBI+ is around 550bps (9.5%–4%).

When the yield is useful to estimate the country risk premium

High default risk scenario: Suppose political, macroeconomic, and financial conditions change: the fiscal imbalance increases and international reserves decrease, raising questions about the country's ability to meet its obligations. When investors start selling their bonds, the interest rate rise and the yield curve flattens. In this scenario, bond prices reflect a probability of default. In developed countries, a flat yield curve indicates uncertainty about the future inflation rate and whether the Fed will raise the federal funds rate. In emerging markets, the interpretation is quite different: a flat yield curve reflects investors have concerns about whether the country will be able to pay its obligations. When the EMBI+ overpasses 600bps, short-term rates rise more rapidly than long-term rates, and the yield curve flattens. Under this scenario, the EMBI+ usually fluctuates around 750/900 basis points (for example, on September 6, 2024, the EMBI+ of Mexico was 770bps while the yield curve was flat at 11%). *In this scenario, the yield is no longer a reference for investors since it is the result that they price the bonds assuming a possible haircut.* The R^2 is neither informative. However, a flat yield curve is always transitional; it lasts a short time. You will notice in Figure 12.7 that the long end of the yield curve corresponds to a modified duration of 11 years. Remember that when the interest rises, the duration and the modified duration decrease.

Default/Debt restructuring scenario: In developed countries, the yield curve inverts if the economy goes into a recession or is at risk of entering a recession. Investors expect a reduction in the federal funds rate and the long-term interest rates drop. In an emerging country, an inverted yield curve means that investors expect the country will force a restructuring process of their obligations by imposing a similar haircut to all bonds. Assume that investors expect a two-year restructuring period and a 70% haircut. Taking into account a haircut of 70%, bond prices are calculated by investors using a high yield of around 10%, thus, the bond price is $30/(1.10)^2 = 24.79$. Figure 12.8 shows that the long-term bonds yield is around 25%, therefore, the EMBI+ is 2,100bps (25%–4%).

The yield of 25% is absolutely meaningless because only reflect the mathematical effect of compounding interest. For identical prices, the implicit interest rate that equals all bond prices to $24/$25 must be higher for the short-term bonds because they have few years of compound interest in comparison with a 30-year bond, whose yield is lower because it has more years of compound interest.

The EMBI+ loses significance when investors purchase bonds based on their default probability rather than looking their yields. This situation typically occurs when the EMBI+ is between 700/900bps and generally corresponds to a bond yields higher than 20%;

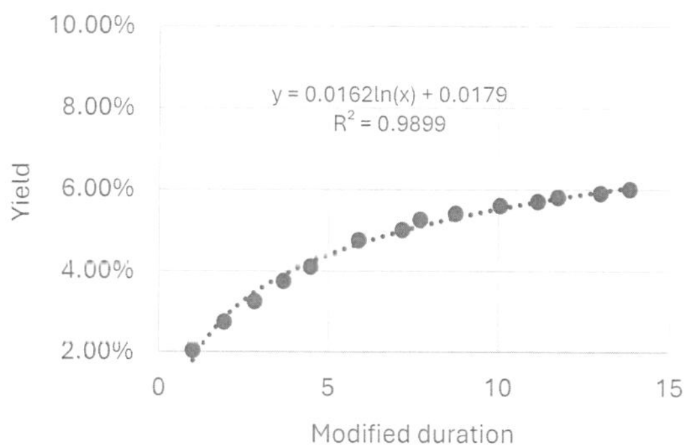

FIGURE 12.5 Yield curve under low default risk

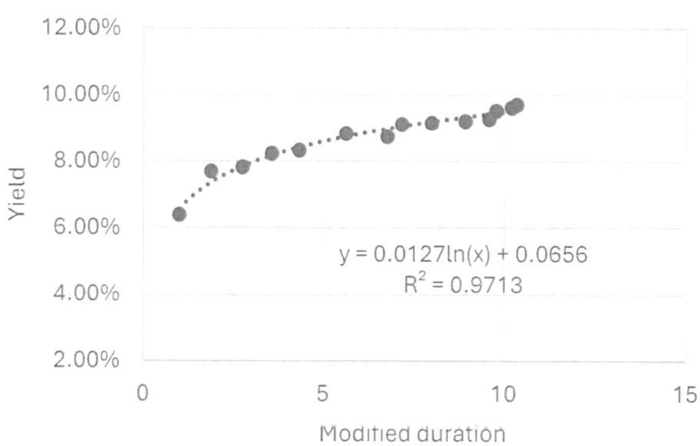

FIGURE 12.6 Yield curve under moderate default risk

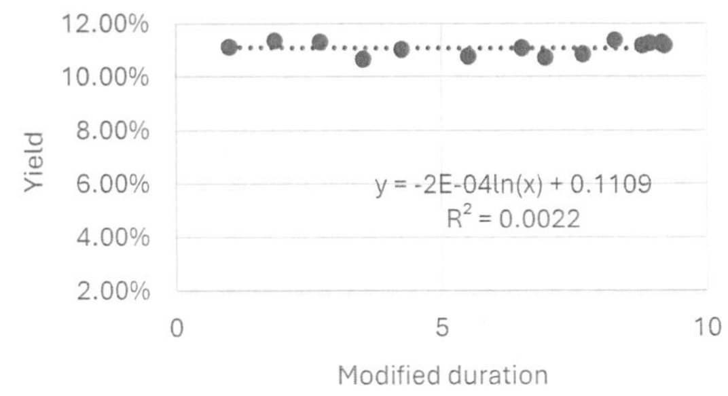

FIGURE 12.7 Yield curve under high default risk

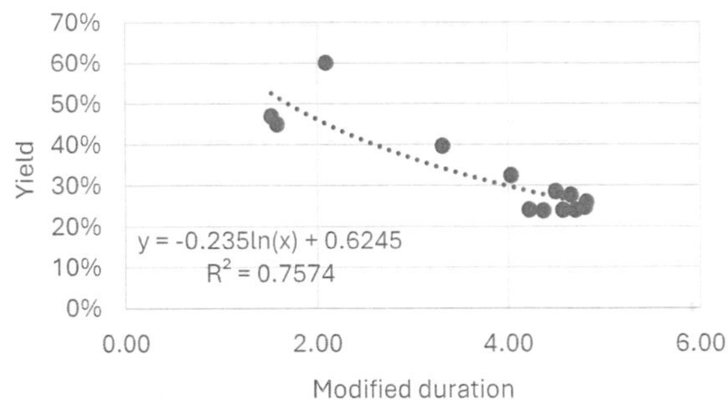

FIGURE 12.8 Yield curve with high default probability

however, investors will never earn 12% at maturity, whether or not the country defaults on its debt. Why? In case of default, all comments are unnecessary. If the debt is redeemed, bond prices will rise, and future cash flows will be reinvested at lower interest rates.[3]

Because the EMBI+ has no meaning when the yield curve is flat or inverted, practitioners who normally add the spot EMBI+ as a country risk premium in the cost of capital should carefully consider a cap or maximum value in these situations, around 600/800bps. In addition, we examine in a next section which is the correspondence with the weighted scenario analysis when nonsensical values of EMBI+ are included in the cost of capital.

Looking for the risk premium in corporate bonds yields

Another fact that tells us that a country's risk premium of more than 800/900bps could be illogical is the emerging corporate bond yields. Although there is a widespread popular belief that a company in an emerging country cannot get credit at a lower cost than the government, high country risk is not necessarily reflected in the bond yields of emerging countries. Figure 12.9 depicts that Argentinean corporate bond yields were about 10% in July 2024, when the Argentinean EMBI+ was near 1,500bps. The country risk premium reflects (essentially) the default risk, but this does not mean that a company that operates in an emerging country will default on its bonds. In summary, "good CFOs, bad politicians".

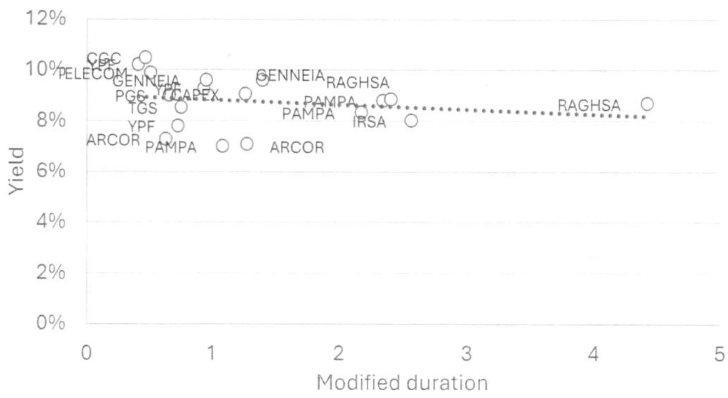

FIGURE 12.9 Yield of Argentinean corporate bonds in July 2024

Country risk premium using probability-weighted cash flows

An alternative to including the country risk premium in the cost of capital is scenario analysis, where analysts try to forecast several possible scenarios for the economy and the industry (e.g., pessimistic, optimistic, and more likely) and then assign probabilities for each scenario. Valuing in emerging markets, we recommend starting by considering the different ways that the business could be affected as a consequence of a unilateral action of the government.

In fact, there is a great debate within the financial community on how, where and when to include country risk factors in the project appraisal process. There has been much research on the subject of the equivalence of the free cash flows adjustments versus discount rates adjustments in discounted cash flow (DCF) models (James and Koller, 2000; Harvey, 2005; Goedhart and Haden, 2003; Brealey et al., 2004).

The inclusion of the country risk using scenario analysis has defendants. Copeland, Koller, & Murrin (2000) suggested that the country risk can be considered constructing company-specific and industry scenarios aligned with macroeconomic scenarios: "we find that having managers discuss these explicit risks and their effect on cash flow provides more insights for managers than a black box". While managers can better plan to mitigate these risks by identifying specific factors that have a large impact on value, not all them can be including in a scenario.

TABLE 12.6 Weighted average country risk premium

Markets	Weights	EMBI+ Dec 04	WACRP (bps)
Latin America	64.70%	460	298
Rest of the world	26.00%	104	27
China	2.50%	57	1
Short-term markets	5.40%	225	12
Potential markets	1.40%	188.6	3
Total			341

TABLE 12.7 Pessimistic scenario: Haircut of 50% on the free cash flow in thousands of US dollars

	Probability	Dec 05	Dec 06	Dec 07	Dec 08	Dec 09	Dec 10	Dec 11	Dec 12	Dec 13	Dec 14
Most likely	60%	5,995	9,297	10,855	12,678	13,279	14,609	15,806	16,863	18,162	304,979
Distressed business	40%	2,998	4,648	5,428	6,339	6,639	7,305	7,903	8,431	9,081	152,489
Expected FCF		4,796	7,437	8,684	10,142	10,623	11,687	12,645	13,490	14,529	243,983
Cost of capital	10.07%										
Firm value	$149,382.28										

Many years ago, we were hired to determine the fair value of "Bio", a biotechnological company in Argentina. Since Argentina defaulted on its obligations, the EMBI+ fluctuated around 5,000 basis points. Because the company has no debt, we estimate an unlevered cost of capital of 10.07% before counting the market risk premium. We forecast the FCF for ten years and calculate the terminal value using a long-term growth rate of 3%. Since it exports 80% of its products to 35 countries, the company's revenue was primarily in dollars. The Government had not introduced export barriers, so its exposure to currency was low. Even more, a sharp devaluation, one of the components of country risk, may operate asymmetrically. As Bio sells its products to other countries that are considered risky, we calculate a weighted average country risk premium (WACRP), using the EMBI+ calculated by JP Morgan and assigning different weights to each country based on the mix of export revenue. Table 12.6 displays the EMBI+ in the third column and the weighted average country risk premium in the fourth column.

Next, we performed two analyses:

1. Scenario analysis using probability-weighted cash flows without computing a country risk premium, considering a 50% haircut on the most likely free cash flow with a 40% chance because of adverse government regulations such as currency controls. We call this pessimistic scenario as "distressed business".
2. Adding a country risk premium in the cost of capital to obtain the identical value of 1.

To obtain an identical value of US$149,382.28 in the pessimistic scenario, an equivalent country risk premium of 3.09% is solved by iteration, leading to a cost of capital of 13.16%. Interestingly, it was similar to the to the weighted average country risk premium of 3.41% that we had previously calculated.

Equivalent country risk premium	3.09%
Cost of capital	13.16%
Firm value	$149,382.28

Some analysts who favor using one of the CAPM-adjusted models could achieve considerably different results. For example, if we had applied the Godfrey-Espinoza model, using the observed volatilities of MERVAL and S&P500 returns, and the R^2 over the January 1995–December 2001 period, the cost of capital would be:

$$r = 4.67\% + 5.75\%\frac{0.45}{0.13}(1-0.24) + 3.41\% = 27.91\%$$

Given that most multinational biotechnological companies at the time had a WACC of 12/13%, this figure seems unreasonable.

Implied probabilities if we add a country risk premium of 1,000bps: We previously commented that it did not make sense to consider more than 600/800 basis points because, beyond that limit, the yield is not a reference for the investors since it has no economic sense. In order to see the illogical probabilities that result from a nonsensical country risk premium, we first calculate the business value by adding a

TABLE 12.8 Implied probabilities with a CRP of 1,000bps in thousands of US dollars

	Probability	Dec 05	Dec 06	Dec 07	Dec 08	Dec 09	Dec 10	Dec 11	Dec 12	Dec 13	Dec 14
Most likely	1.51%	5.995	9.297	10.855	12.678	13.279	14.609	15.806	16.863	18.162	304.979
Distressed business	98.49%	2.998	4.648	5.428	6.339	6.639	7.305	7.903	8.431	9.081	152.489
Expected FCF		3.043	4.719	5.510	6.435	6.740	7.415	8.022	8.559	9.218	154.796
Cost of capital	10.07%										
Firm value	$94.775,93	--> Obtained by iteration									

country risk premium of 1,000 basis points to the cost of capital, and then we solve the implied probabilities using scenario analysis to arrive at the same business value.

Country risk premium	10.00%
Cost of capital	20.07%
Firm value	$94,775.93

The probability for the pessimistic scenario should be 98.49% in order to get the same value! This indicates that including the 1,000bps of country risk premium did not make sense. It's interesting how Copeland, Koller, & Murrin (2000) describe the results of valuing Pão de Açúcar, a Brazilian retail grocery chain, after assessing three macroeconomic scenarios provided by Merrill Lynch:

> The resulting value is 1,207 to 1,288 million Reais. The market value at the time of the valuation was 1,171 million Reais. If we use the base-case cash flows with Brazil's country-risk premium, excluding credit risk, at the time of the valuation (September 1998) of 7.8%, we find a value of 260 million Reais, far below the market value. If, however, we use a long-term perspective on Brazil's country risk excluding credit risk of 2%, the value is a more reasonable 1,044 million Reais.
>
> (p. 385)

A country risk premium of 780 basis points (as in the case of Pão de Açúcar) in the cost of capital leads to an illogical value (or a meaningless pessimistic probability using scenario analysis to obtain the same value).[4] When CRP is around 400/500 basis points, scenario analysis may lead to an equivalent premium in the cost of capital near the current CRP of 700/800bps. Perhaps for this reason and its cost/benefit relationship, practitioners usually add the spot EMBI+ in these circumstances.

Both approaches have pros and cons. If you prefer to include the CRP in the cost of capital, remember that over 700/800bps, the yield is meaningless, simply because the investor no longer uses it as a reference. Harvey (2005) observed that, in addition to choose the model that includes the country risk into the cost of capital, the term structure of country risk must be considered in project evaluation. Risk levels rise during and after the crisis; however, Erb, Harvey, & Viskanta (1996) found evidence of mean reversion in country risk ratings. This suggests that it would be inappropriate to use the current risk to evaluate cash flows for, say, ten years of a project life.

The scenario analysis forces our mind to think in possible events that can affect the business return and assign them subjective probabilities. However, it will never account for every possible outcome (who in their right mind would conceive that a government forbid the export of cheese?).

In conclusion, there is still no definitive answer. While adding country risk to the cost of capital is like a black box, scenario analysis cannot deal with all possibilities. However, comparing the results of one method to another generally provides a more comprehensive perspective.

Box 12.1 The case of LCG of Chihuahua, Mexico

In 2011 we appraised a small, modern milk-processing Mexican company in the state of Chihuahua, which was the only company in Mexico dedicated entirely to social programs. The company has historically provided milk for social programs in several Mexican states, like Chihuahua, Veracruz, Nuevo Leon, Durango, Puebla, San Luis Potosi, Sinaloa, Zacatecas, and Oaxaca. The EMBI+ of Mexico was 200bps at the time, which included as a premium in the cost of capital, resulting in an equity cost of capital of 11.52%.

During discussions with LCG's CEO, we discovered that the EMBI+ was not a good measure of the risk supported by the business because the majority of its revenues came from a sale to one of the aforementioned Mexican states, which was traditionally considered credit high-risk. Furthermore, Bruno recently recommended the board against making a significant transaction to that state due to the high likelihood of default (which ultimately occur). Ex ante, you would undoubtedly believe that it is preferable to apply the scenario technique in this situation instead of adding a premium to the cost of capital, and assign a high probability to the default scenario, which would greatly reduce the company's value, but be clear that this does not solve the default.

Hidden country risk factors

There may occasionally be hidden risks or risks that are impossible to quantify. Even when the senior management procures to secure returns through legal contracts, experience shows that politicians are always able to circumvent them through indirect actions other than changing laws. Henisz & Zelner (2010) describe how the US-based AES Corporation acquired the Georgian electricity distribution company Telasi in 1998. Attorneys allegedly created a set of guarantees that supposedly allowed AES-Telasi to pass the politician risks and other risks on to Georgian consumers. However, due to the government's inaction to cut the supply to nonpaying industrial consumers, to supply fuel to AES-Telasi, and imposition of taxes on electricity, AES's return deteriorated. The result was that AES's "guaranteed" 20% return became a shareholder loss of US$300 million.

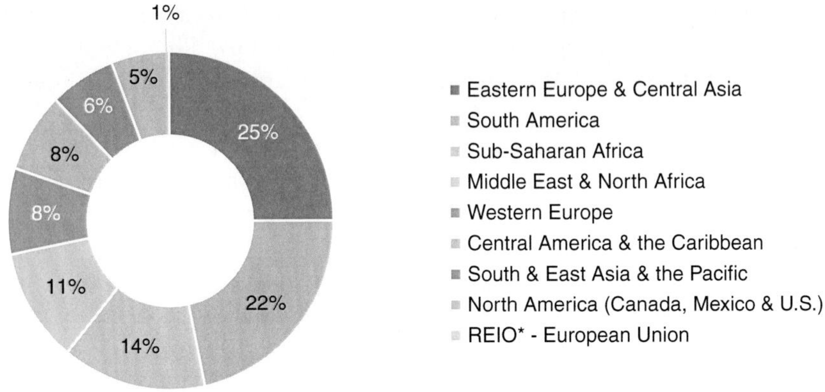

* A REIO may be a party to a proceeding under the 2022 ICSID Additional Facility Rules and Regulations or under the 2022 ICSID Mediation Rules and Regulations

FIGURE 12.10 Distribution of all ICSID cases registered by state party or Regional Economic Integration Organization (REIO) involved. Statistics Issue 2024-2

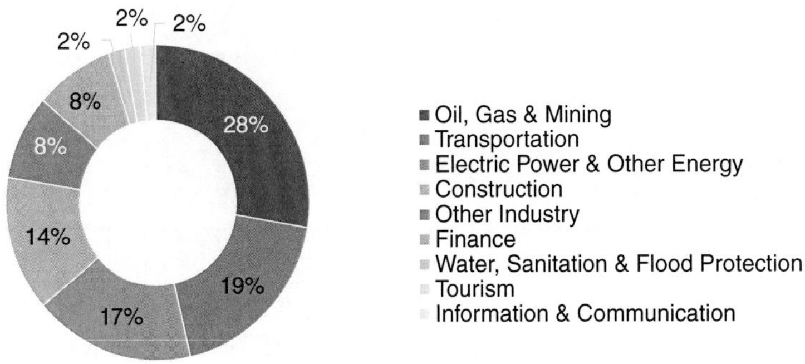

FIGURE 12.11 Distribution by economic sectors involved in ICSID cases 2023-2

When the Argentine Government devalued the peso currency in December 2001, it froze the utility rates for several years to compensate the price increase. Other actions that governments could take include limitations to importations, forbid the exportation of primary products to increase its internal supply or deny the sale of foreign currency to pay importations or dividends. Legal disputes are typically the result of these actions. Regarding legal conflicts involving emerging countries, you can consult the website of The International Centre for Settlement of Investment Disputes (ICSID). Figures 12.10 and 12.11 show the distribution of all ICSID cases registered by the state party and by the economic sectors involved.

How does country risk affect the market value?

We performed a study to explain the ADR's monthly returns of companies of Argentina (13 companies), Brazil (24 companies), and Mexico (18 companies) using a multifactor model that uses three regressors: the stock market return, represented by the S&P500, the country risk premium represented by the EMBI+ and the real exchange rate (RER). For the case of companies in the oil and steel industry, we add the WTI (West Texas Intermediate) return and the HRC steel return, respectively. There is an interrelationship between steel and the oil industry since the former requires large amounts of energy, while the extraction and transportation of hydrocarbons requires steel. Returns were calculated in delta-log form from December 2009 to May 2023 (163 observations). This study is performed and updated every year in my course on econometrics for finance, and Tables 12.9, 12.10, and 12.11 report only the main findings. ★, ★★, and ★★★ denotes significance at the 10%, 5%, and 1% level, respectively. A similar study with ten emerging countries, although with fewer companies in each sample, was carried out by Abuaf (2011) where he states that the ADR returns in most emerging countries are positively related to the S&P500 and negatively to CDS spreads.

In the case of Argentina, only Mercado Libre (MELI) and TENARIS (TS) were sensitive to the SP500 factor. Concerning the CRP factor, it seems that companies with fewer operations in Argentina are less sensitive to the country risk, as in the case of Mercado Libre, which has only 23.75% of its operations in Argentina, 52.77% in Brazil, and the rest of its revenues come from eight countries. Mercado Libre was the only company not affected by the country risk and seems to support the vision that it is firms, not countries or markets that are emerging. TENARIS also has revenues that are well diversified between five countries: Argentina, Brazil, Mexico, Colombia, and EE.UU. TERNIUM (TX), IRSA, and YPF also have operations in other countries of America but are less diversified and are sensitive to the country's risk. This is consistent with Harvey (1995) who found that emerging market returns have a low correlation with developed country returns and are segmented instead of integrated into world capital markets.

TABLE 12.9 Summary statistics of Argentinean ADRs

Firm	Intercept	SP500	CRP	RER	WTI	HRC	F	Adj. R^2
TENARIS	−0.01**	0.62 ***	−0.06	0.03	0.51 ***		42.4	0.61
TERNIUM	−0.01	1.13 ***	−0.16 ***	−0.09		0.29 ***	25.59	0.43
YPF	0.00	0.28	−0.48 ***	−0.37 *	0.30 ***		21.03	0.33
MELI	0.00	1.57 ***	−0.05	−0.09			16.21	0.29
IRSA	0.00	0.54 **	−0.46 ***	−0.20			30.43	0.42
CRESUD	0.00	0.45 **	−0.50 ***	0.00			34.34	0.45
FRANCES	0.01	−0.15	−0.88***	−0.27			67.45	0.62
GALICIA	0.02	−0.00	−0.96 ***	−0.34 *			87.20	0.68
MACRO	0.01	−0.08	−0.86 ***	−0.43 **			60.20	0.65
PAMPA	0.01	−0.12	−0.57 ***	−0.66 ***			32.25	0.49
TELECOM	0.00	−0.07	−0.52 ***	−0.20			26.27	0.52
TGS	0.02	−0.16	−0.55 ***	−0.33 *			27.00	0.15
EDENOR	0.01	−0.05	−0.82 ***	−0.27			26.47	0.39

Brazil has nine companies that were sensitive to the SP500, and most were significant to the country's risk and the real exchange rate. Vale do Rio Doce (VALE), with 44.53% of its sales in Brazil, was significant to the country's risk at a 10% level. Petrobras (PBR) was significant only to the WTI factor at a 10% level.

In Mexico, most companies are sensitive to the SP500 and only a few companies are sensitive to the country risk, maybe due to many companies having diversified

TABLE 12.10 Summary statistics of Brazilian ADRs

Firm	Intercept	SP500	CRP	RER	WTI	HRC	F	Adj. R2
BRASKEM	−0.01	1.15 ***	0.08	−1.47 ***			26.69	0.44
BRF	−0.01	0.80 ***	−0.07	−0.97 ***			27.41	0.45
CBD	−0.01	0.54 ***	−0.18 **	−1.37 ***			44.84	0.58
EMBRAER	−0.00	0.63 ***	0.04	−0.77 ***			23.30	0.41
GERDAU	−0.01	0.70 ***	−0.33 ***	−0.81 ***	0.17 **		41.22	0.56
KLABIN	−0.00	0.75 ***	−0.19 **	−0.41 **			130.45	0.80
SID	−0.02	1.02 ***	−0.36 **	−1.24 ***			31.62	0.53
AMBEV	−0.00	0.34 **	−0.16 **	−0.94 ***			172.80	0.84
ULTRAPAR	0.00	0.43 **	−0.11	−1.29 ***			43.09	0.57
VALE	0	0.41 *	−0.18 *	−1.18 ***			27.68	0.45
BRADESCO	0.00	0.13	−0.32 ***	−1.53 ***			74.76	0.70
CIG	0	0.13	−0.28 ***	−1.53 ***			47.28	0.59
CIGc	0.00	0.23	−0.29 **	−1.37 ***			33.1	0.56
CYRELA	−0.00	−0.05	−0.41 ***	−1.62 ***			53.78	0.62
EBR	0.00	−0.15	−0.42 ***	−1.39 ***			27.42	0.50
ELP	0.00	−0.05	−0.25 ***	−1.36 ***			40.40	0.49
GAFISA	−0.04	0.00	−0.50 ***	−1.30 ***			36.86	0.57
GOL	−0.00	−0.13	−0.71 ***	−2.19 ***			52.07	0.56
ITUB	0.00	0.08	−0.26 ***	−1.53 ***			99.24	0.65
SBS	0.01	0.27	−0.42 ***	−0.96 ***			48.76	0.54
USNZY	−0.01	0.36	−0.55 ***	−0.98 ***		0.24 *	22.39	0.48
TIM	0.00	0.24	−0.19 **	−1.12 ***			42.04	0.56
VIV	−0.00	0.02	−0.09 *	−1.27 ***			55.29	0.63
PBR	0.00	0.50	0.26	−0.55	−0.20 *		24.27	0.50

TABLE 12.11 Summary statistics of Mexican ADRs

Firm	Intercept	SP500	CRP	RER	HRC	F	Adj. R2
ASR	0.01	0.57 ***	−0.02	−0.91 ***		37.77	0.53
CEMEX	−0.01	1.10 ***	−0.19 *	−0.88 ***		37.95	0.53
MXE	0.00	0.43 ***	−0.08 *	−1.14 ***		101.9	0.76
MXF	−0.00	0.36 ***	−0.13 **	−1.08 ***		142.4	0.72
OMAB	0.01	0.57 ***	−0.04	−1.19 ***		55,00	0.57
PUODY	0.01	0.51 ***	0.05	−1.05 ***		28.89	0.41
IPOAF	−0.01	0.82 ***	−0.15	−0.66 **		17.51	0.38
TELEVISA	−0.01	0.73 ***	−0.25 **	−0.56 **		39.45	0.49
AMOV	−0.00	0.32 **	−0.07	−0.96 ***		30.81	0.48
AMX	−0.00	0.36 **	−0.06	−1.00 ***		31.05	0.48
FMX	0.00	0.26 **	−0.15 **	−0.59 ***		36.35	0.52
PAC	0.01	0.42 **	−0.09	−0.93 ***		55.26	0.57
IBA	0.00	0.34 **	−0.01	−0.74 ***		19.12	0.31
GBOOY	0.01	0.21	−0.21 **	−1.45 ***		60.46	0.65
BIMBO	0.01	0.21	−0.10	−0.91 ***		20.67	0.38
FEMSA	0.00	0.27 *	−0.10	−0.81 ***		23.93	0.42
FNLPF	0.00	0.23	0.02	−0.64		5.93	0.13
WMMVY	0.00	0.26 *	−0.08	−0.90 ***		35.8	0.46
SIMECB	0.01	−0.31	−0.42 ***	−0.35	0,24 ***	16.54	0.37

operations in other countries as the case of America Movil (AMOV) (54.79%), CEMEX 22.45%, BIMBO 45.87%, Industrias Penoles (IPOAF) 40.4%, FEMSA 30.77%, Walmart 50% and Fomento Mexicano (FMX) 44.83%.

Concluding thoughts

Measuring country risk is a challenge in emerging countries. Although risk providers can give a good description of risk factors that is certainly useful, we need numbers, measures, or a single number to use in a valuation. We still do not have a scientific model to compute the country's risk, but are aware that it is not fiction; as a result, some approaches have been proposed. The most popular consist in including a premium in the cost of capital; its simplicity makes it widely used by practitioners. The other is scenario analysis, which permits to consider several risk factors in a scenario-weighted probability. However, while we can analyze and asses some risk factors such as expropriation, the effect of a devaluation, and its effect on the business performance, not all risks are susceptible to be modeled. If you are comfortable adding a country risk premium in the cost of capital, remember that EMBI+ values around 700/800bps may give illogical values; if you prefer scenario analysis, be aware to build reasonable assumptions and ask yourself about their quality and their impact on the cash flows implied. A back-and-forth between the two approaches (adjusted discount rate and scenario analysis) can help detect inconsistencies.

Short questions and problems

1. What is the difference between an integrated and a segmented investor?
2. What is the relation between the EMBI spread, CDS, risk factors, and rating?
3. An appraiser has to estimate the cost of equity capital of a firm that has all its operations in an emerging country, and uses the following model:

$$r = rf + (rm - rf)\frac{\sigma_L}{\sigma_{US}} + CRP$$

   Where rf is the US-T bond return, rm-rf represents the American market risk premium, σ_L represents the standard deviation of returns in the local market measured in dollars, σ_{US} the standard deviation of returns in the US equity market, and CRP the country risk premium. What is the appraiser's error?
4. Suppose that 40% of the stock market volatility of an emerging country can be explained by the EMBI+, and that the correlation coefficient between the stock market index and the risk-free bond yields used to calculate the EMBI+ is 0.30. rf = 4%, rm-rf = 5%, $\sigma_L = 30\%$, $\sigma_{US} = 20\%$. Calculate the cost of capital using the Godfrey-Espinosa and Goldman Sachs models and explain the difference.
5. Suppose you are valuing a Mexican company. The EMBI spread for Mexico is 150bps, the risk-free rate is 4%, the market risk premium is 5%, and beta is 0.5. You apply the practitioner model, adding a country risk premium to the cost of equity. Therefore, ke = 4%+5%x0.5+1.50% = 8%. A manager says this number is illogical since the EMBI spread does not reflect the risk the company faces, because their revenues come from other states that have previously defaulted their obligations and are considered risky. Which model do you suggest to estimate the country risk exposure?
6. Calculate the cost of equity capital of XX using the Godfrey-Espinosa and practitioner models. rf = 5%, rm-rf = 6%, β = 1.2, EMBI+ = 500bps, $\sigma_L/\sigma_{US} = 2$; $R^2 = 0.40$.
7. Explain the differences between the "adjusted beta" in the Godfrey-Espinosa model and the CAPM beta.
8. John. XX, a financial analyst, uses the following model to estimate the cost of capital in an emerging country: $r = rf_L + (rm_L - rf_L)\beta + CRP$. Where is the pitfall of John's model?
9. The government of an emerging country has granted the concession to operate the toll of one of the major highways to XX Corp for five years. However, two potential risks were identified by senior management. First, in the past, the government had implemented price controls for some goods and services, and tolls were not the exception. The probability that the government will impose

price controls is 40%, which would result in a 35% free cash flow's reduction. Second, there is a risk of contract cancellation since the experience indicates a probability of 25% cancellation from the fifth year without compensation, which would obligate XX Corp. to enter into a dispute at the CIADI. The cost of capital is 12% without considering any premium for country risk, while the EMBI+ is 300bps. The initial outlay is 90M, and the expected free cash flow is 20M per year for ten years without terminal value. Calculate the NPV of the business considering the following alternatives: a) including the EMBI+ in the cost of capital b) using weighted-probabilities scenarios (40% for the haircut, 25% for an expropriation scenario, and 35% for the free cash flow without any haircut nor expropriation.

10. Suppose XX Corp. is already operating the toll business. However, the government wants to freeze the toll prices. The probability of contract cancellation is higher, and senior management estimates an80% chance of recovering US$100 million in ten years if a claim is initiated at the CIADI right now. Assuming that the required return to calculate the present value of this sum is 15%, would you decide to invest in the business? Which would be the required return that makes the NPV = 0 considering the NPV obtained in exercise 9?
11. XXX is a motorcycle sales company settled in an emerging country. The initial outlay is 40M, and the expected free cash flow is 10M during ten years without any salvage or terminal value. The cost of capital for a similar business is 12% without considering any premium for the country risk, while the EMBI+ is 300bps. The senior management has identified three potential scenarios:

    a) An optimistic scenario. The expected free cash flow is 12M during ten years (probability = 10%).
    b) A sharp devaluation. It would generate a strong recession, causing a haircut on the free cash flow of 50% for the first two years of the projection. From year three to year five, the expected free cash flow is 6M, and from year six to year 10 is 10M per year (probability = 60%).
    c) Motorcycle imports are subject to government restrictions. It would impact the expected sales, causing a haircut on the free cash flow of 40% (probability = 30%).

    Calculate the NPV of the business including the EMBI+ in the cost of capital and using scenario analysis with weighted probabilities.

12. The Godfrey & Espinosa model to estimate the cost of equity capital is

$$r = rf + (rm_{US} - rf)\frac{\sigma_{r_L}}{\sigma_{r_{US}}}(1 - R^2) + CRP$$

    a) If $R^2 = 0$, what does it mean, and what is the cost of equity?
    b) If $R^2 = 1$, what does it mean, and what is the cost of equity?

Notes

1 The stock market volatility of 40% represents an approximate average of the stock market risk in emerging countries, not the bond market.

2 Notice that $R^2 = \rho^2_{r,CRP}$

3 In search of more patterns, the EMBI+ fluctuates between 200 and 700bps when the CDS yield curve is positive, and over 1,000bps when is inverted.
4 Sometimes, the implied probability for the pessimistic scenario could be higher than 100%.

References

Abuaf, N. (2011). Valuing Emerging Market Equities: The Empirical Evidence. *Journal of Applied Corporate Finance, 27*, 77–88.

Banco Central Chile (2024). Available at https://si3.bcentral.cl/Siete/ES/Siete/Cuadro/CAP_DYB/MN_EI11/EI_EMBI/637184958408281857?cbFechaInicio=2024&cbFechaTermino=024&cbFrecuencia=MONTHLY&cbCalculo=NONE&cbFechaBase=

Brealey, R.A., *et al.* (2004) Fundamentals of Corporate Finance, McGraw-Hill/Irwin.

Bruner, R. F., Conroy, R. M., Estrada, J., Kritzman, M., & Li, W. (2002). Introduction to Valuation in Emerging Markets. *Emerging Markets Review*, 310–324.

Copeland, T., Koller, T., & Murrin, J. (2000). *Valuation: Measuring and Managing the Value of Companies*, 3rd edition. New York: Wiley.

Damodaran, A. (2003). *Measuring Company Exposure to Country Risk: Theory and Practice.*

Damodaran, A. (2012). *Investment Valuation Tools and Techniques for Determining the Value of Any Asset*, 3rd edition. New York: John Wiley & Sons.

Erb, C., Harvey, C., & Viskanta, T. (1995). Country Risk and Global Equity Selection. *The Journal of Portfolio Management*, Winter, 74–83.

Erb, C., Harvey, C., & Viskanta, T. (1996). Expected Returns and Volatility in 135 Countries. *Portfolio Management, 46(58)*.

Fama, E. (1984). Forward and Spot Exchange Rates. *Journal of Monetary Economics, 14*, 319–338.

Godfrey, S., & Espinosa, R. (1996). A Practical Approach to Calculating Costs of Equity for Investment in Emerging Markets. *Journal of Applied Corporate Finance*, Fall, 80–89.

Harvey, C. (1995). Predictable Risk and Returns in Emerging Markets. *The Review of Financial Studies, 8(3)*, 773–816.

Harvey, C. (2005, October). Available at https://people.duke.edu/~charvey/Teaching/BA456_2006/Harvey_12_ways_to.pdf

Henisz, W., & Zelner, B. (2010). The Hidden Risks in Emerging Markets. *Harvard Business Review.*

Mariscal, J., & Hargis, K. (1999). A Long-Term Perspective on Short-Term Risk. Goldman Sachs Portfolio Strategy, October 26, pp. 1–23.

O'Brien, T. J. (1999). The Global CAPM and a Firm's Cost of Capital in Different Currencies. *Journal of Applied Corporate Finance, 12*, 73–79.

Pereiro, L. (2001). The Valuation of Closely-Held Companies in Latin America. *Emerging Markets Review*, December, 330–370.

Pereiro, L. (2006). The Practice of Investment Valuation in Emerging Markets: Evidence from Argentina. *Journal of Multinational Financial Management, 16(2)*, 160–183.

Rodriguez, I. M., Dandapani, K., & Lawrence, E. R. (2019). Measuring Sovereign Risk: Are CDS Spreads Better than Sovereign Credit Ratings? *Financial Management, 48(1)*, 229–256.

Schramm, R., & Wang, H. N. (1999). Measuring the cost of capital in an international CAPM. *Journal of Applied Corporate Finance 12*, 63–72.

Stulz, R. (1999). Globalization of Equity Markets and the Cost of Capital. Dice Center Working Paper 99-1.

Sy, A. (2001). Emerging Market Bond Spreads and sovereign Credit Ratings: Reconciling Market Views with Economic Fundamentals. IMF Working Paper, 3–23.

The ICSID Caseload: Statistics. Issue 2024-2. (n.d.). Available at https://icsid.worldbank.org/sites/default/files/publications/2024-2%20ENG%20-%20The%20ICSID%20Caseload%20Statistics%20%28Issue%202024-2%29.pdf

CHAPTER

13

Currency risk in emerging and international equity markets

Introduction

When valuing international equities or business in an emerging market, analysts face an additional set of questions. Companies located in other countries generate sales, expenses, and cash flows in domestic currency, and these currencies have gone through periods of depreciation/appreciation. Therefore, the obvious question when considering an investment is if there are considerable deviations to the purchasing power parity (PPP) or, to put in another way, whether the local currency is overvalued or undervalued. Acquiring a company when the local currency and the business value are overvalued, is not a good deal. A devaluation will eventually be imposed by the government, decreasing the expected cash flow and the business value expressed in dollars. Purchasing a business after a devaluation has the opposite effect because the asset's dollar value. Acquiring a business after a devaluation could be profitable since probably the assets are undervalued.

DOI: 10.4324/9781003628491-16

After reading this chapter, we will be able to:

- Forecast the forward exchange rate and financial projections in a foreign currency;
- Understand the equivalence of valuing a business in different currencies, assuming the fulfillment of the Interest Rate Parity and the Purchasing Power Parity Theory;
- Recognize how the real exchange rate affects a valuation.

Valuing a business in different currencies

Demonstrating the equivalence of valuing a company in different currencies has no importance per se. However, as we'll see, the model will help us to understand that certain relationships between interest rates and inflation rates must be maintained to reach a consistent valuation.

Reasons to perform the valuation in a strong currency

The appraiser in emerging markets must have important reasons for making the analysis using nominal FCF and cost of capital expressed in dollars.

1. The local currency is overvalued or undervalued. If the local currency is overvalued at the moment of the acquisition, there is a danger of a sudden and sharp devaluation, which would result in a lower future cash flow in dollars, at least for a few years until the pass-through process[1] is completed. On the other hand, investing immediately after a sharp devaluation may be a great opportunity because companies could be undervalued, and the later pass-through would result in a larger future cash flow measured in dollars.
2. Reports are required to be expressed in a strong currency. As the currency of emerging markets has observed a tendency towards depreciation and higher inflation rates than developed countries, senior management of a multinational is required to forecast the FCF in dollars, creating a consistent set of macroeconomic assumptions regarding exchange rate, domestic inflation rate, interest rates, and gross domestic product (GDP) growth. This compels the analysis to focus on an inextricably linked tryptic: inflation, exchange, and interest rates.
3. Higher inflation rate. Emerging countries usually have an inflation rate higher than developed. How should we include it to estimate the long-term growth rate and the terminal value? How should we consistently include it in the terminal value and the cost of capital?
4. All inputs of the cost of capital are (consistently) nominated in US dollars.
5. Risk-free rate: since there is no well-defined risk-free rate in emerging countries, practitioners prefer to use the expected return on US Treasury Bonds as a proxy.
6. Market risk premium: as the stock indexes series are generally shorter, the market risk premium in emerging countries is considered not representative of the local market risk premium.[2] Besides, an event in the stock market, such as a financial crisis or a boom, can considerably affect the geometric or arithmetic average return. For these reasons, practitioners usually use the American risk premium as a proxy.

7. Beta: beta is a coefficient not affected by the currency used in the analysis.
8. Country risk premium: if the appraiser prefers to include a country's risk premium in the cost of capital, frequently use the EMBI spread published by JP Morgan.

Selecting the right economic theories and assumptions

By definition, the currency used to forecast cash flows should not affect the DCF value. If the company value is US$100 million, it would be 434 million in Argentinean pesos; 79 million in euros, and so on (quotes from Reuters on 1/19/2011). However, the currency choice affects the inputs. To perform the valuation in dollars, it is preferable to forecast the expected cash flows in domestic currency to incorporate the senior management's forecasts of quantities and prices. Managers are familiar with this information, and most financial statements are more detailed in domestic currency. Once the free cash flow is forecasted in domestic currency, this must be expressed in dollars using the expected market exchange rate. As we'll see, if the interest rate parity (IRP) and the purchasing power parity (PPP) are expected to be fulfilled simultaneously, valuing in dollars or domestic currencies gives identical fair values. The key rule here is that the cash flows and the cost of capital must be expressed in the same currency. Therefore, we have two alternative methods to obtain a fair value for the company:

1. Firm value in foreign currency: estimate the cash flows and cost of capital in US dollars, as well as the DCF value in dollars.
2. Firm value in domestic currency: estimate the cash flows and cost of capital in domestic currency, as well as the DCF value in domestic currency. Afterward, this can be converted to dollars using the spot exchange rate.

However, each of these choices carries implications. While using the first approach we have to forecast the forward exchange rate, using the second approach we have to forecast the forward inflation rate in the emerging country. Although the currency used to forecast cash flows should not affect the value, establishing the correct assumptions and selecting the economic theories that provide rationale is required. The equivalence of valuing a business in domestic or foreign currency can be demonstrated using a DCF model, which assumes the simultaneous fulfillment of interest rate parity (IRP) and purchasing power parity (PPP) theories (Dumrauf, 2014; Dumrauf, 2015)

About the exchange rate quotes

An exchange rate is usually expressed as a currency pair, for example, USD/BRL – BRL is the abbreviation of Brazilian Real. The first currency that's listed in the pair (USD) always represents one unit of that currency, meaning 1 US$. However, because most examples we use in this chapter involves emerging markets where several units of domestic currency must be exchanged for one dollar, we will express the currency pair as D (domestic)/US$, because the exchange rate is simpler to understand when BRL/US$ = 6 rather than US$/BRL = 0.166.

Forecasting the forward exchange rate assuming the interest rate parity

IRP states a relationship between the interest rates and the currency exchange rates for the two countries. Under the absence of arbitrage opportunities, the interest rate differential is equivalent to the differential [3] between the spot and forward rates, so the IRP must hold for every period of t in equilibrium. To illustrate this for a single year:

$$\frac{F_t^{D/USD}}{S^{D/USD}} = \frac{1+i_t^D}{1+i_t^{USD}}. \qquad [13.1]$$

i_t^D = one period forward domestic interest rate,

i_t^{USD} = one period forward dollar interest rate,

$F_t^{D/USD}$ = forward exchange rate for one period forward.

Therefore, the forward exchange rate is:

$$F_t^{D/USD} = S^{D/USD}\frac{1+i_t^D}{1+i_t^{USD}}. \qquad [13.2]$$

The uncovered IRP refers to the condition where exposure to unanticipated changes in exchange rates is uninhibited. On the other hand, covered IRP refers to the condition where an investor uses a forward contract to eliminate the risks concerning the exchange rate. Since the forward contract reflects the differential between the interest rates, there is no opportunity for arbitrage.

The relative purchasing power parity theory and the domestic inflation rate

According to the law of one price, if there are no transaction costs, nor taxes and trade barriers for any good, then the prices of these goods should be the same at every country. For example, if a computer costs US$1,000 in the US and 5,000 reais in Brazil, the PPP exchange rate would be five reais for every US dollar, and so with re rest of all other goods. The relative PPP theory is formally stated in terms of inflation rates: the expectations theory of forward exchange rates maintains that the expected spot exchange rate t periods in the future equal the t-period forward rate, so the PPP must hold for every period of t in equilibrium:

$$\frac{F_t^{D/USD}}{S^{D/USD}} = \frac{1+\pi_t^D}{1+\pi_t^{\star}}. \qquad [13.3]$$

Therefore, the forward exchange rate for one period forward is:

$$F_t^{D/USD} = S^{D/USD}\frac{1+\pi_t^D}{1+\pi_t^{\star}}. \qquad [13.4]$$

IRP, coupled with PPP and the expectations theory of forward exchange rates, implies the international Fisher effect (Fisher, 1896). These relationships are mutually consistent, so both theories should be predicting the same forward exchange rate:

$$F_t^{D/USD} = S^{D/USD}\frac{1+i_t^D}{1+i_t^{USD}} = S^{D/USD}\frac{1+\pi_t^D}{1+\pi_t^{\star}}. \qquad [13.5]$$

Since the inflation rate fluctuates much less and is lower in developed countries than in developing countries, staying around 2.2% and 5.5%, analysts can assume the international inflation rate remains constant during the forecast period (Central

Intelligence Agency, 2012). Thus, analysts can obtain the expected domestic inflation rate from Equation 13.5 for one period forward:

$$\pi_t^D = \frac{F_t^{D/USD}}{S^{D/USD}}(1+\pi_t^*) - 1. \qquad [13.6]$$

π^D represents an implicit or expected inflation rate in the emerging country since it is solved using the equilibrium condition of the formula [13.3].

Regarding the empirical evidence on the IRP and PPP

IRP and PPP have been extensively researched since the 70s. The conventional view is that are appealing in theory but rejected empirically. Bansal and Dahlquist (2000) and Flood and Rose (2001) found evidence supporting UIP for emerging market currencies. After doing an overview, Taylor (2002) and Taylor and Taylor (2004) came to the conclusion that there is some degree of confidence in the PPP's long-term viability. Using bonds with maturities ranging from five to ten years, Chinn and Meredith (2004), Chinn (2006), and Zhang (2006) showed that yield differentials explain future currency movements. Cheung, Chinn, and Garcia (2005) found that UIP performs well in predicting exchange rate movements at long horizons relative to other structural models. Mehl and Cappiello (2009) found support in favor of uncovered interest rate parity for dollar rates vis-à-vis major mature economy currencies but far less against emerging market currencies. Skinner and Mason (2011) found that while covered IRP holds for large and small triple-A-rated economies, it does not hold for longer maturities for Brazil, Chile, Russia, and South Korea.

Box 13.1 Purchasing power parity in emerging markets

Figures 13.1 to 13.4 show the evolution of the nominal exchange rate and the theoretical PPP value for three emerging countries (Argentina, Brazil, and Mexico from December 1992 to December 2023. Although we can see deviations from the theoretical value suggested by the PPP, the exchange rate seems to converges to the theoretical PPP value after periods of appreciation/depreciation.

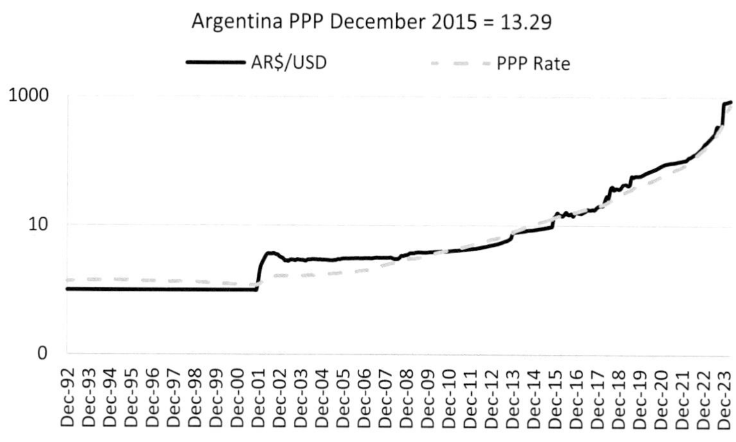

FIGURE 13.1 Argentina EX and theoretical PPP EX on the base December 2015 = 13.29

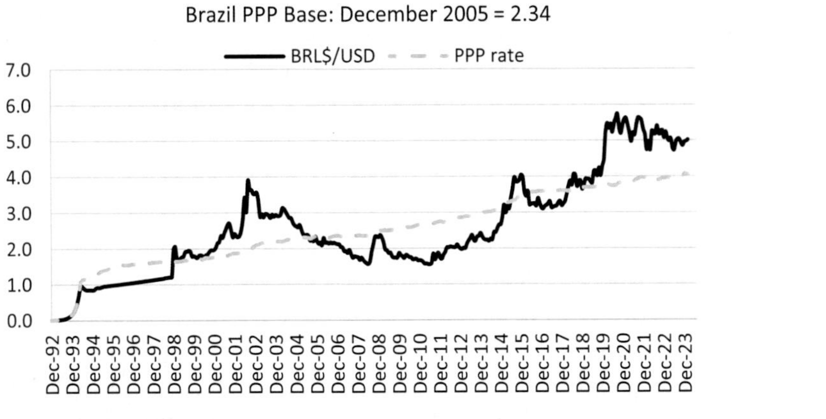

FIGURE 13.2 Brazil EX and theoretical PPP exchange rate on the base December 2005 = 2.34

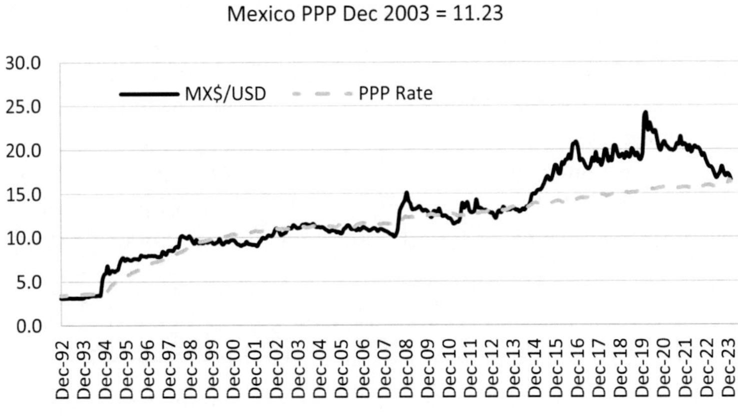

FIGURE 13.3 Mexico EX and theoretical PPP exchange rate

The equivalence of the DCF value using different currencies

Analysts can perform a valuation using the nominal FCF and WACC expressed in dollars to obtain the fair value of the business in dollars:

$$V^{USD} = \sum_{t=1}^{\infty} \frac{FCF_t^{USD}}{(1 + WACC_t^{USD})^t}. \quad [13.7]$$

Otherwise, analysts could perform the valuation using the nominal FCF and WACC expressed in domestic currency to obtain the fair value in domestic currency:

$$V^{D} = \sum_{t=1}^{\infty} \frac{FCF_t^{D}}{(1 + WACC_t^{D})^t}. \quad [13.8]$$

The fair value in domestic currency divided by the spot exchange rate $S^{D/USD}$ must be equal to the fair value in dollars:

$$V^{USD} = \frac{V^D}{S^{D/USD}}. \quad [13.9]$$

The inflation rate observed in emerging countries is higher than the international inflation rate observed in developed countries. Therefore, the WACC expressed in dollars must consider the inflation rate differential to obtain the discount factor expressed in domestic currency:

$$(1+WACC_t^D)=(1+WACC_t^{USD})\frac{(1+\pi_t^D)}{(1+\pi_t^{\star})}. \qquad [13.10]$$

π_t^D = t–period domestic inflation rate

$\pi_t^{\star}$ = t–period international inflation rates.

For the same reason, the long-term growth rate in an emerging country must consider the inflation rate differential adjustment[4]:

$$g^D=g^{\star}\frac{(1+\pi_T^D)}{(1+\pi_T^{\star})}. \qquad [13.11]$$

g^D = nominal long-term growth rate in the emerging country,
$g^{\star}$ = nominal long-term growth rate in the developed country,
π_T^D = last forecast period domestic inflation rate,
$\pi_T^{\star}$ = last forecast period international inflation rate.

Next, the terminal values in dollars and domestic currency are expressed as:

$$TV^{USD}=\frac{FCF_T^{USD}(1+g^{\star})}{WACC_T^{USD}-g^{\star}}. \qquad [13.12]$$

$$TV^D=\frac{FCF_T^D(1+g^D)}{WACC_T^D-g^D}. \qquad [13.13]$$

The forecasted FCF expressed in domestic currency is equal to the forecasted FCF in dollars multiplied by the forward foreign exchange rate:

$$FCF_t^D=FCF_t^{USD}F_t^{D/USD}. \qquad [13.14]$$

We now prove the equivalence of valuing a company in domestic or foreign currency. According to equation 13.9, the fair value in dollar equals the fair value in domestic currency divided by the spot exchange rate: $V^{USD}=\frac{V^D}{S^{D/USD}}$. The free cash flow in domestic currency, according to equation 13.4 is $F_t^{D/USD}=S^{D/USD}\frac{1+\pi_t^D}{1+\pi_t^{\star}}$, and the WACC expressed in domestic currency, according to equation 13.10 is $(1+WACC_t^D)=(1+WACC_t^{USD})\frac{(1+\pi_t^D)}{(1+\pi_t^{\star})}$.

Replacing equations 13.4, 13.9 and 13.10 in equation 13.8:

$$V^D=\sum_{t=1}^{\infty}\frac{FCF_t^D}{(1+WACC_t^D)^t}=\frac{V^{USD}}{S^{S/USD}}=\frac{1}{S^{S/USD}}\sum_{t=1}^{\infty}\frac{FCF_t^{USD}S^{D/USD}\frac{\left(1+\pi_t^D\right)^t}{\left(1+\pi_t^{\star}\right)^t}}{(1+WACC_t^{USD})^t\frac{\left(1+\pi_t^D\right)^t}{\left(1+\pi_t^{\star}\right)^t}}$$

$$=\sum_{t=1}^{\infty}\frac{FCF_t^{USD}}{(1+WACC_t^{USD})^t}=V^{USD}. \qquad [13.15]$$

The simultaneous fulfillment of IRP and PPP assumes that the interest rate differential equals the inflation rate differential, implying the fulfillment of Fisher's effect. Why the forward exchange rate is estimated using IRP rather than PPP? Because we can observe market's forward interest rates but not expected inflation rates. The process of obtaining forward interest rates to forecast the exchange rate using market bond data is explained in the next section. If both theories predict the same exchange rate, the real exchange rate (RER) can be subtracted from equation 13.4. In rearranging terms, if the PPP holds, the RER remains constant along the projection. To illustrate for one single year:

$$RER_0^{D/USD} = F_t^{D/USD} \frac{1+\pi_t^*}{1+\pi_t^D}. \qquad [13.16]$$

Forecasting the exchange rate using the sovereign bond yield spread

The equivalence stated by equation 13.15 assumes a flat yield curve, where the interest and inflation rates remain constant over the length of the forecast period. There are some corporate finance textbooks (Berk & DeMarzo, 2007; Brealey, Myers, & Marcus, 2008; Emery & Finnerty, 2007; Graham, Smart, & Megginson, 2010; Ross, Westerfield, & Jaffe, 2009; Brigham and Erdhardt, 2010; Damodaran, 2012) that use the IRP to forecast the exchange rate using interest rates across two countries, assuming a flat yield curve. However, a flat yield curve is transitional.

In emerging markets, even though forward exchange rates are not liquid or available beyond 12/18 months, emerging market borrowers are able to issue bonds in domestic and foreign currency. Bonds issued in domestic currency pay a higher return than dollar-denominated bonds; the premium reflects the expected depreciation of the domestic currency. To forecast the forward exchange rate, is more appropriate using the sovereign bond yield spread from the same issuer since the only risk difference between bonds nominated in domestic currency and dollars is the currency risk. Since the issuer and the jurisdiction are the same and differ solely in the currency, the yield spread reflects the market opinion about the forward exchange

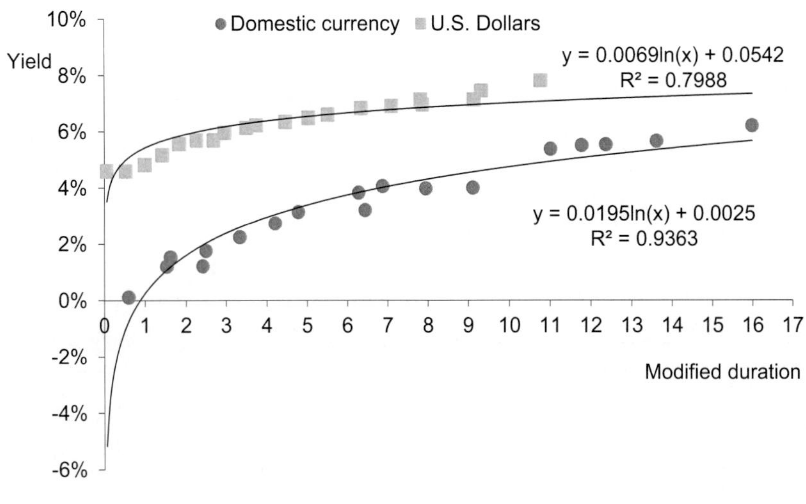

FIGURE 13.4 Yield curves for sovereign Mexican bonds

rate. Figure 13.4 shows yield curves for the Sovereign Mexican Bonds in Mexican pesos and American dollars in June 2011 (Source: Reuters). While there are several sophisticated techniques for constructing yield curves, these are beyond the scope of this paper. We obtain the best-fit curves by adjusting a logarithmic trend line to illustrate expected returns for sovereign bonds in domestic currency and dollars.

Notice that bonds nominated in domestic currency have higher yields than bonds nominated in dollars. Since the market requires a currency premium for the devaluation risk, the yield spread reflects the market opinion about the expected exchange rate. Analysts easily obtain the yield for a specific year using the yield curve equations. For example, to calculate the required return in domestic currency and dollars for one year from now:

$$i_1^D = 0.0542 + 0.0069\ln(1) = 5.42\%$$

$$i_1^{USD} = 0.0025 + 0.0195\ln(1) = 0.25\%$$

To obtain the yields for subsequent years, we only change the number of the year for which we want the forecast yield. For example, the expected yields for three years from now:

$$i_3^D = 0.0542 + 0.0069\ln(3) = 6.18\%$$

$$i_3^{USD} = 0.0025 + 0.0195\ln(3) = 2.39\%$$

Then, to forecast the forward exchange rate for a specific year, we solve for the forward interest rate f. Given the two-year spot rate, there could be a rate on a one-year instrument one year from now that will make the investor indifferent between two alternatives:

$$(1 + i_1^{USD})(1 + f_2^{USD}) = (1 + i_2^{USD})^2. \qquad [13.17]$$

Solving equation 13.17 for f_2^{USD} :

$$f_2^{USD} = \frac{(1 + i_2^{USD})^2}{(1 + i_1^{USD})} - 1. \qquad [13.18]$$

The expected exchange rate one year from now is calculated with the spot rates:

$$F_1^{D/USD} = S^{D/USD} \frac{(1 + i_1^D)}{(1 + i_1^{USD})}. \qquad [13.19]$$

To forecast the expected exchange rate for two years from now:

$$F_2^{D/USD} = S^{D/USD} \frac{(1 + i_1^D)(1 + f_2^D)}{(1 + i_1^{USD})(1 + f_2^{USD})}. \qquad [13.20]$$

Notice that this expression is equal to

$$F_2^{D/USD} = F_1^{D/USD} \frac{(1 + f_2^D)}{(1 + f_2^{USD})}. \qquad [13.21]$$

In general, to forecast the future exchange rate for a given year t:

$$F_t^{D/USD} = F_{t-1}^{D/USD} \frac{(1 + f_t^D)}{(1 + f_t^{USD})}. \qquad [13.22]$$

As the yield curve is upward sloping rather than flat, we must calculate the WACC for each period. For example, the WACC for the t-period will be equal to the WACC for the t-1 period plus the change in the interest rate observed in the yield curve:

$$WACC_t^{USD} = WACC_{t-1}^{USD} + (i_t^{USD} - i_{t-1}^{USD}). \quad [13.23]$$

TABLE 13.1 DCF equivalence with domestic and foreign currencies

	Yr 0	Yr 1	Yr 2	Yr 3	Yr 4	Yr 5	Yr 6	Yr 7	Yr 8	Yr 9	Yr 10
FCF ^{D}		100.00	108.54	117.04	125.69	134.56	143.71	153.17	162.98	173.16	183.72
Terminal value ^{D}											1,417.85
FCF ^{D}		100.00	108.54	117.04	125.69	134.56	143.71	153.17	162.98	173.16	1,601.57
FCF ^{USD}		8.11	8.52	8.96	9.41	9.89	10.39	10.91	11.46	12.04	12.65
Terminal value ^{USD}											97.64
FCF ^{USD}		8.11	8.52	8.96	9.41	9.89	10.39	10.91	11.46	12.04	110.29
$F^{D/USD}$	11.72	12.32	12.73	13.07	13.36	13.61	13.84	14.04	14.22	14.38	14.52
f^{D}		5.42%	6.38%	6.74%	6.97%	7.15%	7.29%	7.40%	7.50%	7.59%	7.67%
f^{USD}		0.25%	2.97%	3.99%	4.65%	5.15%	5.54%	5.87%	6.15%	6.39%	6.61%
p^{D}		7.26%	5.38%	4.70%	4.26%	3.94%	3.69%	3.48%	3.30%	3.15%	3.01%
p^{*}		2.00%	2.00%	2.00%	2.00%	2.00%	2.00%	2.00%	2.00%	2.00%	2.00%
Q		10.00	10.30	10.61	10.93	11.26	11.59	11.94	12.30	12.67	13.05
P		10.00	10.54	11.03	11.50	11.96	12.40	12.83	13.25	13.67	14.08
1 + $WACC^{USD}$		1.15	1.35	1.57	1.82	2.10	2.42	2.79	3.22	3.71	4.27
WACC disc. factor ^{USD}		0.87	0.74	0.64	0.55	0.48	0.41	0.36	0.31	0.27	0.23
PV cash flow USD	69.76	7.06	6.30	5.70	5.18	4.71	4.29	3.91	3.56	3.25	25.81
1 + $WACC^{D}$		1.21	1.47	1.75	2.07	2.44	2.86	3.34	3.90	4.55	5.30
WACC disc. Factor ^{D}		0.83	0.68	0.57	0.48	0.41	0.35	0.30	0.26	0.22	0.19
PV cash flow ^{D}	817.54	82.69	73.80	66.83	60.70	55.22	50.27	45.80	41.74	38.05	302.45
Real exchange rate	11.72	11.72	11.72	11.72	11.72	11.72	11.72	11.72	11.72	11.72	11.72

Model example

Foreign Investor Corp. is a multinational company considering an acquisition in México. Senior management is required to forecast the FCF in dollar amounts, designing a consistent set of macroeconomic assumptions regarding the exchange rate, the domestic inflation rate, the interest rates, and the growth rate:

1. The target acquisition's FCF is forecasted for ten years, assuming a real growth rate of 3% plus the domestic inflation rate, until the company reaches a steady state at the end of year 10.
2. The long-term growth rate is assumed to be 2% per year, plus the domestic inflation rate.
3. The spot exchange rate is $S^{D/USD} = 11.72.$, and the WACC expressed in dollars is 15%.

Table 13.1 shows the forecasted FCF in millions of domestic currency and US dollars, domestic and dollar interest rates, domestic and international inflation rates, and the forward exchange rate. The last row shows the real exchange rate (RER), which, as mentioned earlier, remains constant along the explicit forecast period, assuming the IRP and PPP hold.

Using equations 13.7, 13.8, and 13.9, these are the equivalence values:

$$V^{USD} = 69{,}76$$

$$V^{D} = 817.54$$

$$V^{USD} = \frac{817.54}{11{,}72} = 69.76$$

Summarizing, you must follow the following steps:

1. Forecast the FCF in domestic currency; this allows senior management to work with prices and quantities they deal with every day.
2. Using the IRP theory, forecast the forward exchange rate.

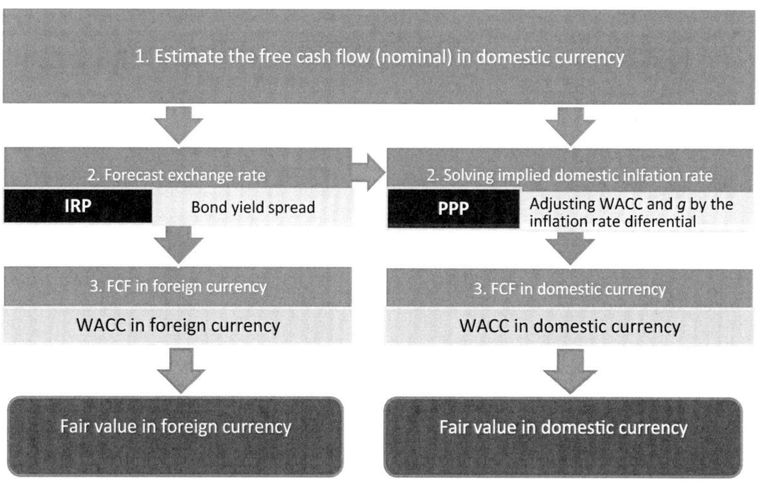

FIGURE 13.5 Steps of valuation in domestic and foreign currency

3. Convert the FCF expressed in domestic currency to dollars using the forward exchange rate and then calculate its present value using the cost of capital expressed in dollars.
4. The WACC in dollars and the nominal long-term growth rate observed in developed countries must be adjusted by the inflation differential rate in order to obtain the WACC and the long-term growth rate in domestic currency. To do this, you must first estimate the expected inflation rate in order to compute the inflation rate differential.

The model provides a framework to analyze the consistency of the inputs and projections. It can be extended to analyze different economic scenarios such as devaluation, different pass-through rates, and different real exchange rates. This analysis is valuable in emerging markets since the exchange rate has observed periods ranging from strong appreciation to periods of strong depreciation.

The real exchange rate momentum for acquisitions

A sudden devaluation in emerging markets may present an investment opportunity since it may be the best time to acquire a business. Argentina serves as an excellent example. Figure 13.6 shows the relationship between the real exchange rate[5] and GDP growth rate along four periods. The first period goes from 1979 to 1991, which is characterized by a strong depreciation of the peso and by a sharp decline int the GDP growth rate. Argentina pegged the peso to the dollar from 1992 to 2002, during which time the peso appreciated and the GDP increased for most of the year. The third period goes from 2003 to 2010. After a strong depreciation of 2002, the peso appreciated and GDP grew fast. The final time frame, which runs from 2011 to 2023, was marked by currency controls and a sudden devaluation in 2017. During this time, GDP growth grew about 0%. The stars represent the peso's most severe depreciation during those years.

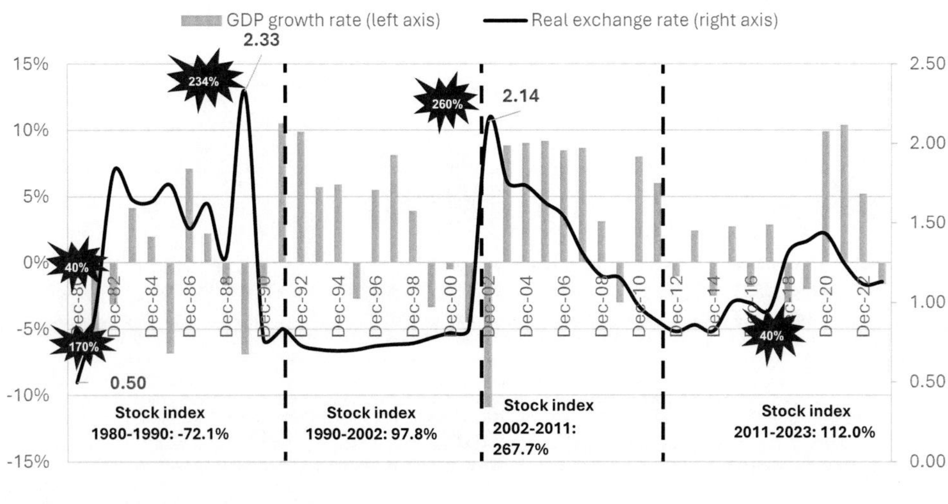

FIGURE 13.6 GDP growth rate, real exchange rate and stock index return

We can identify two well-defined processes within the 1979–2023 timeframe. A devaluation's impact on inflation and GDP growth rate is measured in the first, while the pass-through effect on the same variables is measured in the second. After a devaluation, GDP, real wages, and the inflation rate all decline. At this time, the stock market typically rises. The second and third periods were like this. Because the stock market usually anticipates the economic cycle, despite the Argentinean economy performs bad during the fourth period, the stock market grew 112%, in anticipation of the introduction of a new government. When the domestic currency appreciation is significant, a new devaluation takes place and the process begins again. Notice that in periods of peso appreciation the Argentinian GDP grew, and the stock market return increased.

We conducted a speculative experiment taking into account the 1980 to 2023 timeframe. As if we were an advisor standing at the beginning of each of the four periods described, we estimate the present value of a notional free cash flow of $100, growing at the expected inflation rate observed at that moment, plus a real growth rate of 3% over ten years without terminal value. We use a cost of capital of 15% for all periods and the free cash flow was forecasted in US dollars. For periods of peso appreciation, we assumed a gradual depreciation until reaching the real exchange rate of 1 on base December 2015 = 1 at the end of the ten-year projection. In contrast, if the peso was depreciated, we assumed a gradual appreciation until reaching the real exchange rate of 1 at the end of the ten-year projection. Then, we compare the expected present value with the present value calculated using the observed inflation rate, GDP growth rate, and exchange rate for this period. An investor who acquires a business before a sharp devaluation (such as in early 1981[6] or in 1998, faced a "Double Nelson" since the GDP dropped, cash flows in dollars were less than expected, and the PV ex-post was less than the PV ex-ante. If the acquisition was made at the beginning of 1991, or in 2002, following a sharp devaluation, the opposite occurred because the assets price was a bargain, and the subsequent pass-through improved the cash flow in dollars. The last period, from December

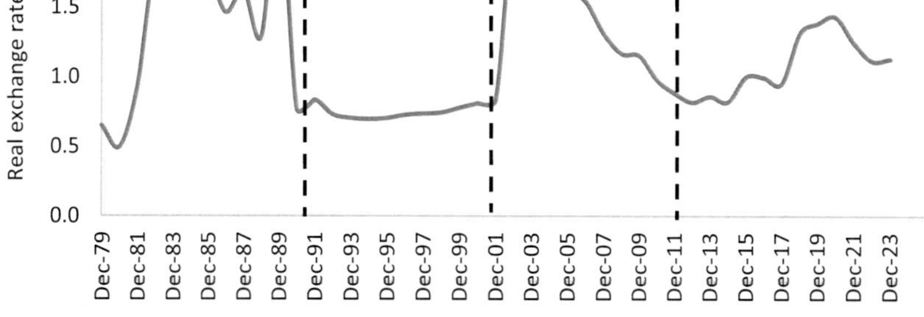

FIGURE 13.7 Differences between the present values of the expected and observed cash flow

2011 to December 2023, which was characterized by the peso depreciation and the fall of the GDP, show similar results to the first period.

Similar consequences result from a devaluation in other emerging markets. Glen (2002) analyzed the performance of 18 stock markets around 24 devaluation events. He found that devaluations had a negative impact, often followed by high interest rates and poor economic performance. Stock markets anticipate the devaluation and deliver negative returns (in both local and dollar terms) in the few months preceding a devaluation, though the trend reverses after this event.

Empirical evidence of currency effect on business value

It is a common belief among practitioners that unexpected changes in foreign exchange rates should affect the market value of some firms. Shapiro (1975) stated that factors affecting a multinational firm's exchange risk include the distribution of its sales between domestic and export markets, the amount of import competition it faces domestically, and the degree of substitutability between local and imported factors of production. The economic exposure to exchange rate changes can be interpreted as the regression coefficient of unexpected firm value changes on unexpected exchange rate changes (Adler & Dumas, 1984; Adler & Simon, 1986; Hodder, 1982; Abuaf & Jorion, 1990). Bartram and Bodnar (2007) suggested that the hedging behavior of firms could explain the lack of exposure.

Concerning the relationship between the exchange rate and stock returns, Bae, Kwon, & Li (2008) found that exchange rate changes had negative impact on the underlying share returns of ADRs. Abuaf (2011) recognizes the importance of deviations to the PPP for international investors when analyzing an investment in an emerging country and states that a significant overvaluation of the real exchange rate is correlated with a positive carry for the currency. Conversely, an overvaluation/undervaluation could end in a maxi depreciation/appreciation. However, he suggests that asymmetric currency expectations should be modeled in cash flows and does not include the real exchange rate as a factor in the model. Esqueda & Jackson (2012) examined how ADRs behaved throughout the currency crises in Argentina, Brazil, Chile, and Mexico and concluded that prices are determined by the underlying stock, exchange rates, and US index, in that order. We discussed and clarified the key findings of a multifactor model in Chapter 12, which uses the real exchange rate as one of the factors to explain the ADR's return in Argentina, Brazil, and Mexico. The real exchange rate was significant for 45 out of 55 companies, with the majority of companies in Brazil and Mexico are significant at the 1% level.

Concluding thoughts

Since the model we presented assumes the simultaneous fulfillment of IRP and PPP, the play instrumental roles in an arbitrage-free valuation to forecast the expected exchange and inflation rates. It provides a framework for valuation in emerging markets and for multinationals that analyze to acquire a business in another country. Managers should be interested in a model that helps them to analyze the effect of a sudden devaluation or appreciation of the domestic currency, exploring different economic scenarios and combinations of devaluation and pass-through rates. Appreciated currencies in emerging countries generally lead to sharp devaluations that generate a fall in the GDP and sales measured in domestic currency, affecting the business value.

Short questions and problems

1. IRP states that the variation in the exchange rate is equal to the differential between the...................interest rate and the.....................interest rate. Equivalently, it implies that the forward exchange rate equals the............... exchange rate multiplied by the interest rate................... PPP states that the change in the exchange rate is equal to the differential between the............... inflation rate and the...............inflation rate. If the forward exchange rate was estimated using the IRP, then the domestic inflation rate must be equal to the quotient.............. F_1/S_0 multiplied by 1 +.................inflation rate minus one.
2. If the Brazilian one-year treasury yield in reais is 11.13%, the Brazilian one-year treasury yield in dollars is 6.09%, the spot exchange rate is BRL$/US$ = 5.09, the forward exchange rate one year from now is (mark the correct answer):

    a) 5.3318
    b) 5.3621
    c) 6.3621

3. If the Brazilian inflation rate in August 2023 is 4.21%, the US inflation rate is 3.7% for the same month, and the spot exchange rate is BRL$/US$ = 4.90, the forward exchange rate one year from now, according to PPP is (mark the correct answer):

    a) 4.903%
    b) 4.924%
    c) 4.856%

4. The US inflation rate is 2.67%, the 1GBP/US$ spot is 1.209, the one-year forward exchange rate is 1.211 (source: Refinitiv at October 3, 2023), assuming the fulfillment of purchasing power parity, the implied/expected domestic inflation rate is (mark the correct answer):

    a) 2.839%
    b) 5.254%
    c) 2.00%

5. Suppose the expected inflation rate is 2.7% in US and the Mexican observed inflation rate was 3.7% in the last 12 months. If the spot exchange rate of MX$/US$ = 17.8030 and the one-year forward rate MX$/US$ = 17.8032, which is the implied/expected Mexican inflation rate? Is it consistent with the PPP taking into account the observed inflation rate?
6. Using the following data, calculate the company value in dollars and domestic currency assuming perpetual cash flows.

TABLE 13.2 Data for calculating company value

Free cash flow^D	100
Spot Exchange rate (S_0)	10
WACC^{USD}	10%
Yield emerg. Bond^D	7%
Yield emerg. Bond^{USD}	5%
International inflation rate	2%

7. Suppose you are valuing Itaunas Ltd. You want to perform the valuation in domestic currency but also in dollars. The spot exchange rate is BRL$/US$ = 5, the WACC in dollars is 10.61%, the international inflation rate is 2%, the long-term growth rate g* observed in developed countries is 4%, and the sovereign bond yields in Brazilian reais and dollars are 7% and 5% respectively, and are expected to remain constant. You have to demonstrate the equivalence of valuing in foreign and domestic currency using the following free cash flow, where FCF^D represents the free cash flow expressed in Brazilian reais.

TABLE 13.3 Annual figures for Itaunas Ltd.

	Year 1	**Year 2**	**Year 3**	**Year 4**	**Year 5**	**Year 6**	**Year 7**	**Year 8**	**Year 9**	**Year 10**
FCF^D	15	17	19	20	22	24	26	28	30	31

8. Using the sovereign Brazilian bond yields in reais and dollars, obtain the respective yield curves and calculate the forward interest rates and the future exchange rate. The spot exchange rate is BRL$/US$ = 5.

TABLE 13.4 Data on Brazilian bond yields

Mod. Duration	**Yield R$**	**Yield US$**
0.6	2.30%	1.00%
1.5	4.20%	2.61%
1.9	4.50%	2.90%
2.6	5.12%	3.30%
3.5	5.55%	3.60%
4.3	5.90%	4.10%
5.2	6.30%	4.30%
6.1	6.50%	4.70%

(*Continued*)

TABLE 13.4 (Continued)

Mod. Duration	Yield R$	Yield US$
6.9	6.81%	4.92%
7.5	6.88%	5.01%
8.6	7.15%	5.30%
9.1	7.20%	5.35%
10.2	7.21%	5.45%

9. Recalculate the DCF value in dollars obtained in exercise 7 using the exchange rate forecasted in exercise 8. Is the difference significant?
10. What can we learn from the yield curve and how does it relate to the yield to maturity?
11. Calculate the DCF value in domestic currency of exercise 9, considering how the inflation rate differential change period by period.
    If the expected American inflation rate is 2.67%, the GBP/US$ = 1.209, and the future exchange rate is 1.211 (Refinitiv 2023-10-3), what should be the inflation rate in United Kingdom if the purchasing power parity holds?

    a) 2.839%
    b) 5.254%
    c) 2.00%

Notes

1 The exchange-rate pass-through refers to the impact on the domestic inflation rate caused by a devaluation. After a devaluation, a country makes its goods cheaper; as a result, its exports increase while importer goods become more expensive. As a result, a percentage of devaluation is reflected in local prices.

2 In some cases, their composition could have undergone important changes due to the entry of new companies and the delisting of others.

3 If we assume a world where interest rate capitalizes continuously, the equation must be expressed using the difference between the interest rates instead of the differential.

4 The long-term growth rate to calculate the terminal value in domestic currency for a company that operates in an emerging market will be much higher than the long-term growth rate expressed in dollars, due to the different inflation rates.

5 The real exchange rate is a nominal exchange rate adjusted for the ratio of prices between two countries. In this case, we use the Argentinean Consumer Price Index and the US Consumer Price Index, expressed on the base 2015=1. The election of the base period to calculate the real exchange rate is a matter of convention and has been a debatable question (jokingly, we can say that if you have ten economists to express their opinions, we would have eleven opinions).

6 In February 1981, the economy minister was quoted in newspapers as saying, "Whoever bets on the dollar loses". The author of this textbook, a teenager at the time, sold a Yamaha 400 Daytona and, along with some savings, purchased dollars. The following week, the dollar rose more than 100% and he acquired a Honda CB900F. Thanks LS!

References

Abuaf, N. (2011). Valuing Emerging Market Equities: The Empirical Evidence. *Journal of Applied Corporate Finance, 27*, 77–88.

Abuaf, N., & Jorion, P. (1990, March). Purchasing Power Parity in the Long Run. *Journal of Finance*, 157–174.

Adler, M., & Dumas, B. (1984). Exposure to Currency Risks: Definition and Measurement. *Financial Management, 13* (Summer), 41–50.

Adler, M., & Simon, D. (1986). Exchange Risk Surprise in International Portfolios: Some Equity Markets Are Super-Nominal! *Journal of Portfolio Management*, Winter, 44–53.

Bae, S. C., Kwon, T. H., & Li, M. (2008). Foreign Exchange Exposure and Risk Premium in International Investments: Evidence from American Depositary Receipts. *Journal of Multinational Financial Management, 18*(*2*), 165–179.

Banco Central de la República Argentina (2023). Available at www.bcra.gob.ar/Publicaciones-Estadisticas/Currency_rates.asp

Bansal, R., & Dahlquist, M. (2000). The Forward Premium Puzzle: Different Tales from Developed and Emerging Economies. *Journal of International Economics, 51*, 115–144.

Bartram, M., & Bodnar, G. (2007). The exchange Rate Exposure Puzzle. *Managerial Finance, 33*(*9*), 642–666.

Berk, J., & DeMarzo, P. (2007). *Corporate Finance: The Core*, 2nd edition. Boston: Pearson.

Brealey, R., Myers, S., & Marcus, A. (2008). *Fundamentals of Corporate Finance*, 9th edition. New York: McGraw-Hill.

Brigham, E., & Erdhardt, M. (2010). *Financial Management, Theory and Practice*. Mason: South-Western Cengage Learning.

Central Intelligence Agency (2012). Available at https://www.cia.gov/the-world-factbook/field/inflation-rate-consumer-prices/

Cheung, Y., Chinn, M., & Garcia, P. (2005). Empirical Exchange Rate Models of the Nineties:AreAny Fit to Survive? *Journal of International Money and Finance, 24*, 1150–1175.

Chinn, M. (2006). The (Partial) Rehabilitation of Interest Rate Parity in the Floating Rate Era: Longer Horizons, Alternative Expectations, and Emerging Markets. Journal of *International Money and Finance, 26*, 7–21.

Chinn, M., & Meredith, G. (2004). Monetary Policy and Long- Horizon Uncovered Interest Rate Parity. Washington D.C.: IMF Staff Papers, Vol. 51, No. 3.

Damodaran, A. (2012). *Investment Valuation Tools and Techniques for Determining the Value of Any Asset*, 3rd edition. New York: John Wiley & Sons.

Dumrauf, G. L. (2015). *Currency Choices in Valuation: An Approach for Emerging Markets*. Discussion paper. World Finance Conference. Buenos Aires.

Dumrauf, G. L. (March 2014). Currency Choices in Valuation: An Approach for Emerging Markets. *JCC, The Business and Economics Research Journal*, 7(*1*), 11–22.

Emery, D., & Finnerty, J. (2007). *Corporate Financial Management*, 3rd edition. New Jersey: Prentice Hall.

Esqueda, O. A., & Jackson, D. O. (2012, July). Currency Depreciation Effects on ADR Returns: Evidence from Latin America. *Journal of Economics and Finance, 36*(*3*), 691–711.

Fisher, I. (1896, 1 December). Appreciation and Interest: A Study of the Influence of Monetary Appreciation and Depreciation on the Rate of Interest, with Applications to the Bimetallic Controversy and the Theory of Interest. *The Economic Journal, 6*(*2*), 567–570.

Flood, R., & Rose, K. (2001). Uncovered Interest Parity in Crisis: The Interest Rate Defense in the 1990s. IMF Working Paper, 01/207.

Glen, J. (2002). Devaluations and Emerging Stock Market Returns. *Emerging Markets Review, 3*(*8*), 409–428.

Graham, J., Smart, S. B., & Megginson, W. L. (2010). *Corporate Finance: Linking Theory to What Companies Do*, 3rd edition. Mason: South-Western Cengage Learning.

Hodder, J. (1982). Exposure to Exchange Rate Movements. *Journal of International Economics, 13* (November), 375–386.

Koller, T., Goedhart, M., & Wessels, D. (2010). *Valuation: Measuring and Managing the Value of Companies*, 5th edition. Hoboken, New Jersey: JohnWiley & Sons, Inc.

Mehl, A., & Cappiello, L. (2009). Uncovered Interest Parity at Long Horizons: Evidence on Emerging Economies. *Review of International Economics, 17(5)*, 1019–1037.

Ross, S., Westerfield, R., & Jaffe, J. (2009). *Corporate Finance*, 9th edition. New York: McGraw-Hill/Irwin.

Shapiro, A. (1975, May). Exchange Rate Changes, Inflation, and the Value of the Multinational Corporation. *The Journal of Finance, 30(2)*, 485–502.

Skinner, F., & Mason, A. (2011, July 2). Covered Interest Rate Parity in Emerging Markets. Available at http://papers.ssrn.com/sol3/papers.cfm?abstract_id = 1869974

Taylor, A. (2002). A Century Of Purchasing-Power Parity. *Review of Economics and Statistics*, 139–150.

Taylor, A., & Taylor, M. (2004). The Purchasing Power Parity Debate. *The Journal of Economic Perspectives, 18(4)*, 135–158.

The National Institute of Statistics and Censuses (INDEC) (2023). Available at www.indec.gob.ar/indec/web/Nivel4-Tema-3-5-31

Zhang, Y. (2006). Does the Horizon Matter? The Uncovered Interest Parity Reconsidered. *International Journal of Applied Economics, 3(2)*, 61–79.

CHAPTER

14

Control premium and marketability discount

Introduction

Acquiring a controlling number of shares in public companies involves paying a premium over the current market price per share to induce existing shareholders to sell. The size of the premium depends on the maximum value an acquirer would be willing to pay based on its belief and expectations that under its management, the business´ performance will improve. The statistics tell us that the control premium can be significant: sometimes over 50% of the company value before the acquisition. For example, if the company has a market value of $100 million and is acquired for $150 million, the control premium is 150 – 100 = 50 million. From the minority shareholders' side, it can be viewed as a discount for lack of control or minority discount, since the difference between the business optimally managed and the business poorly managed is also $50 million.

The discount for lack of marketability (DLOM) proceeds when we consider the value of a private company. Because there is no marketplace for private companies, selling the company could be a very difficult task, more costly and time-consuming

DOI: 10.4324/9781003628491-17

than selling a position in a public company. The consequence is that a private company should sell at a lower price concerning intrinsic value because of the uncertainty of selling it. The statistics, as in the case of the control premium, indicate that the DLOM can be considerable.

That the control premium and the discount of lack of marketability have value is just as certain as there is no single and standard method for estimating their fair value. However, we have empirical data and some methodologies have been proposed, ranging from regression analysis to option theory.

After reading this chapter, you will be able to:

- Recognize the factors influencing the value of the control premium;
- Recognize the factors influencing the value of the lack of marketability;
- Be aware of the empirical data.

Control premium

When an acquisition of a publicly traded company is done at a price higher than the current market price, the difference is considered a control premium (CP) since the buyer is willing to pay a premium over the market value to acquire a controlling share. It is motivated by the acquirer's belief that, with a best management, the company's profits and cash flow will improve as the market value, especially if the acquirer thinks that the company suffers poor management. In the majority of acquisitions, the managers of the acquiring firm, not the shareholders, decide to acquire a company and the price to pay for it. Therefore, the motive for some acquisitions may not be stockholder wealth maximization but rather managerial self-interest. Other motives to pay a control premium are related to the synergy that supposedly arises from operating economies of scale in management, production, marketing, or distribution[1] and increased market power due to reduced competition.

The size of the premium is usually large in hostile takeovers. The firm's management presumably tries to negotiate the greatest price for the company in hostile scenarios, while in a friendly takeover, the management might be influenced by the positions they could get in the surviving company.

Damodaran (2012) mentioned as motives for acquisitions the management's intention to make their firm the largest and most dominant in their industry rather than diversification, the managerial ego when there are multiple bidders for the same firm, and the potential compensations to the managers from the transaction, that might blind them in the negotiation and generate an agency cost for their stockholders.

Box 4.1 Case study: Barugel & Azulay and the overconfidence in valuation

The managerial ego was the basis for a number of acquisitions made in Argentina in the 1990s. For example, Barugel y Azulay, a company involved with the sale of bathroom accessories, was acquired for more than double the fair value estimated at that time. The context of optimism that prevailed at that time greatly influenced the acquirer's expectations. After the devaluation of the Mexican peso in 1994, Argentina suffered the "tequila effect", and investors began withdrawing deposits from banks. Despite losing 20% of deposits in just three months, the Argentine financial system resisted, and the GDP grew strongly again in 2006. Investors come back and the M&A activity re-emerged. Ernesto Barugel, the main shareholder of Barugel y Azulay, commissioned two valuations from two consulting firms. Since the difference between estimated values was 8%, there was reason to believe that the company's fair value was very close.

However, four potential acquirers have expressed an interest in acquiring the company, whose plans involve an aggressive expansion of the business financed with debt. Maybe these expectations were influenced by the macroeconomic context at the time, which changed drastically a few months later due to the depreciation the Brazilian real. They used a cost of capital between 13% and 15%, but the most striking thing was that some of the potential acquirer's forecasted cash flow exceeded the consulting firm's forecasts by three times.

The bidding between two private equity funds finally drove the price by 170% above the original estimated fair value. Another potential strategic acquirer, who knew the industry well, withdrew from the fight. Ernesto always tells me that he congratulates himself every day when he shaves in the morning.

The belief that they are better at managing the company sometimes can justify considerable premiums. Additionally, the control establishes a series of privileges in favor of the controlling share.

The reasons for considering a control premium

Having a controlling share, the acquirer gets a series of prerogatives to determine the direction of the company, for example:

- Register stock for a public offering
- Transform into a private company
- Liquidate, sell, or merge the company, seeking to cash out the minority investor instead of offering that investor the opportunity to continue with her investment
- Select management and set their compensations
- Perquisites. The controlling party can pay for trips, retirement plans, education, medical care, and other expenses to benefit her or her designee. These expenses benefit the majority shareholder at the expense of the minority shareholder.
- Buy, sell, and pledge assets
- Declare dividends
- Make capital distributions
- The majority shareholder may borrow funds from the company at a lower-than-market interest rate or lend funds to the company at a higher-than-market interest rate.

These prerogatives reduce the influence and the return on minority stockholder´s investments, although sometimes the controlling party and the minority stockholder sign contracts to mitigate their effects, as we´ll explain later. According to Pereiro (2006), due to the limited protection to minority investors, the controlling shareholders of private companies may be commanding high control premiums that more than compensate the discount for the lack of marketability and it may explain the decrease of the number of quoting companies in the Argentinean stock market. In addition, the recurring crises in Argentina have conspired against the sustainable growth of companies and their need to issue new shares. Several of them became private companies, because they believe (and state) that there is no advantage to remaining public.[2]

Owens, Grossman, & Fackler (2014) offered an additional justification for the importance of maintaining control. In their studies, they conducted experiments where the participants had to select among different assets with various payout conditions. According to the findings, individuals place on having control over their financial outcomes, suggesting that this preference can lead to a different behavior predicted by traditional economic theory based solely on expected utility.

Value of control premium

The control premium, as we stated before, is frequently based on the self-confidence of the acquirer to enhance the target company's performance. The premium increases if the target company is perceived as poorly managed.

Suppose AM Corp. reported an EBITDA of $20 million, and its market capitalization was $100 million at the time, equivalent to a P/EBITDA of 5x. TDT, the potential buyer, believes that under its management, EBITDA might reach $25 million by removing the current management and reducing some inefficiencies. The enterprise value will improve from $100 million to $125 million (5 x 25) and assuming that TDT is willing to pay $125 million, the control premium value is:

$$\text{Control premium} = \text{Value of firm well-managed} - \text{Value of firm poorly managed}$$
$$\text{Control premium} = 125 - 100 = 25$$

The control premium is typically expressed as a percentage rather than in absolute values. In this case, the control premium is 125/100 – 1 = 25% or 25% of the current value. This percentage does not change if AM Corp. acquires a portion that allows it to have the controlling interest. For example, if AM Corp. acquires the 60% of TDT, the difference in values between the 60% and 40% shares:

$$\text{Value of controlling interest} = 125 \times 60\% = 75 \text{ million}$$
$$\text{Value of noncontrolling interest} = 100 \times 40\% = \$40 \text{ million}$$
$$\text{Control premium: } 75 - 40 = 25 \text{ million}$$

Control premium using stock price

The control premium can be also calculated from the share price. For example, suppose Firm A wants to acquire Firm B. Firm B's share price is $10 per share, and firm A offers $14 per share. The control premium is: 14/10 – 1 = 40%. The excess amount paid over the equity book value of an acquired company is reported on the balance sheet as part of the goodwill. The goodwill represents an intangible value associated with the future expected value of earnings and cash flows of the target, including factors like brand reputation, customer relationships, and synergies.

Minority discount, marketability discount and total discount

A minority shareholder in a publicly traded company can be considered a passive investor with little influence on the way the company is run. Therefore, the shareholding of the minority shareholder in a closely held company is worth less than the same shareholding in a publicly traded company. Even worse, minority shareholders in a private company faces the additional difficulty of finding a willing buyer if they decide to sell, so, the minority shareholder's value is less than the shareholder control value.

Example: Suppose KF has a marketable minority value of \$100 million; if a control premium of 25% is applied, the control value will be \$125 million, which is equivalent to a minority discount of 20% since a discount of 20% applied on \$125 million gives a marketable minority value of \$100 million. In addition, as KF is a private company, a potential acquirer would apply a discount for lack of marketability (DLOC) of 30% in an eventual deal.

Figure 14.1 shows how a premium or a discount is applied. The horizontal line in the middle of the drawing represents the marketable minority value; then, the control value is obtained by adding a control premium, represented by the horizontal line at the top of the chart. To obtain the nonmarketable minority value (represented by the horizontal line at the bottom of the chart), a lack of marketability discount is applied to the marketable minority value.

Note that the minority discount, also known as discount for lack of control (DLOC) is the inverse of the control premium and is calculated with the following formula:

$$\text{DLOC} = \frac{\text{Control Premium}}{1 + \text{Control Premium}}. \qquad [14.1]$$

$$\text{DLOC} = \frac{0.25}{1.25} = 20\%$$

Conversely, DLOC can be used to determine the control premium:

$$\text{Control Premium} = \frac{\text{DLOC}}{\text{1-DLOC}}. \qquad [14.2]$$

$$\text{Control Premium} = \frac{0.20}{1 - 0.20} = 25\%$$

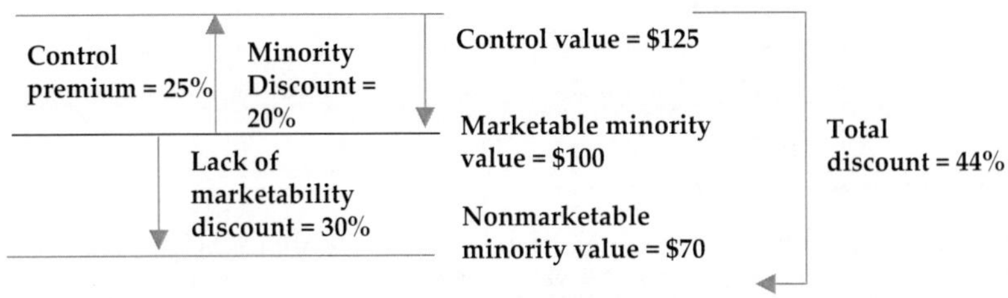

FIGURE 14.1 Minority discount and discount for lack of marketability

It is evident that there is a 25% upside from 100 to 125 and a 20% downside from 125 to 100.

Total discount

The total discount represents the discount applied to the control value to find the nonmarketable minority value. Taking the control value, the minority discount and the lack of marketability discount are applied in this way:

$$\text{Total discount } (\%) = 1 - (1 - \text{DLOC}) \times (1 - \text{DLOM}). \quad [14.3]$$
$$1 - (1\text{–}20\%) \times (1\text{–}30\%) = 44.00\%$$
$$\text{Company value: } 125 \star (1 - 0.44) = 70$$

Notice that the process is multiplicative rather than additive: the total discount is 44.00% and not 20% + 30% = 50%.

Control premium, minority discount, and marketability discount are related since the synergies perceived by the acquirer could be offset by the discounts.[3]

Mechanisms to protect the minority position

There are various ways to protect the minority shareholders from the majority shareholders, taking several forms such as restrictions, rights, and agreements, which reduce the discount amount for lack of control.

Shareholder agreements

A shareholder agreement is a contract among shareholders that describes the rights and responsibilities of each of the shareholders under various circumstances. It may, for instance, impose restrictions on transferring shares and pre-emptive rights for current shareholder to acquire shares to maintain ownership percentages. The shareholders' agreement is intended to guarantee equitable treatment and protection of shareholder's interests. For example, a buy-sell agreement could require that, in the event of a certain circumstance, such as the death or retirement of the shareholder, either the majority shareholder or the corporation to buy back the minority shareholder's stock at a set price or formula. Also, a minority shareholder could force the company or the majority shareholder to buy stock at a set price under a "put" option.

Shareholder agreements differ from company bylaws and work in conjunction with the articles of incorporation, which is a collection of documents that typically contain relevant information such as the type of corporate structure, duration of the corporation, and the amount and type of stock to be issued with each class entitled to elect certain directors.

In September 2003, Telecom Italia and W de Argentina Inversiones SL signed an agreement establishing a call option in favor of Telecom Italia to acquire the W stake exercisable in January 2009. The Italians paid to W de Argentina Inversiones SL US$60 million for the call option and to retake control of the company from January 2009. In the event that Telecom Italia decides to exercise the call, it must pay a fixed value for 30% of the shares and the market value for the rest of the shares at the moment of the transaction. In May 2008, W de Argentina filed a lawsuit against Telecom Italia to declare the nullity of the contract that granted the call option in favor of Telecom Italia to acquire the stake owned by W de Argentina. The case's details are covered in Chapter 17, where we value Sofora Telecomunicaciones.

Straight voting

Under this voting system, each share is entitled to one vote per director seat. For example, if three directors are up for election and a minority shareholder, David, owned 500 shares, the shareholder can cast up to 500 votes per director for a total of 1,500 votes. David can therefore cast 500 votes for each director under straight voting, but not 1,500 votes for each of them. The disadvantage of straight voting is the minority shareholder representation. For example, a majority shareholder with 1,000 shares can vote up to 1,000 times per director, while the minority shareholder can only vote up to 500 times per nominee. An alternative to address this problem consist in using cumulative voting.

Cumulative voting

In cumulative voting each share gives the right to as many votes as there are directors to be elected, so, it may be possible for the minority party to elect some board member even if the majority part opposes their election. While the maximum that David can vote for each director in the case of straight voting was 500, under cumulative voting David is allowed to vote 1,500 for each director. Other agreements can combine voting rights. For example, a group of shareholders, typically minority shareholders, may form a voting trust, agreeing to vote their stock as a block and thereby achieving a majority position (Hichtner, 2017).

Supermajority

A supermajority is a percentage of support higher than a simple majority to approve certain actions, specified using a percentage or fraction greater than one-half. For example, a company might require 75% approval for a merger, instead of requiring 51%. Other actions that usually require a supermajority include the decision to go public or leave the stock market and go private, liquidation, and the hiring or firing of a CEO.

Preemptive rights

Preemptive rights give to existing shareholders the opportunity to acquire additional shares in a new offering in an amount equal to their original ownership before the shares are offered to the public. The preemptive right cushions the shareholders' loss if additional shares are priced lower than the original shares they bought, and protect from having their interest diluted by the majority shareholder.

Right of first refusal (ROFR)

A ROFR is a contractual right that someone hast to match or decline to match an offer for an asset after other offers have been made. It assures the holder that they will not lose their right to an asset if others express interest in it, and preventing the majority party from negotiating with third parties' offers before the minority party. In joint venture situations, the ROFR gives the right to minority shareholders to purchase shares or sell shares of the partners who leave the venture before they are offered to the public.

Appraisal rights

An appraisal right gives the minority shareholder the right to demand a judicial proceeding or independent valuation of the company's shares to determine the fair value of the stock price. Shareholders can invoke their appraisal rights when they will be force to give up their shares at an unreasonable price, usually in a merger or acquisition, and demand that a court for an independent valuation. Analysts may use some of the valuation methods such as discounted cash flow or relative valuation, and if the valuation determines that the value of shares is higher than was offered, the court may require either to the company or to the majority shareholder to pay the shareholder the fair value.

Employee shareholder agreement

An employee shareholder is an employee who has agreed to receive shares in the employer's company in exchange for various employment rights. The agreement defines the rights and protections to employee-shareholders, including resolution of conflict of interest, confidentiality, intellectual property, provisions on minority protection, and provision for non-competition. Many shareholders agreements[4] require that an individual must remain employed by the firm to remain a shareholder. Although this provision may appear to be an innocuous safeguard against absentee ownership, according to Briol & Benson (2019) a professional limited liability company (PLLC) this provision can create a "trap" for the minority shareholders when couple with another provision that requires a departing shareholder to sell his interest at a buyout price determined by a fixed formula – book value or perhaps even a fixed price. For example, if the majority party knows that per share fair value exceeds the price set by the shareholder agreement, it could use its power to control employment decisions and probably force the minority party to sell her shares at the shareholder agreement price below their fair value, harming the minority shareholder and obtaining a benefit for himself.

Marketability discount

Private companies may face limitations in finding an acquirer or might take a long time to convert the ownership interest into cash at minimal cost. As a result, potential investors would claim a percentage reduction in business value to compensate for this risk. This discount is known as a discount of lack of marketability (DLOM), which leads to a nonmarketable value.

The marketability varies with the type of securities. For example, publicly traded securities are more marketable than the securities of private concerns, and securities with restrictions are generally less marketable than securities without restrictions. Besides, the lack of marketability discount varies across potential investors because the desire for liquidity varies with investors. For example, an owner of a private company acquiring another private business may not be worried about the lack of marketability and would consider a lower discount, if any.

Minority discount and marketability are related since the majority shareholder may be able to affect marketability through a merger or an initial public offering. Therefore, you have to consider both discounts in conjunction with each other. Simpson (1991) described as factors leading to a smaller or larger discount, the equity interest to suppress a merger, the capacity of cumulative voting to affect the Board of Directors, and the concentrated or fragmented ownership of the remaining interest in the company.

Methods to estimate the lack of marketability value

The most popular methods to estimate the lack of marketability are the restricted stock method and the IPO method. Both methodologies consist of establishing the difference between the stock prices at which private transactions took place and the stock prices after they became public. From a more scientific perspective, the option pricing method and the regression analysis have been also suggested.

Restricted stock method

When a company issues common stock with certain restrictions on the timing of the sale, such as non-transferable stocks issued to employees and restricted stocks for executives and directors ("letter stock"), the DLOM is reflected in the price differential between restricted and freely tradable shares. The restrictions usually include a vesting period that may last several years.

IPO method

The initial public offering (IPO) allows a business to register as a pre-IPO company, which allows potential investors to invest in the business before it goes public. Therefore, we know the pre-IPO price and then, when the IPO takes place, the IPO price. The difference between the two prices, expressed as a percentage, is considered the DLOM. This method assumes that the price difference reflects the market's perception of the lack of marketability associated with the pre-IPO shares.

Box 4.2 Case study: InsuAgro

In 2006, we estimated the fair value of InsuAgro, a private small company involved with the agrochemicals sales for an IPO. The DLOM was calculated over our DCF value estimation. It was a pleasant and successful experience. A DLOM of 20% over our fair value estimation was agreed between the company's owner, the brokers, and the Small Companies Department of the Buenos Aires Stock Exchange. The business had three years of life at this moment, and was founded by two former managers of a Japanese company, ISHIHARA SANGYO KAISHA, LTD., involved with the agrochemical company. Today,

InsuAgro is quoting its shares on the Panel Pyme of Buenos Aires Stock Exchange under the acronym INAG. When we told the history during a valuation course, a student raised his hand and told me: "I am a shareholder of InsuAgro since I bought 10% of the IPO shares, and I almost recovered the investment with the dividends paid". The company has been successful since then, driven by soil prices, and it continues to grow strongly.

Regression analysis

This methodology was proposed first by Silber (1991), who found that the lack of marketability had a median value of 33.75%. He found that more time required to sell the asset, a poor financial performance, restrictions on transferability, the small the company size, and economic downturns lead to higher DLOM. Hertzel and Smith (1993) analyzed 106 private placements between 1980 to 1987 and came to the conclusion that an appropriate discount for lack of marketability was 13.5%. Bajaj, Denis, Ferris and Sarin (2001) examined 88 private placements from 1990 through 1995 finding that registered shares were issued at a median discount of 9.85% while placements of unregistered shares had a median discount of 26.47%. Comment (2012) stated that DLOM should be approximately 5.5% based on an analysis of over 1,100 private placements that took place between 2004 and 2010. This small discount could be due to the shortening of the period under Rule 144 where trading restrictions were changed from two years to six months.

Option pricing method

Under this method, the DLOM is estimated as the option price/strike price ratio. The reasoning is as follows: since a put option gives to its holder the possibility to sell the stock at the strike price, therefore, the put price on the restricted stock represents a proxy for the DLOM. One of the first proponents to use the option price to estimate the DLOM was Chafee (1993), who based upon the volatility of small publicly traded companies, concluded that the discount for the lack of marketability for private equity interests with a two-year holding period were 28% to 41%. A variant of this methodology is the lookback put option that allows the user to look back at the stock prices over the life of the option after its purchase and exercise it at the maximum beneficial price of the stock. For example, Longstaff (1995) used a lookback put to estimate the upper bound on the marketability value for a private company based on the price of a lookback option.[5] Barenbaum, Schubert, & Garcia (2015) point out that the put option overstates the DLOM because not only protects the holder from downside risk but also allows the benefit for upside potential, which is included in the cost of a put. Instead of using the put price of an estimation of DLOM, they proposed a different hedging strategy, employing an at-the-money equity collar plus the interest cost of borrowing funds to monetize the underlying asset. The collar protects both the downside risk of receiving less than the strike price as well as the potential upside of receiving more than the strike price. Then, the DLOM is represented by the cost of borrowing money for monetizing the underlying asset at its current value less the earnings of the equity collar.

This method leads to a significantly low and non-observed DLOM supported by empirical evidence on restricted stock and IPO transactions. When the underlying asset is non-traded, they suggest the creation of a portfolio consisting of the non-trade asset and a stock index for creating a hedge. Since the asset's volatility cannot be observed they assume a correlation coefficient between the non-traded asset and the stock index and then perform a Monte-Carlo simulation to estimate the probability of receiving less than the assumed current value of the non-trade asset. However, for the case of not perfect correlation, they recognize the effectiveness of the equity collar depends on the correlation between the assets included in the portfolio, while a higher correlation would lead to a lower DLOM and an increased likelihood that a loan can be obtained.[6] A comprehensive review of empirical research of DLOM is Vianello (2019). He provides an insightful analysis of historical research, discusses the strengths and weaknesses of existing models, and offers extensions, evaluating their performance using objective empirical standards.

Other methods

While restricted stock studies and pre-IPO studies are frequently recognized as the top approaches for estimating DLOM, the Johnson/Park empirical method is used by roughly 27% of respondents in a recent Business Valuation Resources poll (2021). It enables appraisers to generate rate of return measures that may be used in many valuation scenarios.

Finally, the specific method for estimating the DLOM may vary depending on the circumstances and the asset being valued. For example, a large private company, with a good credit reputation, may have a lower discount for lack of marketability. Other factors influence DLOM are legal and compliance with relevant laws and regulations. Market conditions as volatility, industry trends and changes in market sentiment also can impact the asset's liquidity and marketability. The method to be used should be complemented with professional judgement based on their expertise and knowledge to consider the unique characteristics and circumstances of the asset being valued.

Empirical evidence of control premium

The first series of data comes from *Mergerstat Review*,[7] based on the stock prices observed five working days after the company's sales was announced. The mean of the control premium was close to 40%, and a second study from 1980 to 1994 gave a similar value.

Pratt (2009), a recognized authority on business valuation discounts and premiums, explain how different discounts or premiums may be applicable, depending on the valuation approach used. The Mergerstat/Shannon Pratt's Control Premium Study, a quarterly publication from Mergerstat, L.P. tracks acquisition premiums for completed transactions and provides data and insights involving publicly traded companies where a controlling interest was acquired.

Dyck & Zingales (2004) constructed a measure of the private benefits of control in 39 countries using 393 controlling block sales and data from 1990 to 2000, finding an average control premium of 14%, within a range from −4%/+65%. Private benefits of control are larger in countries where the capital markets are less developed and ownership is more concentrated. For example, they found similar control premiums for Argentina, Colombia, and Venezuela (27%); Chile was 18%, and Brazil was 65%.

Paglia & Harjoto (2010) created a database of 1,328 matched-pairs and 9,765 matched-industry pairs using transactions from 1995–2008 to study DLOMs. They found discounts that average 65–70%, significantly larger than those reported in other databases and from other studies, while larger and profitable companies, and those with lower risk of financial distress exhibit lower DLOMs. According to an analysis of 403 made worldwide between 2007 and 2015 by Baldi & Salvi (2022), overconfident, cash-generating acquirers overpay the targets. While operational and financial synergies are not usually priced up front, higher premia are justified for larger-sized, high-growth targets, non-conglomerate acquisitions, and when the consideration is paid in stock. Novak (2022) from Willamette Management Associates reviewed 24 years of transactions from 1998 through 2021. They distinguish between a strategic acquirer, who operates in the same industry and generally wants to acquire the target to hold it, and an acquirer who acquires a business for investment purposes and exits their investment within a short time frame. For example, the mean equity acquisition premium for a strategic buyer was 34.8% while for the case of a financial buyer was 30.2%. For the case of invested capital acquisition premium, the mean was 24.7% for a strategic buyer and 18.0% for a financial buyer. They also distinguish the premiums among companies that have different capital structures: the control premium decreased as the target leverage increased, mainly in the case of the invested capital acquirer. The study found lower premiums for industries like construction (23.2%) and agriculture (17.1%), while higher premiums were found for manufacturing (38.4%) and services (39.2%), although there was high variability across all industry groups.

Control premiums are determined on a case-by-case basis and depend on factors such as market conditions, industry, and leverage. The DCF analysis with controlling-owner projections must identify potential changes and synergies that would improve the business performance (for example, expense reduction, eliminating employee compensation, improving the working capital management, whether there are opportunities to increase the customer base, opening new markets.).

Empirical evidence of marketability discounts

Since 1980, John D. Emory has been researching the value of stocks before and after they became public companies. In his first eight studies and expanded studies from 1980 to 1997, Emory analyzed 593 transactions. The mean and median discounts for lack of marketability that occurred five months before an IPO were 44 and 43%, respectively. After making minor data adjustments to previous IPO from 1980 through 2000, Emory (2002) found the overall mean discount and median discount were 46% and 47%. They also found that the DLOM increases as the time between a transaction and the IPO increases. For example, when there were 0–30 days between transactions and the IPO, the DLOM was 30%, increasing to 55% for transactions up to five months before the IPO. However, the discounts found were for cases where a high degree of marketability is likely; other businesses with extremely limited marketability might be eligible for a bigger discount. The Silber study (1991) found a median DLOM of 33.75% for restricted stock. However, the discount varies with the company's revenues since firms with higher revenues and positive earnings have significantly lower discounts than firms with lower revenues and negative earnings.

Willamette Management Associates has published the results of 18 studies (periods) that analyze IPO transactions from 1975 to 1997 using the IPO method to determine DLOM. The difference with Emory's studies was that Willamette reviewed transactions from one to 36 months before the initial public offering instead of transactions up to five months before the IPO. To reflect differences in market conditions between the dates, Willamette used an industry P/E multiple at the time of offering and compared it to the Industry P/E multiple at the time of the private transaction. The majority of the discounts are in the range of 40 to 60%.

Concluding thoughts

The control premium is frequently based on the self-confidence of the acquirer to improve the target company's performance. The size of the premium depends on the maximum value that an acquirer would be willing to pay, which should be based on an objective projection of the company's future performance. If the target company is perceived as poorly managed, the greater the premium. The control gives prerogatives in favor of the majority party that reduces the influence and the return on minority stockholder´s investments. However, there are mechanisms to protect the minority shareholders against the majority shareholders, which take several forms such as restrictions, rights, and agreements, to mitigate the discount for lack of control.

Private companies may face limitations in finding an acquirer or would take a long time to convert the ownership interest to cash at minimal cost. This lack of marketability implies a risk for potential investors; therefore, they would claim a percentage reduction in an asset value to compensate for this risk. The methodologies proposed to estimate DLOM range from data-based methods (restricted stock method and IPO method) to less common, more scientific methods (regression analysis and option pricing).

Short questions and problems

1. The control premium is:
   a) The difference between the price paid over the market price in an acquisition
   b) The price paid in an acquisition due to the advantages that gives the control of a company
   c) The controlling value minus a reduction due to the lack of control
2. When a control premium is claimed?
   a) When valuing the minority interest in a business
   b) When valuing the majority interest in a business
   c) When valuing the illiquidity of a company

3. Economic reasons that influence to pay a control premium include:
   a) The transform to a private company
   b) Increased market power due to reduced competition
   c) The senior management's belief that the target is poorly managed
4. The discount for lack of marketability (DLOM) is
   a) The reduction in value of an ownership interest due to lack of control
   b) The discount applied to a minority interest in a company
   c) The reduction in an ownership interest's value because it is not marketable
5. Typical factors to estimate the discount for lack of marketability include:
   a) Risk of not finding an acquirer or taking a long time to find it
   b) Return of the investment
   c) Management's quality
6. If the control premium is 40%, the minority discount or discount of lack of control (DLOC) is:
   a) 66.66%
   b) 28.57%
   c) 33.33%
7. Estimate the total discount given a DLOC of 30% and DLOM of 40%.
8. For a company with a DLOC of 25% and a DLOM of 30%, the total discount is closest to:
   a) 47.50%.
   b) 18.66%.
   c) 46.35%
9. Suppose WWW Corp. considering acquire Alfabeta, a private company. The estimated fair value of the current operations is $100 million. Alfabeta is managed by three brothers, who are the owners of the business. WWW believes that a single, distinctive general manager could take their place. In addition, they expect gains for inefficiencies reduction and synergies derived from an integration with the WWW operations. The present value of each savings after taxes is as follows:
   a) Savings in salaries and compensations: $10 million
   b) Savings of inefficiencies reduction: $20 million
   c) Savings from synergies:10 million

   At the same time, WWW Corp. considers a discount for lack of marketability of 30%. What is the company value and the total discount considering DLOC and DLOM?
10. The argument to consider the put option's cost as a proxy for DLOM is:
    a) Represent a percentage of the strike price that gives to its holder the possibility to transform its holding in cash at the strike price.
    b) Do not overstate the option fair value since does not consider the upside situation
    c) Represents a percentage of the stock price

11. Complete the following sentences:
 The process of compute both the control premium and the discount for the lack of marketability is ....rather than additive. For instance, if the control premium is 40%, and DLOM is 35%, the total discount is.....................
12. How is it possible to defend what seems like an excessive control premium?
13. Discuss the implications of a high control premium for minority shareholders.

Notes

1 Synergy calculations work well in Excel. In mergers, expected synergies are frequently more than offset by the impact of the operative income resulting from the clash of cultures between the employees of the merged companies
2 In 1998 there were 180 companies listed in the stock market.
3 We participated in negotiations in emerging markets where the potential buyer, fascinated by the expected synergies, did not even put the argument of discounts on the table.
4 Shareholder agreements are common among owners of private companies, especially for companies with many shareholders and when there is a close relationship between the owners and management.
5 Lookback options are expensive and not traded on major exchanges but over the counter.
6 When the underlying asset's volatility cannot be observed, it is difficult to believe in obtaining a loan to finance this kind of hedging. Perhaps, in extractive industries such as oil, the volatility of the petroleum price could be a better proxy of the underlying asset's volatility rather than assuming any correlation.
7 Mergerstat L. P. publishes the *Mergerstat Review,* which provides data and statistics on mergers and acquisitions transactions that involve US companies, including privately held, publicly traded and cross-border transactions.

References

Baldi, F., & Salvi, A. (2022). Disentangling acquisition premia: Evidence from the global market for corporate control. *Finance Research Letters, 48*(C).

Barenbaum, L., Schubert, W., & Garcia, K. (2015). Determining Lack of Marketability Discounts: Employing an Equity Collar Collar. *The Journal of Entrepreneurial Finance, 17*(1), 65–81.

Briol, S. & Benson, M. (2019, June 7). Shareholder Agreement Trap for Shareholder Employees. Available at https://briollaw.com/a-shareholder-agreement-trap-for-shareholder-employees/

Business Valuation Resources (2021, July 28). Available at www.bvresources.com/articles/bvwire/dlom-survey-reveals-methods-of-choice

Chafee, D. (1993, December). Option Pricing as a Proxy for Discount for Lack of Marketability for Private Company Valuations. *Business Valuation Review*, 182–186.

Comment, R. (2012). Revisiting the Illiquidity Discount for Private Companies: A New (and Skeptical) Restricted Stock Study. *Journal of Applied Corporate Finance, 24*(1), 80–92.

Damodaran, A. (2012). *Investment Valuation*. New York: John Wiley and Sons.

Dyck, A., & Zingales, L. (2004). Private Benefits of Control: An International Comparison. *Journal of Finance, 59*, 533–599.

Emory, J. D. (2002). Discounts for Lack of Marketability, Emory Pre-IPO Studies 1980–2000 as Adjusted October 10, 2002. *Business Valuation Review, 21*(4), 190.

Hichtner, J. (2017). *Financial Valuation: Applications and Models*, 4th edition. New York: John Wiley & Sons.

Longstaff, F. (1995). How Much Can Marketability Affect Security Values? *Journal of Finance*, *50(5)*, 1767–1774.

Novak, N. P. (2022, May 16). *Evaluating and Applying Control Premiums*. Available at chrome-extension://efaidnbmnnnibpcajpcglclefindmkaj/https://willamette.com/835/Control_Premiums_2022.pdf

Owens, D., Grossman, Z., & Fackler, R. (2014). The Control Premium: A Preference for Payoff Autonomy. *American Economic Journal: Microeconomics*, *6(4)*, 138–161.

Paglia, J., & Harjoto, M. (2010). The Discount for Lack of Marketability in Privately Owned Companies: A Multiples Approach. *Journal of Business Valuation and Economic Loss Analysis*, *5(1)*, 1–26.

Pereiro, L. (2006). The practice of investment valuation in emerging markets: Evidence from Argentina. *Journal of Multinational Financial Management*, *16(2)*, 160–183.

Pratt, S. P. (2009). *Busines Valuation Discounts and Premiums*, 2nd edition. New York: Wiley.

Silber, W. L. (1991). Discounts on Restricted Stock: The Impact of Illiquidity on Stock Prices. *Financial Analysts Journal*, *47(4)*, 60–64.

Simpson, D. W. (1991). Minority Interest and Marketability Discounts: A perspective: Part I. *Business Valuation Review*, *10(1)*, 7–13.

Vianello, M. (2019, July). Empirical Research Regarding Discounts for Lack of Marketability. Volume 1.1.

CHAPTER

15

Company performance measures and value creation

Introduction

Alfred Marshall coined the term economic profit in the nineteenth century. At the beginning of 1991, the consulting firm Stern & Stewart from New York redirected,

DOI: 10.4324/9781003628491-18

expanded the concept in many ways, and added valuable insights to the economic profit, promoting a new method for measuring business performance called economic value added (EVA), which is strongly related to finance theory. Economic profit is also proposed as a valuation method, and we discuss the equivalence with the free cash flow method.

After reading this chapter, you will be able to:

- Calculate economic profit;
- Perform the most common adjustments to the financial information;
- Use economic profit in valuation;
- Understand how traditional financial metrics can induce wrong decisions.

Economic profit and performance

Conceptually, economic profit (EP) represents the net operating profit of a business after taxes on operations. The EP is determined as the return on invested capital (ROIC) minus WACC, multiplied by the capital invested. The calculation makes sense and appears to be quite simple at first glance.

$$EP = (ROIC - WACC)C. \qquad [15.1]$$

C = capital invested
ROIC = return on invested capital

$$ROIC = \frac{NOPAT}{C}. \qquad [15.2]$$

In practice, we need to adjust the accounting information to obtain the NOPAT and capital, and taxes on operations are not equal to the reported income taxes. For now, we keep it simple and we'll assume that tax on operations is equal to EBIT times the legal tax, until we address the required adjustments.

Economic profit is not cash flow

As its name suggests, EP is a measure of earnings rather than cash flow. Since the cost of capital charge is equal to WACC x C, we can express EP using the standard income statement format.

Operative revenues
– Operative costs
EBIT
– Income taxes on operations
NOPAT
– Cost of capital charge (WACC x C)
Economic Profit

TABLE 15.1 Income statement and NOPAT structure

Income statement structure		**NOPAT structure**	
Sales	2,000	Sales	2,000
Operative expenses (COGS, admin. & commercial expenses)	500	Operative expenses (COGS, admin. & commercial expenses)	500
EBIT	1,500	EBIT	1,500
Interest from debt	500	-	
Interest from securities	300	-	
Extraordinary income	100	-	
EBT	1,400	EBT	1,500
Income taxes 30%	420	Adjusted taxes 30%	450
Net income	980	NOPAT	1,050

Notice that we compute only the operative income and expenses to calculate the NOPAT, and to be consistent, the invested capital, or simply capital, must consider only the operative assets and noninterest-bearing current liabilities. According to Alfred Marshal (1842–1924) "What remains of his (the owner's or manager's) profits after deducting interest on his capital at the current rate may be called his earnings of undertaking or management".

NOPAT and invested capital calculation

The best way to explain how to assess EP is with an introductory example. Cleaning Corp. is engaged in the manufacturing of consumer tissue products, such as bathroom tissue, paper towels, and napkins. It sells its products to supermarkets, warehouse clubs, and other retail outlets. The first column of Table 15.1 shows the income statement structure, and the second column shows the items considered to calculate the NOPAT.

Notice how the NOPAT differs from the net income. It only considers operative revenues and expenses; therefore, neither financial results nor extraordinary income count to calculate the NOPAT. Concerning the income tax, we have to consider the taxes only attributable to operations. For the case of Cleaning, we assume adjusted taxes equals the operative income times the legal tax rate[1]:

Adjusted taxes = EBIT x t

In practice, NOPAT and taxes are subject to many adjustments we explain later. One way to calculate adjusted taxes is

Adjusted taxes = Income tax provision + tax shield – taxes on non-operating income + taxes on non-operating expenses
Adjusted taxes = 420 + 500 x 30% – 400 x 30% = 450

TABLE 15.2 Balance sheet and capital structure

	Balance sheet structure	Capital structure
Cash and banks	118	20 (*)
Marketable securities	1,000	-
Accounts receivable	1,200	1,200
Inventory	2,500	2,500
Total current assets	4,940	3,720
Buildings, land, and equipment	6,100	6,100
Construction in progress	680	-
Total assets	13,200	9,820
Accounts payable	2,200	2,200
Fiscal and social liabilities	300	300
Total current liabilities	2,500	2,500
Long term financial debt	500	-
Total liabilities	3,000	Operating liabilities 2,500
Total owner's equity	10,200	-
Total liabilities and owners' equity	13,200	Capital employed 7,320

(*) Operative cash and banks are considered to be 2% of sales

Thus, adjusted taxes, or income taxes on operations, represent the hypothetical income tax the company would have paid without considering financial effects and non-operating income/expenses. We will now compute the capital invested. Table 15.2 shows the balance sheet and the capital structures of cleaning.

The general rule to calculate the capital is subtracting all non-operative assets from the total assets (cash in excess, marketable securities, buildings, houses, land, and other non-operative assets that do not generate operative revenues or expenses) and subtracting only noninterest-bearing current liabilities. Which assets and liabilities should not be taken into account when calculating capital? The following are the more common non-operative assets:

- Cash in excess. To manage the cash as effectively and efficiently as possible, managers have an optimum cash balance to meet the liquidity needs. To address this issue, I ask CFOs during an executive program: What is the cash balance that makes you feel comfortable with? What proportion of annual sales does it represents? Before listening to their response, I write down my hunch (1.5%/2%) on the blackboard and cover it with one hand. They are really surprised when they see that their ratio is very close to 2%. Even though each company has a different cash balance to annual sales ratio, all cash in excess must be subtracted from the optimum cash balance since it is not operative.

- Marketable securities. Since marketable securities do not generate EBIT, they must not be considered part of the capital invested; to be consistent, interest from marketable securities must not be considered in the NOPAT calculation.
- Construction in progress. A construction is not an operative asset because it does not yet generate NOPAT. It will be when completed, and the asset placed into service.
- Properties and lands. Sometimes, companies have non-operative fixed assets as properties (i.e., a house for holidays, lands or departments for rent).
- Other non-operative assets, such as artworks.[2]
- Noninterest-bearing current liabilities. Operative liabilities, such as commercial, fiscal, and social liabilities, must be subtracted from the operating assets to calculate the working capital since they do not require an interest payment. For example, a company purchasing large amounts of inventory on credit has a free source of capital.

Considering the capital, NOPAT, and a WACC of 10%, the economic profit is

$$ROIC = \frac{NOPAT}{C} = \frac{1.050}{7,320} = 0.1434$$

$$EP = (0.1434 - 0.10)7,320 = 317.69$$

Most common adjustments to the financial information

To calculate both the economic profit and capital, we need to make some adjustments to the accounting information to reflect the "true" economic result of the company. The adherence to the accounting GAAP rules generates some accounting distortions. One of the typical distortions is the research and development costs (R&D); because GAAP requires record R&D costs as incurred, the earnings decline immediately in the short run, making managers' performance appear poorly.

All adjustments involve modifications to both the capital and the NOPAT. Since these adjustments affect earnings multiples, we shall revisit them in Chapter 16. Typical adjustments include:

- Capitalize intangible investments. Although US GAAP requires that R&D and advertising costs be expensed as incurred[3], these costs typically benefit the company in future periods. Thus, we must record R&D and advertising costs as long-term assets and amortize them over the estimated useful life. This adjustment means an increase in capital investment and NOPAT.
- Capitalize employee training costs. Companies invest money to train their employees to improve their skills and productivity. Employee training is an investment in human capital and should be considered a long-term asset, and amortizing these costs over the period is estimated to benefit the company's performance.
- Depreciation methods. The depreciation of a fixed asset is an operating expense that represents the decrease in the value of an asset through its useful life due to the passage of time and obsolescence. Its recording follows the straight-line

depreciation method, which is generally unrelated to the economic life of the fixed asset and can be affected by a revaluation. One way to mitigate this effect is to consider a maintenance capital expenditure that constitutes an economic or standardized depreciation unaffected by accounting differences and is forward-looking.

- Treat leased assets as if they were owned. The interest component of rents is added back to NOPAT, after taxes. As Mauboussin & Callahan (2022) point out, from 2019, most companies reporting under US generally accepted accounting principles (GAAP) or international financial reporting standards (IFRS) must reflect leases on the balance sheet. For companies reporting using GAAP, the interest paid for the lease must be treated as a financing cost; that means the interest expense after taxes must be added back to EBIT to calculate NOPAT. To be consistent, the estimated present value of rents must be added to capital.
- LIFO Reserve. The LIFO method (Last in, First Out) is a method to price ending inventories on the balance sheet. Since the last prices are usually higher than the initial prices, under LIFO, ending inventories are undervalued, meaning a higher cost of goods sold,[4] less profit, and less taxes. External financial reports are usually prepared using the LIFO method, which means that lower income taxes are included in the report. The LIFO method is particularly beneficial in periods of price increases because it lowers income taxes.[5] The same company can then use the FIFO method to price ending inventories, which reports a lower COGS and higher profit, which appeals to investors. The difference between the LIFO and FIFO (First in, First Out) is recorded as a LIFO reserve account.

$$\text{LIFO reserve} = \text{FIFO inventory} - \text{LIFO inventory}. \qquad [15.4]$$

Analysts look at a public company's LIFO reserve to see if earnings need to be adjusted for changes in LIFO reserve, as in adjusted EBITDA. The LIFO reserve must be added back to capital and the change in reserves after taxes is added to NOPAT. It also effectively shifts COGS from LIFO to FIFO while preserving the tax benefit of deducting the more expensive LIFO costs (Stewart, 2018).

Other Reserves and Allowances. Besides the LIFO Reserve, we may find other types of reserves and allowances, such as Reserve for Inventory Obsolescence and Allowance for Doubtful Accounts. These accounting transactions would be treated similarly to the LIFO Reserve.

Capitalize goodwill impairment. Goodwill is an intangible asset that accounts for the difference between the price of an acquisition minus the value of tangible assets and intangible assets net of liabilities. Although under GAAP and IFRS goodwill is not amortized,[6] companies are required to periodically test goodwill for impairment. Assume that company A acquires company B for $100 million, valuing its assets at $80 million and recognizing a goodwill of $20 million on its balance sheet. The acquisition price was based on an expected NOPAT of $10 million and a cost of capital of 10%. After some time, company A tests its assets for impairment and discovers the NOPAT is $9 million; as a result, the fair value of company B declines from $100M to $90M, and company A will record an impairment charge of $10 million on the income statement, which will also affect the value recorded on the balance sheet, but there is no impact on the cash flow. However, the impairment charge is not necessary using economic profit because the method registers a profit loss of $1 million (NOPAT – cost of capital charge = 10-10x10%), and the present value of $1 represents a loss of $10 million (1/0.10). Since impairment charges have already been considered in the economic profit, we have to reverse the impairment charge by adding $1 million to the NOPAT and $10 million to the capital. The same treatment rule should be applied for restructuring charges and non-recurring items.

Capitalize restructuring charges. Because restructuring charges distort earnings in the period incurred, they must be added back to earnings and to capital.

Capitalize non-recurring items. Extraordinary items like discontinued operations, gains and losses on debt extinguishments, and other non-recurring items, after tax, must be added back to EBIT, and are also added to capital.

Remove excess cash, lands, artworks, marketable securities and equity investments in other companies, financial subsidiaries and tax loss carryforwards. All non-operating assets must not be included in the invested capital and their rents must not be included in NOPAT.

Deferred income taxes. The deferred income tax constitutes a liability that results from the difference in income recognition between tax laws and accounting methods. The typical case of a deferred income tax is the depreciation method since most companies use straight-line depreciation for reporting and accelerated depreciation for taxes. As the accelerated depreciation method allows for more significant depreciation during a few years, cash taxes are lower than the company's reported taxes, generating a difference that must be paid in the future, which eventually will be classified as either current or long-term liability. A deferred tax asset is the opposite of a deferred tax liability. For instance, a carryover of tax losses: if a business incurs a loss during a fiscal year, the tax authority allows it to compensate its taxable income in the following years. Another possible situation is when there is a difference between tax and accounting rules. For example, when expenses are recognized in the income statement before they are required to be recognized by the tax authorities, as in the case of prepaid expenses (insurances) or revenues that were taxable before they must be recorded in the income statement. There are many ways to recognize the effects of deferred taxes on economic profit. Mauboussin & Callahan (2022) proposed to convert the book tax provision to cash taxes. For example, if a company has a net deferred tax liability balance of $100 and ends the year at $200, the difference of $100 is added to the NOPAT, and the $200 net deferred tax liability is added to capital. Adding back $100 to the NOPAT or reducing the tax provision by $100 gives the same result. By adding net deferred taxes back to the capital invested and added back to income in arriving at NOPAT, we reverse the distortion for taxes not paid. This adjustment means an increase in the capital invested and NOPAT.

Stewart (2013) is emphatic in not recommending this approach for companies that occasionally negotiate tax settlements that trigger a one-tax-time payment or credit. Instead, he proposed adding the net deferred tax liability to capital and then reducing the tax on NOPAT by the cost of capital saved from the net deferred tax liability. For example, if a company has $200 of net deferred tax liability and the cost of capital is 10%, then $200 is added to capital, and $20 is deducted from the NOPAT tax. In summary, the key rule is adding back to capital and NOPAT the following concepts:

- All expenses that will benefit the company's performance over the long run, such as R&D, employee training, advertising costs, even they were recognized as an expense in the year they were incurred.
- Goodwill impairments, restructuring cost, and non-recurring items.
- Interest after taxes paid for the lease to NOPAT and the estimated present value of rents to capital.
- The LIFO reserve must be added back to capital and the change in reserves after taxes is added to NOPAT
- The undepreciated depreciation to capital and the difference between the standardized depreciation and accounting depreciation to NOPAT.

Example: Conundrum Company

Conundrum Company's senior management has decided to use economic profit as a metric for evaluating division managers' performance. The cost of capital is 10%. Assume that management will calculate EP using the following adjustments:

1. Marketable securities must be deducted from the average operating assets since they are not operating assets.
2. Land and properties held for sale are not operating assets and must receive the same treatment as marketable securities.
3. Marketing costs will be capitalized and amortized over three years since they will benefit the performance during that time.
4. Fixed assets depreciation expense is $600, while the economic depreciation is $400: the difference of $200 must be added to capital assets and operating income. Assume no adjustments are necessary for depreciation expenses from previous years.
5. Deferred taxes. As the company has deferred taxes of $200, we must add this amount to capital. Assuming that the deferred taxes at the end of the previous year are $100, the increase of $100 is subtracted from the income tax provision.
6. All current liabilities are non-interest bearing and thus are subtracted from average operating assets.
7. Since the company uses the LIFO method to price the inventories, it has a LIFO reserve account of 80 in year 1 and $100 in year 2. The LIFO reserve must be added to capital and the change in reserves must be added to NOPAT.
8. Tax shield. Since the company saves taxes from interest on debt and pays taxes from interest on marketable securities, the next tax shield is considered to calculate the adjusted cash taxes.

Tables 15.3 and 15.4 show the income statements and balance sheet.

TABLE 15.3 Income statement

Sales	6,700
COGS	1,920
Gross margin	4,780
Allocated overhead	434
Marketing expenses	150
Administration expenses	2,480
EBIT	1,716
Interest from debt	48
Interest from securities	25
Earnings before taxes	1,693
Income tax 30%	508
Net income	1,185

TABLE 15.4 Balance sheet

Cash and banks	119
Marketable securities	562
Accounts receivable	1,022
Inventory	2,781
Total current assets	4,484
Property, plant and equipment (net)	6,780
Goodwill	1,000
Land and properties (held for sale)	1,000
Total assets	13,264
Accounts payable	1,269
Fiscal and Social liabilities	470
Total current liabilities	1,739
Financial Debt	648
Deferred taxes	200
Total liabilities	2,587
Total owner's equity	10,677
Total liabilities and owners' equity	13,264

Capital calculation

TABLE 15.5 Adjustments to arrive at capital

Total assets	13,264
Adj. 1: subtract marketable securities	562
Adj. 2: subtract land and properties	1,000
Adj.3: Add unamortized marketing costs	100
Adj.4: Add unamortized depreciation	200
Adj.5: Add deferred taxes	200
Adj. 6: Deduct non-int. bearing current liabilities	1,739
Adj.7: add LIFO reserve	100
Capital	10,563

Adjusted taxes calculation

After multiplying EBIT by the tax rate of 30%, the income tax provision amounts to \$507.9 million. As the income tax provision contains the tax savings and the taxes on interest from marketable securities, to eliminate these effects, we must calculate the net tax shield, adding to the income tax provision the interest tax shield and subtracting the tax on interest from marketable securities. The net interest tax shield is (Interest from debt minus interest from securities) x t = (48 – 25)0.30 = 6.9

In addition, we must add the change in reserve after taxes is (100 – 80)0.30 = 6, and subtract the increase in net deferred taxes, which implied an increase in NOPAT.

TABLE 15.6 Adjusted taxes

Income tax provision	507.9
+ Net interest tax shield	6.9
+ Change in reserves	6
– Increase in deferred taxes	100
Adjusted Taxes	420.8

NOPAT calculation

TABLE 15.7 Adjustments to arrive at NOPAT

EBIT	1,716
Adj. 3a: Add back marketing expenses	150
Adj. 3b: Deduct marketing amortization	50

(Continued)

TABLE 15.7 (Continued)

Adj. 4a: Add back depreciation	1,200
Adj. 4b: Deduct economic depreciation	1,000
Adj. 5: Add back goodwill amortization	100
Adjusted EBIT before tax	2,116
Adjusted taxes	420.8
NOPAT	1,695

Economic profit calculations

TABLE 15.8 Economic profit

NOPAT	1,695
Cost of capital charge 10%	1,056
Economic Profit	639

Notice that ROIC = NOPAT/C = 1,695/10,563 = 16.05% and EP = (ROIC – WACC)C = (16.04% – 10%)10,563 = 639. Since the Economic profit is positive, the interpretation would be that Conundrum would have created value for $639 million.

Economic profit in valuation and the free cash flow equivalence

Economic profit has been proposed as another method in valuation arguing that gives identical results to the free cash flow method. While using perpetuities – and after making a little algebraic arrangement - is easy to demonstrate the equivalence, when the cash flow is uneven, as it is in practice, some setups are required.

The equivalence using perpetuities

Assume that a company has reached a stationary state and does not grow anymore. Using EP, the company value is calculated as the capital invested plus the perpetuity of economic profit.

$$V = C + \frac{EP}{WACC}, \qquad [15.5]$$

$$V = C + \frac{(ROIC - WACC)\,C}{WACC},$$

$$V = \frac{C \times WACC + ROIC \times C - WACC \times C}{WACC},$$

$$V = \frac{NOPAT}{WACC}. \qquad [15.6]$$

The expression [15.6] is equal to $V = \frac{FCF}{WACC}$, as we explain in Chapter 8. Since the net investments in working capital and capital expenses are zero in a perpetuity (CAPEX equals depreciation over time), the only items of free cash flow are the EBIT and taxes on EBIT, thus, NOPAT is always equal to free cash flow.

For purposes of valuation, a company that does not grow distributes the NOPAT as dividends. Therefore, EP and FCF give the same value. Note that after rearranging and simplifying, the capital invested C disappeared from the EP valuation formula!

Now suppose the company grows at a long-term growth rate forever. Therefore, we use the growing perpetuity formula:

$$V = C + \frac{EP}{WACC - g}, \qquad [15.7]$$

$$V = C + \frac{(ROIC - WACC)C}{WACC - g},$$

$$V = \frac{C \times WACC - g \times C + ROIC \times C - WACC \times C}{WACC - g},$$

$$V = \frac{NOPAT - NI}{WACC - g} = \frac{FCF}{WACC - g}. \qquad [15.8]$$

As NI represents the net investments in working capital and CAPEX, the NOPAT less NI represents the free cash flow. After rearranging and simplifying, C vanishes once more, and both methods give the same value. Since the book value is cancelled out and only the cash flows are left to give the result, EP is equivalent to the cash flow valuation methods such as DCF and NPV. Remember that the operating asset value is implicitly considered in the expected free cash flow, as we explained in Chapter 1 when we introduced the main ideas of valuation. Notice how the expressions [15.7] and [15.8] are connected with the idea of the NPV. We accept an investment only if its NPV is positive; and the NPV would be positive if the present value of EP is higher than the capital C. In the case of the expression [15.7], the NPV of a project is calculated as

$$NPV = -C + \frac{EP}{WACC - g}. \qquad [15.9]$$

Value driver formula and the return/growth relation

An alternative formula to [15.8] is known as the value driver formula, which expresses the firm value through three value drivers: NOPAT, long-term growth rate, and WACC:

$$V = \frac{NOPAT(1 - \frac{g}{ROIC})}{WACC - g}. \qquad [15.10]$$

Rearranging terms and replacing, we have

$$V = \frac{NOPAT\left(\frac{ROIC - g}{\frac{NOPAT}{C}}\right)}{WACC - g},$$

$$V = \frac{ROIC \times C - g \times C}{WACC - g},$$

$$V = \frac{NOPAT - NI}{WACC - g} = \frac{FCF}{WACC - g}.$$

Therefore, the value driver formula equals the formula [15.6] of economic profit. With growing perpetuities, the equivalence between EP, value drivers' formula and the FCF method is easy to demonstrate. Does the equivalence between EP and FCF valuation methods hold when the cash flow is uneven? The answer is a great conditional "IF" since it requires some conditions hold and any setup. The equivalency also holds if ROIC exceeds WACC; however, a setup is required if the ROIC-WACC convergence is assumed.

The equivalence for uneven cash flows when ROIC>WACC

The formula to calculate the value a company using the EP method was possibly inspired by the 1961 Miller-Modigliani paper: "Adding in the present value of the (uniform perpetual) earnings, on the assets currently held, we get as an expression for the value of the firm" (pp. 416–417). The first term of the formula represents the present value of a constant perpetual earnings and the second term represents the present value of economic profit from the investments in some future period t:

$$V = \frac{X}{k} + \sum_{t=0}^{\infty} I(t) \frac{r - k}{k(1+k)^{t+1}}. \qquad [15.11]$$

X = expected net operating profit
k = cost of capital
r = return on invested capital
I(t) = investment in period t

Adding the capital invested in assets in place C and decomposing the second term of the MM formula in the economic profit generated by the assets in place and the economic profit generated from future investments, we can express the firm value as the sum of the three terms: C, the present value of the expected EP from the assets in place and the present value from the EP generated by future investments:

$$V = C + \sum_{t=1}^{\infty} \frac{EP_{t\ Assets\ in\ place}}{(1+WACC)^t} + \sum_{t=1}^{\infty} \frac{EP_{t\ Future\ investments}}{(1+WACC)^t}. \qquad [15.12]$$

Example: Fructus Corp. is a company that generates value for its shareholders because the ROIC exceeds the WACC and grows at a vigorous rate, until reaching a steady state at the end of year five. Once the company matures, the expected long-term growth rate is 3%. Table 15.9 and Figures 15.1 and 15.2 show that firm value, represented by the PV of free cash flow plus terminal value, is always higher than Invested Capital, while FCF is lower than NOPAT in the first two years, because of the higher investment requirements. Notice that it is assumed that net investments, composed of CAPEX and working capital, will be made at the beginning of each year and thus are shown in the previous year (for example, the net investment of 3,500 in year 2 is shown in year 1, the net investment of year 3 is shown in year 2, and so forth. Stewart (1991) makes the same assumption in some introductory examples[7] and then applies the economic profit to Wal-Mart. The free cash flow is the difference between NOPAT and net investment, and the WACC is assumed to be 10%. We calculate the terminal value of EP and FCF methods with the growing perpetuity formula as 376.4/(10% – 3%) = 5,377 and 1,644.6 (1 + 3%)/(10% – 3%) = 24,199, respectively.

So far, so good. However, our projection does not take into account a very long-standing logic assumption on valuation: once the company reaches a steady state, the competitive advantages become exhausted and the company cannot create value for its shareholders anymore, since the ROIC should converge to the WACC. If Fructus Corp. gets to maintain the ROIC above the cost of capital, would create value for shareholders forever, which is note feasible since the company value would grow indefinitely.

TABLE 15.9 Economic profit and FCF in valuation

Year	**1**	**2**	**3**	**4**	**5**	**T+1**
Growth rate		35%	15%	10%	7%	3%
NOPAT	1,200	1,620	1,863	2,049	2,193	2,259
Capital	10,000	13,500	15,525	17,078	18,273	18,821
Net investment	3,500	2,025	1,553	1,195	548	565
FCF	–2,300	–405	311	854	1,645	1,694
ROIC	12%	12%	12%	12%	12%	12.00%
WACC	10%	10%	10%	10%	10%	10%
EP spread	2%	2%	2%	2%	2%	2%
Ec. profit calculations						
Economic profit	200	270	311	342	365	376
Terminal value					5,377	
	200	270	311	342	5,743	
PV economic profit	4,437					
Capital	10,000					
C + PV economic profit	14,437					
FCF calculations						
Free cash flow	–2,300	–405	311	854	1,645	1,694
Terminal value					24,199	24,925
FCF + terminal value	–2,300	–405	311	854	25,843	26,618
PV FCF per year	14,437	18,181	20,404	22,134	23,494	24,199

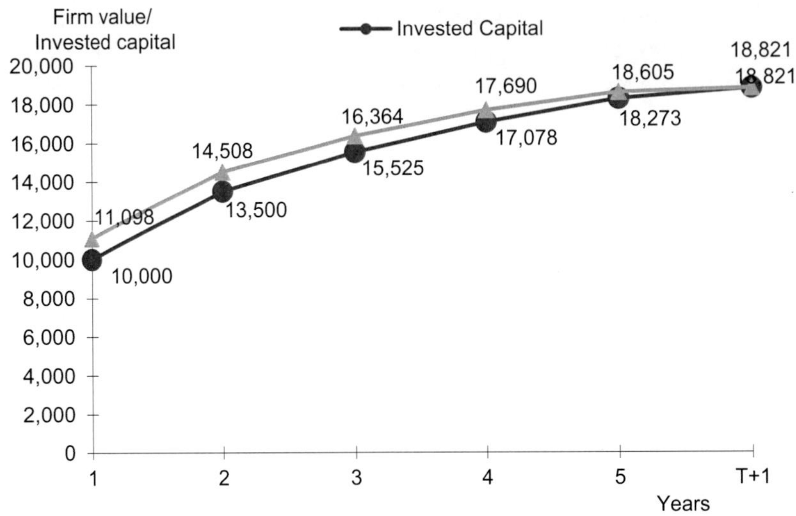

FIGURE 15.1 Invested capital and firm value

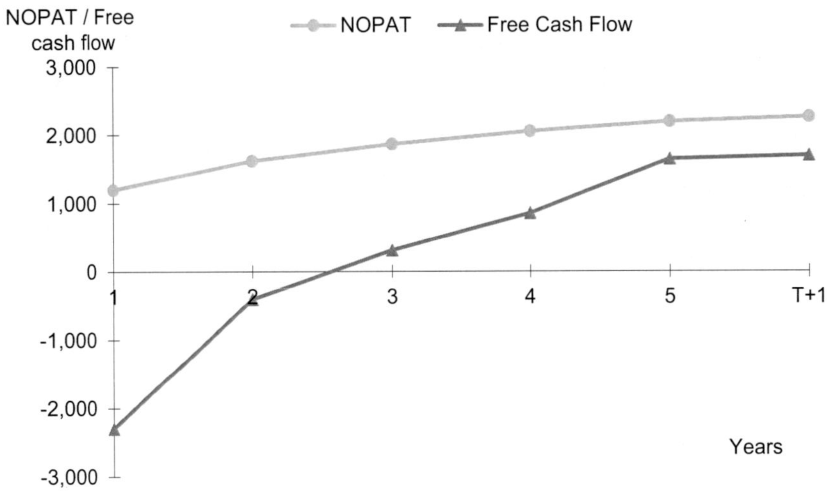

FIGURE 15.2 NOPAT and free cash flow

EP and FCF valuation equivalence assuming that ROIC and WACC converge

If the company cannot create value beyond the steady state, the fulfillment of this condition requires introducing setups for some relationships hold at the end of the explicit forecasted period:

1. The NOPAT/Capital ratio (ROIC) equals WACC.
2. The terminal value must match the invested capital.

   Damodaran (2012) provides an example of valuing a firm as the sum of three terms: the capital assets in place, the present value of the EP from assets in place, and the present value of a series of new investments. Since it is expected the new investments equal depreciation, it constitutes an application of the formula [15.3].

Finally, to match the equivalence with the free cash flow method, he assumes the return on new investments that start at the beginning of the terminal year will be equal to the cost of capital, while the growth in NOPAT would be 5% a year beyond the steady state. However, in order for the ROIC to match the WACC, it would require setting up a considerable increase in the invested capital or a decrease in NOPAT.

Following with the example of Fructus Corp., we set up the NOPAT for year T+1 at $1,882 for the ROIC equals 10% (1,882/18,821); notice that the terminal value of free cash flow equals the Capital of $18,821 at the beginning of the year T+1 and both methods provide the same company value. We can also set up a higher capital rather than a lower NOPAT or a combination of the two; however, it is counterintuitive that NOPAT decreases while capital increases or that capital increases while NOPAT decreases from year T to year T+1. This result happens because we consider a drop in the ROIC from 12%

TABLE 15.10 Economic profit and FCF in valuation setting up the NOPAT/capital ratio

Year	**1**	**2**	**3**	**4**	**5**	**T+1**
Growth rate		35%	15%	10%	7%	3%
NOPAT	1,200	1,620	1,863	2,049	2,193	1,882
Capital	10,000	13,500	15,525	17,078	18,273	18,821
Net investment	3,500	2,025	1,553	1,195	548	565
FCF	−2,300	−405	311	854	1,645	1,317
ROIC	12%	12%	12%	12%	12%	10%
WACC	10%	10%	10%	10%	10%	10%
EP spread	2%	2%	2%	2%	2%	0%
Ec. profit calculations						
Economic Profit	200	270	311	342	365	0
Terminal value					0	
	200	270	311	342	365	
PV Economic Profit	1,098					
Capital	10,000					
C + PV Economic Profit	11,098					
FCF calculations						
Free cash flow	−2,300	−405	311	854	1,645	1,317
Terminal value					18,821	19,386
FCF + Terminal value	2,300	405	311	854	20,466	20,703
PV FCF per year	11,098	14,508	16,364	17,690	18,605	18,821

to 10%, rather a gradual, asymptotic convergence over a longer forecast period, allowing the present value difference between two methodologies to disappear.

We discussed some of the ROIC-Capital relationship's shortcomings in Chapter 10, and provide examples about firms with revenues compounded by services could overstate ROIC since they don't use fixed capital for its generation and ROIC could be extremely large or negative. These issues could make the setup unreliable.

Size does not always matter: Bianca Co. and the mirage of growth and earnings

Any CEO wants the business grows and profits measures increase (EBITDA, net income, earnings per share). Growth is typically associated with something good; the higher the sales, size, and profits, the better, and the business is supposedly in good shape. However, the expansion requires new investments in working capital and CAPEX; thus, growth means more investments. The growth of sales, assets, and earnings could be a mirage if the company value increases less than the new investments or even decreases. This issue is not always understood, mainly in the case of private companies.

Bianca Company was a small company that operated in an emerging market. It was involved with the production of vanillas, and to be honest, they were the best vanillas made in the industry. At the beginning, Bianca sold their products to small supermarkets, keeping a respectable EBITDA margin and a reasonable DOS ratio – two factors that significantly affect a company's value since they affect free cash flow. Leo, the owner, dissatisfied with the business' growth, decided to expand it and started selling vanillas to large supermarkets, despite the fact that they imposed several conditions on their suppliers. As a result, revenues increased sharply, but at the same time, considerable investments in working capital and capital expenditures were necessary.[8] Was the growth favorable? Profits and assets had increased. The bad news is that supermarkets traditionally impose some conditions on their suppliers that affect negatively the cash cycle and the EBITDA margin. The cash cycle is affected because supermarkets delayed payments to suppliers. EBITDA margin is affected because supermarkets impose fees on their suppliers to get the best place on the shelves. As a result, both the free cash flow and the return on invested capital are negatively affected. Although Leo learned that investing at a rate of return lower than its cost destroys value, he believed this was very theoretical, and there was no point in being worried about such a situation. After all, Bianca was a private company, so "it would never be penalized by the stock market".

Table 15.11 and Figure 15.3 show the NOPAT and free cash flow evolution over a five-year period. At first, the free cash flow is negative due to the investment requirements to finance the rapid growth. Once it achieves a steady state, investment requirements cease, and the free cash flow collapses into NOPAT (we assume here that the growth rate will be 0% from year six and beyond). Net investments are assumed to occur at the beginning of each year. Notice that both methods give identical results, since the company value is $65 million and when the expected long-term growth rate is zero, the condition that establishes the terminal value equals the invested capital at the end of the explicit period T is not required.

TABLE 15.11 NOPAT and free cash flow of Bianca Company

	Year 0	Year 1	Year 2	Year 3	Year 4	Year 5
NOPAT	9.0	11.7	13.8	14.8	15.7	16.2
Invested Capital	110.0	143.0	171.6	188.8	203.9	214.1
Net Investment	33.0	28.6	17.2	15.1	10.2	0.0
FCF	–24.0	–16.9	–3.4	–0.3	5.5	16.2
ROIC	8%	8%	8%	8%	8%	8%
WACC	10%	10%	10%	10%	10%	10%
Economic Profit	–0.02	–0.02	–0.02	–0.02	–0.02	–0.02
PV EP	–45					
PV EP + C	65					
PV FCF per year	65	96	122	138	152	162

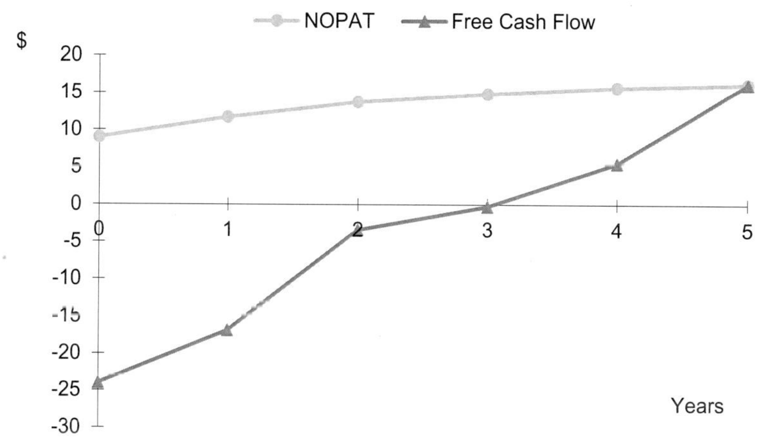

FIGURE 15.3 NOPAT and free cash flow

Figure 15.4 shows the capital and firm value evolution for each year. Notice two important things: 1. Firm value is always inferior to capital 2. The increase in DCF value is always lower than the increase in the capital invested over the forecast period (at the beginning the difference is about $45 million and at the end is a bit more than $52 million. Therefore, the increase in NOPAT and firm value is only a mirage; the more the company invests, the more value it destroys since the present value of the outstanding free cash flow is lower than the invested capital.

Owners do not care or do not realize until they want to sell the business when they receive an offer or are required to express how much they want for the company. The latter is what happened with Bianca. One day, a potential buyer made an offer for a much lower value than the capital invested in the business. Surprised, the first thing Leo got to say was: "I invested $110 million here, and you are offering less than that sum of money?"

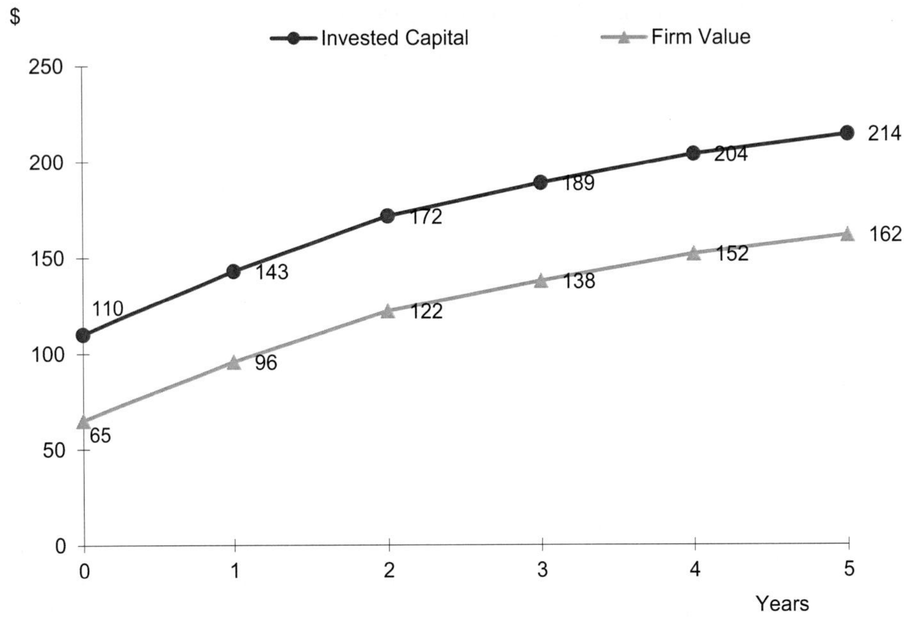

FIGURE 15.4 Firm value and capital invested

The immediate answer was: "The replacement value of the assets or the capital you invested here may be higher than my offer. But we are interested in the expected cash flow, not in the cost of starting the business from scratch. The present value of the expected free cash flow is around $65 million. Thus, paying $110 million for your company is not much of a deal".

The lesson is that a business can increase its size, but this does not mean it increases its fair value. So simple as to invest your money to receive a return of 9% when the opportunity cost for an investment that involves the same risk is 10%. In such a case, each dollar invested in the business will destroy shareholders' value. Size does not always matter.

The depreciation effect on economic profit

Because of the straight-line depreciation method, an investment may have a lower EP and ROIC at the beginning of the project's life and a higher one in later years, as the NOPAT raises while the capital decreases. It has been proved many times in financial literature that accounting return measures are a poor estimator of the underlying rate of return. Harcourt (1965) stated that the accounting measure of the rate of profit is misleading since it is affected by the method of depreciation used whether or not the stock of capital is growing. Fischer and McGowan (1983) argued that only the economic rate of return on investment is relevant for inferring monopoly returns and stated that the accounting data used to construct returns are inappropriate for capturing the true rate of return. Suppose you are applying the EP method to evaluate a single project. Table 15.12 displays the expected free cash flow, including a salvage value in year 10. Its internal rate of return is 21.82%, and the cost of capital is 12%. As the NPV is positive, and the IRR is greater than

TABLE 15.12 Internal rate of return of the investment

	Year 0	Year 1	Year 2	Year 3	Year 4	Year 5	Year 6	Year 7	Year 8	Year 9	Year 10
Sales		1,560	2,652	3,448	3,965	4,559	5,015	5,517	5,793	6,082	6,387
Operative expenses		1,014	1,724	2,241	2,577	2,964	3,260	3,586	3,765	3,954	4,151
Depreciation		260	260	260	260	260	260	260	260	260	260
EBIT		286	668	947	1,128	1,336	1,495	1,671	1,767	1,869	1,975
Income Taxes (40%)		114	267	379	451	534	598	668	707	748	790
NOPAT		172	401	568	677	801	897	1,003	1,060	1,121	1,185
+ Depreciation		260	260	260	260	260	260	260	260	260	260
- Incr. Working capital		68	62	159	103	119	91	100	55	58	61
CAPEX		130	130	130	130	130	130	130	130	130	130
Free Cash Flow	−3,000	234	469	539	703	813	936	1,032	1,135	1,193	1,254
Salvage value											3,000
FCF + Salvage value	−3,000	234	469	539	703	813	936	1,032	1,135	1,193	4,254
Cost of capital	12.00%										
NPV	$1,851.25										
IRR	21.82%										

TABLE 15.13 ROIC and economic profit of the investment

	Year 0	Year 1	Year 2	Year 3	Year 4	Year 5	Year 6	Year 7	Year 8	Year 9	Year 10
Working Capital	400	468	530	690	793	912	1,003	1,103	1,159	1,216	1,277
Fixed assets	2,600	2,470	2,340	2,210	2,080	1,950	1,820	1,690	1,560	1,430	1,300
Capital		2,938	2,870	2,900	2,873	2,862	2,823	2,793	2,719	2,646	2,577
ROIC		5.8%	14.0%	19.6%	23.6%	28.0%	31.8%	35.9%	39.0%	42.4%	46.0%
Economic Profit		-181	56	220	332	458	558	667	734	804	876
PV Economic Profit	1,964.10										

the cost of capital, the two rules lead us to the same decision: accept the project. However, Table 15.13 shows the ROIC is 5.8% in year 1 and 46% in year 10. The economic profit is negative in the first year and increases from year 2 to the end of the project's useful life in year 10. The present value of EP is \$1,964.10, higher than the NPV.

It has been suggested that one approach to addressing this issue is adopting an economic depreciation plan rather an accounting depreciation schedule over the life of the investment. However, it doesn't solve the difference. At this point, one might ask: if we have to establish some setups for NPV and EP to give the same result, why not use NPV directly? Even recognizing that there are no bulletproof metrics, we see some advantages and disadvantages of using economic profit. For example, the internal rate of return (IRR) and the net present value give us a unique measure, calculated considering several years/periods (since they use a stream of cash flows); in that sense, they are complex weighted averages since we can have a low cash flow in a year and a high cash flow in another. On the other hand, EP permits focusing on the performance in every period. The anomaly that comes from the depreciation method deserves attention and must be carefully explained and discussed with the senior management that uses the EP to evaluate projects or adopts a bonus system based on economic profit.[9] Finally, if you are measuring the company's performance, the evolution of the economic profit could be more important than the absolute level.

Box 15.1 The case of Ipiranga

In 2006, we were hired to analyze the performance of Ipiranga, a Brazilian Petroleum Company. The management wanted to know if its ROIC was in line with the performance observed by American companies in the petroleum industry as well as to that of other Brazilian companies in different industries. In addition, the senior management was interested in the relationship between economic profit and market value added (MVA). The total market value is equal to the market capitalization plus debt value. The MVA is the difference between the total market value and the invested capital:[10]

$$MVA = Total\ Market\ Value - Capital\ Invested \quad [15.11]$$

The first part of the analysis consisted in comparing the Ipiranga's ROIC to the ROIC of the top 25 Brazilian companies operating in various industries as well as the ROIC of a sample of 15 American petroleum companies at the time. Its ROIC was below the average sample in both instances.

TABLE 15.14 ROIC of Ipiranga and Brazilian companies of different industries

	ROIC	ROIC 3 yr average
Ipiranga	11.5%	10.4%
Average sample	14.9%	15.0%
25th percentile	7.99%	10.09%
75th percentile	21.37%	21.24%

TABLE 15.15 ROIC of Ipiranga and American petroleum companies

	ROIC	ROIC 3 yr average
Ipiranga	11.5%	10.4%
Average sample	16.5%	13.9%
25th percentile	11.3%	9.2%
75th percentile	20.9%	18.5%

The second requirement was to compare the present value of the expected economic profit with the market value added. We first forecasted the stream of economic profit for ten years, including the terminal value, and then we calculated the present value for each year using a WACC of 12%. The present value of the expected economic profit only explained a small part of the MVA. The gap between the market value and invested capital indicates that the market expected a better performance of the business than economic profit indicated.

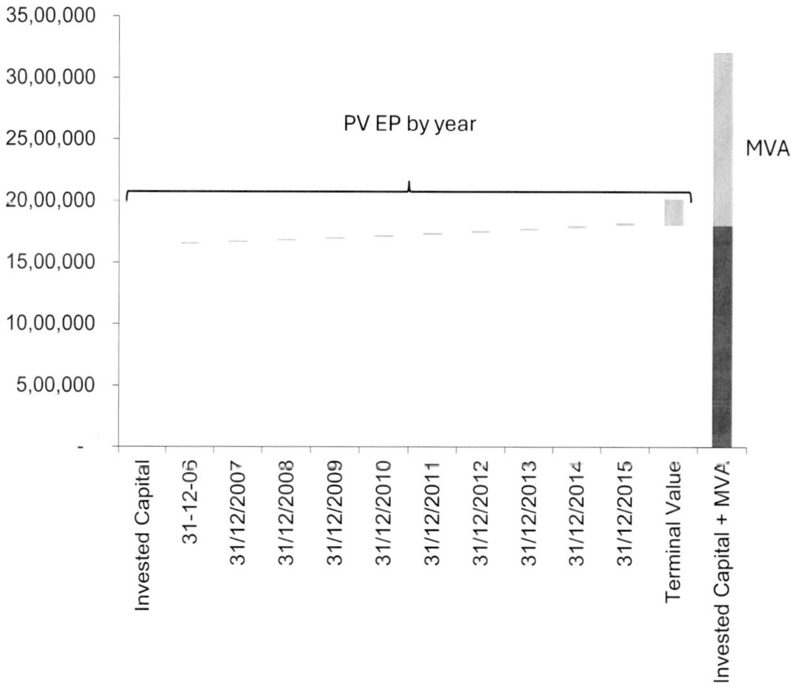

FIGURE 15.5 Economic profit and MVA of Ipiranga

Traditional metrics may lead to wrong investment decisions

Many companies use metrics such as earnings per share, net income, ROE, ROA or ROIC to measure their performance. Although there are no bulletproof metrics, some metrics are better than others. Smart Corp. is a full-equity finance

TABLE 15.16 ROIC, EPS, economic profit and NPV of Smart Corp.

	Business as actual	Investment	Metrics after investment
NOPAT	160	24	184
Capital	1000	200	1200
ROIC	16,0%	12,0%	15,3%
Cost of capital charge	100	20	120
EPS	0,16	0,12	0,15
Economic Profit	60	4	64
NPV	600	40	640

company with a ROIC of 16% and a cost of capital of 10%; thus, the current operations create value for shareholders. Suppose Smart has an opportunity to invest 200M in a project to expand its operations with a return of 12%. While Economic Profit and NPV are positive, the ROIC decreases from 16% to 15.3%, and EPS decreases from 0.16 to 0.15. The investment is good and must be accepted, however, someone who relies on traditional metrics may be inclined to reject the investment, since it reduces earnings metrics. Rejecting the investment would be a mistake because its return exceeds the cost of capital, resulting in a positive NPV of 40 (–200 + 24/0.10) and Economic Profit (0.12 – 0.10)200 = 40, calculated assuming perpetuities.

Suppose Bewildered Corp. is fully equity financed and has a cost of capital of 12%. Since its ROIC is 10%, the current operations are destroying shareholders' value. However, the management is comfortable using earnings per share as a metric performance; any investment decision should increase the earnings per share to be accepted. Let's say Bewildered gets the chance to invest 200M in a project with a return of 11.5%. A Bewildered manager recommends making the investment since once the project is running, the ROIC and EPS will increase. However, both economic profit and NPV show that the investment destroys value. The value increases only when new investments cover the cost of capital, although the ROIC and EPS could increase or decrease if the new projects earn more or less than the existing average return on capital. Although ROIC would be a good metric of the return on capital for this case, it does not count the cost of capital. In addition, the EPS has many flaws since managers can manipulate earnings per share to demonstrate profitability by) deferring or cutting discretionary spending to meet short-term goals and transitory share repurchases or by splitting stocks. As Economic Profit counts the cost of capital, it would be a better measure of company performance than EPS, ROIC, ROA, and ROE since they fail due to not considering the cost of capital, and are not consistent with the objective of a firm, which is to maximize the net present value of all existing and projected investments.[11] Stewart (2012) explained that ROIC, ROA, RONA, and its variants fail due to this inconsistency and states that economic profit automatically deducts the capital charge that must be earned to recover the amount of capital that has been invested.

TABLE 15.17 ROIC, EPS, economic profit and NPV of Bewildered Corp.

	Business as actual	Investment opportunity	Metrics after investment
NOPAT	160	23	183
Capital	1600	200	1800
ROIC	10,0%	11,5%	10,2%
Cost of capital charge	192	24	216
EPS	0,100	0,115	0,102
Economic Profit	-32	-1	-33
NPV	-266,7	-8,3	-275,0

Decisions to create value

The value drivers to create (or destroy) value are related to investment, financial, and divestiture decisions.

Creating value through investment decisions

The company can create value with the assets in place (reducing operative expenses, increasing efficiency) and select projects with a positive NPV. This is nothing new.

Creating value with divestitures

The management can create value through divestitures by identifying and selling the business segments that don't fit their objective. A divesture allows companies to generate cash flow, cut costs, and focus on their core businesses. Divestments are also a source of capital to fuel growth. Many years ago, we advised Alfa Corp., an enterprise group of three companies: the first was related to the software industry, the second to the publishing industry, and the third was a printer. The software and publishing businesses performed well, but the printing company did not; we recommended selling the business since it was destroying value. Senior management argued right once that the company had been in business for years, and recently it outsourced products to other companies to increase revenues and covering the operative expenses. Our advice was ignored because emotional reasons prevailed over rational arguments. We conducted the group's second valuation six years later. In this opportunity, we perceived that the senior management would think seriously about the printing company's performance and were determined to sell the business. Initially, they claimed for a liquidation value, close to the assets market value minus liabilities. Although the printing company had some fixed assets, they are highly illiquid. Its employees were older, too. After a short discussion, senior management acknowledged that they were willing to sell the company for free in order to avoid having to pay workers' compensation!

TABLE 15.18 Monthly economic profit of two sales on credit

	A	B
Revenues	1,000	1,000
Operative expenses	741.0	742.0
Earnings before taxes	259.0	258.0
Taxes (40%)	103.6	103.2
NOPAT	155.4	154.8
Account payables (capital)	166.7	83.3
Cost of capital charge	1.67	0.83
Economic profit	165.0	154.0

Creating value through intelligent capital structure decisions

In previous chapters, we describe the fiscal advantages of debt financing. Occasionally, you may face a situation where the interlocutor is not convinced to use debt on the capital structure. Donald is the sole owner of a very profitable, unlevered company. The business was able to finance its expansion using internal funds in the past, and it is still able to finance the growth to do so now. When I explained the tax advantages of debt, he answered: "You mean that the business would save taxes with a leveraged capital structure; so, I should go into debt and use the money to repurchase shares to myself. Then what? What should I do with the funds? Since I don´t get a similar return, thus, I should reinvest the funds in other businesses, receiving a lower return". The answer seems quite challenging, but the issue is not whether Donald should do it but whether someone has the ability to design an intelligent capital structure.

Account receivables as capital employed and economic profit

Recently, the CFO of SRP Corp. analyzed two operations. The company sold its products under different schemes: operation A has a higher NOPAT; however, DSO is 60 days, while DSO of Operation B takes half, 30 days. Since the company invests in customers, the account receivables balance represents the capital invested in these operations. The cost of capital is an annual 12% or monthly 1%. Although the NOPAT of A is higher, after recognizing a cost of capital charge, the Economic Profit of B is higher. If SRP performs one operation B for each month, the difference would be (165.0–154.0) x 12 = $132 million. Computing a cost of capital, even in accounts receivable, is particularly important in emerging countries, where the inflation and interest rates are usually higher than in developed.

Managing the short-term and long-term profits tradeoff

The tradeoff between short-term and long-term profits involves balancing short-term profits against potential greater profits in the future. Managers are typically influenced by external pressures, such as delivering short-term result to satisfy investors' expectations, which may lead to postpone investments in innovation, research and development, and employee training which in turn can lead to substantial gains in the future. Constraints on quarterly reporting could therefore work as the enemy of long-termism. Rappaport (1986) alerts managers not to accept short-term earnings as guidance and stated they should make strategic decisions and acquisitions that maximize shareholders' value, even if short-term earnings are negative. Firms that invest in R&D, such as technology and pharmaceuticals typically not see results right away, but they are better positioned for future growth. For example, Apple consistently invest in R&D to create new technologies and products, like the iPhone and Apple Watch, which, in addition to generate immediate sales and profits, enhance brand loyalty and market position over time. CEOs must balance duration and level of returns: a company that delivers high shareholder returns in the short term (maybe two or three years) does not ensure future success, while focusing solely on the long-term returns can lead to shareholder activism.

Concluding thoughts

The economic profit strictly focuses on computing the "true" capital that produces the "true" operating income. It could be considered a better metric than ROA, ROE, and other similar since they don't compute the cost of capital. As a measure of performance, it can clarify some situations. For example, when the company invests in projects with a positive NPV while at the same time, the traditional metrics, such as ROIC or ROE exhibit a decrease. On the other hand, EP is affected by the depreciation schedule, and the equivalence with the free cash flow method requires the ratio NOPAT/Capital setup to reach the ROIC-WACC convergence.

Short questions and problems

1. The senior management of WW must calculate the EP of an investment. The NOPAT is \$100 million, operating assets totaling \$500 million and operating liabilities totaling \$150 million. The WACC is 10%. Calculate the economic profit.
2. Spring company incurred \$20 million in R&D expenses, \$1 million in employee training, working capital of \$10 million, has off-balance sheet operating leases of \$10 million, and fixed assets of \$40 million. Let's assume R&D expenses and employee training will benefit the next five years. The NOPAT is \$5 million, and the WACC is 10%. Calculate the economic profit.
3. Describe how these items should be adjusted and the impact on NOPAT and Capital:

   a) Expenditures on R&D expenses and employee training
   b) Construction in progress
   c) Allowances for doubtful debts
   d) Deferred tax provisions
   e) Operating leases

4. Aluminum Corp. is a mature company with low business risk. The management recently decided to acquire a competitor, arguing that the acquisition will increase the earnings as follows:

TABLE 15.19 ROIC before and after a new acquisition

	Business as actual	Acquisition	Business as actual+ acquisition
Operative income	1,000	500	1,500
Income taxes 40%	400	200	600
NOPAT	600	300	900
Capital	3,000	1,900	4,900
ROIC	20%	16%	18%

The cost of capital is 15%, and the net income is distributed as dividends. JM, a manager, does not agree with the acquisition since the consolidated ROIC decreases. What do you think?

5. Concerning problem 4, which would be your answer if the cost of capital would have been 18% rather than 15%?
6. Fill in X in Table 15.20 and describe which of the three firms creates more value and why.

TABLE 15.20 ROIC and FCF of A, B, and C companies

	A	B	C
NOPAT	100	120	120
Growth rate	10%	10%	25%
Capital	1,000	1,000	1,000
Net investment/NOPAT	100%	80%	200%
Change in NOPAT	10	10	25
Net investment	100	96	X
ROIC	10%	12%	X
FCF = NOPAT-I	0	24	X

7. Assuming that Coffice has a NOPAT of $200, its capital is $1,000 and its cost of capital is 10%, calculate:

   a) The economic profit
   b) The consolidated economic profit supposing Coffice invests $1,000 in a project with an expected return of 25% and a cost of capital of 15%.
   c) The same as b), but assuming the project has a return of 9%.

d) The economic profit assuming a new management gets efficiencies that reduce the working capital investment by \$40.

8. Determine the average capital using US Steel's financial data for 2021 and 2022 (remember that construction in progress is still not an operative asset):

TABLE 15.21 US Steel's financial data

	2021	2022
Total assets	16,988	16,931
Construction in progress	2,470	885
Operating liabilities	3,896	3,824

9. Determine the NOPAT, ROIC, and EP based on Microglobal's operating income of \$3,160M, its 2022 income tax provision of \$782, and its WACC of 12.7%.
10. El Puerto de Liverpool is a Mexican department store chain with an extensive retail offering that includes shopping, boutiques, and financial businesses. Calculate the economic profit for 2022 based on the following financial data. The WACC is 12.80%, and the statutory tax rate is 30%.

TABLE 15.22 El Puerto de Liverpool's financial data

	2022	2021
Total assets	235,875	221,971
Construction in progress	4,629	5,963
Short term deposits	20,712	30,248
Operating liabilities	54,713	50,191
Operating income	25,515	

11. The management of Skyline Corp. acquired Granite Peak for \$4,000 based on an expected NOPAT of \$400 in perpetuity and a cost of capital of 10%. As the equity book value of Granite Peak is \$3,000, goodwill of \$1000 is registered. Once the management of Skyline takes control of the business, notes the NOPAT is lower, around \$300. Therefore, it decides to register an impairment of \$100 and writes down the asset value to \$1,000. What is the economic profit? What is the effect on the fair market value? Which adjustment should be performed to calculate the NOPAT?
12. Tables 15.23 and 15.24 show the total assets, current liabilities, and income statement of OIL-DRI Corporation of America. Determine the ROIC considering an operative cash balance of 2% of revenues, a tax rate of 21%, and any other adjustments that you believe are necessary to determine the capital invested.

TABLE 15.23 ODC total assets and current liabilities

	July 2023
Cash and cash equivalents	31,754
Accounts receivable	59,287
Inventories	42,612
Other assets	2,854
Property, Plant and Equipment	120,872
Goodwill	3,618
Trademarks and patents	1,399
Customer list	22
Deferred income taxes	7,201
Operating lease right-of-use assets	9,386
Other non-current assets	7,230
Total assets	286,235
Accounts payable	17,101
Dividends payable	1,927
ST Notes payable	1,000
Operating lease liabilities	1,872
Accrued expenses	36,868
Current liabilities	58,768

TABLE 15.24 ODC income statement

	July 2023
Total revenue	413,021
Cost of goods sold	309,794
Gross margin	103,227
Selling and admin. expenses	62,187
EBIT	41,040

Notes

1 Although NOPAT and NOPLAT (net operating profit less adjusted taxes) are used interchangeably, the latter considers deferred taxes. If a company does not carry deferred taxes, NOPAT equals NOPLAT.

2 Artwork on the balance sheet of a company is strange. We have seen a case where the company's owner wanted to include the collection of artworks in the company's price. The buyers told him they were only interested in the company and not art collectors.

3 The accounting rules rely on a prudence criterion. Spending money on R&D does not mean there will be future benefits, and when any future benefits will occur. As such, R&D, employee training, and advertising costs do not meet the definition of an asset for GAAP purposes.

4 The cost of goods sold is determined by the value of the beginning inventories plus purchases, minus the ending inventories.

5 LIFO inventory method is forbidden in The United Kingdom, New Zealand, most countries in the European Union because it's not allowed under the International Financial Reporting Standards (IFRS)

6 If under other accounting norms, the goodwill is amortized, the amortization charge must be added back to capital, and also must be added back in arriving at NOPAT. Although it is a non-cash expenditure, differences in goodwill accounting affect profit measures, capital invested, and ROIC.

7 These examples assume that the long-term growth rate is zero, thus the NOPAT collapses to the free cash flow. In this case, both methods give the same value and no setups are required.

8 Leo knew the industry very well since his father was the owner of the largest vanilla producers, finally acquired by Nabisco.

9 Economic profit is a component of executive compensation at a well-known European automotive company. Compensation, however, is not only determined by EP; rather, it accounts for about 20% of a weighted average of performance metrics.

10 Sometimes, it is calculated as the difference between the market capitalization and the equity book value.

11 It appears that macroeconomists are out of touch with the objective of the firm. Any financial economist knows that the main objective of the firm is to maximize the shareholder's value, but it is still possible to find any book (not finance textbooks) where the author says or suggests that the objective of the firm is to maximize profits (perhaps influenced by the microeconomic textbooks and the marginal rule). Try googling "objective of the firm" to check it. Profit's objective is caveman and erroneous; otherwise, finance would not exist.

References

Damodaran, A. (2012). *Investment Valuation Tools and Techniques for Determining the Value of Any Asset*, 3rd edition. New York: John Wiley & Sons.

Harcourt, G. (1965). The Accountant in a Golden Age. *Oxford Economic Papers, 17*, 66–80.

Marshall, A. (1890). *Principles of Economics*. London: Macmillan.

Mauboussin, M. J., & Callahan, D. (2022). Return on Invested Capital, How to Calculate ROIC and Handle Common Issues. *Consilient Observer*, 1–44.

Miller, M., & Modigliani, F. (1961). Dividend Policy, Growth, and the Valuation of Shares. *The Journal of Business, 34(4)*, 441–433.

Rappaport, A. (1986). *Creating Shareholder Value: The New Standard for Business Performance*. New York: The Free Press.

Stewart, B. (1991). *The Quest for Value: A Guide for Senior Managers*. New York: Harper Business.

Stewart, B. (2013). *Best-Practice EVA: The Definitive Guide to Measuring and Maximizing Shareholder Value*. New York: Wiley.

Stewart, B. (2018). The EVA Measurement Formula. A Primer on Economic Value Added (EVA). Available at chrome-extension://efaidnbmnnnibpcajpcglclefindmkaj/https://www.shareholderforum.com/access/Library/20181108_ISS-Stewart.pdf

CHAPTER

16

Relative valuation

DOI: 10.4324/9781003628491-19

Introduction

Another valuation method that is frequently applied in M&A transactions is relative valuation. At first glance, it seems very straightforward: as we mentioned in Chapter 4 when we estimated the fair value of Geenworth, all we need to do is select a set of comparable companies, choose the appropriate multiple, which is typically a measure of company earnings like EBITDA, and then multiply the sample mean by the target's estimated EBITDA to estimate the fair company value.

The basic assumption underlying the relative valuation is that there are firms with similar characteristics that can be grouped into similar classes. For instance, it appears natural to compare a firm that produces soft drinks and sparkling waters with similar businesses, such as Coca-Cola, PepsiCo, National Beverage, Nestle, and Keurig Dr. Pepper.

After reading this chapter, you will be able to:

- Select the peer group and choosing the right multiple;
- Analyze the connections between a multiple and the company fundamentals;
- Make adjustments to the financial information to make useful comparisons;
- Recognize the limitations of the relative valuation.

What is a multiple?

A multiple is simply a ratio of the market value of an asset relative to a key statistic – usually some measure of the company's earnings – that is assumed to have a logical relationship to the market value observed. One of the most popular multiples used by capital markets analysts is the price–earnings ratio or P/E ratio. The P/E ratio relates the price per share with the earnings per share:

$$P/E = \frac{\text{Price per share}}{\text{Earnings per share}}. \qquad [16.1]$$

According to Refinitiv Eikon's July 2023 quotes, Exxon Mobil Corp.'s P/E ratio in December 2022 was 8.31 (earnings per share excluding extraordinary items):

$$P/E = \frac{110.30}{13.27} = 8.31$$

The immediate interpretation is that investors were willing to pay a multiple of 8.31 times the current earnings per share (EPS) for one share of Exxon Mobil. The metric in the numerator is typically higher than the one in the denominator because the former is supposed to be many times larger than the latter. The enterprise value/EBITDA or price/EBITDA multiples are the most widely utilized multiples to determine the fair value of a non-financial company, despite the fact that the P/E ratio is frequently used in security analysis. A few multiples use the cash flow, the book value of a share, or the company sales instead of a measure of the earnings.

Consistency between the market value and the earnings measure

The connection between the market value and the earnings measure is the most important. For example, equity value multiples, such as P/E, are calculated using a denominator relevant to equity holders. Notice that it relates the share price with the earning per share,[1] which makes sense.

Enterprise value/EBITDA (EV/EBITDA) multiple also makes sense because relates the total company market value (market cap plus the outstanding debt minus cash equivalents)[2] with EBITDA, which is relevant to all stakeholders.

$$EV/EBITDA = \frac{\text{Market Cap} + \text{Debt} - \text{Cash equivalents}}{\text{EBITDA}}. \qquad [16.2]$$

The most typical multiples

There is a wide variety of multiples: multiples of earnings, sales, cash flow, and multiple of book value. We'll go over the most commonly utilized in practice.

Price earning

Price earning is the most popular multiple in the capital markets, and traders use it to establish comparisons between companies and suggest arbitrage strategies. For example, if two similar comparable companies are traded at different price earnings, to take advantage of this discrepancy, a trader would probably suggest selling the share with the higher P/E and purchasing the one with the lowest in order to profit from the difference.

In mergers and acquisitions, once the P/E of the peer group is estimated, then the equity value is calculated by multiplying the net income of the target by the P/E of the peer group:

$$\text{Equity value} = \text{P/E of the peer group x net income}$$

We do not use P/E for non-financial companies since the net income is not always a good measure of the business's performance since it is affected by financial results and other non-operative items. P/E, on the other hand, can be representative in the case of financial entities. Why? Because the net income is a reasonable measure of its performance since a bank is a highly leveraged business. Similar to a non-financial company's sales, interest earned on loans constitutes the main operative revenue, while interests paid for deposits represent the main expense, which is comparable to the cost of goods sold for a non-financial company. Therefore, the net income is a more accurate indicator of the success of financial entities than the net income of a non-financial company.

Trailing price earning

The trailing P/E is the most common and uses the net income for the last 12-month period. Since monthly earnings data are not available, we use the previous four quarterly earnings reports, which are updated quarterly.[3] Some databases give the option to calculate the P/E using the last 12-month period or another period.

Forward P/E

In December 2022, Exxon Mobil's P/E ratio was 8.31; however, multiples relate the stock price, which reflects expectations, with earnings, which are based on accounting and influenced by the economic cycle and accounting conventions, as we will explain later. Perhaps for these reasons, analysts estimate other versions of the P/E ratio that differ in the way the earnings are calculated, and whether realized or projected earnings are used.

Analysts calculate the Forward P/E by estimating net income over the next 12 months instead of using the historical net income. Therefore, forward P/E is based on expectations about the expected earnings for next year. For instance, on 2023-15-09, Exxon Mobil's P/E was 9.34 for the last twelve months (LTM), whereas the forward P/E for the next 12 months (NTM) was 12.74 (Source: Refinitiv Eikon).

Price/EBITDA and enterprise value/EBITDA

In mergers and acquisitions, the most widely multiples for determining the fair value of non-financial companies are the EBITDA multiples. Why are they preferred over the other multiples? EBITDA is an earning measure less distorted than the net income, which is affected by non-operative items such as interest expense, interest income, and results from holding non-monetary assets – over which senior management has less control than operating expenses and revenues – EBITDA is a less distorted earnings metric. Furthermore, is not skewed by depreciation and amortization methods and usually represents a percentage of revenues.[4] In practice, two EBITDA multiples are utilized, namely PRICE/EBITDA and enterprise value/EBITDA:

$$P/EBITDA = \frac{\text{Market Cap.}}{\text{EBITDA}}. \qquad [16.3]$$

$$EV/EBITDA = \frac{\text{Market Cap.} + \text{Total Debt} - \text{Cash equiv.} + \text{Minority Interest}}{\text{EBITDA}}. \qquad [16.4]$$

The former relates the Market Capitalization or Equity Market Value to EBITDA, whereas the latter links the Enterprise Value (the sum of Market Capitalization and Debt Value or Firm Value) to EBITDA.

Example: Exxon Mobil

Suppose you want to calculate the EBITDA multiples for Exxon Mobil in 2022 Q4. At that time, the market values and company fundamentals were:

Market Cap: $450,245MM
Debt: $41,193MM
Cash & Equivalents: $29,640MM
Minority Interest: $7,424MM
Enterprise value: $469,222MM (450,245 + 41,193 – 29,640 + 29,640)

EBITDA: 87,586MM

$$P/EBITDA = \frac{450,245}{87,586} = 5.14$$

$$EV/EBITDA = \frac{469,353}{87,586} = 5.36$$

EBITDA multiples and capital structure

Keep in mind that EBITDA is available to all investors in the company, including equity holders and debt holders, rather than just equity holders. As a result, P/EBITDA does not count the capital structure, only the part available to equity holders. Some analysts consider this fact a disadvantage of P/EBITDA; as with any ratio, there is no direct interpretation. Suppose two firms, A and B, have identical EBITDA but different capital structures. While firm A is highly leveraged, B is moderate.

Firm B's P/EBITDA is doubled, but its EV/EBITDA remains the same. We obtain the equity fair value directly by multiplying P/EBITDA by the firm's EBITDA:

Firm A = 4 x 5 = 20 Firm B = 8 x 5 = 40

If we used EV/EBITDA, the equity fair value would be obtained by deducting the debt from the firm value:

Firm A = 12 x 5–40 = 20 Firm B = 12 x 5–40 = 20

When there are companies in the peer group with different leverage levels. Issues occur. Suppose you are valuing a company whose EBITDA is 100, and the peer group has an EV/EBITDA and P/EBITDA of 10 and 5, respectively. Using EV/EBITDA, the firm value is 10x100 = 1,000. Supposing the target company has a debt of 600, then the equity fair value is E = 1,000–600 = 400. P/EBITDA would lead to an equity fair value of 5 x 100 = 500. While P/EBITDA appears to be affected by the capital structure, EV/EBITDA appear to be capital structure-neutral.

EV/EBITDA is not infallible, despite being regarded as capital structure-neutral. Suppose that during an economic downturn, both companies' EBITDA drops from \$5 million to \$4 million, and that Firm A's market cap drops from \$20 million to \$10 million and Firm B's from \$40 to \$25 million.

TABLE 16.1 EBITDA multiple with different capital structures

	A	B
EBITDA	5	5
Market cap.	20	40
Debt	40	20
Firm value	60	60
P/EBITDA	4	8
EV/EBITDA	12	12

TABLE 16.2 EBITDA multiple after a downturn with different capital structure

	A	B
EBITDA	4	4
Market cap.	10	25
Debt	40	20
Firm value	50	45
P/EBITDA	2.5	6.25
EV/EBITDA	12.5	11.25

Common sense would indicate that the higher the financial leverage, the greater the probability of financial distress; as a result, Firm A's market cap may decline more. However, although Firm A's market cap decreased more than Firm's Bs (by 50% compared to37.5%), its EV/EBITDA is 12.5 as opposed to 11.25 because the numerator contains the book value of debt. Ironically, if this figure is not adjusted to reflect the fair value of debt, the financially distressed company could observe a higher EV/EBITDA, which is the opposite to what common sense and intuition would suggest indicate. Given that Firm A now generates $4 million in EBITDA and has $40 in debt, assuming an interest rate of 8% and hypothetical interest payments of $3.2 million on that debt, basic math indicates that the company is barely making ends meet and may be on the verge of financial distress.

EBITDA multiples and CAPEX

Another issue related to EBITDA multiples is that they exclude the net investment in working capital and capital expenditures. In industries where capital expenditures are considerable, there could be a large gap between EBIT and EBITDA; therefore, you are more likely to use EV/EBIT instead of EV/EBITDA, and using this multiple for industries where fixed assets are less important and where D&A is comparatively low.

Warren Buffett once famously said, "Does management think the tooth fairy pays for capital expenditures?"[5] He dislikes EBITDA because it excludes the often-sizable capital expenditures companies make and leaves out the significant capital expenditures they undertake.

Adjusted EBITDA

EBITDA multiples are widely used for comparing companies with different capital structures. It ignores non-operating expenses and focuses on operational profitability. However, adjusted or normalized EBITDA, as opposed to the standard EBITDA, is usually calculated for valuation purposes and is useful for better understanding the true earnings by eliminating non-recurring income and expenses, and compensations paid to owners. Especially for private companies, it is necessary to eliminate abnormalities or idiosyncrasies such as owners' personal expenses, and rentals above or below fair market value. The comparison with other companies in the same industry is made easier by these adjustments.

Common adjustments

- Non-recurring income and expenses (Litigation expenses, repairs or maintenance, insurance claims, unrealized gains or losses, legal or financial advice fees, discontinued services)
- Depreciation and amortization methods
- Owner's salaries or other compensation (for example, health or life insurance) that is higher than the market average
- Gains or losses on foreign exchange
- Goodwill impairments
- Share-based compensation
- Salary payments to family members who are not involved in the business

Non-recurring expenses or one-time costs reduce EBITDA and need to be added back, while non-recurring expenses need to subtract back, such unrealized gains. Goodwill impairment occurs when for example, company A acquires company B for $10 million valuing its assets at $8 million and recognizing a goodwill of $2 million on its balance sheet. If after a while company A tests its assets for impairment and discovers the value of company B declining from $8M to $7M, it will recognize an impairment charge of $1 million on the income statement. It affects also the value recorded on the balance sheet, but there is no impact on the cash flow.

Example of how to use adjusted EBITDA

Calculating the adjusted EBITDA requires research on the composition of the income statement and reading notes to obtain an accurate metric that valuation specialists use to estimate the firm value and also as an indicator of the company's performance.

Although some databases have a metric called "normalized EBITDA", since the adjustments are often not available to the public, frequently this measure is equal to the standard EBITDA. For this reason, and especially for the case of private companies, if you want to estimate the business value using a multiple of EBITDA, adjustment must be performed under much scrutiny, since the value could change significantly after add-backs. The adjusted EBITDA is typically calculated on an annual basis for valuation purposes, sometimes using a three-year or five-year average.

Assume Vanilla Prime Corp. is being valued for a sale transaction, using an EBITDA multiple of 5x to arrive at the purchase price estimate. The standard EBITDA of the last fiscal year is $9 million. However, after disentangling the financial information, you discover the following discrepancies:

- Owner's salaries and other compensations above the market average to perform a similar task of 0.4 million
- Unusual expenses including financial consultant, impairments, and legal fees of $0.2 million
- Unrealized foreign exchange loss of $0.2 million[6]
- Goodwill impairment losses of $0.4 million

TABLE 16.3 EBITDA's adjustments

Standard EBITDA	**9.0**
+Salaries and compensations	0.4
+Unusual expenses	0.2
+Unrealized FX loss	0.2
+Goodwill impairment	0.4
Adjusted EBITDA	10.2

Since the company added back 1.2 million of adjustments, this adds 1.2 x 5 = 6 million to its purchase price:

Firm value using standard EBITDA: 5 x 9 = 45
Firm value using adjusted EBITDA: 5 x 10.2 = 51

Lastly, Adjusted EBITDA is superior than standard EBITDA because it provides a more accurate view of a company's true earnings, by harmonizing the different line-item expenses to reflect ongoing profitability and simplifying comparisons between companies in in the same industry.

Enterprise value to operative cash flow

Because earnings are vulnerable to accounting conventions and could be manipulated, some analyst prefer to use cash flows. The price-to-cash flow (P/CF) ratio compares the Market Cap. to its operating cash flow. For example, in December 2022, Exxon Mobil´s operative cash flow was estimated by the Refinitiv Database to be 76,987MM. Therefore, the enterprise value to operative cash flow was

$$EV/OCF = \frac{\text{Enterprise Value}}{\text{Operative Cash Flow}}. \qquad [16.5]$$

$$EV/OCF = \frac{469,222}{76,987} = 6.11$$

Enterprise value to free cash flow

The EV/FCF ratio is similar to the P/OCF ratio, although it subtracts capital expenditures from the operative cash flow. It avoids the problem of ignoring differences in capital intensity since companies must spend on fixed assets to maintain profitability and competitive position in the market. The Refinitiv Database estimate of the free cash flow of Exxon Mobil in December 2022 was 43,641MM. Therefore, the enterprise value to free cash flow was

$$EV/FCF = \frac{\text{Enterprise value}}{\text{Free Cash Flow}}. \qquad [16.6]$$

$$EV/FCF = \frac{469,222}{43,641} = 10.75$$

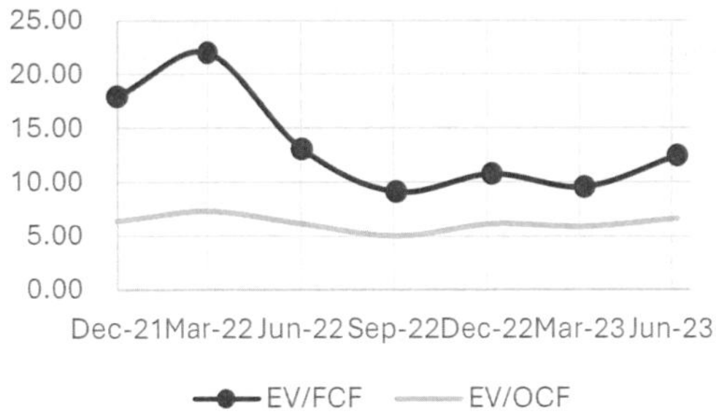

FIGURE 16.1 Cash flow multiples of Exxon Mobil

Since two businesses may have identical operating cash flows but distinct CAPEX requirements, you should first think about the demands of capital expenditures before employing cash flow multiples. Besides, capital expenses requirements could occur at different times. Second, and perhaps most crucially, keep in mind that cash flow statements reflect earnings and changes in assets and liabilities; as a result, there may be a larger OCF in one year and a smaller one in another. To mitigate the effect of measuring the cash flow at a single point in time, consider using cash flow average measures. Figure 16.1. shows the series of EV/OCF and EV/FCF multiples of Exxon Mobil from December 2021 to June 2023. Notice that while the EV/OCF is stable around 5/6, the EV/FCF peaked in March 2022, possibly due to an investment in fixed assets.

Price/book value

Price/book value, or P/B ratio, relates the stock price to its book value. Analysts calculate the P/B ratio by dividing the current closing price of the stock by the latest quarter's book value per share.

$$P/B = \frac{\text{Stock price per share}}{\text{Book value per share}}. \quad [16.7]$$

Since the stock price is equal to the market cap divided by the total number of shares, price/book value can also be calculated as

$$P/B = \frac{\text{Market capitalization}}{\text{Shareholders' equity}}. \quad [16.8]$$

The P/B can be interpreted as how much times the investor is willing to pay for the equity book value. To determine the P/B, analysts may make additional adjustments. For example, for distressed companies, the book value is usually calculated without the inclusion of intangible assets that would have no resale value.

The market cap of Exxon Mobil in December 2022 was 450,245MM, and the equity value was 195,049MM. Therefore, the P/BV was

$$P/B = \frac{450{,}245}{195{,}049} = 2{,}31$$

Financial institutions like banks and other financial services firms may find the P/B ratio more helpful. The liquid assets that make up a financial entity's asset base are cash, marketable securities, loans, and reserves; their book values are close to their market values. Liabilities are deposits that ought to be roughly worth their market value as well.

Furthermore, regulations and technical relationships must be met, which restricts dividend distribution. The book value might therefore be more in line with its market value.

Price to sales ratio

P/S ratio, or PSR, relates the market capitalization to its revenues. It is calculated by dividing the company's market capitalization by the company's total sales over the past 12 months.[7]

$$P/S = \frac{\text{Market capitalization}}{\text{Sales}}. \qquad [16.9]$$

Revenues of Exxon Mobil in December 2022 was 398,675 million. Therefore, the P/S ratio was

$$P/S = \frac{450{,}245}{398{,}675} = 1{,}13$$

The P/S ratio can be interpreted as how much an investor is willing to pay for each dollar of revenue. Some argue that the advantage of using P/S is the lower accounting distortion of sales numbers, and that it can still be used with negative or abnormally high/low earnings. However, P/S does not consider the profitability or the ability of the company to manage the operative costs. It is therefore preferable to utilize P/S in conjunction with an eye in an earnings measure. Table 16.3 shows the historic five-year average PSR and EBITDA margin for Exxon Mobil peers, calculated August 8th, 2023. Notice the dispersion of the sample: the PSR goes from a minimum of 0.11 to a maximum of 2.06, while the corresponding EBITDA margin goes from 4.6% to 39.6%.

TABLE 16.4 PSR Exxon Mobil peers, five-year average

Company Name	PSR	EBITDA margin
PBF Energy Inc	0.11	4.6%
Valero Energy Corp	0.30	6.2%
Marathon Petroleum Corp	0.35	10.3%
Phillips 66	0.36	4.2%
Total Energies SE	0.74	21.4%
Exxon Mobil Corp	1.07	15.5%
Chevron Corp	1.49	22.9%
Conoco Phillips	2.06	39.6%

Source: Refinitiv Eikon

The comparable approach in practice

Perhaps because of its low complexity and purportedly lowest cost-benefit connection, analysts often abandon comprehensive valuation models like DCF in favor of a relative valuation approach (Lie & Lie, 2002). The market multiples strategy is used by 92.8% of the 1,980 stock analyst members of the CFA Institute, according to a survey conducted by Pinto, Robinson, & Stowe (2015).

When utilizing multiples to value stocks, there are two primary comparable approaches: market comparable and precedent transactions comparable.

Precedent transactions comparable

Comparable transactions consider past deals of similar firms that have been acquired. In principle, the Precedent Transaction Comparable method or "transaction comps" has an advantage related to the Market Comparable method; while the later used prices observed in a certain period, the former represents the actual price paid in a deal. However, the difficulty with this approach is the limited availability of financial data regarding past transactions between private companies, especially in emerging markets.

The drawback to the comparable approach is its implementation. The first is choosing a set of comparable companies or comparable transactions. The second is determining the right multiple, such as EBITDA, sometimes revenues, cash flow, or another measure of operating performance.

Market comparable and the case of "Petroleum Services"

This approach looks at market comparables for a firm and its peers. Although analysts, traders, and appraisers use multiples to estimate the fair value of a business, there are some differences in how they use the multiple and its significance.

In mergers and acquisitions, advisors on both sides of the transaction often use multiples and negotiate based on multiples. They are also used in a variety of litigation contexts. Other consultants use the multiples to compare the previous value obtained with the DCF methodology with the market opinion.

Traders use multiples more actively to take advantage of the discrepancies in the market value between similar firms. For instance, if we have two comparable companies traded by different multiples, the lower multiple would be interpreted as an opportunity for investment, and a trader could suggest a strategy consisting of selling the overvalued stock (the company that has the lower multiple) and buying the undervalued stock (the company that has the lower multiple) and held it until the value increases.

To identify the peer group ("equity comps" or "trading comps"), a preliminary study of the candidates is required. Although you will never find a perfect comp because no company is ever 100% similar, it is possible to narrow down our search using a database and operational and financial filters in three steps:

Step 1: Selecting the "Comps" peer group

The natural step for your analysis is to look for companies that operate in the same industry or/and have similar characteristics as the company you are trying to value;

you can use a database like Reuters or Bloomberg that searches and screens for relevant criteria you input. The natural operational filters could be:

- Industry/sector
- Product & services
- Customers/distribution channel
- Geography

Some researchers think that it is better to combine the industry information with the company information; for instance, Cheng & McNamara (2000) state that using industry is an effective way of identifying peers and that with a combination of industry and profitability, the analysis improves to get more accurate valuations. This conclusion is also supported by Eberhart (2001) who found that when the industry classification is combined with the information provided by a firm, more accuracy in valuation.

In 2023, we estimated the fair value of "Petroleum Services", a small, South American non-public company primarily involved in the Oil Related Services and Equipment industry. The first step is looking for comps of our target in a database. The Refinitiv Eikon database suggests eight peers in a similar business line providing similar services.

To establish a comparison, we have tried to find the exact business description by looking at company websites and research reports; the company's website helps visualize all the products and services the company provides, while research reports provide actual segment data. We must search each company, what the company does, what kind of product the company produces, and compare some financial filters. After performing the research, we stayed with Schlumberger NV, Nov Inc., Baker Hughes Co, Haliburton Co, TechnipFMC PLC, and Helmerich and Payne Inc., eliminating two companies from the sample, CGG SA, and PGS ASA. Regretfully, there is a tradeoff in selecting the right comps: to improve the comparability is inevitable to lose some companies in the peer group.

TABLE 16.5 Oil-related services and equipment peers

Identifier (RIC)	Company name
SLB	Schlumberger NV
NOV.N	Nov Inc
BKR.OQ	Baker Hughes Co
HAL.N	Halliburton Co
FTI.N	TechnipFMC PLC
HP.N	Helmerich and Payne Inc
GEPH PA	CGG SA
PGS.OL^G24	PGS ASA

Financial ratio comparison

Financial filters can help us with our comparison, basically to check if our company has ratios similar to the peers or if it deviates too much from the average, and perhaps we have to eliminate some from the sample. We prefer ratios that measure profitability, return on capital, and asset management, such as EBITA margin or EBIT margin, return on capital, and cash cycle. While EBIT margin tells us about the operating income as a percentage of sales, return on capital relates the net operating profit after taxes (usually calculated as EBIT minus taxes on operations) with the invested capital to produce it. The cash cycle integrates days sales outstanding (DSO), days sales of inventory (DSI), and days payable outstanding (DPO), in only one measure since the DSO + DSI – DPO = cash cycle. EBITDA margin and cash cycle are determinants of the company's free cash flow. We do not forget how much the company invests in fixed assets and how much depreciates, so we must consider the CAPEX requirements. While some companies have a respectable EBITDA, they have considerable capex requirements; therefore, the EBIT margin could be distant from the EBITDA margin. Profitability is not all; we also must consider how much the company invests in working capital and capital expenditures to obtain EBITDA. Of course, these indicators vary from company to company and from industry to industry. Table 16.6 shows some financial ratios of the Comps, the sample average, and our company target. Petroleum Services has considerably better profitability ratios and better liquidity and leverage ratios. While the cash cycle of PS is closer to the sample average, the asset turnover and profitability are considerably higher than the average, maybe due to Petroleum Services being a small "growth company", usually more nimble than larger companies. Apart from the profitability and asset turnover, we see no reason for eliminating some peers from the sample.

Step 2: Selecting the right multiples and organizing the information

Once we have the set of traded comparables, the next step is the choice of the multiple to make the comparison and organize the information so that you can easily see valuation across your custom-defined universe. The choice depends on the nature of the business and the industry in which the business operates. While the appropriate multiple is not the same for all industries, looking at equity research reports of comparable companies to see what multiples analysts are using can be useful to figure out which multiples apply to a business you are considering. For this case, we select the EV/EBITDA multiple obtained from the Refinitiv Eikon database on February 15, 2023.

Since there are no significant differences between the mean and the median for EBITDA multiples, we will use the average EBITDA multiples to estimate the fair market value in the next step.

Step 3: Calculating the value of Petroleum Services

Once you have spread the multiples for the peer group, the final step is to use this information to estimate the fair value of Petroleum Services. Suppose we select EV/EBITDA as the proper multiple. But which EV/EBITDA? The LTM EV/EBITDA,

TABLE 16.6 Peers' financial ratios

	SLB	NOV.N	BKR.OQ	HAL.N	FTI.N	HP.N	Sample Average	Petroleum Services
Liquidity								
Current Ratio	1.2	2.3	1.3	2.0	1.2	2.5	1.8	2.5
Leverage								
Total Debt to Equity	69.1	38.6	46.2	101.5	43.8	19.6	53.2	35.9
Interest Coverage Ratio	8.5	5.3	-	6.2	1.5	1.5	4.6	4.3
Profitability								
EBITDA Margin	22.4	9.9	14.8	19.8	8.8	19.9	15.9	26.9
EBIT Margin	14.8	5.7	9.7	15.1	3.2	1.4	8.3	25.1
Activity								
Days sales outstanding	80.4	106.4	100.4	74.8	130.0	61.1	92.2	109.0
Days sales of inventory	58.0	97.5	93.7	56.9	70.4	22.1	66.4	41.0
Days on payable	56.9	47.1	88.0	59.0	81.3	25.5	59.6	49.0
Cash cycle	81.6	156.8	106.1	72.7	119.1	57.7	99.0	91.0
Asset Turnover	0.7	0.7	0.6	0.9	0.7	0.4	0.7	1.6

TABLE 16.7 Peers' E/V EBITDA

Company	EV/EBITDA
Schlumberger NV	13.40
Nov Inc	10.76
Baker Hughes Co	11.16
Halliburton Co	9.16
TechnipFMC PLC	14.06
Helmerich and Payne Inc	5.31
Mean	10.64
Median	10.96

Source: Refinitiv Eikon

the forward EV/EBITDA? An adjusted EV/EBITDA? The current EBITDA could be different from the last audited EBITDA, especially if the company is re-emerging from a recession and the EBITDA is expected to grow considerably in the current year. Or maybe the company is at the peak of the cycle and is expecting a decrease in EBITDA. In these cases, we need to make a "crunch number" analysis, using economic science but accompanied by discussions with the senior management, asking about the last numbers, and analyzing the consistency of the expectations. Since the senior management of Petroleum Services forecasted an EBITDA of $10.2 million in 2023, and the comp universe is trading on average at 10.64 EV/EBITDA, then the implied equity value would be

$$V = 10.64 \times 10.2 = 108.52$$

Since the EV/EBITDA gives us the firm value or enterprise value, to determine the equity fair value, the net debt of $2.5 million must be subtracted

$$E = V - D = 108.52 - 2.5 = 106.02$$

In practice, we will not be so lucky to find truly[8] comparable companies; this is the most challenging part of the relative valuation since the classifications available are very broad ones, and the industry names can be different in various sources. If you are not sure about the company classification, try to identify some keywords relevant to the business descriptions of the companies.

Multiples and company value drivers

Higher-quality businesses should deserve higher valuation multiples. For instance, there could be available investment opportunities, strategy, and qualitative differences such as quality of management. These differences can be translated into numbers considering three value drivers: return on capital, cost of capital, and growth. Multiples can be related to the firm value drivers making the correct assumptions and fundamentally assuming the market value responds to the discounted dividend model, in the case of price earning, or to the free cash flow model, in the case of EV/EBITDA multiple.

We can re-formulate the multiple formulas to relate them with the cost of capital, growth rate, ROE, and ROIC. Although it allows us to visualize relationships with the company fundamentals, in practice, the values obtained using value driver formulas usually differ from the conventional multiple formulas, as we explain with some examples.

Price earning and company fundamentals

ROE and payout are two examples of corporate fundamentals that can be used to determine earnings multiples. For example, the P/E can be represented in terms of payout and long-term growth rate if you think the Gordon dividend growth model accurately captures the stock price:

$$P = \frac{DPS}{ke - g}. \quad [16.10]$$

Where *DPS* represents the expected dividend per share for next year. We explained this formula in Chapter 3. Replacing [16.10] in [16.1]:

$$P / E = \frac{DPS}{EPS(ke - g)}. \quad [16.11]$$

Since DPS/EPS represents the payout ratio, we can express the P/E ratio as

$$P / E = \frac{Payout}{ke - g}. \quad [16.12]$$

Dividends and related dates are determined on a quarterly basis after the board of directors meets to review the company's financial statements. For example, Coca-Cola normally pays dividends four times a year, usually April 1, October 1, and December 15. If we know the last dividend and we have an estimated DPS growth rate, the expected DPS for the next year is expressed as $DPS = DPS_{t-1}(1 + g)$.

Example: Coca-Cola

On December 30, 2023, Coca-Cola was trading at 23.75 times earnings, smart estimated earnings per share and dividend per share were 2.69 and 1.84, respectively, the cost of equity capital was 8.2% (source: Refinitiv Eikon), the long-term expected growth rate was expected to be 4%, and the expected inflation rate was 2.67%. The following are some queries we could pose to ourselves:

a) Given the observed P/E – 23.75, what growth rate would justify the P/E calculated using formula [16.11]?
b) What is the implicit real long-term growth rate considered on the P/E ratio?
c) Which P/E should be fair?
d) It is evident that the implicit growth rate in the formula [16.11] is higher than 4% given the observed P/E of 23.75. Perhaps the market might anticipate a faster growth rate in the near future and an organic growth rate of about 3% to 4% in the long run.

$$23.75 = \frac{1.84}{2.69(0.082 - g)}$$

$$g = 5.32\%$$

Observe that the nominal growth rate g is a multiplicative process rather than additive, which includes the inflation rate plus a real growth rate, similar to the GDP growth rate:

$$g = (1 + g_R)(1 + \pi) - 1. \quad [16.13]$$

For simplicity, we use an additive process since, unless the inflation rate is high, an additive or a multiplicative process gives a similar nominal growth rate while the inflation rate is low:

$$g = g_R + \pi. \qquad [16.14]$$

Given that the nominal growth rate is 5.32%, the real growth rate is 5.32%-2.67% = 2.65%, which seems to be reasonable, similar to the GDP growth rate.

The payout ratio is 1.84/2.69 = 0.6840. P/E is calculated using formula [16.12] repeated here for ease in the explanation.

$$P/E = \frac{Payout}{ke - g}. \qquad [16.12]$$

$$P/E = \frac{0.6840}{(0.082 - 0.04)} = 16.29$$

Dividend yield and the payout ratio relationship

Dividend yield is determined by dividing the dividend per share (DPS) by the stock price.

$$DY = \frac{DPS}{P}. \qquad [16.15]$$

The payout ratio is also obtained by dividing the dividend yield by the inverse of P/E.

$$Payout = \frac{\frac{DPS}{P}}{\frac{E}{P}} = \frac{DPS}{E}. \qquad [16.16]$$

We can solve the implicit growth rate on the P/E of Coca-Cola using the dividend yield. Notice that it is the same value obtained with formula [16.12].

$$23.75 = \frac{0.6840}{0.082 - g}$$

$$g = 5.32\%$$

Price earnings and ROE

As the equity or company value, the P/E ratio also depends on the growth rate and the cost of capital. An increase in the P/E requires the fulfillment of two conditions:

1. The return on equity must be higher than the cost of capital
2. The company should keep a portion of its earnings to finance its growth.

Consequently, we can connect the ROE and growth rate to the P/E ratio. More growth means more value if, and only if, the company reinvests its earnings with a return higher than the cost of capital and vice versa. As the retention rate is the inverse of the payout ratio, one way to express the growth rate is

$$g = ROE(1 - Payout). \quad [16.17]$$

This growth rate is sometimes called as the sustainable growth rate, the maximum rate a business can sustain without additional external sources like equity or debt. Substituting and rearranging terms:

$$g = ROE - ROE \times Payout,$$

$$Payout = \frac{ROE - g}{ROE}. \quad [16.18]$$

Lastly, the P/E value driver formula is

$$P/E_F = \frac{ROE - g}{ROE(ke - g)}. \quad [16.19]$$

This formula must be used carefully since the way to calculate the growth rate, ROE (1 – payout), can conduce to illogical values when ROE is greater and payout/retention rate is low/higher or when g>ke. For example, Coca-Cola was trading at 23.75 times earnings on December 30, 2023. The ROE smart estimate was 44%, Payout = 68.40%, and it's cost of equity capital = 8.2%.

$$g = ROE(1 - payout) = 0.44(1 - 0.6857) = 0.1390$$

$$P/E_F = \frac{ROE - g}{ROE(ke - g)} = \frac{0.44 - g}{0.44(0.082 - g)}$$

Notice that we cannot use the growth rate of 13.87% because it would result in a negative denominator. However, we can calculate the implicit growth rate on the observed P/E:

$$23.75 = \frac{0.44 - g}{0.44(0.082 - g)}$$

$$g = 4.41\%$$

When g>ke, neither formula [16.12] nor formula [16.19] may be applied. For example, Microsoft was trading at 38.83 times earnings on December 30, 2023 (Source: Refinitiv Eikon). The cost of equity capital can be estimated as 8.68% and the payout ratio = 26.92% according to smart estimates. Using formula 16.12 results in an implicit growth rate of 7.99%, and although it is possible that Microsoft can grow at a higher rate in the short term, a growth rate of 7.99% would not be sustainable over the long run.

$$38.83 = \frac{0.2692}{0.0868 - g}$$

$$g = 7.99\%$$

Price earning and the multiples stages formula

Sometimes, when using formulas [16.12] or [16.19], the implicit growth rate is too high compared to a long-term growth rate of 3 to 4%. It can occur not just with growing companies but also with mature companies when their performance is recovering after a recession; as a result, the short-term growth rate may exceed the more organic growth rate of 3%. In these cases, we can assume that the market anticipates more growth in the near future, perhaps over the next three, four, or five years, and an organic growth rate starting from year six and beyond, utilizing the two or three stages formula described in Chapter 3. Formula 16.21 depicts two growth stages: the first term considers a short-term growth which is supposed to hold during T periods, which was described in Chapter 3, and the second term uses the formula [16.10] with the DPS capitalized by T periods and discounted with the cost of capital ke for T periods. The expected next year's dividend is estimated as:

$$DPS = EPS \times Payout(1 + g_{ST}). \qquad [16.20]$$

And the price is

$$P = DPS\frac{1 - \frac{(1+g_{ST})^T}{(1+ke)^T}}{ke - g_{S1}} + \frac{DPS(1+g_{ST})^{T-1}(1+g_{LT})}{(ke - g_{LT})(1+ke)^T} \qquad [16.21]$$

The multiples stage formula permits us to consider that the market is expected a higher growth rate in the short term (g_{ST}). Let's go back to the case of Coca-Cola, which has an implied growth rate of 5.32%, according to formula [16.11]. Analysts predict growth rates of 4.06 in 2024 and 5.38% in 2025 (source: Refinitiv Eikon). To estimate the stock price, we'll use a short-term growth rate of 5% for the next five years and a 3% for the growing perpetuity:

$$P = 1.84\frac{1 - \frac{(1+0.05)^5}{(1+0.082)^5}}{0.082 - 0.05} + \frac{1.84(1+0.05)^{5-1}(1+0.03)}{(0.082 - 3\%)(1+0.082)^5}$$

$$P = 8.01 + 29.87 = 37.89$$

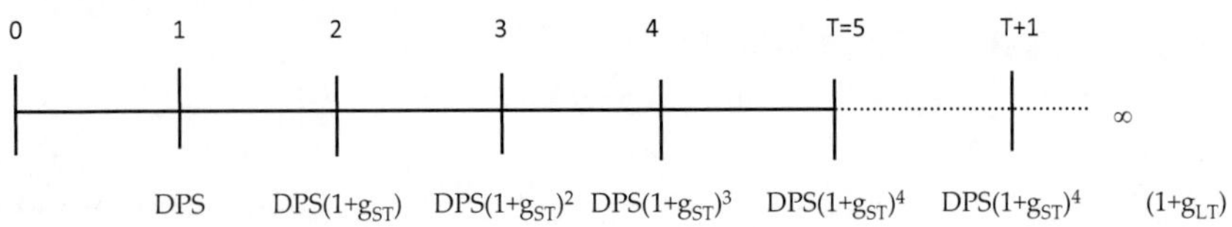

FIGURE 16.2 Stream of dividends per share

Year	1	2	3	4	5	
DPS	1.84	1.93	2.03	2.13	2.24	
Perpetuity					44.30	=+F2*(1+3%)/(8.2%-3%)
DPS + perpetuity	1.84	1.93	2.03	2.13	46.54	

$37.89 =NPV(8.2%;B4:G4)

FIGURE 16.3 Present value of the stream of dividend per share

When performing these calculations by writing the formula on a spreadsheet, there is room for mistakes. It is preferable to define the DPS stream in a row using a quick and safer calculation, as we describe below:

- The projected DPS growth rate is 5% until year five, as shown in the second row of Figure 16.3. The DPS of period T+1 is found in cell G2, which is growing at a long-term growth rate of 3%.
- A perpetuity's value can be found in cell F3.
- Lastly, cell A6 shows the present value of the dividend stream. Cell F4 shows the value of perpetuity plus the DPS for year five.

Finally, dividing the stock price by the earnings per share

$$P / E = \frac{39.44}{2.69} = 14{,}66$$

Coca-Cola's P/E of 23.75 indicates that the stock price is overvalued if the long-term growth rate is 3% from year six and beyond, the cost of equity capital would remain constant, and earnings and dividends grow at the expected growth rate. On the other hand, Coca-Cola grew at a rate of 4.91% from 1983 to 2022 and 7.89% from 1925 to 2022 (source: Gurufocus and Refinitiv Eikon). Coca-Cola achieved $28.5 million in 1925, $6,641 million in 1983, and $43,004 million in 2022). If we calculate the respective geometric means:

$$(43{,}0004/6{,}641)^{1/39}\text{-}1 = 4.91\%$$
$$(43{,}0004/28.5)^{1/97}\text{-}1 = 7.84\%$$

EV/EBITDA and value drivers

To perform an analysis of the EV/EBITDA using company's fundamentals, we must consider the NOPAT, ROIC, and long-term growth rate. Remember that the firm value can be calculated using the economic profit formula, which was discussed in Chapter 15 and repeated here for ease in the explanation.

$$V = \frac{NOPAT - I}{WACC - g},$$

The net investment *I* represents the increase of invested capital g x C, because of the rise in working capital and CAPEX above depreciation needs:

$$V = \frac{NOPAT - g \times C}{WACC - g},$$

$$V = NOPAT \frac{\frac{NOPAT - g \times C}{NOPAT}}{WACC - g},$$

$$V = NOPAT \frac{1 - \frac{g \times C}{ROIC \times C}}{WACC - g},$$

$$V = \frac{NOPAT\left(1 - \frac{g}{ROIC}\right)}{WACC - g} \quad [16.22]$$

Given that V is the enterprise value, rearranging

$$EV = \frac{NOPAT\left(ROIC - g\right)}{ROIC(WACC - g)} \quad [16.23]$$

The formula of value drivers assumes the company is already in the steady state. Lastly, the EV/EBITDA ratio is

$$EV / EBITDA_F = \frac{NOPAT\left(ROIC - g\right)}{ROIC(WACC - g)EBITDA} \quad [16.24]$$

Table 16.8 shows the P/E ratio for three companies when all net income is distributed as dividends, so the long-term growth rate is zero. The shareholder´s common stock is composed by 100 shares with a par value of $1. Using formula [16.19], repeated here for ease in the explanation, the P/E is equal to 1/ke:

$$P / E_F = \frac{ROE - g}{ROE(ke - g)}. \quad [16.19]$$

$$P / E_F = \frac{10\% - 0\%}{10\%(10\% - 0\%)} = \frac{1}{10\%} = 10$$

When the firm reinvests a portion of its earnings, the growth rate is determined as ROE(1-payout), and the market capitalization is calculated using the formula [16.10]. For example, Firm B's P/E and market capitalization are:

$$P / E_F = \frac{12\% - 3\%}{12\%(10\% - 3\%)} = 10.71$$

$$Market\ cap = \frac{8}{10\% - 3\%} = 114.28$$

TABLE 16.8 Price earning and growth rate

	Firm A	Firm B	Firm C
P/E zero growth			
Cost of equity capital (ke)	10%	10%	10%
Shareholders' common stock	100	100	100
Net income	10	12	8
ROE	10%	12%	8%
Dividends	10	12	8
EPS (Net income/100)	10	8.33	12.50
Market cap. (Dividends/ke)	100	120	80
P/E	10	10	10
P/E with growth			
Growth rate = ROE x (1 – payout)	2.5%	3%	2%
Dividends	5	8	4
Payout	75%	75%	75%
Market cap.	66.7	114.3	50.0
P/E = ROE-g/ROE(ke – g)	10.0	10.7	9.4

As we see in the earlier examples, the P/E depends on the growth rate and cost of equity capital. The P/E increases when the firm grows if ROE>ke, remains constant if ROE = ke, and decreases if ROE<ke. The last happens because how much the company invests with a return lower than the cost of capital, more value is destroyed.

Table 16.9 describes the EV/EBITDA value drivers' formulas when the firm does not grow and when the firm reinvests part of its earnings and grows. EBITDA changes in the same proportion of NOPAT (for example, the NOPAT of Firm C is 7.69% higher than the NOPAT of Firm B). The net investment is calculated by multiplying the growth rate by the invested capital, using the same growth rate of Table 16.6 (2.5%, 3%, and 2%). Firm value is calculated with the formula [16.23]. Notice that Firm C creates value since ROIC >WACC and Firm D destroys value because ROIC>WACC.

The P/E and EV/EBITDA value drivers' formulas assume a constant relationship between the value drivers to be valid. For example, the P/E formula assumes the fulfillment of conditions to apply the Gordon dividend growth model and constant relationships between ROE, ke, and g. The EV/EBITDA formula also assumes

TABLE 16.9 EV/EBITDA and growth rate

	Firm A	Firm C	Firm D
EV/EBITDA zero growth			
WACC	9%	9%	9%
CAPITAL	140	140	140
NOPAT	13	14	10
ROIC	9.3%	10.0%	7.1%
Free Cash Flow	13.00	14.00	10.00
EBITDA	12	12.92	9.23
EV (Firm Value)	144.44	155.56	111.11
EV/EBITDA	12.04	12.04	12.04
EV/EBITDA with growth			
Growth rate	2.5%	3.0%	2.0%
g x Capital	3.5	4.2	2.8
Firm Value	146.15	163.33	102.86
EV	146.15	163.33	102.86
EV/EBITDA	12.18	12.64	11.14

that the firm achieves a steady state and a constant relationship between EBITDA, NOPAT, ROIC, and g.

Use caution when putting these formulas into practice. While they may be helpful for mature companies, where these relationships are more stable, they do not always hold true, as we demonstrate with a public company example.

Example: Exxon Mobil

Company fundamentals in December 2022 (source: Reuters Refinitiv)

ROE = 6.7%; ke = 8.96%; g = 2.1%

First, we use the formula [16.19] repeated here for ease in the explanation to calculate the P/E ratio:

$$P / E_F = \frac{ROE - g}{ROE(ke - g)}. \quad [16.19]$$

$$P/E = \frac{6.7\% - 2.1\%}{6.7\%(8.96\% - 2.1\%)} = 10.00$$

Nonetheless, the P/E ratio from December 2022 to March 2023 Q1 fluctuated between 8.31 and 7.42 (2023Q1). Making a similar analysis with the EV/EBITDA:

EV = 469,353MM
NOPAT = 57,547
Average LT Capital = 283,886MM
ROIC = 20.23%
EBITDA = 88,500MM
Growth rate oil and gas industry 5Y = 10.9% (annual 2.1% geometric average)
WACC at 30-12-22 = 8.15%

Because the D/V ratio is a low 11.21%, the WACC is similar to the cost of equity capital. Calculating the EV/EBITDA with the formula [16.24] repeated here for ease in the explanation.

$$EV/EBITDA_F = \frac{NOPAT(ROIC - g)}{ROIC(WACC - g)EBITDA} \quad [16.24]$$

$$EV/EBITDA = \frac{57,547(20.3\% - 2.1\%)}{20.3\%(8.15\% - 2.1\%)88,500} = 9.63$$

According to P/E and EV/EBITDA derived using fundamentals, market values should precisely represent the formulas of the various value drivers if the ROE, ROIC, long-term growth rate, and risk-adjusted cost of capital remain constant. However, market expectations change more rapidly than accounting measures, which reflect historical earning measures. All earnings-multiple are affected by expectations and economic events, such as the economic cycle and a crash or boom. The next section deals with this issue.

Multiples and empirical evidence

Although multiples have been used for decades in the marketplace, a few studies have examined the theory behind valuation multiples. The line of research has focused in two primary areas: a) which multiples better describe the capital market performance of companies, and b) what are the determinants that explain the multiples observed in a certain industry.

Using similar firm multiples based on PE, price to sales, enterprise value to sales, and enterprise value to operating cash flow, Kim & Ritter (1999) looked at IPO pricing and found that using earnings forecasts outperform the use of historical multiples. Additionally, they also found that although PE and Market to book value ratio perform poorly, MTB outperformed PE. A similar conclusion is sustained by Liu, Nissim, & Thomas (2002) who found that multiples based on earnings forecasts explain better stock prices for US equity market than historical earnings measures, cash flow measures, book value of equity and sales multiples. These overall rankings hold true for nearly all of the industries that were studied, despite the common belief that different industries have different multiples. In a subsequent 2007 study, they examined nine markets in addition to the United States (Australia, Canada, France, Germany, Hong Kong, Japan, South Africa, Taiwan, and the United Kingdom) and suggest that valuations derived from industry multiples based on reported earnings outperform those based on reported operating cash flows and the accuracy improved when they considered forecasts earnings instead reported. Schreiner & Spremann (2007) also discovered that forward-looking multiples, particularly the two-year forward-looking PE, outperform historical multiples.

Harbula (2009) tested the accuracy of forecasted earnings using a sample of 400 companies chosen from the DJ STOXX 600 index, with a market capitalization greater than €200 million, spanning various industries. They found that enterprise value multiples are typically more accurate than equity multiples and that prospective multiples provide more accurate valuation results than current or historical multiples, particularly when taking earnings drivers into account.

With respect to the determinants of multiples, only a few articles have addressed this topic in the financial literature. Among them, it is worthwhile to mention that Cheng & McNamara (2000) stated that PE outperforms MTB and reported that using return on equity is a relevant criterion for selecting appropriate P/E and P/BV multiples. Dittman & Weiner (2005) in a study of a sample of European and American companies in 16 countries concluded that the use of return on asset (ROA) or a combination of ROA and total assets are the best criteria to select the peer group. Harbula (2009) analyzed various potential determinants of multiples and concludes that growth was a major determinant of the level of multiples and stability of results and stability of growth also appeared to be significant factors that drove mainly profit based multiples Finally, suggest not underestimate the importance of the homogeneity and relevance of the sample of peers for the valuation results. This factor appeared to have a strong significance across all multiples.

Plenborg & Coppe Pimentel (2016) conducted a comprehensive literature review and outlined the key findings for eight implementation issues: the choice of comparable firms, the choice of value driver, the use of reported versus forecasted earnings, the measurement of averages of peers' multiples, the accounting differences, normalization of earnings, the impact of size, and the adjustments for the illiquidity discount and control premium.

Pros and cons of relative valuation

Relative valuation is thought to be simpler than DCF valuation, the main advantage of the comparable approach is providing a single number that permits making value judgments and fast comparisons; however, since multiples can differ for a variety of reasons, we must avoid falling into the trap of a simplistic interpretation.

As described in the previous section, it is erroneous to believe that we do not need to consider value drivers such as risk, cost of capital, accounting conventions, and growth; a multiple represents a snapshot of a specific ratio at a certain or during a period, which sometimes can experiment with considerable changes due to multiples' vulnerability to the economic cycle and crash events such as financial crises or market booms.

The economic cycle effects

Two renowned investors, Benjamin Graham, and David Dodds, were the first to detect the inconsistency of the P/E ratio in their legendary 1934 investment tome *Security Analysis.* The investors attributed illogical P/E ratios to temporary and sometimes extreme fluctuations in the business cycle. To smooth a firm's earnings over a period, they recommended using an average of earnings per share over five or ten years when computing P/E ratios. Years later, Molodovsky (1960) stated that at the bottom of the economic cycle, earnings are low and P/E is high. At the peak of the economic cycle, it is the opposite: earnings are high and P/E ratios are low, because the stock prices represent expectations and earnings reflect past earnings.

Suppose that following an expansion, the economy peaks and then starts to decline. As a result, investors sell their shares in anticipation of the recession, which lowers the market values and all earnings multiples. At this point in the business cycle, the effect on earnings multiples is doubly dire, as financial statements reflect past high EPS while prices decline rapidly in anticipation of recession, resulting in exceptionally low multiples. When the business cycle approaches the lowest point of a downturn, on the other hand, investors buy stocks because they expect a re-emergence, which raises stock prices. This, along with low historical earnings per share, results in larger multiples. Consequently, in a poor year, a company may have a high P/E while in a good year, it may be low or negative.[9]

P/E ratios are automatically calculated every day by Bloomberg, Reuters, or FactSet by dividing the current price of a stock by its earnings, using the most recent four quarters of earnings available. This method of calculating multiples is known as forward-looking; they also calculate forward P/E ratios using forecasted earnings and prices.

In 1998, the Nobel Prize in Economics Robert Shiller and Professor John Y. Campbell introduced the CAPE® ratio as an improvement upon the classic price/earnings "PE" ratio. The CAPE ratio, also known as the Shiller P/E ratio, calculates

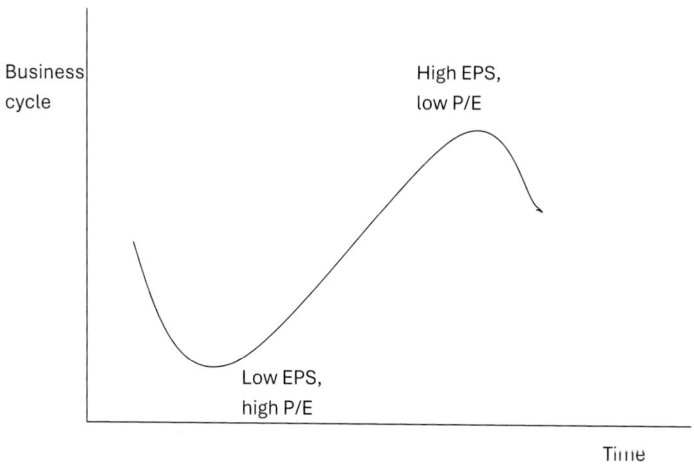

FIGURE 16.4 Price earning and the business/economic cycle

a cyclically adjusted price earning, dividing the stock price by the average earnings over the past ten years to smooth out fluctuations in profits that occur over different periods of a business cycle.

$$CAPE = \frac{\text{Share price}}{\text{10-year average, inflation-adjusted earnings}} \qquad [16.25]$$

The CAPE ratio is calculated by taking the earnings per share of the S&P500, for the past ten years, then adjusting them by the inflation rate to today's dollars, and taking the average of the series. Finally, by dividing the current level of the S&P500 by the ten-year average, we obtain the CAPE ratio. The CAPE ratio for a stock is calculated in the same way, using the EPS and the current stock price. Although the P/E 10 ratio has been questioned as a predictor of market tops and bottoms, the average may mitigate anomalies, seasonal changes in stock, and the effect of the economic cycle identified by Molodovsky.[10]

Box 16.1 Case study: Burford and Eton Park funds and the litigation over the 2012 expropriation of YPF

The P/E ratio is also widely employed in courts. For instance, dissident shareholders may file a lawsuit to dispute the proposed price for their shares in a merger. At the time of writing, US District Judge Loretta Preska ruled in favor of Burford Capital, Petersen Energia Inversora, and Eton Park Capital Management LP, ordering Argentina to pay US$16.1 billion to minority shareholders of state-controlled oil company YPF as a result of the government's nationalization of the controlling party. The compensation calculated by the plaintiff expert was based on the highest P/E ratio observed on the Q-4 2008 earnings, along a lookback period of two years, arguing that this was the information available to investors deciding whether to invest in YPF as of February 22, 2010, the date considered as the time Argentina took control of YPF. The Q-4 2008 earnings were affected by many international and local events, such as the subprime mortgage crisis, which had severe consequences for the US and all global capital markets, and Argentina's confiscation of retirements and pension funds, which had a negative impact on Telecom's EPS from Q-4 2008.

Figure 16.5 depicts the P/E calculated according to the Supreme Court guidelines for a two-year lookback period from February 22, 2008, to February 22, 2010, as well as the observed P/E for a ten-year lookback period (source: Refinitiv Eikon). The observed P/E ranged from a minimum of 5.09 to a maximum of 23.49, while the average was 12.87. The illogic of a P/E of 27.1 is even more evident when we look at the observed P/E returning to 10/12 a year later. Calculations may vary slightly, but the truth is that no investor was seriously thinking about paying 25/27 times earnings per share for a YPF share on February 22, 2010.

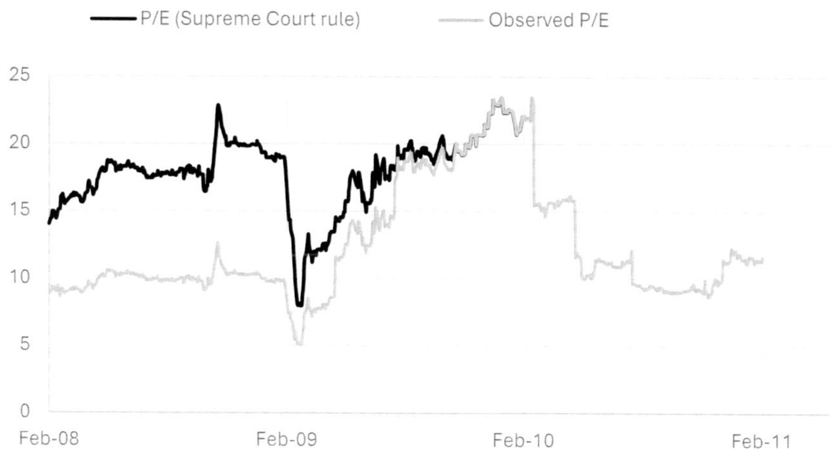

FIGURE 16.5 YPF P/E ratio

Differences in accounting practices

In Chapter 15, we addressed the adjustments to the financial information since some accounting practices could affect the performance measures such as ROIC and economic profit. Most of these adjustments also must be considered to calculate appropriate earnings multiples. Divergent accounting practices can make similar firms appear different and different firms appear similar (Young & Zeng, 2015), thereby resulting in a biased sample of peers. While the cash flow is not affected by accounting practices, earnings can be affected by several accounting practices, for instance:

- Goodwill (and other aspects of business combinations)
- Amortization methods for intangibles and R&D expenditures
- Depreciation methods
- Provisioning and deferred tax

Goodwill

Goodwill is not amortized or depreciated like other assets. However, it is periodically tested for impairment. When a goodwill impairment charge is recognized, it reduces the equity book value and the company's earnings, affecting multiples such as the P/BV ratio and the P/E ratio. While the earnings decrease can lead to a higher P/E and a higher P/BV ratio, on the other hand, goodwill impairment charges also represent a signal to investors that the company overpaid for an acquisition or that the acquired business is not performing as expected, which could negatively affect the investor perception, potentially leading to a decrease in the company stock price and thus, a reduction in P/E and P/BV ratios. Adjusting for impairment charges is recommended for a more accurate comparison by reflecting the impact of reduced asset values.

Example: suppose two firms, Firm A and Firm B, operate in the same industry and have recently recognized goodwill impairment charges. Table 16.10 shows the P/BV and P/E ratios calculated with the adjusted book values. Notice that without considering the goodwill impairment charge, both firms have the same P/BV, while after calculating the adjusted book value, Firm A has the higher P/BV. Concerning the P/E, without considering the goodwill impairment charge, Firm B has the higher P/E, while after adjusting the net income, Firm A has the higher P/E.

TABLE 16.10 Adjusted multiples for impairment charges

	Firm A	**Firm B**
Book value	100	150
Market cap	200	300
Net income	12	15
P/BV	2	2
P/E	16.67	20
Goodwill impairment charge	8	3
Adjusted book value	92	147
Adjusted net income	4	12
Adjusted P/BV	2.2	2.0
Adjusted P/E	50.0	25.0

To adjust for the goodwill impairment charges, we need to subtract the impairment charges from the book value and net income of each company. For instance, the adjusted book values and net income are as follows:

- Adjusted book value of Firm A: \$100 million – \$8 million = \$92 million
- Adjusted book value of Firm B: \$150 million – \$3 million = \$147 million
- Adjusted net income of Firm A: \$12 million – \$8 million = \$4 million
- Adjusted net income of Firm B: \$15 million – \$3 million = \$12 million

Then we calculate the multiples for each company using the adjusted book values and net income:

- P/BV of Firm A: \$200 million / \$92 million = 2.2x
- P/BV of Firm B: \$150 million / \$147 million = 2.0x
- P/E of Firm A: \$200 million / \$4 million = 50.0x
- P/E of Firm B: \$150 million / \$12 million = 25.0x

After adjusting for the goodwill impairment charges, we can see that the P/BV ratio and the P/E ratio for Company A are higher than that of Company B, which means that Firm A is valued more highly than Firm B.

R&D amortization. Research & development amortization consists of spreading the deductions of R&D expenses over time rather than deducting them immediately. The accounting treatment can affect the company's earnings and therefore, valuation multiples.

For example, consider two identical companies in the same business, having $10M of R&D expenses on the balance sheet. While company A amortizes the R&D expenses over ten years, company B does not.

TABLE 16.11 Price earning under different accounting conventions

	A	B
EBITDA	20	20
Amortization	1	0
R&D expenses	0	10
EPS after amortization	19	10
Share price	90	100
Price earning	4.74x	10x

Observing the P/E of both companies, one could deduce that Company B is cheaper than Company A, however this is incorrect. According to Schreiner & Spremann (2007), adjusted accrual-based earnings, calculated by adding back amortization of intangible and R&D expenditure to EBIT, provide more accurate estimates than reported earnings multiples. Analysts will often make adjustments to harmonize the P/E and make a better comparison, for example:

- Convert accounting data to a common format; for instance, if company B had amortized the R&D expenses over ten years, both companies would have identical P/E.
- Use other measures less affected by accounting differences, such as EBITDA or Sales multiples.

Deferred tax

Deferred tax assets or liabilities arise from disparities between accounting income and taxable income, which can have impact on tax expense and, consequently, net income and P/E and P/BV ratios.

Companies typically use the straight-line method to depreciate an asset, while tax regulations allow companies to use an accelerated depreciation method. Since the straight-line method produces a lower depreciation expense than the accelerated method, the accounting income is temporarily greater than its taxable income. Accounting recognizes the difference as a deferred tax liability, which can increase future tax expenses and reduce net income, resulting in a higher P/E ratio.

If a company has recognized deferred tax assets, future tax benefits will reduce tax expense while increasing net income, resulting in a lower P/E ratio. Deferred taxes arise from differences between the accounting values of assets and liabilities for reporting purposes and their tax basis. When the accounting value of certain assets exceeds their tax basis, the difference creates a deferred tax asset, increasing the book value and resulting in a lower P/BV ratio. The opposite happens if the accounting value is lower than their tax basis, generating a deferred tax liability, which can decrease the book value of assets and equity, potentially resulting in a higher P/BV ratio.

Plenborg & Coppe Pimentel (2016) addressed eight implementation concerns regarding the usage of multiples, most of them related to the earnings measure. Some of them were discussed in this book, including the selection of comparable firms, the selection of value drivers, accounting differences and their effects, normalization of earnings, and the elimination of non-recurring items. They also discuss the impact of size, noting that larger firms yield more accurate value estimates than smaller firms and that the harmonic mean and median values outperform mean values.

DCF or multiples?

For analysts that use the DCF method and multiple analysis in tandem, it serves as a check between the two methodologies and aids in the formulation of appropriate queries, digging into the company fundamentals. The utility of the DCF and multiple techniques has been highly researched; the seminal study in this respect is the paper by Kaplan & Ruback (1996). Numerous subsequent studies confirmed the validity of the DCF model (Penman & Sougiannis, 1998; Francis, Olsson, & Oswald, 2000; Berkman, Bradbury, & Ferguson, 2000; Gilson, Hotchkiss, & Ruback, 2000).

DCF, in our opinion, is the most detailed method of valuing a business; it forces the appraiser to describe consistent assumptions and check the consistency of the projections (for example, whether the sales growth rate is compatible with the GDP growth rate, the industry growth rate, and the company market share; the consistency of margins and cash cycle). Multiples' defendants argue that DCF is more complex and requires many assumptions, while multiples do not. However, this vision is not totally accurate because the usage of multiples necessitates adjustments to reconcile accounting disparities and the analyst must be aware of multiple's vulnerability to the business cycle. If we accept that both techniques are prone to forecast error, the question becomes which has the lowest forecast error. Kaplan and Ruback (1996) conducted a study comparing the deviations between the forecasted value from both methodologies concerning the final price of 51 leverage transactions. DCF values were calculated using three different beta versions: a) asset betas, b) industry betas, and c) observed betas. On the other hand, multiples were calculated using two versions: a) market comparable, b) similar transactions, and market comparable and similar transactions. The DCF technique performed marginally better than the multiples methodology, with a higher percentage of transactions falling within a 15% deviation of the effective transaction price. The mean squared error was also lower, except for comparable transactions. Finally, Kaplan and Ruback concluded that when both methods were used together, the results were more reliable.

What method should be used? Our suggestion is similar with what we do in practice: perform a discounted cash flow valuation and then utilize multiples to compare your fair value to the market vision.

Concluding thoughts

Multiples provide a quick way to make value judgments and establish comparisons between companies in the same industry/sector. However, they must avoid simplistic interpretations that have the potential to be misused, including accounting conventions and economic cycle effects. Sometimes, the relative valuation approach could be still more complicated. We should consider some additional issues, for example, the stock market can become over or undervalued at times, which would make a comparable approach less meaningful. In these cases, it is better look at the company's historic multiple over the years. For firms experimenting rapid growth, past EBITDA is inaccurate; for these cases, it is better to estimate a forward multiple. In general, multiples for mature companies are more stable.

There is not a multiple that is invulnerable; all have limitations. EBITDA multiples are more robust to accounting conventions since they do not depend on depreciation and amortization schedules. Multiples of cash flows are affected by CAPEX and the working capital investments; fundamental or value driver formulas depend on exact relationships among value drivers.

Finally, we always prefer to perform a DCF first, followed by a multiple analysis, as we believe both approaches are more beneficial when used in tandem.

Short questions and problems

1. When comparable companies differ in capital structure, which multiple would you recommend to estimate the fair value of the target company and why?
   a) Price/EBITDA
   b) EV/EBITDA
2. Table 16.12 shows some ratios for not-distressed and distressed companies. Is the EV/EBITDA multiple reliable in the context of companies?

TABLE 16.12 EV/EBITDA ratios

	Not distressed	Distressed
EBITDA	100	50
Market cap	1000	350
Debt	100	600
EV/EBITDA	11	19.0
Interest	7	60
EBITDA/Int.	14.3	0.8
D/E	10%	171%

3. The S&P500 was trading at 21.78 times earnings on October 5, 2023. On the same day, the USTB ten-year rate was 4.71%, the assumed market risk premium was 5%, and the expected growth rate in real GNP was 2.5%. The EPS mean estimate and dividends estimate were 216.94 and 91.60, and the S&P500 = 4,259.66

   a) Assuming that the market is correctly priced, what is the inflation rate implied in the PE ratio? Is it reasonable taking into account that the expected inflation rate is 2.7%?
   b) You assume that for December 2023, the USTB 10y rate will increase to 5%, and the expected growth rate in real GNP will decrease to 2%. What is the P/E assuming the payout ratio will remain unchanged and the expected inflation rate is 2.7%?

4. On April 2023, El Puerto de Liverpool, a Mexican company, had an estimated EPS of 13.03 and dividends per share of 2.25 to be paid one year from now. Earnings had grown at a geometric growth rate of 8.23% a year over the prior five years. Assume a market risk premium of 5.5%, a risk-free rate of 5%, a beta of 1.28, and an expected Mexican inflation rate of 3.67%. The stock price on October 5, 2023, was 90.17, and therefore, the observed P/E is 90.17/13.03 = 6.92

   a) If the Mexican inflation rate is 3.67%, what is the real long-term growth rate implied in the current P/E ratio if you use the Gordon formula?
   b) Calculate the intrinsic P/E assuming two stages of growth: assume a growth rate of 8% with the current payout ratio of 17.26% for the first five years, and from year six and beyond, a growth rate of 4% together with a payout ratio of 75%.

5. Now calculate the fair P/E of El Puerto de Liverpool using the formula [16.19]. The estimated ROE is 13%, g = 4%, and the observed P/E ratio on October 5, 2023 was 6.92. Use the cost of equity capital calculated in exercise 4 a).
6. On December 29, 2023, the stock of PepsiCo was traded at 28.34 times earnings, the expected EPS and DPS were 7.36 and 4.94, and the cost of equity capital 8.15%.

   a) What implicit growth rate justifies a P/E ratio of 28.34 using the current payout?
   b) If the estimated GDP growth rate is 2.4% for 2023 and the expected inflation rate is 3.1%, is the implicit growth rate sensical?
   c) As the smart estimate for the EPS growth rate is 9.37% for 2025 and 8.7% for 2026 (source: Refinitiv Eikon), use the two stages formula to calculate the stock price considering a short-term growth rate of 9% for the first three years projection and a long-term growth rate of 4% for 2027 and beyond. Compare the result with the P/E of 28.34; does it make sense?

7. Microsoft was traded at 38.83 times earnings on December 30, 2023 (Source: Refinitiv Eikon). The cost of equity capital is 8.68%, and the payout ratio is 26.92%, according to smart estimates. Assuming that the market is correct, calculate the implicit growth rate using Gordon's dividend formula.

8. According to Gufufocus, on January 5, 2024, the SP&500 was trading at 25.93 times earnings with a dividend yield of 1.46%. The US10YT on that date was 4.05%. Consider a market risk premium of 5.7%.

   a) What growth rate in dividends/earnings would justify the P/E ratio? Since the GDP is expected to grow 1.4% a year, and the consensus estimate for inflation, in the long term, is 2.5%, is the implicit growth rate reasonable?
   b) Estimate the fair P/E ratio using the GDP expected growth rate and the consensus estimate of the inflation rate of 2.5% and compare it with the observed P/E of 25.93.

9. On October 5, 2023, Trust Company has the following financial data: EBITDA = 30,326,961,000; ROIC = 10.1%; g = 6%; WACC = 11.81%; EBIT = 25,515,379,000; effective tax rate = 25%; NOPAT = 19,136,534,250; EV/EBITDA = 4.97. Calculate the EV/EBITDA using the formula [16.24] to check if the market is closest or not to the observed ratio.
10. Table 16.13 shows the quarterly EBITDA of Tyrius Corp. over twelve months. Recently, Tyrius received a tender offer of 6xEBITDA, which would lead to a firm value of 6 x 237.1 = 1,422.34, based on the annual standard EBITDA. However, the company takes one quarter to sell its inventory, valued under the FIFO method, in which assets purchased or acquired first are disposed of first, while the revenues reflect the quarterly inflation rate of 5%. This situation generates a gap between costs and revenue, which underestimates the cost of goods sold, and OPEX, which represents 48% of the revenues, overstating the company's profits. Supposing the inflation rate drops to zero at the end of the year, how much do you pay for the company based on EV/EBITDA?

TABLE 16.13 Quarterly and annual EBITDA of Tyrius Corp.

	Q1	Q2	Q3	Q4	Year
Revenues	105.0	110.3	115.8	121.6	452.6
OPEX before D&A	50.0	52.5	55.1	57.9	215.5
EBITDA	55.0	57.8	60.6	63.7	237.1

11. VVV Corp. has $100 million in revenues and $50 million in operative expenses, and depreciation and amortization of $12 million in the last fiscal year. The senior management has recognized adjustments for unrealized losses of $8 million from litigation expenses and goodwill impairment. Calculate the standard EBITDA and the normalized EBITDA.
12. TTT company wants to calculate the normalized EBITDA for the last year. The net income is $100,000, interest expenses are $20,000, depreciation and amortization are $10,000, income taxes are $70,000, and adjustments of $45,000 for unrealized forex losses and litigation expenses. Calculate the standard EBITDA and the normalized EBITDA.

13. Historic multiples. Suppose you are valuing Papelera Lujan, a private company located in an emerging country. The firm produces paperboard, tissue paper, and other paper products. Looking for comparables in the NAICS, we found seven in the paperboard mills and toilet manufacturing industry. First, we calculate the DCF value and then the implicit EV/EBITDA ratio as DCF value/normalized EBITDA = 6.98. This multiple seemed high for a private company in an emerging country, especially when the comparison was established, for example, with Kimberly-Clark de Mexico, a public company, having an EV/EBITDA of 6.8. However, if you look for a ten-year EV/EBITDA, an EV/EBITDA of 6.98 looks not unreasonable. What do you think?

TABLE 16.14 EV/EBITDA of Papelera Lujan 1999–2008

	Dec-99	Dec-00	Dec-01	Dec-02	Dec-03	Dec-04	Dec-05	Dec-06	Dec-07	Dec-08
International Paper Co.	10.3	7.9	10.1	9.7	13.1	12.4	11.1	7.8	6.7	3.5
Sonoco Products Co.	6.6	6.0	9.3	7.4	8.0	8.8	8.0	8.8	7.7	5.5
Graphic Packaging Holding Co.	-	6.0	9.0	7.9	11.0	10.0	8.3	9.7	7.3	7.6
Kimberly-Clark de Mexico SAB de CV	6.6	4.8	5.4	4.9	5.9	7.1	7.2	7.7	7.9	6.8
Avery Dennison Corp.	-	15.1	10.8	11.4	12.7	11.4	11.5	12.0	15.0	10.5
Industrias Forestales Sa	9.4	5.3	5.2	7.7	13.7	13.7	9.0	10.6	8.8	12.4
Amcor Flexibles North America Inc.	7.2	6.9	8.3	8.1	8.3	8.1	7.9	8.7	7.0	6.7
Mean	8.0	7.4	8.3	8.2	10.4	10.2	9.0	9.3	8.6	7.6

Notes

1 The relevant denominator must be computed after interest, preferred dividends, and minority interest expense.

2 Cash equivalents are marketable securities and (eventually) excess cash. They are subtracted from the outstanding debt since they can be used immediately to pay the obligations.

3 There is an alternative to Trailing P/E that uses operating earnings, excluding earnings from discontinued operations, extraordinary items, and accounting changes.

4 Remember that operative expenses usually represent a percentage of sales; therefore, EBITDA also can be expressed as a percentage of sales.

5 http://www.forbes.com/sites/tedgavin/2011/12/28/top-five-reasons-why-ebitda-is-a-great-big-lie/
6 Foreign exchange losses (gains) represent losses from changes in the value of assets or liabilities that have not been paid/applied by the end of the accounting period. Realized gains or losses arising from completed transactions. Foreign exchange losses are reported on the income statement and may appear as a separate line item; under IFRS9, are included in operating profit.
7 It can also be calculated on a per-share basis by dividing the stock price by sales per share for 12 months.
8 Many years ago, we performed the valuation of American Plast, an Argentinean company that produces thermoformed packaging for food and beverages. A few months later, we performed the valuation of "Petropackaging", another Argentinean company that also manufactures thermoformed packaging for food and beverages, but mainly for pet food. Both companies were in a "similar business line", and had similar financial ratios, capital structure, and profitability margins during the last five years. Interestingly, Petropackaging sales did not suffer during the recession, while American Plast's did. The owners treated their pets well.
9 When earnings like net income or EBITDA are negative or excessively small, databases do not report P/E and EBITDA multiples, because they are not economically useful.
10 If a company has negative EPS in any of those years, the cumulative earnings over the ten-year period could be negative and the CAPE ratio would reflect a negative value.

References

Berkman, H., Bradbury, M., & Ferguson, J. (2000). The Accuracy of Price-Earnings and Discounted Cash Flow Methods of IPO Equity Valuation. *Journal of International Financial Management and Accounting, 11(2)*, 71–83.

Cheng, C., & McNamara, R. (2000). The Valuation Accuracy of the Price-Earnings and Price-Book Benchmark Valuation Methods. *Review of Quantitative Finance and Accounting, 15(4)*, 349–370.

Dittman, I., & Weiner, C. (2005). *Selecting Comparables for the Valuation of European Firms*. SFB 649 Discussion paper 2005-002.

Eberhart, A. C. (2001). Comparable Firms and the Precision of Equity Valuations. *Journal of Banking & Finance, 25*(7), 1367–1400.

Francis, J., Olsson, P., & Oswald, D. R. (2000). Comparing the Accuracy and Explainability of Dividend, Free Cash Flow, and Abnormal Earnings Equity Value Estimates. *Journal of Accounting Research, 38(1)*, 45–70.

Gilson, S. C., Hotchkiss, E. S., & Ruback, R. S. (2000). Valuation of Bankrupt Firms. *Review of Financial Studies, 1(1)*, 43–74.

Graham, B., & Dodds, D. (1934). *Security Analysis*. New York: McGraw-Hill Companies, Inc.

Harbula, P. (2009). Valuation Multiples: Accuracy and Drivers Evidence from the European Stock Market. *Business Valuation Review, 28(4)*, 186–200.

Kaplan, S., & Ruback, R. (1996). The Market Pricing of Cash Flow Forecasts: Discounted Cash Flow vs. the Method of Comparables. *Journal of Applied Corporate Finance, 8(4)*, 45–60.

Kim, M., & Ritter, J. R. (1999). Valuing IPOs.. *Journal of Financial Economics, 53*, 409–437.

Lie, E., & Lie, H. (2002). Multiples Used to Estimate Corporate Value. *Financial Analysts Journal, 58(2)*, 44–54.

Liu, J., Nissim, D., & Thomas, J. (2002). Equity Valuation Using Multiples. *Journal of Accounting Research*, 135–172.

Liu, J., Nissim, D., & Thomas, J. (April 2007). Is Cash Flow King in Valuations? *Financial Analyst Journal, 63(2)*, 56–68.

Molodovsky, N. (1960). Stock Values and Stock Prices. *Financial Analysts Journal, 16(3)*, 9–12.
Penman, S., & Sougiannis, T. (1998). A Comparison of Dividend, Cash Flow, and Earnings Approaches to Equity Valuation. *Contemporary Accounting Research, 15(3)*, 343–383.
Pinto, J. E., Robinson, T. R., & Stowe, J. (2015). Equity Valuation: A Survey of Professional Practice. Working paper, CFA Institute.
Plenborg, T., & Coppe Pimentel, R. (2016). Best Practices in Applying Multiples for Valuation Purposes. *The Journal of Private Equity, 19(3)*, 55–64.
Schreiner, A., & Spremann, K. (2007). *Multiples and their Valuation Accuracy in European Equity Markets. Working paper.* Available at http://ssrn.com/abstract = 957352
Shiller, R. (2022). *Online Data Robert Shiller.* Available at www.econ.yale.edu/~shiller/data.htm
Young, S., & Zeng, Y. (2015). Accounting Comparability and the Accuracy of Peer-Based Valuation Models. *Accounting Review, 90(6)*, 2571–2601.

PART

4

Real-world cases

This part contains four real valuation cases that our firm was hired to estimate the fair value. The methodology used for each case is very similar for three of them – with some variations according to the specifics of the case – while it is something different for the case which deals with a financial entity.

The first case was about Sofora Telecomunicaciones, which is the controller company of Telecom, one of the two companies which provide the telecommunications services and one of the most important companies in Argentina. It involved litigation between the partners, was rich in analysis, and involved all of the techniques that we describe in the previous chapters.

The second case is about a financial entity. Since the business of a financial company is totally different to that of a non-financial company, a different DCF model is built for this case. The business operated in an emerging market which experienced a big financial crisis. After that, it was compelled to reduce its operations, stopping to receive deposits and give loans. The European controller expressed its desire to operate the company, so, a fair value had to be determined to compensate the local operator. We had to consider industry regulations and also valuing non-operative assets.

The third case was "Cars Recovery", a company involved in stolen vehicle recovery services (SVRS). In 2008, we were hired by JJ Corporation, an American company, to estimate the fair value of its subsidiary "Cars Recovery" which operates in Argentina. JJ Corporation is the parent company, which had a 25% of the CR at this time.

The fourth case was "American Packages", a listed Argentinean company primarily involved in the production of plastic packages for the dairy products industry, with a particular focus on the yogurt segment. It controls approximately 55% of the local market, being the major packaging manufacturer in the region, and exports to many countries across Latin America. The majority interest of American Packages is owned by "Dix", a Brazilian company which held 62% of the shareholding, while RR held the remaining 38%.

Except for the Sofora case – which involved a public company – the others cases used fictitious names for the companies involved, to protect their confidentiality.

DOI: 10.4324/9781003628491-20

CHAPTER

17

Sofora Telecomunicaciones SA

Introduction

Argentina's Convertibility Plan, which put the country's currency on par with the US dollar, collapsed in early 2002. The government found itself unable to keep the currency on par with the dollar, thus it depreciated the local currency. Like most large Argentinean companies, Telecom Argentina had taken on most of its debt in dollars. As a result of the dollar's rise to 3ARS = 1US$, the company was forced to suspend payments on its debt of about ARS3.2 billion in April 2002, which

DOI: 10.4324/9781003628491-21

put it in default. The inflation rate rose to 41% in 2002 following the devaluation, and the government frozen the utility rates in an effort to stabilize prices. Due to its frozen rates and inflation-driven cost increases, Telecom loss ARS4.39 billion (US$1.38 billion), depleting its retained utilities and legal reserves.

France Telecom and Telecom Italia (through subsidiaries) have their shares of common stock in Nortel Inversora (totaling 67.8%) to a company created for this purpose, Sofora Telecomunicaciones S.A. The France Telecom subsidiaries would then sell 48% of this company's share capital to W de Argentina-Inversiones S.L, along with an option to purchase the remaining 2%, exercisable between 2008 and 2013. Telecom Italia became the new exclusive operator of Telecom Argentina, in which Nortel continued to hold a 54.74% stake. The company's name was shortened to Telecom Argentina S.A.

In September 2003, France Telecom shed its half-interest in Nortel Inversora, and sold its stake to a private Argentine Group, W de Argentina (1) for US$165 million. W de Argentina-Inversiones was owned by the Werthein Group, a leading Argentine investment company. The other partner, Telecom Italia, accepted that a local partner had bought the share of France Telecom, but for a limited time.

An agreement was signed by Telecom Italia and W de Argentina establishing a call option in favor of Telecom Italia to acquire the W de Argentina stake exercisable from January 2009. The Italians paid the Whertein Group 60 million dollars for the call option and to retake control of the company from January 2009. If Telecom Italia decide to exercise the call, it should pay a fixed value agreed on in 2003 for 30% of the shares and the market value for the rest of shares at the moment of the transaction. The agreement also established a call option in favor of Argentina Inversiones SL to acquire the 2% remaining owned by France Telecom. Thus, if W de Argentina decide to exercise the option, Telecom Italia and W de Argentina would each have a 50% share of Telecom Argentina.

In 2003, the Argentinian economy recovered and Telecom Argentina back to be profitable. However, in 2007 started legal battle between the two owners of Sofora Telecomunicaciones SA ("Sofora") for the control of Telecom Argentina.

In May 2008, W de Argentina filed a lawsuit against Telecom Italia to be declared the nullity of the contract that granted the call option in favor of Telecom Italia to acquire the stake owned by W de Argentina.

W argued that the acquisition of TELCO, the controlling party of Telefonica de España ´ the only local competitor of Telecom de Argentina – constituted a monopoly practice. Since the National Commission of Defense of the Competency recognizes the argument, W de Argentina rejected the sale of its share and hired three consultants to estimate the fair value of Sofora's common shares.

The following sections describe the process to obtain the fair value of Sofora that we performed in May 2008, presented as documentary proof by W de Argentina in its lawsuit with Telecom Italia before the National Judge Commercial N° 8, Secretary N° 15, Buenos Aires.

Sofora's holding

Figure 17.1 shows the structure of Sofora's holding in 2008. W de Argentina acquired 48% of Sofora's common share in December 200, while in February 2008

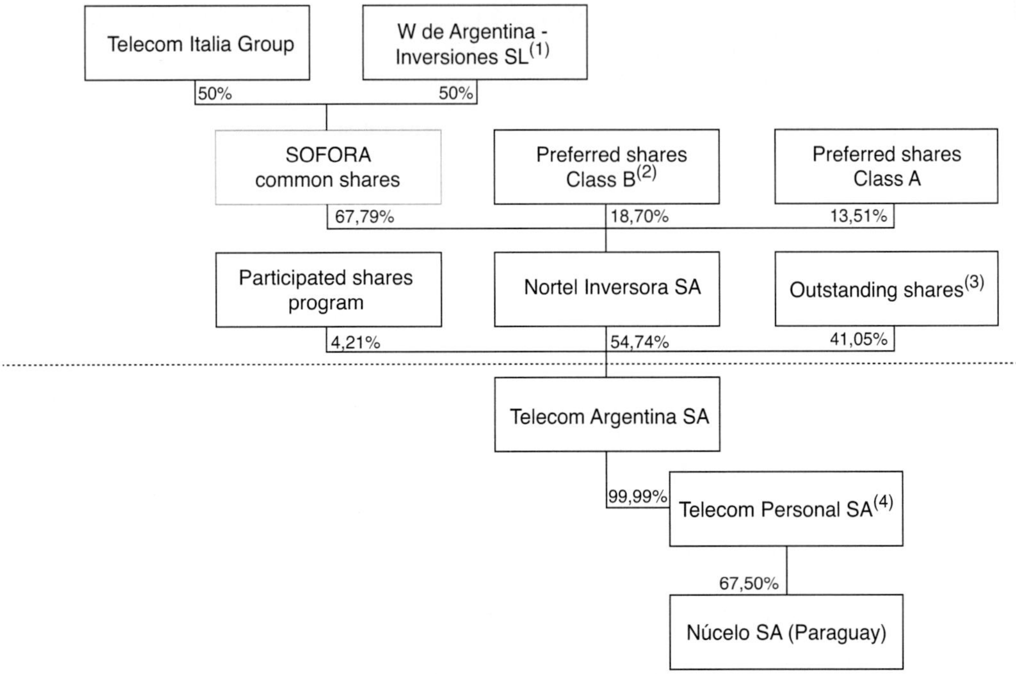

FIGURE 17.1 Sofora's holding in 2008

1. W de Argentina acquired the 48% common stocks of Sofora in December 2003. In February 2008 it manifested its desire to exercise a call option on 2% common stocks of Sofora, achieving a shareholding of 50%.
2. Traded on the New York Stock Exchange.
3. Traded on the New York Stock Exchange and Bolsa de Comercio de Buenos Aires.
4. Nortel Inversora owns 0.01% of the Telecom Personal common stocks.

manifested its desire to exercise a call option to buy the remaining 2%. Telecom Argentina holds a controlling interest in Telecom Personal[1] and is "the cash flow made" of the holding.

Since the objective was to estimate the fair value of Sofora's common shares, it was necessary to describe the cash flow trajectory that the company takes until its shareholders get their dividends.

First, Nortel Inversora receives 54.74% of the Telecom's dividends; the capital and dividends corresponding to the class A preference shares shall be redeemed before distributing dividends to Sofora's common shareholders. The class A preferred shares' principal paid a cumulative dividend of 6% annually and included an inflation-adjusted clause. The class B preference shareholders (48.96%) and the Sofora common shareholders (51.04%) might receive dividends immediately following the amortization of the capital and the payment of the equivalent dividends to the class A preference shareholders. Dividends may be paid to class B preference shareholders (48.96%) and Sofora's common shareholders (51.04%) immediately following the payment of capital and associated dividends to class A preference shareholders.

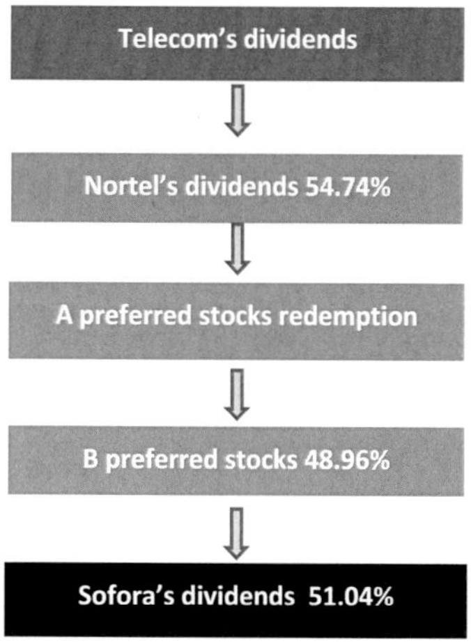

FIGURE 17.2 From Telecom's dividends to Sofora's dividends

Historical performance analysis and projected cash flows

Before creating the assumptions to forecast Telecom's financial statements, a thorough study of the past performance is required. We examined the company's performance throughout a 12-year period (1996–2007) in order to gather data that would support our financial statement and cash flow forecasting assumptions. There is no set length for the historical period that needs to be examined; the general rule is that the company's performance occurred in a uniform environment. For instance, if a company was ruled by inept management during one of the previous decades, which skewed the performance of all ratios, it would not make sense to evaluate it today using financial data from those two decades.

Despite the fact that the company has had its rates for the landline telephone frozen since 1999, it managed to boost its revenues and earnings in other segments. First, the landline telephone segment had declined due to the advancement of mobile network technology, to the point that it represents a small percentage of Telecom's revenues. Second, the use of cell phones has been increasing (in Argentina, there is more than one cell phone for every person). Third, the revenues for internet services increased. Thus, Telecom got more revenues from mobile phones and internet services since the Government allowed some adjustments to keep up with inflation.

The recession that started at the end of 1998 affected the company sales, which had 0% growth in 1999 and a fall of 5% in 2001. Telecom experienced a negative EBIT of 5% of revenues and a negative EBT of ARS5.67 billion following the devaluation of the domestic currency in early 2002 and the collapse of Argentina's Convertibility Plan, which put the domestic currency on par with the dollar. This resulted in a tax loss of nearly ARS1 billion, the first in many years. The company defaulted on its bonds as a result of the peso's devaluation, which caused the debt and interest payments to quadruple. The GDP fell by 10.6%, the largest decline in history, and the country was devasted. However, the GDP rebounded and expanded quickly in 2003, which helped Telecom Argentina recover and achieve a net profit of ARS351 million (118 million dollars) and net sales of

TABLE 17.1 Historical income statement in millions of Argentine pesos

	Dec 96	Dec 97	Dec 98	Dec 99	Dec 00	Dec 01	Dec 02	Dec 03	Dec 04	Dec 05	Dec 06	Dec 07
Sales	1.983	2.585	3.173	3.183	3.226	3.049	3.983	3.753	4.494	5.718	7.437	9.074
COGS	1.168	1.391	1.586	1.538	1.729	1.488	2.872	2.640	2.950	3.704	4.510	4.963
Gross margin	816	1.194	1.587	1.645	1.497	1.561	1.111	1.113	1.544	2.014	2.927	4.111
Administ. expenses	118	178	208	238	235	246	279	222	244	249	272	342
Commercial expense	207	331	562	661	631	903	1.034	784	900	1.261	1.743	2.133
EBIT	491	685	817	746	631	412	–212	107	400	504	912	1.636
Interest expenses	106	152	188	237	300	285	3.722	1	1.394	106	570	503
Interest revenue	67	40	43	73	83	56	–1.541	49	222	-200	88	62
Related companies	–2	–1	–7	–7	–8	–11	–23	2	–2	7	5	
Other income								208	131			
Other expenses	70	107	85	73	52	74	175			165	186	98
Extraordinary items	0	0	0	0	0	0	0	0	0	1.424	0	102
Earnings before taxes	379	465	580	502	354	98	–5.673	365	–643	1.464	249	1.199
Income taxes	119	158	208	147	85	51	–1.294	–7	26	122	–17	292
Minority interest	0	0	2	3	2	0	25	–21	–3	8	22	23
Net income	260	307	374	358	271	47	–4.354	351	-666	1.334	244	884

ARS3.75 billion (US$1.26 billion) for the year. Voice, data, and Internet transmission made up 68% of its net sales, followed by cellular (31%), and its printing and publishing subsidiary for telephone directories and other similar materials, as well as the sale of advertising in these publications, which made up 1%.

OPEX, EBIT and EBITDA

It should be noted that the COGS/Sales and EBITDA/Revenues ratios consistently tend to stay at 50% and 20/22% respectively. Both of these ratios declined during Argentina 1999–2002 recession, although they eventually recovered to their historical levels.

TABLE 17.2 Historical operative costs as sales percentage

	Dec 96	Dec 97	Dec 98	Dec 99	Dec 00	Dec 01	Dec 02	Dec 03	Dec 04	Dec 05	Dec 06	Dec 07
Sales growth	-	30%	23%	0%	1%	–5%	31%	–6%	20%	27.2%	30.1%	22.0%
COGS	59%	54%	50%	48%	54%	49%	72%	70%	65.6%	64.8%	60.6%	54.7%
Adm. expenses	6%	7%	7%	7%	7%	8%	7%	6%	5.4%	4.4%	3.7%	3.8%
Commercial expenses	10%	13%	18%	21%	20%	30%	26%	21%	20.0%	22.1%	23.4%	23.5%
EBIT	25%	26%	26%	23%	20%	14%	–5%	3%	9%	9%	12%	18%
EBITDA	51%	51%	50%	47%	45%	41%	47%	53%	46%	35%	31%	34%

Generally speaking, operating expenses generally represent a percentage of sales, as we discuss in Chapter 2. In the 1990s, for instance, the cost of goods sold (COGS) was roughly 50%, and the domestic inflation rate was close to the international inflation rate and even low (1 to 2% annually). However, in 2002, all operating expenses increased as a percentage of sales because of the Government's frozen rates and the devaluation, which caused the inflation rate to rise to 40%. In 2002, COGS accounted for 72% of sales; however, between 2003 and 2007, COGS, administration costs, and commercial expenses began to decline, reaching 54.7%, 3.8%, and 23/23.5% of sales in 2007, respectively. Between 2003 and 2007, the rate of inflation decreased once again, and at the end of 2007, earnings before interest and taxes accounted for 18% of sales, which is close to the historical 21/22%.

Income taxes

In the 1990s, income taxes paid as a percentage of pre-tax revenue were nearly equal to the legal tax rate of 35%. This dropped following the 2002 devaluation, and in 2007 the effective tax rate was 24.4% because the business was once again successful.

TABLE 17.3 Historical balance sheet in millions of Argentine pesos

	Dec 96	Dec 97	Dec 98	Dec 99	Dec 00	Dec 01	Dec 02	Dec 03	Dec 04	Dec 05	Dec 06	Dec 07
Cash and banks	10	17	12	17	30	57	89	26	32	46	31	45
Marketable securities	206	344	292	655	708	153	1.316	2.441	3.630	596	631	947
Accounts receivable	440	532	767	740	849	678	596	581	612	705	783	898
Inventories	13	15	33	25	58	22	12	14	79	104	176	157
Other assets		7	5	7	6	6	3	3	3	5	18	5

(Continued)

TABLE 17.3 (Continued)

	Dec 96	Dec 97	Dec 98	Dec 99	Dec 00	Dec 01	Dec 02	Dec 03	Dec 04	Dec 05	Dec 06	Dec 07
Other receivables	63	56	94	63	114	290	76	150	78	76	128	332
Current assets	732	971	1.203	1.507	1.765	1.206	2.092	3.215	4.434	1.532	1.767	2.384
Fixed assets	4.209	4.618	4.700	4.999	5.185	4.827	9.618	8.001	6.895	5.959	5.741	5.738
Investments	242	37	30	67	24	54	59	47	2	2	1	2
Accounts receivables	3	12	9	4	6	4	1					
Intangibles	24	99	220	538	577	478	937	845	773	764	783	760
Other assets	7	56	36	25	22	57	138	193	228	269	413	282
Non current assets	4.485	4.822	4.995	5.633	5.814	5.420	10.755	9.086	7.898	7.015	6.948	6.787
Total assets	5.218	5.793	6.198	7.140	7.579	6.626	12.847	12.301	12.332	8.547	8.715	9.171
Accounts payable	478	442	482	664	854	491	391	451	548	824	1.494	1.640
Salaries and wages	70	90	82	93	68	61	61	77	79	104	132	164
Fiscal liabilites	103	146	168	72	64	85	117	151	114	222	229	266
Debt	577	598	429	638	985	1.161	11.053	9.996	9.434	905	1.395	1.474
Other liabilites	6	22	56	136	122	21	25	25	22	31	36	50
Contingencies	0	0	0	13	10	6	9	15	30	110	87	49
Current liabilities	1.234	1.298	1.217	1.616	2.103	1.825	11.656	10.715	10.227	2.196	3.373	3.643
Debt	1.401	1.767	2.033	2.389	2.509	2.089	144	86	1.219	3.996	2.703	1.724
Contingencies	67	82	95	58	53	60	141	210	214	247	241	243
Fiscal and social liabilities	0	22	43	58	47	246	29	30	38	122	95	332
Other liabilities	24	21	33	98	17	13	65	39	71	78	102	120
Non current liabilities	1.504	1.920	2.268	2.737	2.689	2.419	379	365	1.549	4.443	3.141	2.419
Total liabilities	2.738	3.218	3.485	4.353	4.792	4.244	12.035	11.080	11.776	6.639	6.514	6.062
Shareholders' Equity	2.480	2.575	2.713	2.787	2.787	2.382	812	1.221	556	1.908	2.201	3.109
Total liabiities and shareholders' Equity	5.218	5.793	6.198	7.140	7.579	6.626	12.847	12.301	12.332	8.547	8.715	9.171

Fixed assets

In the 1990s, the corporation made investments in fixed assets to maintain a fixed assets/sales ratio greater than one; however, after 2002, these investments significantly decreased, and in 2007, the fixed assets/sales ratio was 0.63.

Other assets and other liabilities

One of Telecom's advantages is that it typically has a negative cash cycle and working capital since its days sales inventory (DSI) is too low and its days accounts payable (DAP) exceed its days sales outstanding (DSO).[2] Together with an EBITDA margin of over 30%, the negative cash cycle enables Telecom to generate a large enough cash from operations. Between 2001 and 2005, CAPEX was low, but in 2006 and 2007, it started to rise once more. Although the company actually reduced CAPEX because of the crisis, the 2002 CAPEX figure appears completely distorted by an accounting revaluation[3], but in reality, the company limited its capital expenses to a minimum.[4]

Like any other company, Telecom had other operative assets, mainly composed of tax credits, which fluctuated around 2% to 4% of the sales. Other operative liabilities, such as fiscal and social liabilities, represented around 5% of the sales. The last column of Table 17.4 summarizes the accumulated values of the main categories of the free cash flow. Explained in a nutshell, Telecom had a positive EBITDA of ARS20.3 billion, it carried loss forward for ARS0.23 billion,[5] its net investments including working capital and CAPEX was of 16,528–587 = ARS15.9 billion, and a free cash flow of ARS4.9 billion.

Cash conversion cycle

The other value driver in a valuation usually is the cash cycle. Given that it takes less time to collect its bills than it takes to pay its purchases to its suppliers, and the inventories are not significant – just wires and cell phones – Telecom's cash cycle is significantly negative as a result. By the end of 2007, the company's cash cycle was negative by –73 days due its DSO of 36 days, DSI of 12 days, and a DAP of 121. Every ratio that corresponds to the past performance is displayed in Table 17.5.

Financial statement forecasting assumptions

As with all valuation procedures, the statement of assumptions that follows is a condensed version of a much more involved and possibly tiresome process that reflects:

a) Examining historical performance
b) Reviewing research studies, and
c) Having internal discussions with senior management.

TABLE 17.4 Historical cash flow in millions of Argentine pesos

	Dec 97	Dec 98	Dec 99	Dec 00	Dec 01	Dec 02	Dec 03	Dec 04	Dec 05	Dec 06	Dec 07	Accumulated
EBIT	685	817	746	631	412	–212	107	400	504	912	1.636	6,638
Depreciation & Amortization	624	778	763	833	830	2.101	1.877	1.646	1.498	1.392	1.416	
EBITDA	1.309	1.595	1.509	1.464	1.242	1.889	1.984	2.046	2.002	2.304	3.052	20,396
Accounts receivables	92	235	–27	109	–171	–82	–15	31	93	78	115	
Inventories	2	18	–8	33	–36	–10	2	65	25	72	–19	
Accounts payable	–36	40	182	190	–363	–100	60	97	276	670	146	
Fiscal liabilites	43	22	–96	–8	21	32	34	–37	108	7	37	
Other receivables	–7	38	–31	51	176	–214	74	–72	–2	52	204	
Salaries	20	–8	11	–25	–7	0	16	2	25	28	32	
Other liabilities	16	34	–31	–14	–101	4	0	–3	9	5	14	
Other assets	7	–2	11	–1	0	–3	0	0	2	13	–13	
Working capital	51	201	80	49	419	–245	–49	–35	–300	–495	58	–587
Income taxes	158	208	147	85	51	–1.294	–7	26	122	–17	292	–229
Cash from operations	1.100	1.186	1.603	1.330	772	3.428	2.040	2.055	2.180	2.816	2.702	21,212
CAPEX	1.033	860	1.062	1.019	472	6.892	260	540	562	1.174	1.413	
Cash from investments	1.040	922	1.780	1.068	–152	8.521	1.279	1.612	–2.460	1.216	1.702	16,528
FREE CASH FLOW	37	356	2	97	1.030	–5.344	688	470	4.763	1.430	1.348	4,877
Financing results	–152	–188	–237	–300	–285	–3.722	–1	–1.394	–106	–570	–503	
Cash flow from financing	–30	–361	3	–84	–1.003	5.376	–751	–464	–4.749	–1.445	–1.334	–4,842
Increase/decrease in cash	7	–5	5	13	27	32	–63	6	14	–15	14	
Cash at the beginning	10	17	12	17	30	57	89	26	32	46	31	
Final cash	17	12	17	30	57	89	26	32	46	31	45	

TABLE 17.5 Historical performance ratios

	Dec 97	Dec 98	Dec 99	Dec 00	Dec 01	Dec 02	Dec 03	Dec 04	Dec 05	Dec 06	Dec 07
Sales growth	30%	23%	0%	1%	−5%	31%	−6%	20%	27.2%	30.1%	22.0%
OPEX											
COGS	54%	50%	48%	54%	49%	72%	70%	65.6%	64.8%	60.6%	54.7%
Administrative expenses	7%	7%	7%	7%	8%	7%	6%	5.4%	4.4%	3.7%	3.8%
Commercial expenses	13%	18%	21%	20%	30%	26%	21%	20.0%	22.1%	23.4%	23.5%
EBIT	26%	26%	23%	20%	14%	−5%	3%	9%	9%	12%	18%
Borrowing interest rate	7%	9%	8%	3%	8%	12%	6%	7%	9%	11%	9.7%
Effective tax rate	34%	36%	29%	24%	52%	23%	−2%	−4%	8%	−7%	24.4%
CAPEX & Depreciation											
Depreciation	14%	17%	15%	16%	17%	22%	23%	24%	25%	24%	25%
Fixed assets/sales	1.8	1.5	1.6	1.6	1.6	2.4	2.1	1.53	1.04	0.77	0.63
CAPEX (in millions of ARS)	1,033	860	1,062	1,019	472	6,892	260	540	562	1,174	1,413
Other assets and liabilities											
Other ST assets	2%	3%	2%	4%	10%	2%	4%	2%	1%	2%	4%
Fiscal liabilities	5.6%	5.3%	2.3%	2.0%	2.8%	2.9%	4.0%	2.5%	3.9%	3.1%	2.9%
Social liabilities	3.5%	2.6%	2.9%	2.1%	2.0%	1.5%	2.1%	1.8%	1.8%	1.8%	1.8%
Management ratios											
Days on sales	62	73	70	79	67	45	47	50	45	38	36
Days on inventory	4	8	6	12	5	2	2	10	10	14	12
Days on payables	116	110	158	177	123	50	62	66	81	119	121
Cash cycle	−50	−29	−82	−83	−51	−3	−14	−7	−25	−66	−73

1. Revenues: After experimenting with different models and discussing with W de Argentina's senior management the company's forward plan, we decided to use the linear tendency to forecast the first seven years. Assuming a declining rate of inflation, we projected a nominal growth rate of 5% in the tenth year.
2. Cost of goods sold: It was forecasted to be 54% of sales in 2008, before gradually decreasing to 50% of sales by the end of 2011.
3. Administration expenses: 3.7% of sales from 2008 to 2010, with a target of 3.5 of sales by the end of 2010.
4. Commercial expenses: Assuming the business will continue to maintain the ratio seen over the previous three years, commercial expenses accounted for 23% of sales for the projected timeframe.
5. Effective income tax rate: For the whole forecasted period, was set at 35%, which is the legal tax rate in Argentina. This resulted in an EBIT/Sales ratio of 21/22%
6. Fixed assets, CAPEX, and depreciation: Since the global depreciation rate was 25%, we adopted this ratio for the forecasted period. Capital expenses were considered to be 15% of the annual sales, the standard in the global telecommunications industry. These assumptions lead to a fixed assets/sales relation of 0.40
7. Day sales outstanding, days on inventories, and days accounts payable: These were estimated as 36, 10, and 120 days respectively, based on historical performance. These assumptions result in a –76-day negative cash cycle.
8. Other assets, fiscal liabilities, and social liabilities: These were estimated as 2%, 3%, and 2% of the annual sales.

Forecasted free cash flow

We used the methods we outlined in Chapter 2 to forecast the balance sheet, income statement, and free cash flow while taking into account all of the assumptions mentioned in the preceding section.

TABLE 17.6 Forecasted free cash flow in millions of Argentine pesos

	Dec 08	Dec 09	Dec 10	Dec 11	Dec 12	Dec 13	Dec 14	Dec 15	Dec 16	Dec 17
EBIT	2.036	2.588	3.069	3.569	3.933	4.297	4.660	4.986	5.285	5.550
Depreciation & amortization	1.830	1.826	1.881	1.980	2.113	2.270	2.446	2.630	2.816	2.998
EBITDA	3.866	4.415	4.951	5.549	6.046	6.567	7.106	7.617	8.101	8.547
Accounts receivables	143	152	152	152	153	152	152	137	126	111
Inventories	–1	16	18	17	21	21	21	19	17	15

(Continued)

TABLE 17.6 (Continued)

	Dec 08	Dec 09	Dec 10	Dec 11	Dec 12	Dec 13	Dec 14	Dec 15	Dec 16	Dec 17
Accounts payable	233	201	220	209	256	254	254	227	209	184
Fiscal liabilites	50	46	46	46	47	46	46	42	38	34
Other receivables	–121	31	31	31	31	31	31	28	25	22
Salaries	47	31	31	31	31	31	31	28	25	22
Income taxes	713	906	1.074	1.249	1.377	1.504	1.631	1.745	1.850	1.942
Cash from operations	3.463	3.587	3.972	4.386	4.798	5.190	5.602	5.985	6.356	6.697
CAPEX	1.582	1.814	2.046	2.278	2.511	2.743	2.974	3.183	3.374	3.542
Cash from investments	1.577	1.814	2.046	2.278	2.511	2.743	2.974	3.183	3.374	3.542
Free cash flow	1.886	1.773	1.926	2.108	2.287	2.447	2.628	2.802	2.982	3.154

We delivered a seminar about valuation in emerging markets at the end of 2013. Since we had already completed Sofora's valuation in May 2008 and were aware of the financial performance for the 2008–2012 timeframe, we thought it would be interesting to compare the projected and actual cash flows for that time frame. Figure 17.3 displays both cash flows, with the total cash flow for 2008–2012 shown in the final column.

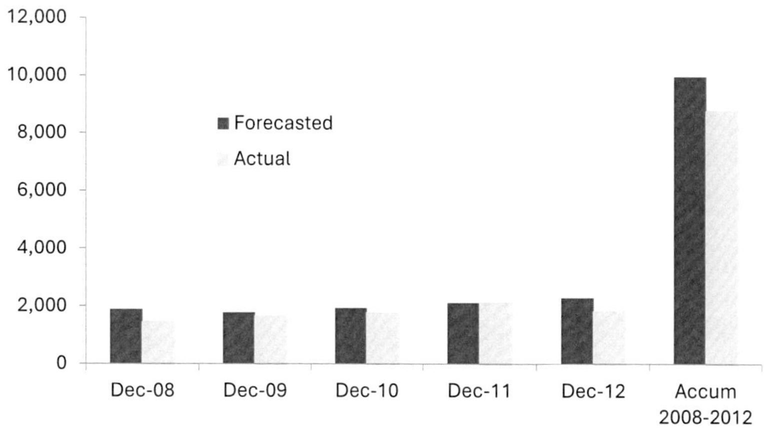

FIGURE 17.3 Forecasted and actual free cash flow in millions of Argentine pesos

Cost of capital estimation

All of the of the cost of capital inputs were estimated in dollars, as we discussed in Chapter 13.

Risk-free rate: Using the US T-Bond return with a ten-year maturity, the average for the previous year was calculated to be 3.8%

Market risk premium: We consider a Premium of 6.7%, based on the American stock market return from 1925 to 2007.

Beta: We estimate the beta by regressing the monthly returns of Telecom and the Argentine stock market for the last 60 months, between June 2003 and May 2008.

Country risk premium: We add 480 basis points to the cost of equity capital. The EMBI+ average from the previous year was used to compute the country risk premium.

Cost of equity capital: Using the CAPM model, we calculate a cost of equity capital of 13.49%.

$$ke = rf + \left[E(rm) - rf\right]\beta + RP$$

$$ke = 3{,}8\% + [6.7\%]0{,}73 + 4{,}8\% = 13{,}49\%$$

Cost of debt after taxes: The expected yield on the Telecom corporate bonds was considered as the marginal cost of debt. It was 10% before taxes and 6.5% after taxes.

$$kd(1-t) = 10\%(1-35\%) = 6{,}5\%$$

WACC: We estimate the expected capital structure using the circularity approach outlined in Chapter 11. It yields a D/V ratio of 15% and an E/V ratio of 85%.

$$WACC = kd(1-t)\frac{D}{D+E} + ke\frac{E}{D+E}$$

$$WACC = 10\%(1-0{,}35) \times 0{,}15 + 13{,}49\% \times 0{,}85 = 12{,}4\%$$

As of December 31, 2007, the Telecom debt was around 1,000 million US dollars, and the D/V ratio, measured using market values, was roughly 18%/20% (the market cap fluctuated between US$4 to 4.6 billion in 2008).

Telecom's fair value

After estimating the free cash flow and the cost of capital, we obtained the fair value of operations (V). We then added the marketable securities and subtracted the financial debt to determine the equity fair value. Since marketable securities can pay off a portion of the debt right once, the net financial debt is considered as the difference between marketable securities and debt. At the end of valuation, the market cap was US$3,560 million, and the equity fair value was US$4,309 million, as shown in Figure 17.4.

You should definitely include a graph like this in your value report. See Appendix A for an easy-to-follow design guide.

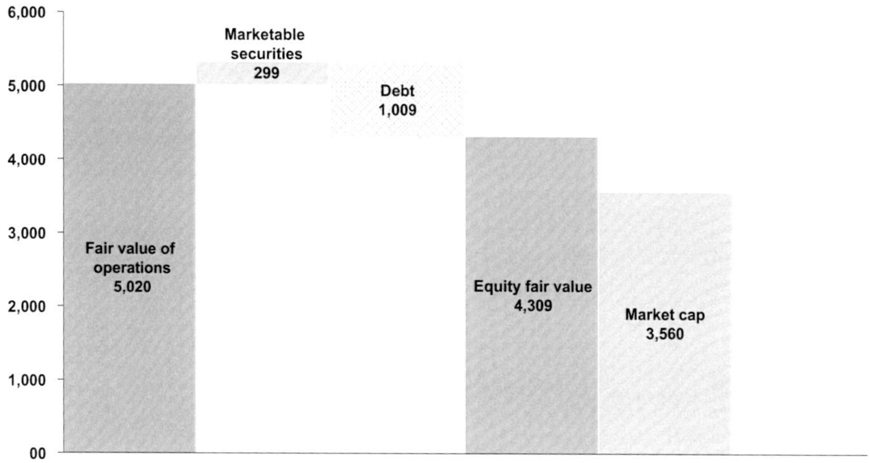

FIGURE 17.4 Telecom fair value flow in millions of US dollars

Valuation in domestic and foreign currency: The equivalence

Even though the financial statements and free cash flow were first projected in Argentine pesos, we used the interest rate and purchasing power parity theories to convert them to dollars, as we explain in Chapter 13. Tables 17.7 and 17.8 demonstrate that when the simultaneous fulfillment of the purchasing power parity and the interest rate parity is assumed, the results of valuing in domestic or foreign currency are equivalent. As we previously stated, the equivalence is not important per se; rather, it works as a double check to ensure that the relations between the real exchange rate, inflation rates, and forecasted interest rates are all consistent.

TABLE 17.7 Firm value and equity value in millions of Argentine pesos

	Dec 08	Dec 09	Dec 10	Dec 11	Dec 12	Dec 13	Dec 14	Dec 15	Dec 16	Dec 17
FCF	1,886	1,773	1,926	2,108	2,287	2,447	2,628	2,802	2,982	3.154
Terminal value										25,808
FCF + Terminal value	1,886	1,773	1,926	2,108	2,287	2,447	2,628	2,802	2,982	28,962
Firm value	15,912									
– Net financial debt	2,251									
Equity value in ARS at December 2007	13,661									
Equity value in US$ at December 2007(*)	4,309									

(*) Equity value in ARS/spot exchange rate

TABLE 17.8 Firm value and equity value in millions of US dollars

	Dec 08	Dec 09	Dec 10	Dec 11	Dec 12	Dec 13	Dec 14	Dec 15	Dec 16	Dec 17
FCF	572.8	518.5	542.5	571.7	597.5	615.6	636.5	653.6	669.8	682.2
Terminal value										5,582.0
FCF + Terminal value	572.8	518.5	542.5	571.7	597.5	615.6	636.5	653.6	669.8	6,264.2
Firm value	5,019.5									
– Net financial debt	710.1									
Equity value at December 2007	4,309									

Sources: Banco Central de la República Argentina, The National Institute of Statistics and Censuses (INDEC), Ministerio de Economia de la Nacion Argentina, and ROFEX (Rosario Future Exchange).

Country risk and its effect on the Telecom market value

Figure 17.5 shows the relation between the Telecom Market Capitalization and the EMBI+. It appears that market capitalization falls as the EMBI+ rises. We are interested in the response of our DCF model if we were to incorporate the spot EMBI+ for a specific date. Alongside this relationship, we calculated the DCF value for several dates during the valuation process, including the spot EMBI+ value in a cell of our spreadsheet DCF model. It is noteworthy that in a number of days, the DCF values that are displayed on the rectangles were similar to the market capitalization.

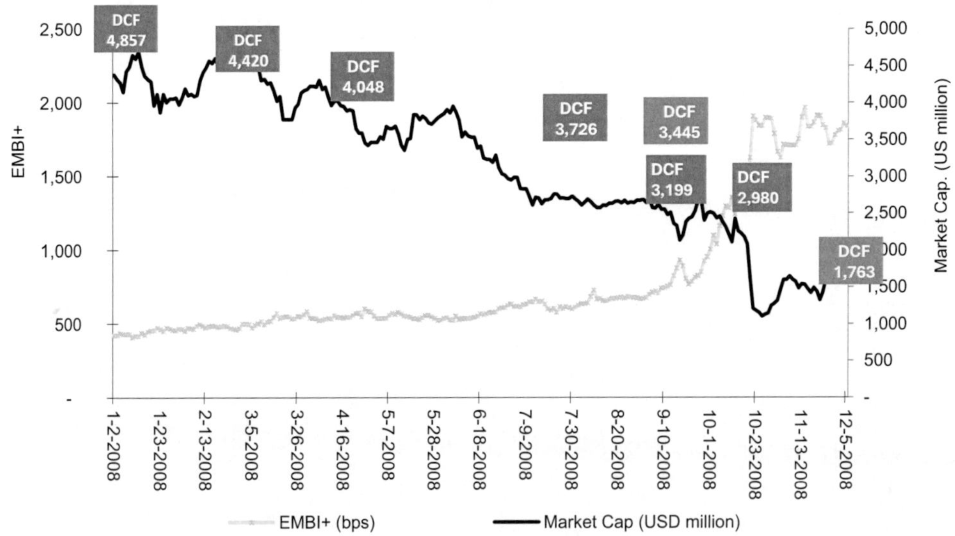

FIGURE 17.5 EMBI+, DCF, and market value in millions of US dollars

Relative valuation

Using a peer group of 13 companies, including a sample of wireline/integrated companies and a sample of mobile companies, we calculate the EV/EBITDA for 2007 and estimations for 2008 and 2009. The weighted average EV/EBITDA multiple[6] for 2008 was 5.0X, a similar value of the implicit EV/EBITDA of our valuation, which was around 5.28 calculated as the Firm value of operations divided by an estimated EBITDA of US$950 million at the time of the valuation.

$$\frac{\textit{Firm value of operations}}{\textit{Estimated EBITDA}} = \frac{5.029}{950} = 5.28$$

TABLE 17.9 Peer group and EV/EBITDA

Company	Enterprise Value – US$ MM	EBITDA Margin			EV / EBITDA		
		FY 07	FY 08 E	FY 09 E	FY 07	FY 08 E	FY 09 E
Wireline/Integrated							
Telecom Argentina	4.669	34%	34%	35%	4.8x	4.0x	3.5x
Telmex	43.749	41%	42%	43%	5.9x	5.0x	5.0x
Axtel	3.188	34%	35%	37%	8.5x	7.0x	6.3x
CTC	2.692	45%	42%	42%	4.7x	4.4x	4.5x
Brasil Telecom Part.	8.120	34%	35%	37%	3.8x	3.6x	3.4x
Tele Norte Leste Part.	12.506	37%	37%	37%	3.4x	3.3x	3.3x
Telesp Fixed	14.162	42%	43%	42%	4.0x	4.5x	4.5x
Average		39%	40%	41%	5.0x	5.0x	4.9x
Mobile							
America Movil	118,092	41%	41%	42%	10.2x	8.8x	7.9x
NII Holdings Inc.	7,350	28%	28%	30%	8.0x	6.2x	4.6x
Vivo Holdings	10,963	25%	25%	27%	6.2x	5.6x	5.5x
Telemig Celular	886	33%	36%	36%	3.5x	3.0x	2.8x

(Continued)

TABLE 17.9 (Continued)

Company	Enterprise Value – US$ MM	EBITDA Margin			EV / EBITDA		
		FY 07	FY 08 E	FY 09 E	FY 07	FY 08 E	FY 09 E
TIM Part.	8,860	23%	24%	26%	5.5x	4.7x	4.2x
Entel	4,908	40%	41%	42%	6.7x	6.2x	6.1x
Average		38%	38%	39%	9.4x	8.1x	7.3x
		Latam weighted average			7.8x	7.0x	6.4x

Source: Merrill Lynch, Deutsche Bank & Bloomberg

Preferable stocks and Sofora's common stocks valuation

To estimate the dividends to Class A and Class B preferred shares, it was necessary to establish when Telecom may distribute dividends to Nortel, the parent company. We complete the following steps:

1. Forecast the net income of Telecom.
2. To forecast dividends to Nortel was used the historical payout of Telecom, which was about 75% before the collapse of the convertibility plan in 2002. Nortel would receive 54.74% of dividends distributed by Telecom once the legal reserve and retained earnings for ARS1,109.9 million were re-constituted. The remaining 25% of excess cash should be used to purchase marketable securities, whose amount was based on the forecasted equity cash flow, which is equal to the free cash flow minus interest charges plus tax savings. Since the forecasted dividends of Telecom in 2008 would be 197 million, Nortel would receive 108 million (197 x 54.74%).
3. According to its expected dividends, Nortel could redeem the principal to Class A preferred shares for ARS108 million in 2008, 605 million in 2009, and 657 million in 2010. This stream of payments must also consider that the capital of preferred A shares was adjusted using a coefficient that reflected the annual inflation rate known as "CER".[7]
4. After the redemption of the principal of Class A preferred stocks, the remaining cash flow become the cash disposable (row 11) to pay dividends to the Class B preferred shareholders (row 17) and the common shareholders of Sofora (row 18), almost in similar percentages (48.96% for the former and 51.04% for the latter). The last column shows the terminal value for both stream of dividends.

TABLE 17.10 Dividends cash flow in millions of Argentine pesos

	Dec 07	Dec 08	Dec 09	Dec 10	Dec 11	Dec 12	Dec 13	Dec 14	Dec 15	Dec 16	Dec 17
Net income Telecom	884	1,116	1,475	1,787	2,112	2,349	2,585	2,821	3,033	3,228	3,399
Dividends distribution date	Apr 08	Apr 09	Apr 10	Apr 11	Apr 12	Apr 13	Apr 14	Apr 15	Apr 16	Apr 17	Apr 18
Telecom's dividend	0	197	1,106	1,340	1,584	1,762	1,939	2,116	2,275	2,421	2,549
Marketable securities		1,481	459	377	316	318	301	304	319	353	397
Nortel dividends (54,74%)	0	108	605	734	867	964	1,061	1,158	1,245	1,325	1,396
Nortel mark securities (54,74%)	811	251	207	173	174	165	166	175	193	217	
Expected CER	2.12	2.3	2.6	2.8	3.1						
Pref. A – Adj. capital		1,110	1,169	657	0	0	0	0	0	0	0
Pref A – rescue		108	605	657	0						
Div. Pref. B (48,96%)	0	0	0	38	425	472	520	567	610	649	683
Terminal value										7,356	
Div. Sofora (51,04%)	0	0	0	39	443	492	542	591	636	676	712
Terminal value										7,669	

Sofora's fair value

After estimating the Telecom fair value on December 31, 2007, we capitalize it with the cost of equity until the precise valuation date, which was May 2008:

$$4{,}302.1\text{x } (1 + 0.1349 \text{ x } 121/365) = 4{,}502.1$$

To consider the participation of Nortel Inversora, we multiply the prior value by 54.74% and add a Control Premium of 20%. After that, we determine the fair value of Sofora common stocks by subtracting the present value of the streams of dividends of Class A and B preferred shareholders.

TABLE 17.11 Sofora common stock fair value in millions of US dollars

Sofora fair value	
Telecom Argentina	4,502.1
Nortel Inversora participation (54,74%)	2,464.5
+ Control Premium of Nortel (20%)	492.9
– Nortel preferable stock value class A	282.0
– Nortel preferable stock value class B	1,047.8
Sofora common stock fair value	1,627.6

Therefore, the portion of W de Argentina was determined to be 1,627.6 x 50% = 813.8

Final discussions and intriguing story

I would like to discuss the events of a 2008 meeting with one of Sofora Group's partners. It took a long time, but we were finally satisfied and prepared to give the Valuation Report after nearly finishing the analysis. I explained how we had obtained the fair value of Telecom, and the expected dividend policy, since before Sofora's common shareholders received their dividends, preferred shareholders should receive their dividends first. Our methodology consisted in calculating the DCF value of Telecom first, then adding a control premium, and lastly the preferred shareholder's fair value-obtained by discounting the forecasted dividends – to achieve the fair value of Sofora.

Suddenly, I was questioned by one of the board members: "If you calculate the fair value of Sofora common stocks as the present value of its expected dividends, rather than using your approach, both values should be the same, right?"

I instantly responded "yes" to the question since it made sense, but I was unaware that they had asked the same question of one of the other consultant firms they had engaged, and they were unable to explain the difference. "The whole is equal to the sum of its parts", I thought. "The whole in MM theory, is always equal to the sum of its parts, with or without taxes", I stated. Uncomfortable in front of the other board members' curious looks, I started doing the calculations in the meeting using my notebook. About US$293 million separated the two techniques, or, to put it another way, a ridiculous 5% discount rate was required to make them equal. I requested additional time to complete the analysis. "Maybe I have lost any part on the way," I thought. The anecdote about the pizza story we mentioned in Chapter 6 came immediately to my mind. After glancing around, I recalled that, as is customary in practice, we considered that all of the forecasted free cash flow would be distributed as dividends to shareholders, when we performed the valuation of Telecom. If eventually, the free cash flow is ultimately not fully distributed as dividends, the difference is referred as "excess marketable securities" which have no impact on the firm's value, since marketable securities have zero net present value, as the theory of finance learnedly postulates.

After revising the analysis, we noted that to calculate the preferred shareholders' dividends we took into account Telecom's historical payout of 75%; however, for the case of Telecom fair value, we assumed that 100% of free cash flow would be distributed as dividends. If the "excess marketable securities" belonged to the Telecom shareholders, the corresponding share also would belong to the preferred and common shareholders. Therefore, we made a second analysis adding to the Sofora DCF the present value of marketable securities. After adding both excess forecasted marketable securities and the securities Telecom held at the time of valuation, both approaches matched, and the double-check satisfied us all.[8]

TABLE 17.12 Sofora common stock fair value including marketable securities and control premium in millions of US dollars

Sofora fair value	
Sofora DCF	841
Marketable securities	217
Marketable securities at December 2007	83.47
Control premium	492.9
Sofora common stock fair value	1,635.26

The lack of equivalency would cast doubt on the research even though our initial estimate was accurate. And when considering MM Propositions, the answer was found. Many skeptics believe that it belongs to the realm of "blackboard economics", where there is little correspondence between the theory and the real world. However, MM theorem has practical applications as well. This is not surprising, since there is nothing more practical than a good theory. [9]

Concluding thoughts

Two things happened in September 2008 that made an update to our valuation necessary. One was Argentina's nationalization of pension funds, and the other was the American subprime mortgage crisis, which ultimately turned into a global financial disaster.

The dispute was resolved in large part thanks to our valuation. W de Argentina and Telecom Italia reached an agreement following difficult talks. W de Argentina would remain a partner, holding over 30% of the company's shares. Given that W de Argentina spent US$105 million to be involved in the firm and that Telecom's market value at the time was approximately US$4 billion, it was a great deal from their point of view.

In 2011, at the request of an investor, we once more valued the Sofora Group. Sofora's partners have changed over time.

Notes

1 Nucleo is a subsidiary of Telecom Personal.
2 Inventories are cables and equipment and only represent a low percentage of total assets.
3 Under revaluation accounting, the fixed asset's value is adjusted to its fair market value as of the revaluation date.
4 Regular maintenance costs to keep fixed assets in operational condition were also low this year, in addition to capital expenses.
5 In Argentina, companies with negative earnings before taxes can carry forward their losses to offset the positive taxable income for five years, lowering their tax obligations during those years.
6 The average EV/EBITDA multiples were obtained weighting the enterprise value of each company over the total enterprise value of the sample.
7 The acronym CER appears to be a complete joke at the time. Its meaning is "Reference Stabilization Coefficient", but rather than stabilizing, it complicates contract fulfillment.
8 A minimum difference persists due to the different dates for the dividend distribution.
9 Do you believe that all practitioners are aware that all of the CAPM and MM assumptions with taxes are required by the popular Hamada formulas?

References

Banco Central de la República Argentina (2008). Available at Currency rates: www.bcra.gob.ar/PublicacionesEstadisticas/Currency_rates.asp

Dumrauf, G. L. (March 2014). Currency Choices in Valuation: an Approach for Emerging Markets. *JCC, The Business and Economics Research Journal*, *7*(*1*), 11–22.

Hamada, R. (1972). The Effect of the Firm's Capital Structure on the Systematic Risk of Common Stocks. *The Journal of Finance*, *27*(*2*), 435–452.

Ministerio de Economía de la Nación Argentina (2008). Available at www.mecon.gov.ar/peconomica/basehome/infoeco.html

The National Institute of Statistics and Censuses (INDEC) (2008). Available at www.indec.gob.ar/indec/web/Nivel4-Tema-3-5-31

Rosario Future Exchange (ROFEX)

Research reports of Merrill Lynch, Deutsche Bank, JP Morgan, Raymond James, SBS Group, Allaria Ledesma, and Goldman Sachs.

Appendix A How to design fair value chart with stacked columns

The exact arrangement of the values required to create the company value stacked column chart is depicted in Figure 17.6. In Excel, select the range B2:F5. After selecting "Insert" and selecting "Recommended charts" and "Stacked column", click "OK", and Graph 1 will show up. The fair value of operations is listed in the first column, followed by the value of operations and marketable securities in the second, the equity fair value and debt value in the third, the equity fair value in the fourth, and the market capitalization in the final column. The idea is to stack the values in the chart according to how we would like them to appear after leaving some parts of the columns unfilled.

After obtaining Graph 1, click left in any column, then right-click, choose "format data series", choose 0% for Gap Width, and Graph 2 will show up. The filling in of columns 2 and 3's lower part must be removed as the last step. To accomplish this, right-click on column 2's lower part, then select "fill" and "no fill". Repeat for column 3. Finally, you can complete Graph 3 by adding the appropriate numbers and values.

Fair value of operations	5,020	5,020			
Marketable securities		299	4,309	4,309	
Debt			1,009		
Market cap					3,560

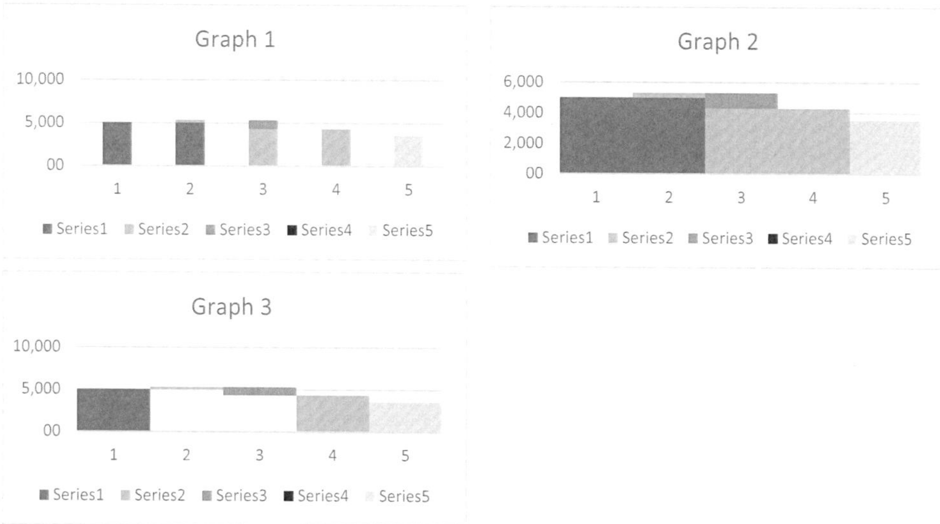

FIGURE 17.6 Fair value chart with stacked columns design

CHAPTER

18

Automotive Financial

Introduction

In October 2006, we performed the valuation of "Automotive Financial" (AUF), the financial branch company of "Latin American Automotive" (LAA), a subsidiary company of a well-known European multinational automotive manufacturer that operates in some South American emerging countries. Through its dealer network and consumer loans, the company was financing the purchase of automobiles sold

DOI: 10.4324/9781003628491-22

by LAA. Argentina went through a severe economic crisis in January 2002, which resulted in a sharp devaluation of the local currency and a decrease in the GDP of 10.6%. The worst was that banks were forced to convert dollar deposits into Argentine pesos at an exchange rate of 1.4 to one, while all dollar loans would be switched to pesos at a one-to-one rate.[1]

Dollar deposits would be converted to pesos at a rate of 1.4 to one, while all dollar loans, no matter how large, would be switched to pesos at a one-to-one rate. Fares and contracts were converted to pesos at different exchange rates, and the government adopted a free-floating regime in February 2002.

With the banking system paralyzed, social distress, the asymmetric "pesification", and a strong recession, the parent company decided to shut down the AUF operations. From that moment, AUF was only a banking structure without operations at the time, dedicated to recovering its loans and paying the bank deposits.

However, the economy started a rapid recovery in the midyear of 2003, and the GDP grew at 8 to 9% from 2003 to 2005, and the trend was accompanied by the automobile industry. People became more confident and sought out other credit alternatives when purchasing a car, and LAA's competitors like Fiat, GM or Ford released new lines of credit for buying cars. The shift in expectations influenced the parent company, which in early 2006 decided to assume full control of the AUF operations. Retail and wholesale activities were re-established on a small scale. The new business would not accept deposits, and the funding would be provided by local banks in the form of a loan paid at maturity.[2] Senior management of LAA, which had developed AUF from scratch, gave it advice and obtained authorizations to operate, proposed that the parent company must provide compensation, and claimed for an independent valuation. Even though there would not be a real transaction – the funds would leave the pocket of one parent company and enter another – the senior management of Latin America Automotive needed to finance other projects.[3]

Methodology used for the analysis

A financial entity is very different to a non-financial company, since the business is entirely leveraged, thus, to estimate the fair value of the target we use the "equity residual method" that consists in calculating the present value of available cash flows to equity holders and then discounting it at the cost of equity capital.

$$E = \frac{ECF_1}{(1+ke)} + \frac{ECF_2}{(1+ke)^2} + \frac{ECF_3}{(1+ke)^3} + \ldots + \frac{ECF_T}{(1+ke)^T} + \frac{ECF_T(1+g)}{(ke-g)} \times \frac{1}{(1+ke)^T}$$

ECF = Cash flow to equity holders
ke: cost of equity capital
g: long-term growth rate

We use an equity approach for a conceptual reason: *liabilities management is part of business operations and is not purely financing.* Thus, the deposit franchise given by the government to the financial entity, potentially allows it to *create value from the liabilities side of its balance sheet.* Therefore, the equity approach makes more sense for banks than the WACC approach used for non-financial companies. In addition, because AUF is a privately-held company and no betas are published, we had to adapt the CAPM model and adding a country risk premium to estimate a risk-adjusted cost of capital. To overcome the lack of beta, we use the bottom-up beta technique we described in previous chapters, identifying the publicly traded competitors most similar to the target. Once the DCF value was obtained, we made a multiple analysis to establish a comparison with a peer group composed by some banks which operate in Argentina. Due to the discontinuation of its operations, AUF had many non-operating assets such land, a building, bonds and foreign currency.[4] Non-operating assets do not generate operative income or business cash flow, any rent from them were excluded from the projections and their values are added to the DCF value.

Historical financial statements

The financial statements of financial and nonfinancial entities differ in certain ways due to the nature of the business. Banks operate on storing customer deposits and lending them out, earning the difference between the interest they earn on lending and the cost of storing customer deposits. Another distinction is that, whereas non-financial companies usually have accounts receivables, accounts payable, net fixed assets, research and development, a bank would not have these items but instead have deposits, loans, and property. Furthermore, banks are meant to keep reserve requirements, which represent a percentage of their deposits that are unencumbered overnight. However, the bank is the owner of these reserves.

A bank's income statement has two main components: interest income and interest expense. The former represents the money earned the financing. The latter is the expense related to storing customer deposits, which would be deducted from interest related revenue. The difference represents the "intermediation margin". Non-interest income includes credit card fees, underwriting fees, fees from overdrawn accounts, transaction fees, and any other non-interest income that a bank earns. Another important item on a bank's income statement is the provisions relate to loans that have defaulted, typically referred to as "loan loss provision." Table 18.1 shows the historical income statements for the 2003–2006 period, where we can observe a strong decline in nearly every item, reflecting the lack of activity as AUF was currently solely dedicated on recovering loans and paying customer deposit. Financial statements corresponding to 2006 reflects the last information presented by AUF to Banco Central de la Republica Argentina (BCRA).

With respect to the balance sheet, loans are considered assets because since lending is a bank's primary source of revenues. Customer deposits are considered liabilities, since they are not owned by the bank and must to be disbursed to clients upon request. The bank pays a small interest rate to the customer deposits, lending a portion of those deposits to other customers charging a higher interest rate. The interest rate spread represents the bank´s revenue.

Bank's usually purchase marketable securities in their trading business. These securities are assets and are acquired or sold depending on the available entity's cash flow and expectations for appreciation or depreciation. When the loans demand is strong, banks usually sell their securities to get cash and lend money, and the opposite occurs when loan demand is low. Loans and customer deposits usually are the most important assets and liabilities.

TABLE 18.1 Historical income statements in thousands of Argentine pesos

	Dec 03	Dec 04	Dec 05	Aug 06
Interest revenue	8,091	9,732	10,394	2,495
Interest expense	20,295	15,848	737	104
Financial margin	–12,204	–6,116	9,657	2,391
Income from services	4,961	1,954	359	131
Dealer commission	622	457	196	43
Administrative expenses	8,861	9,771	8,793	6,277
Provision for credit losses	2,181	1,599	–505	–392
Others	1,143	-	-	-
Financial income	6,552	8,328	7,081	6,976
Financial expenses	6,095	12,507	1,810	1,021
Income taxes	-	-	-	-
Net income	–19,593	–20,168	5,793	1,765

TABLE 18.2 Historical balance sheet in thousands of Argentine pesos

	Dec 03	Dec 04	Dec 05	Aug 06
Cash and equivalents	120,299	1,802	12,214	11,416
Loans – financial sector	12,002	-	16,630	16,259
Loans – private sector	13,886	7,918	557	1,435
Other credits	20,461	19,155	3,354	4,886
Inventories	-	-	2,960	5,240
Net fixed assets	297	201	114	97
Intangibles	2,904	2,221	1,816	1,388
Other assets	10,384	11,209	6,472	3,839
Total assets	180,233	42,506	44,117	44,560
Customer deposits	2,830	1,505	782	396
Financial debt	7,000	2,100	1,095	483
Fiscal liabilities	-	248	353	-
Other liabilities	6,040	14,356	13,568	13,597
Total liabilities	27,540	19,980	15,798	14,476
Equity	152,693	22,526	28,319	30,084
Total liabilities + Equity	180,233	42,506	44,117	44,560

TABLE 18.3 Shareholder's equity statement in thousands of Argentine pesos

	Dec 04	Dec 05	Aug 06
Shareholder's equity at the beginning	152,693	22,526	28,319
Net Income	–20,168	5,793	1,765
Dividends	-	-	-
Reimbursement to shareholders	–109,999	-	-
Shareholder's equity at the end	22,526	28,319	30,084

TABLE 18.4 Historical cash flow in thousands of Argentine pesos

	Dec 04	Dec 05	Aug 06
Operative income	–15,989	522	–4,190
Depreciation & amortization	1,849	1,511	-
Loans – financial sector	–12,002	16,630	–371
Loans – private sector	–5,968	–7,361	878
Deposits	–1,325	–723	–386
Financial debt	–4,900	–1,005	–612
Other financial debt	–9,899	–1,771	-
Social and fiscal liabilities	248	105	–353
Inventories	-	2,960	2,280
Capital expenditures	-	-	–17
Intangibles	268	312	–428
Others assets	1,627	–4,030	–2,633
Other credits for financial intermediation	–1,306	–15,801	1,532
Others liabilities	8,316	–788	29
Other financial income	8,328	7,081	6,976
Other interest expenses	12,507	1,810	1,021
Reimbursement to shareholders	–109,999	-	-
Cash increase/decrease	–118,497	10,412	–798

Remember that loans are an asset of the financial entity and its increase/decrease follows the same rule we describe in Chapter 2 and represent an outflow/inflow. Deposits, on the other hand, are liabilities and their increase/decrease represents an inflow/outflow. Reimbursement refers to the procedure by which a company reimburses its shareholders for certain expenses incurred on behalf of the company.

Automotive industry historical performance

The automotive industry and GDP growth rates are highly correlated. The regression analysis in Figure 18.1 shows that over the 24-year period from 1982 through 2006, the industry sales growth rate was very correlated with the GDP growth rate.

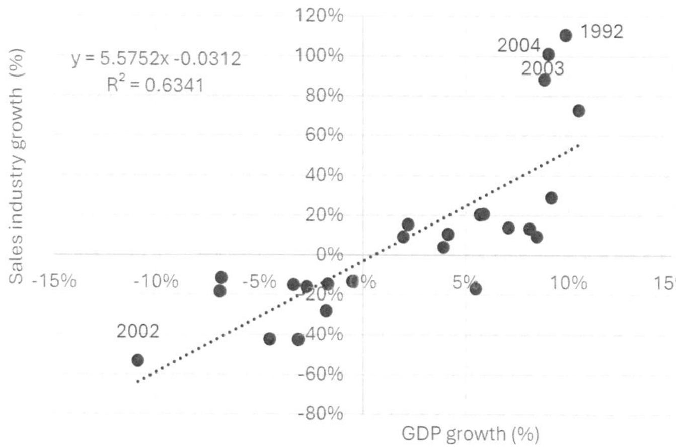

FIGURE 18.1 Emerging country's GDP growth rate and industry sales growth rate: Regression analysis
Source: INDEC, Ministry of Economics of Argentine Republic, and ADEFA

A strong decline in industry sales was observed in 2002, followed by a strong rebound in 2003 and 2004 and then a convergence to a lower growth rate that was more in line with the GDP long-term growth rate (around 3%). The sharp falls in GDP in 1989 (–6.9%), 1990 (–1.8%), 1999 (–3.4%), 2000 (0.5%), 2001 (–4.5%, and 2002 (–10.9%) were followed by strong rebounds in 1991 (10.5%), 1992 (9.9%), 2003 (8.8%%), and 2004 (9%). These recoveries in turn led to a strong increase in automobile sales in 1991 (73%), 1992 (111%), 2003 (88%), and 2004 (101%). We are well aware of this rebound effect in Argentina. When a recession hits, car sales drop sharply; if the recession lasts, cars get old and depreciate. When the economy reborn, the beneficial effect of growth is reinforced by people's desire to renew their cars. To control these outliers, we include an intercept dummy variable that shift the constant term and modify the coefficient slope from 5.57 to 3.76 and the R^2 increases from 0.63 to 0.80.

Figure 18.2 shows the cumulative moving average geometric growth rate (CMAGR) of the Argentinian GDP and car sales industry, along with their strong falls and recoveries. The cumulative moving average returns the moving average of all data up to the current data point. For example, to calculate the CMAGR from 1971 to 1975, we must compose the growth rate for the period 1971–1975 and then calculate the annual geometric growth rate as:

$$CAGR_{1971-1975} = \left[(1+g_{1971})(1+g_{1972})(1+g_{1973})(1+g_{1974})(1+g_{1975})\right]^{1/5} - 1 \qquad [18.1]$$

Loans from major automaker's financial institutions experimented a strong increase as a result of the economy's recovery.

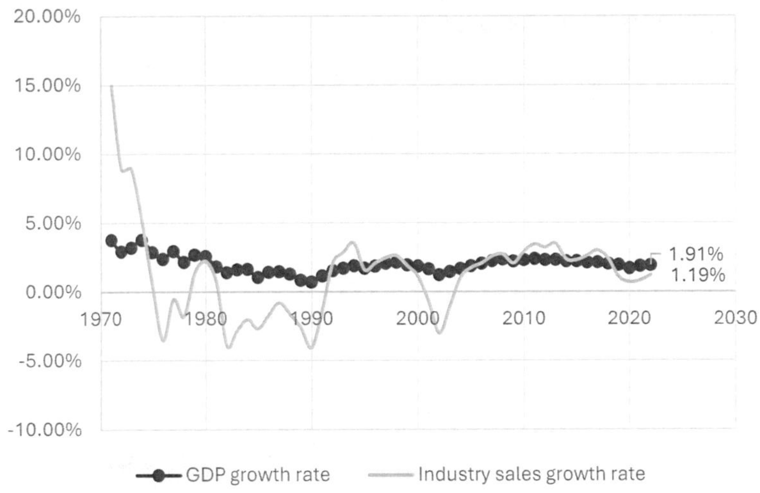

FIGURE 18.2 CMAGR of the GDP and car sales industry

TABLE 18.5 Loans in the financial sector in thousands of Argentine pesos

	Dec 04	Dec 05	Aug 06
Fiat	11,339	21,934	42,265
Ford	62,711	92,157	187,435
Rombo	52,960	103,689	213,546
Toyota	0	0	54,279
Chrysler	1,506	3,342	218,137

Source: BCRA

Assumptions

We used a "top-down approach" to develop the forecast's assumptions, starting with macroeconomic assumptions and moving on to industry and company assumptions. All of them were designed and subsequently discussed with the senior management.

Macroeconomic assumptions

GDP growth rate

We forecasted the GDP values for 2007 and 2008 using an autoregressive model.[5] The forecasted growth rate was 7.03% and 5.3%, respectively. For 2009 and beyond, we expect a growth rate of 3.5%.[6] Figure 18.3 depicts the observed and the forecasted GDP values expressed in 1993 prices.

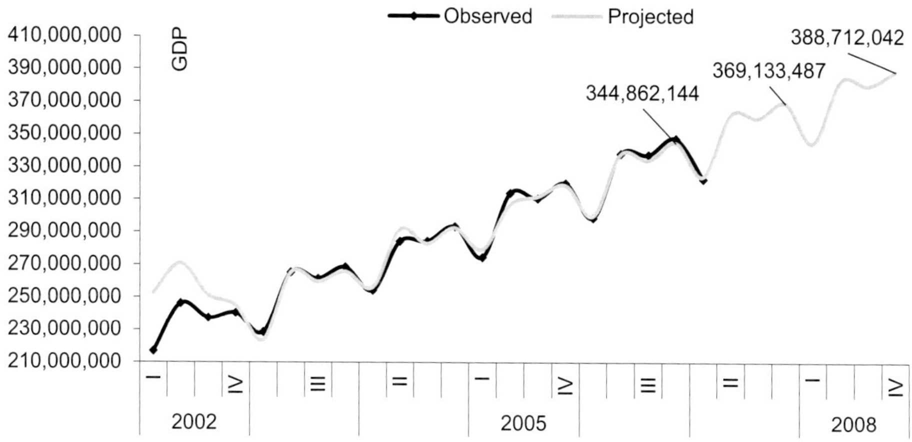

FIGURE 18.3 Observed and projected GDP

Source: INDEC and Ministerio de Economia de la Nacion Argentina

TABLE 18.6 Macroeconomic assumptions

	Dec 07	Dec 08	Dec 09	Dec 10	Dec 11	Dec 12	Dec 13	Dec 14	Dec 15	Dec 16
PBI growth rate	7.03%	5.3%	3.5%	3.5%	3.5%	3.5%	3.5%	3.5%	3.5%	3.5%
Exchange rate	3.25	3.4	3.5	3.6	3.7	3.7	3.8	3.9	4.1	4.2
Inflation rate (Arg)	10%	9%	8%	7%	6%	5%	5%	4%	4%	4%
Inflation rate (USA)	3%	2.5%	2.0%	2.0%	2.0%	2.0%	2.0%	2.0%	2.0%	2.0%
Arg. Infl. rate 2001–2006	110%	120%	130%	139%	147%	155%	162%	169%	176%	183%
US infl. rate 2001 2006	18%	18%	18%	19%	19%	20%	20%	20%	21%	21%
Real exchange rate	1.82	1.82	1.80	1.79	1.78	1.74	1.74	1.74	1.80	1.80

Source: BCRA, Ministerio de Economia de la Nacion Argentina, INDEC, and Rosario Future Exchange (ROFEX)

Exchange rate

After the abandonment of the peg 1 ARS = 1 USD and the adoption of a free-floating system in February 2002, the peso depreciated to nearly 4 pesos per dollar. The devaluation in 2002 left the peso depreciated, leaving room for gradual appreciation since the domestic inflation rate from December 2001 to December 2006 was 91.26%, while the American inflation rate was 14.20% in the same period. In fact, after the overshooting, Argentina received capital inflows and the BCRA had to buy dollars every day to prevent its fall. Therefore, taking into account that the current real exchange rate expressed an important depreciation of the domestic currency, we expect a slightly increase for the nominal exchange rate, above the domestic inflation rate, reaching ARS4.2 = US$1 at the end of the projection.

It is important to clarify that our forecasts about inflation rate, international inflation rate and nominal currency exchange rate, lead to a real exchange rate (RER) about ARS1.80 per dollar at the end of the projection. This should be considered as conservative since the consensus of the economist at the time was around 1.4/1.5 using December 2001 = 1 as the year base for the comparison. Therefore, the expected RER is around 30% higher than the consensus, and 80% higher than the RER of December 2001, when peso devaluated.

The real (bilateral) exchange rate was calculated in a similar way we explained in Chapter 13. The exchange rate is multiplied by the ratio of the accumulated international inflation divided by the accumulated domestic inflation rate from December 2001 to the t-year forecast.

$$RER = \frac{ER}{(1+\pi_t^D)}(1+\pi_t^\star)$$

$\pi_t^\star$ = accumulated international inflation rate

π_t^D = accumulated domestic inflation rate

For instance, the real exchange rate of 1997 is [3.25★(1 + 14%)/(1 + 110%)] = 1.82. If we had received a rate lower than 1.5, then we could conclude the peso is appreciated. However, it is not the case.

This is a crucial point in emerging markets, where the domestic currency observed periods of overvaluation and undervaluation. Furthermore, a valuation based on an appreciated domestic currency may be overpriced because of the potential for a significant future depreciation, which would result in a lower free cash flow in dollars as we discussed in Chapter 13.

Domestic inflation rate

The expected inflation rate was estimated about 10% for 2007, taking into account the tendency observed in the consumer price index published by The National Institute of Statistics and Censuses (2006), as long as some price distortions are corrected,[7] declining slowly until converging to a lower level of 3% for 2012 and beyond. The inflation rate for each year was forecasted taking into account the term structure of bond´s yields expressed in domestic currency. Nominal interest rate reflects lenders' expectations of future inflation and provides a market-based estimation of expected inflation over time. These estimations were based assuming an expected real interest return of 2% per year, therefore the expected inflation rate is calculated as the difference of each yield and a real interest rate of 2%.

The international inflation rate for 2007 was estimated to be 3% and declined along the projection until reaching 2%.

TABLE 18.7 Expected inflation rate

Security	Yield	Duration	Expected inflation rate
T-Bills	11.3%	0.9	9.3%
T-Bills	11.5%	1.2	9.5%
Bonds	14.0%	1.5	12.0%
Bonds	2.1%	1.6	10.1%
Bonds	2.9%	2.0	10.9%
T-Bills	12.3%	2.0	10.3%
T-Bills	12.2%	2.0	10.2%

Source: BCRA

Industry and company assumptions

The assumptions for the explicit forecasted period are detailed in Table 18.8.

1. Industry sales. They include both retail and wholesale sales and were projected to grow at a rate of 4.5%/5% from 2007 to 2011 and at a similar rate of GDP growth rate from 2012 and beyond.
2. AUF loans contracts. They were projected taking into account the historical LAA market share and industry sales expressed in units. It was 19.1% in 2007, over the historical 16% because LAA would launch a couple of car models that were too successful; however, senior management tells us that they observed that the market share gradually returns to the historical share. Therefore, it was forecasted that it would decline to 18% in 2008 and stay at 16% in 2009 and beyond.
3. Retail sales/total sales ratio. We expect a 5% for 2007, 10% in 2008 and reaching the historical ratio of 15% for 2009 and beyond.
4. Revenues. Financial companies' revenues could be split between loan interest and service revenue:

   - Interest from new loans (pledges) and forecasted loan contracts. The projection of new loans is based on the expected industry growth rate and the market share of LAA. Retail contracts were projected using a capital contract of ARS20,000 per loan and a retail sales/total sales ratio for each forecasted. The loan interest rate is assumed to be 14.5%, following a loan amortization schedule through 36 monthly fixed installments.[8] Because additional loans would be granted, capital and interest payments were calculated with an amortization schedule[9] for each year of the forecasted period, which would then be linked to a consolidated amortization schedule for a forecast period of ten years.
   - Income from services. AUF receives a commission of 30% from the insurance company for two concepts: car insurance and life insurance, both calculated over a capital contract. Car insurance is collected as a fixed payment of ARS180 in each installment and a 0.30% on loan balance.

TABLE 18.8 Company and industry assumptions

I	Dec 07	Dec 08	Dec 09	Dec 10	Dec 11	Dec 12	Dec 13	Dec 14	Dec 15	Dec-16
Industry sales growth rate	7.07%	5.30%	3%	3%	3%	3%	3%	3%	3%	3%
Industry car sales (units)	490,500	516,497	531,991	547,951	564,390	581,321	598,761	616,724	635,226	654,282
VW market share	19.1%	18.5%	16%	16%	16%	16%	16%	16%	16%	16%
VW total sales (units)	93,686	95,552	85,119	87,672	90,302	93,011	95,802	98,676	101,636	104,685
Retail/total sales	5%	10%	15%	15%	15%	15%	15%	15%	15%	15%
Retail contracts	4,684	9,555	12,768	13,151	13,545	13,952	14,370	14,801	15,245	15,703
Capital contract per unit (thousands of ARS)	20,000	20,200	20,000	20	20	20	20	20	20	20
Loans contracts (thousands of ARS)	93,686	191,104	255,356	263,017	270,907	279,034	287,405	296,027	304,908	314,056
Maturity (months)	36	36	36	36	36	36	36	36	36	36
Lending interest rate	14.5%	14.5%	14.5%	14.5%	14.5%	14.5%	14.5%	14.5%	14.5%	14.5%
Borrowing interest rate	12%	12%	12%	12%	12%	12%	12%	12%	12%	12%
Capital per unit (thousands of ARS)	30	30	30	30	30	30	30	30	30	30
Life insurance	0.30%	0.30%	0.30%	0.30%	0.30%	0.30%	0.30%	0.30%	0.30%	0.30%
Service margin intermediation	30%	30%	30%	30%	30%	30%	30%	30%	30%	30%
Dealer commission	2%	2%	2%	2%	2%	2%	2%	2%	2%	2%
Administrative expenses (thousands of ARS)	8,500	8,951	9,219	9,496	9,780	10,074	10,376	10,687	11,008	11,338
Credit loss	2%	2%	2%	2%	2%	2%	2%	2%	2%	2%
Turnover tax rate	4.5%	4.5%	4.5%	4.5%	4.5%	4.5%	4.5%	4.5%	4.5%	4.5%
Income tax rate	35%	35%	35%	35%	35%	35%	35%	35%	35%	35%

5. Financing/borrowing. Financing is assumed to have been provided by local banks, according to the Company's operating needs. New financial debts are created automatically in our model to balance the sources and uses of cash, especially in the two first years, when the business launches and the revenues from interest loans and income services still not cover the operative expenses. As the interest rate on new loans is forecasted as a 14.5% and the borrowing interest rate is forecasted to be 12%, we predict a spread of 2.5 percentage points.[10] Additional borrowing was projected taking into account the new loans granted by AUF.
6. Dealer commission. According to the current practice in the market, we forecast a dealer commission of 2% of each loan contract.
7. Administrative expenses. It has been considered ARS8.5 million for 2007 (an amount similar to 2006) and is expected to grow at a rate comparable to that of the sales industry.
8. Credit loss. New loans have been projected assuming a non-collectability rate of 2% (net of recoveries) of the loan portfolio.
9. Fixed Assets and depreciation expenses. The target owns some fixed assets like facilities, computers, furniture and some other fixed assets taken as a guarantee of loans. We assume it takes a stable amount of fixed assets to generate each dollar of "sales" (loans) so capital expenditures have been projected through the forecast period in order to maintain the ratio of revenue to property and equipment.
10. Income tax rate. Our projections assume a company earning money that pays a full income legal tax rate of 35%, except in the two first years, when the business is launching. At the time, the business had a tax loss carry-forward that was considered as a non-operating asset, and added to the DCF value, as we explain later.
11. Marketable securities, dividends and BCRA regulations. The discounted cash flow to equity is the available cash flow that can be paid as dividends to equity holders. But they are not the actual dividends that were forecasted to be paid. As a consequence of BCRA regulations,[11] the company has to keep some ratios of equity to total assets. For this reason, only a part of net income after taxes can be paid as dividends to equity holders. But this doesn't mean that this cash flow is not property of the equity holders and a regulation should not affect the business value. We handled the problem considering the difference as an "excess marketable security" which in fact, are potential dividends that will be distributed in the future. In the meanwhile, they assume the form of marketable securities, which have zero net present value. Remember that the fact that a marketable security has zero NPV means that the investors get their cost of capital (the yield to maturity), and therefore, it conserves its value. Therefore, for our purposes, marketable securities are a part of cash flow to equity, and also disbursed to shareholders in the year it is acquired.
12. Fiscal liabilities. It was projected taking into account the forecasted income taxes.
13. Old loans, inventories, old customer deposits, intangibles, other assets, financial debt, other liabilities, and other credits for financial intermediation, were not forecasted as were considered as non-operating assets and liabilities. Their

historical values were maintained so that they don't affect the forecasted free cash flow. The net value of the non-operating assets and liabilities was added to the DCF value as we explain later.

Forecasted financial statements and cash flow

Table 18.9 shows the forecasted balance sheet where can be appreciated that the new loans and additional borrowing are the primary items. The former represents the loans granted to the private

TABLE 18.9 Projected balance sheet in thousands of Argentine pesos

	Dec 07	Dec 08	Dec 09	Dec 10	Dec 11	Dec 12	Dec 13	Dec 14	Dec 15	Dec-16
Cash and equivalents	12,820	14,430	17,430	19,593	29,416	42,082	55,249	68,903	82,966	97,331
Loans – financial sector	16,259	16,259	16,259	16,259	16,259	16,259	16,259	16,259	16,259	16,259
Loans – private sector	1,435	1,435	1,435	1,435	1,435	1,435	1,435	1,435	1,435	1,435
New loans	93,479	229,099	351,006	409,063	435,037	448,088	461,531	475,377	489,638	504,327
Other credits	4,886	4,886	4,886	4,886	4,886	4,886	4,886	4,886	4,886	4,886
Inventories	5,240	5,240	5,240	5,240	5,240	5,240	5,240	5,240	5,240	5,240
Net fixed assets	147	157	167	227	207	187	257	237	217	317
Intangibles	1,388	1,388	1,388	1,388	1,388	1,388	1,388	1,388	1,388	1,388
Others assets	3,839	3,839	3,839	3,839	3,839	3,839	3,839	3,839	3,839	3,839
Total assets	139,493	276,733	401,650	461,929	497,707	523,404	550,084	577,564	605,868	635,022
Customer deposits	396	396	396	396	396	396	396	396	396	396
Additional borrowing	104,697	247,198	366,801	413,153	435,037	448,088	461,531	475,377	489,638	504,327
Financial debt	483	483	483	483	483	483	483	483	483	483
Fiscal liabilities	279	556	2,054	5,594	6,821	6,813	7,018	7,228	7,445	7,668
Other liabilities	13,597	13,597	13,597	13,597	13,597	13,597	13,597	13,597	13,597	13,597
Total liabilities	119,452	262,230	383,332	433,223	456,334	469,377	483,024	497,081	511,559	526,472
Equity	20,042	14,503	18,318	28,706	41,373	54,027	67,059	80,483	94,309	108,550
Total liabilities + Equity	139,493	276,733	401,650	461,929	497,707	523,404	550,084	577,564	605,868	635,022

TABLE 18.10 Projected income statements in thousands of Argentine pesos

	Dec 07	Dec 08	Dec 09	Dec 10	Dec 11	Dec 12	Dec 13	Dec 14	Dec 15	Dec 16
Interest from new pledges	6,737	23,383	43,166	56,561	62,365	64,793	66,737	68,739	70,801	72,925
Interest expense	6,282	21,114	36,840	46,797	50,891	52,988	54,577	56,214	57,901	59,638
Financial margin	455	2,270	6,326	9,763	11,474	11,805	12,159	12,524	12,900	13,287
Car insurance	1,644	8,147	16,954	23,718	25,875	25,988	26,768	27,571	28,398	29,250
Life insurance	502	1,742	3,215	4,213	4,645	4,826	4,971	5,120	5,273	5,432
Dealer commission	1,874	3,822	5,107	5,260	5,418	5,581	5,748	5,921	6,098	6,281
Administrative expenses	8,500	8,951	9,219	9,496	9,780	10,074	10,376	10,687	11,008	11,338
Provision for Credit losses	1,874	3,822	5,107	5,260	5,418	5,581	5,748	5,921	6,098	6,281
Turnover taxes	117	547	1,192	1,696	1,890	1,918	1,975	2,035	2,096	2,159
Operative income	9,763	4,983	5,870	15,982	19,488	19,466	20,050	20,652	21,271	21,910
Earnings before taxes	9,763	4,983	5,870	15,982	19,488	19,466	20,050	20,652	21,271	21,910
Income taxes	279	556	2,054	5,594	6,821	6,813	7,018	7,228	7,445	7,668
Net Income	–10,043	–5,539	3,815	10,388	12,667	12,653	13,033	13,424	13,826	14,241

It should be noted that the operative income is primarily contingent upon the financial margin and car insurance, as this is a defining characteristic of the banking industry.

TABLE 18.11 Projected cash flow in thousands of Argentine pesos

	Dec 07	Dec 08	Dec 09	Dec 10	Dec 11	Dec 12	Dec 13	Dec 14	Dec 15	Dec 16
Operative income	–9,763	–4,983	5,870	15,982	19,488	19,466	20,050	20,652	21,271	21,910
Depreciation & amortization	80	90	90	100	120	120	120	120	120	120
New loans – private sector	93,479	135,620	121,907	58,057	25,975	13,051	13,443	13,846	14,261	14,689
Additional borrowing	104,697	142,501	119,603	46,352	21,884	13,051	13,443	13,846	14,261	14,689
Social and fiscal liabilities	279	277	1,498	3,539	1,227	–8	204	211	217	223
Income taxes	279	556	2,054	5,594	6,821	6,813	7,018	7,228	7,445	7,668
Cash flow from operations	1,534	1,709	3,100	2,323	9,924	12,766	13,357	13,754	14,163	14,585
Capital expenses	130	100	100	160	100	100	190	100	100	220
Equity cash flow	1,404	1,609	3,000	2,163	9,824	12,666	13,167	13,654	14,063	14,365

The primary components of the equity cash flow are the operative income and new loans that would be financed by additional borrowing.

Cost of capital estimation

In order to estimate the cost of capital we apply the Capital Asset Pricing Model (CAPM). Because AUF is a company which get most of their revenues in Emerging Country, a country risk premium must be considered.

The inputs used in the CAPM formula and adjustments for country risks are described below.

Risk free rate

We used a ten-year Treasury-bond rate of 4.80% observed in November 2006, as a risk-free rate return (Source: Federal Reserve of the United States).

Market risk premium

It was estimated using along-time frame to eliminate the effects of short-term anomalies in the measurement, considering the market return series measured by Ibbotson & Associates from 1925 to 2005. The market risk premium was found yielding 6,50% (geometric mean)

Beta

Because AUF is a non-public company, no betas are published. We use the bottom-up approach, that consists in identifying the publicly traded competitors most similar to the company. Because the perfect comparable never exists, we use the domestic industry average beta, using all financial entities publicly in Argentina. Because measurement errors tend to cancel out, industry averages are more stable than company betas. Notice that we do not carry out the process of unlevering and then re-levering the industry beta, since on the financial company business, the liabilities is part of business operations.

TABLE 18.12 Betas banking industry November 2006: 60-month observations

Bank	Beta
Hipotecario	0.31
Macro	0.78
Rio	0.21
Suquia	0.75
Frances	0.98
Galicia	1.05
Industry average	0.68

Country risk premium

In order to compute the country risk, we add a premium of 400 basis points to the cost of capital. According to JP Morgan, the country risk of Argentina was around 380/390bps in October 2007. The parent company had a corporate rule for the country risk premium in Latin America: 400bps for businesses in Argentina and Brazil and 0bps for the case of Mexico. The parent company's WACC was around 9%; therefore, for investments in Argentina, the cost of capital was 13% (9% + 4%).

Cost of capital for Automotive Financial

According to our estimation, the cost of capital was 13.22%.

$$ke = rf + \left[E(rm) - rf\right]\beta + CRP$$

$$ke = 4.8\% + [6.5\%]0.68 + 4\% = 13.22\%$$

Automotive Financial fair value

Even though the financial statements and equity cash flow were first projected in Argentine pesos, we convert them into dollars as discussed earlier. Table 18.13 shows the explicit forecasted the equity cash flow in Argentine pesos and American dollars, as well as the terminal value, and the equity fair value calculated at December 31, 2006, with the cost of capital of 13.22%. Cash flows were originally forecasted in nominal Argentine pesos to reflect the impact of the expected inflation rate and then converted in dollars, dividing the expected cash flows by the expected currency rate for each year of the projection. This procedure guarantees the consistency of the discounted cash flow model, because the cost of capital is a nominal rate expressed in dollars.

TABLE 18.13 Equity fair value in thousands of US dollars

	Dec 07	Dec 08	Dec 09	Dec 10	Dec 11	Dec 12	Dec 13	Dec 14	Dec 15	Dec 16
Equity cash flow (ARS)	1,404	1,609	3,000	2,163	9,824	12,666	13,167	13,654	14,063	14,365
Exchange rate	3.25	3.40	3.50	3.60	3.70	3.70	3.80	3.90	4.10	4.20
Equity cash flow (US)	432	473	857	601	2,655	3,423	3,465	3,501	3,430	3,420
Terminal value (US)										36,418
ECF (US) + Terminal value (US)	432	473	857	601	2,655	3,423	3,465	3,501	3,430	39,838
Equity fair value (US)	$20,140.7									

Non-operating assets and non-operating liabilities

After AUF stop of receiving deposits and granting loans, it accumulated some non-operating assets as cash in excess, government bonds, lands, facilities, tax loss carry-forward, and other assets. Their value was provided by the senior management and we estimate a fair market value for the government bonds. Because non-operative assets don't generate EBIT or free cash flow, their value has been added to DCF value.

TABLE 18.14 Non-operating assets in millions of US dollars

Cash in excess	6.8
Government bonds	3.8
Lands	1.0
Facilities	1.8
Tax loss carry-forward	3.5
Recovery	1.1
Total non-operating assets	18.00

Cash in excess: despite the parent company decided to temporarily discontinue the operations, AUF is still collecting loan payments. As a result, the business had a cash in excess estimated as US 6.8 million in November 2006.

Government bonds: Argentina's currency board, which had pegged the peso to the US dollar at a 1:1 exchange rate since 1991, was abandoned in January 2002. The new exchange rate was set at a 1:1.4 exchange rate for dollar-denominated deposits and 1:1 for dollar-denominated loans. To compensate the asymmetric "pesification", the Argentine government issues bonds to financial institutions, whose capital would be adjusted by the inflation rate. Because these bonds are not yet negotiable, we estimate its fair value discounting its cash flow with an interest rate required for a bond with similar duration. We estimated a fair value of 65.5% of par value. A few months later, the bond was sold to a financial entity for the price we estimated, approximately 65% of par value.

Lands and facilities: their value was provided by broker´s estimations and included a building located in a residential area which was used by AUF as its headquarters. However, it was abandoned and the parent company has the intention to establish the business' operations in the headquarters of Latin American Automotive.

Recovery of loans: according to management estimation, the recovery would reach US 1.1 million.

Tax loss carry-forward: according to the LAA's tax office, at November 2006, AUF has a tax loss carry-forward of US 3.5 million.

Figure 18.4 shows the DCF value increased by the non-operative assets. Finally, the fair value of the business is the sum of the DCF value plus non-operative assets:

Equity fair value = DCF value + non-operative assets = 18.12M + 12.46 = 30.58 million

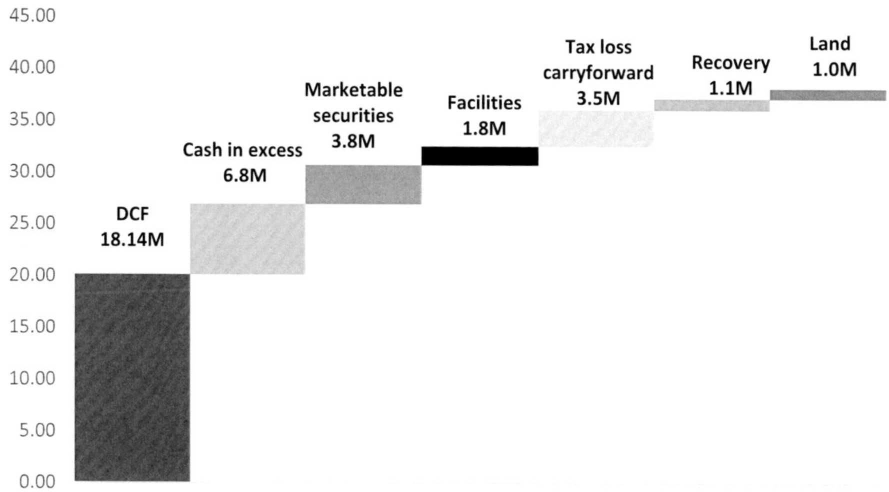

FIGURE 18.4 Telecom fair value flow in millions of US dollars

Relative valuation

Following a DCF analysis, we perform a relative valuation using the price/earnings and price/book value ratios, which are the multiples commonly employed in the banking industry. As we addressed in Chapter 16, multiples provide a fast reference point but have limitations, particularly they are influenced by the business cycle effect.

Price earning and price/book value in Latin America and USA

Based on a sample of 264 financial institutions, we calculate the mean of P/E and price/book value in Latin America and the USA. Table 18.15 and Figure 18.4 present the findings. The average P/E is around 14, while the average price/book value is 1.9. These figures resemble those for Argentina.

TABLE 18.15 P/E and P/BV for Latin America and USA, September 2006

	Sample size	P/E	P/BV
Argentina	5	15.4	1.7
Brazil	9	19.7	1.9
Chile	9	15.6	1.8
Mexico	8	9.2	1.4
Peru	10	14.9	2.7
US	189	17.9	2.8
Venezuela	12	5.8	1.2
Colombia	22	18.8	3.1
Mean		14.1	1.9

Source: Reuters

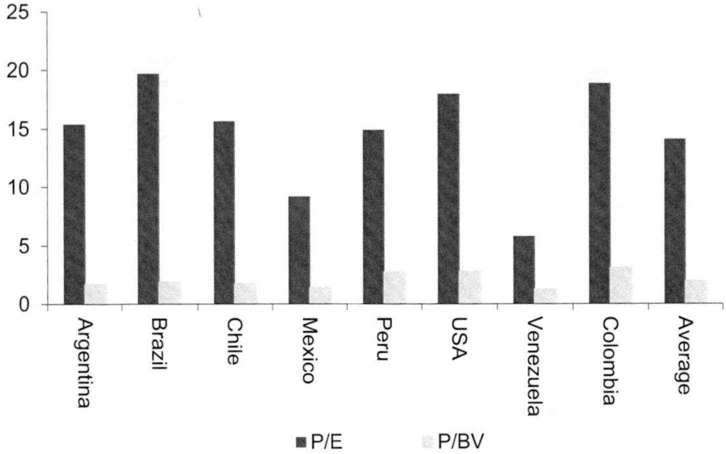

FIGURE 18.5 PE and P/BV in Latin America and USA, September 28, 2006
Source: Reuters

Multiples in Argentina's bank industry

Although we analyze the P/E ratio for Argentina's bank industry from 1997 to 2006, the sample was not considered due to the distortions caused by the effects of the monetary crisis in Argentina that included an asymmetric devaluation of loans and deposits, the abandonment of the peg 1 ARS = 1 dollar, and a default of the sovereign debt in December 2001. As a result, many financial entities exhibited negative P/E for some years. In 2004, the government compensated the banks for the impact of the asymmetric devaluation of deposits and loans through a series of "compensation bonds", and from 2005 the banking industry seemed to begin recovering, and P/E is improving. However, even calculating a ten-year average, multiples exhibited illogical values as Table 18.15 shows. The price/earnings ratio could not be applied to estimate the fair value of AUF.

P/E of Automotive Financial

Even though we decide not to use relative valuation to justify the fair value of AUF, if we estimate the fair value of a business considering only the DCF value plus marketable securities, they totalize US$21.9 million. Since the average P/E for Latin American banks is 14.1, a net income of annual US$1.55 million would support the value, and the truth is that the business would offer much more.

TABLE 18.16 P/E of Argentinean banks 1996–2006

Financial entity	Dec 96	Dec 97	Dec 98	Dec 99	Dec 00	Dec 01	Dec 02	Dec 03	Dec 04	Dec 05	Oct 06	Mean
French Bank	15.2	16.1	13.4	17.4	8	43.8	–1.2	–11.3	–39.1	29.3	25.5	10.6
South Bank	15.4	–79.6	–4.6	–2.5	0.6	0.2	0.6	9.3	11.6	12.4	14	–2.2

TABLE 18.16 (Continued)

Financial entity	Dec 96	Dec 97	Dec 98	Dec 99	Dec 00	Dec 01	Dec 02	Dec 03	Dec 04	Dec 05	Oct 06	Mean
Mortgage Bank	-	-	-	14	−2	5.7	0.1	4.7	5.6	6.9	6.8	5.2
River Bank		7.4	20.7	17.7	7	−59.4	0.6	−3.1	39.1	−2.9	3.8	3.0
Financial Group	-	-	-	-	12.5	4.2	0.5	−10.2	−28.5	24.4	27.1	4.1
Mean	15.3	−18.7	9.8	11.7	5.0	−1.2	0.4	−2.1	−2.3	14.0	15.4	-

Concluding thoughts

The purpose of the valuation was to establish a fair value of Automotive Financial to claim to the parent company funds to finance other projects of LAA. As the operations of AUF were discontinued in 2002, there was only some residual operations and non-operating assets. Therefore, our task was designed a forecast plan taking into account some historical ratios as well as the new business model defined by the parent company.

Since liabilities management is a component of business operations rather than only financing, we use a DCF model that uses the equity cash flow to estimate the AUF's fair value. The parent company provide another valuation after receiving our valuation report that included all the information we discussed in this chapter. After a negotiation, both sides agreed on an intermediate value.

Notes

1 The asymmetric "pesification" generated some unreliable situations. For example, before the peso devaluation, there were cases where people received a loan for one million dollars and immediately made a bank dollar-denominated deposit for the same capital. After the devaluation of the peso and the asymmetric pesification, they owed one million Argentine pesos, had a deposit of 1.4 million Argentine pesos, and at the same time had 1 million dollars in cash or 4 million Argentine pesos, because the exchange rate dropped from 1 peso to 1 US dollar to nearly four pesos per dollar by mid-2002.

2 According to the parent company's senior management "Argentina is like the tide: it raises and falls".

3 Among several new car models that LAA planned to launch on the market, there was a truck that was a complete success.

4 As the loans were collected, the company invested the money in bonds and foreign currency.

5 An autoregressive model uses the past values of the series to predict future values.

6 The observed GDP growth rate from 1900 to 2005 was about 3.3%.

7 In Argentina, as a part of a plan to control the inflation rate, utility rates were frozen in 2002.

8 Fixed installments are a way to repay a loan by making payments of the same amount each month until the loan is paid off.

9 An amortization schedule is a table that lists each monthly payment from the time you start repaying the loan until the loan is fully repaid.

10 Because LAA has an excellent credit rating, local banks provide financing as a "tailor made suit".

11 The regulations established by the Central Bank for financial entities such as Minimum Capital have been considered in the projections, so forecasted net worth carry out with the restrictions. These regulations are not required in the case of borrowing from the local banks.

References

Banco Central de la Republica Argentina (BCRA). (2006). Available at Currency rates: www.bcra.gob.ar/PublicacionesEstadisticas/Currency_rates.asp

Board of Governors of the Federal Reserve System (2006). Available at www.federalreserve.gov/releases/h15/

Ministerio de Economía de la Nación Argentina (2006). Available at www.mecon.gov.ar/peconomica/basehome/infoeco.html

The National Institute of Statistics and Censuses (INDEC). (2006). Available at www.indec.gob.ar/indec/web/Nivel4-Tema-3-5-31

Rosario Future Exchange (ROFEX)

Reuters database

JP Morgan

CHAPTER

19

Automotive Recovery

Introduction

In August 2008, we were hired by "JJ Corp.", an American Company to estimate the fair value of "Automotive Recovery" (AR) which provides stolen vehicle recovery services (SVRS) in Argentina. JJ Corp. owned 25% of AR's shares. A few years ago, AR's management changed. The new leadership worked quite well. They imposed

DOI: 10.4324/9781003628491-23

goals and targets and worked all day to increase operational efficiency, which had an impact on financial performance.

The Argentine GDP grew fast from 2003 to 2008, at an average rate of 8% per year, and the automotive industry sales, which are strongly related to GDP, grew 88% in 2003, 101% in 2004, 29% in 2005, 14% in 2006 and 23% in 2007. Although a robust growth rate was initially expected for 2008, the Argentine government started making moves in March 2008 that impacted expectations. To finance the fiscal deficit, the government decided to increment taxes on soybeans and other crops, which caused angry protests from farmers. The subsequent political upheaval caused the resignation of the Secretary of the Treasury. In the early morning of July 17, after 17 hours of tense debate, the Argentine Senate rejected the government grain exports tax measure by a vote of 37-36. On July 18, the Argentine government officially revoked Resolution 125, so levies on agricultural exports returned to March 10 levels. Despite the increase in uncertainty and political risk, the automotive industry still maintained reasonable expectations, while the new automotive sales continued to expand, as the revenues of AR.

The objective was to estimate the fair equity value for AR, considering the state of the current operations.

Methodology used for the valuation

We use the discounted cash flow model, and the CAPM model was adapted to estimate a risk-adjusted rate in an emerging market.

Since the target is a nonpublic company, no betas are published; therefore, we use the bottom-up beta approach, identifying a publicly traded similar to the target.

We forecast the free cash flow for an explicit period of ten years when the company reaches a steady state; then, we calculate the terminal value with the growing perpetuity formula. The terminal value reflects the present value of cash flows beyond the explicit forecast period. The rationale for performing a ten-year projection is as follows:

- The company achieves a constant growth rate during the continuing-value period, similar to the GDP growth rate.
- Cash flow duration matching the duration of the securities used in the cost of capital.

Expected currency rate

Once all cash flow has been forecasted in Argentinean pesos, we convert them into American dollars before discounting, dividing the expected cash flows expressed in local currency by the expected currency rate for each year of the projection.

We use the future exchange rate observed in the future markets and assume the interest-rate parity works to forecast future spot foreign exchange rates, using the yield curves for Argentina's sovereign bonds in dollars and pesos for the rest of the projection. This procedure guarantees the consistency of the discounted cash flow model because we use a nominal cost of capital expressed in dollars and should be based on current cash flows, which, in turn, should embody inflationary expectations.

Historical performance analysis

Understanding the company's past performance provides an essential perspective for developing and evaluating forecasts of future performance. Tables 19.1 to 19.4 depict the income statement, the balance sheet, the shareholder's equity statement, and the cash flow statement from 2004 to 2007.

TABLE 19.1 Income statement in thousands of Argentine pesos

	Dec 04	Dec 05	Dec 06	Dec 07
Revenues	39,605	60,284	91,786	126,897
Cost of goods sold	18,840	26,248	36,876	49,925
Gross margin	20,765	34,035	54,910	76,971
Administrative expenses	10,194	12,391	17,894	22,431
Commercial expenses	8,648	13,137	21,766	32,643
EBIT	1,923	8,507	15,249	21,897
Financial expenses	1,078	1,182	1,490	3,151
Other income	290	172	-	446
Other expenses	-	-	1,030	-
Extraordinary expenses	-	–992	–29	–275
Income before tax	1,135	6,505	12,701	18,917
Income tax	606	940	3,424	6,645
Net income	529	5,565	9,277	12,272

Revenues increased by 220% in three years, while EBIT increased by 1.038% due to the reduction in the operative cost as a percentage of revenues.

TABLE 19.2 Balance sheet in thousands of Argentine pesos

	Dec 04	Dec 05	Dec 06	Dec 07
Cash and banks	2,109	2,364	5,333	4,186
Marketable securities	-	-	3,938	7,166
Account receivables	2,384	3,971	8,894	12,498
Inventories	2,709	2,080	2,199	5,319
Other assets	-	-	-	143
Other receivables	2,018	2,917	7,917	9,188

(Continued)

TABLE 19.2 (Continued)

	Dec 04	Dec 05	Dec 06	Dec 07
Current Assets	9,220	11,332	28,281	38,500
Net fixed assets	10,034	17,085	22,723	33,401
LT investments	-	3,017	-	-
Intangibles	1,256	1,167	1,185	1,634
Non-current assets	11,290	21,269	23,909	35,035
Total assets	20,510	32,601	52,190	73,535
Account payables	9,317	13,651	19,956	23,114
Social liabilities	970	1,357	2,464	4,331
Fiscal liabilities	1,140	1,595	5,057	8,068
ST financial debt	3,396	2,666	4,658	13,370
Other liabilities	730	396	480	306
Current liabilities	15,553	19,666	32,614	49,189
LT financial debt	1,239	1,490	3,815	5,736
Social and fiscal liabilities	1,238	865	628	435
Other liabilities	948	3,800	209	57
Non-current liabilities	3,425	6,155	4,652	6,227
Total liabilities	18,978	25,820	37,267	55,417
Equity	1,531	6,781	14,923	18,118
Total liabilities + equity	20,510	32,601	52,190	73,535

Net fixed assets constitute the most important asset and are closely related to revenues. Senior management argued that they will represent a lower percentage of revenues in the future.

TABLE 19.3 Shareholder's equity statement in thousands of Argentine pesos

	Dec 05	Dec 06	Dec 07
Equity at the beginning	1,531.1	6,781.4	14,923.1
Net income	5,565.2	9,276.7	12,271.6
Dividends	–315	–1,135.0	–9,076.5
Equity at the end	6,781.4	14,923.1	18,118.2

The company maintained a low payout, except in 2007, when it was near 74%.

TABLE 19.4 Cash flow statement in thousands of Argentine pesos

	Dec 05	Dec 06	Dec 07
EBIT	8,507	15,249	21,897
Depreciation + amortization	4,924	7,141	11,329
EBITDA	13,431	22,390	33,226
Account Receivables	1,587	4,923	3,604
Inventories	−629	119	3,119
Account payables	4,335	6,305	3,157
Fiscal liabilities	454	3,462	3,011
Other receivables	900	5,000	1,271
Social liabilities	386	1,107	1,867
ST other liabilities	−334	83	−173
ST other assets	0	0	143
Income taxes	940	3,424	6,645
Cash flow from Operations	15,475	19,882	26,306
Capital expenses	11,976	12,779	22,007
Intangibles	−89	18	448
Long-term investments	3,017	−3,017	0
Cash flow from investments	14,904	9,781	22,455
LT Social and Fiscal Liabilities	−373	−236	−194
LT other liabilities	2,852	−3,591	−152
Free cash flow	3,050	6,274	3,506
ST financial debt	−730	1,991	8,713
LT financial debt	251	2,325	1,920
Financial expenses	−1,182	−1,490	−3,151
Other income	172	0	446
Other expenses	0	−1,030	0
Extraordinary expenses	−992	−29	−275
Dividends	−315	−1,135	-9,077
Marketable securities	0	3,938	3,228
Cash flow from financing	−2,795	−3,305	−4,652
Incr./decrease in cash	255	2,969	−1,146

There is little difference between EITDA and cash from operation because of the high DAP ratio, which allow the company made a modest net investment in working capital. The capital expenses essentially explain the difference between cash from operations and free cash flow.

Revenue analysis and forecasting

After the strong recession in 2002, the GDP grew at an average of 8% per year. The industry sales grew and experienced a re-emergence in 2003 and 2004, maintaining high growth rates in 2005, 2006, and 2007. Table 19.5 shows the GDP and the automotive industry growth rate from 1988 to 2007.

TABLE 19.5 GDP growth and automotive industry sales growth

Year	GDP	Industry sales
1988	–2%	–15%
1989	–7%	–19%
1990	–2%	–28%
1991	11%	73%
1992	10%	111%
1993	6%	21%
1994	6%	21%
1995	–3%	–35%
1996	5%	15%
1997	8%	13%
1998	3.9%	7%
1999	–3.4%	–17%
2000	–0.5%	–19%
2001	–4.5%	–42%
2002	–10.9%	–53%
2003	8.8%	88%
2004	9.0%	101%
2005	9.2%	29%
2006	8.5%	14%
2007	8.7%	23%

At the end of 2007, Automotive Park had 8 million cars with 716,000 installed devices, which implied a penetration rate of 9%. AR senior management believed that it still had room to continue growing.

TABLE 19.6 Automotive Park penetration

	2007
Automotive park	8,000,000
Insured vehicles	5,700,000
Installed devices	716,000
Insured vehicles penetration	12.6%
Automotive Park penetration	8.95%

AR has been very successful since its revenues have grown at an annual rate of 45% in the last five years, similar to the industry growth rate. There appears to be a strong correlation between new car sales and company revenues, together with the explosive growth observed in Argentina in the same period.

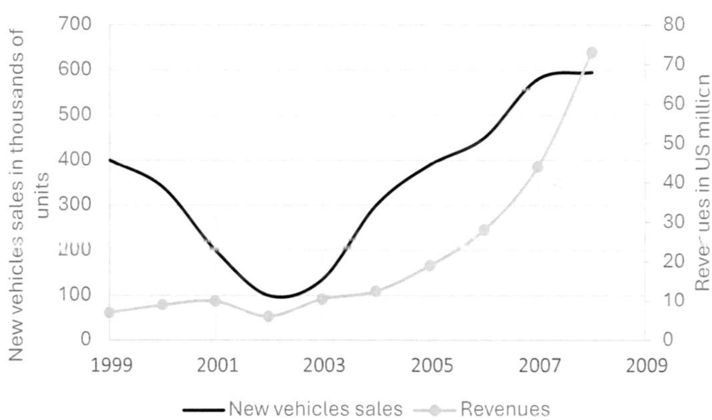

FIGURE 19.1 New vehicles sales and company revenues

To forecast AR's sales, we consider two models: a) a linear regression analysis between the Argentinean GDP growth rate and the automotive industry growth rate and b) an autoregressive model, using the AR's sales monthly data.

Linear regression analysis

We start by analyzing the relation between the GDP growth rate and the automotive industry growth rate in units using a linear regression model that considers the GDP growth rate as the explanatory variable.

We regress the automotive sales growth rate against the GDP growth rate, using data from 1970 to 2007. Notice that the slope of the regression line is 5.386, which means that for a GDP growth rate of 1%, the AR sales growth rate would be 5.39%. Even though the GDP is significant at 0.01%, we can see in Figure 19.2 three outliers surrounded by a circle: AR sales' growth rate for 1992 (111%), 2003 (88%), and 2004(101%), which are growth rates that constitute industry rebounds, since these growth rates were preceded by three severe recessions of 1989 (–7%), 1990 (–1.8%), and 2002 (–10.6%).

TABLE 19.7 Industry growth rate against GDP growth rate regression

	Intercept	GDP growth rate
Coefficient	–0.0456	5.3863
Standard error	(0.0497)	0.6656
p-value	0.2584	0.0000
$R^2 = 0.6517$		

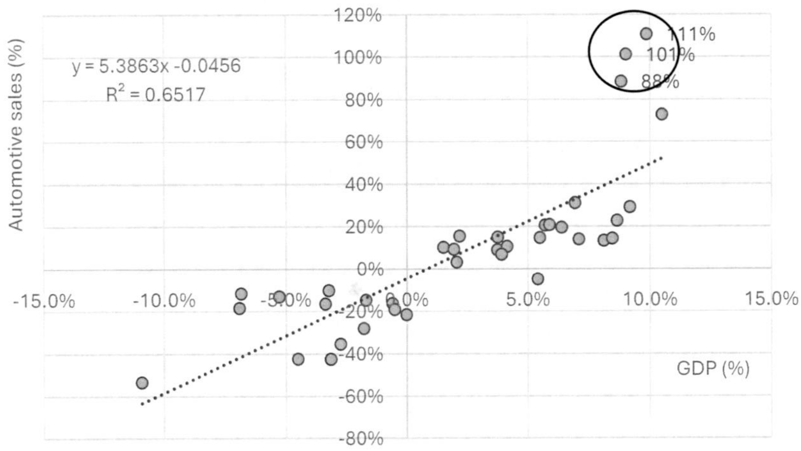

FIGURE 19.2 Automotive industry sales and GDP regression

What is the cause of these outliers? Car sales are too sensitive to the Argentinean GDP, both in the boom and recession. In addition, the GDP growth rate is too volatile; a recession can last two or three years. During a recession, car sales drop sharply, usually by far more than the GDP fall, while the automotive park depreciates. When the economy re-emerges, there is a "rebound effect" as people rush to renew their cars, and car sales grow much more than GDP. However, these outliers were distorting the results. To control this situation, we use a dummy variable D, which takes values of 1 for periods of rebound and 0 for the others, modifying the intercept and the slope of the analysis.[1]

If D = 0:

$$Y_t = \alpha + \delta D_t + \beta_1 GDP_t + e_t \qquad [19.1]$$

If D = 1:

$$Y_t = (\alpha + \delta) + \beta_1 GDP_t + e_t \qquad [19.2]$$

A dummy variable in the intercept has the effect of "knocking" the outlier in equation 19.2, with the advantage of avoiding eliminating the data. Notice that when D = 1, the intercept changes by the value of δ (delta), and the slope decreases from 5.38 to 4.09 in the new regression.

TABLE 19.8 Regression analysis using a dummy variable for the intercept

	Intercept	GDP growth rate	Dummy
Coefficient	−0.0711***	4.0924***	0.6931***
Standard error	0.0235	0.4218	0.0845
p-value	0.0047	0.0000	0.0000
R^2 = 0.883			

How should be interpreted the new coefficients? The effect of including a dummy variable in the intercept represents the value change on the intercept for "times of rebound" and for "times without rebound". Therefore, we should read the equation in this way: if D = 0, the intercept is −0.071 (−7.1%); if D = 1, the intercept is −0.0711 + 0.6931 = 0.62 (62%), which explains the rebound on the industry growth rate. For example, in times of rebound/recovery, if the GDP growth rate is 10%, the industry sales may have an average growth rate of 103%(0.6931 + (−0.0711) + 4.0924 x 10%).

Notice that all coefficients of the new regression are significant at 0.001%, and the R^2 increases to 0.88. Since the forecasted GDP growth rate for 2008 was 8%, using the regression equation, the forecasted automotive industry growth rate for 2008 was:

GDPxbeta + (−0.0711) = 8%*4.0924 – 0.0711 = 25.63%

Then, we check this with the industry projections. In 2007, the industry sales were 564,926 units; if in 2008 they grew at 25.63%, they would be 564,926 x 1.2563 = 709,716 units. However, the industry projections, basically the GM and VW projections, were more prudent and spoke of 650,000 units. In addition, the economy seemed to show signs of moderating its growth due to the Government's intention to impose more taxes on the farmers, entering into a battle with the sector, which generated uncertainty in business.

At the company level, assuming that AR sales would grow at the same industry rate of 25.63% plus the expected inflation rate for 2008, which is 20%, would be:

AR sales growth rate: (1 + 25.63)(1 + 0.20) – 1 = 0.51

The number of devices installed has rapidly increased in recent years, and there is still opportunity to expand market penetration. New car sales kept rising, but it was unable to maintain a growth rate above the GDP growth rate for an extended period of time. That was demonstrated by the industry's geometric average growth rate, which was 2.79% between 1971 and 2007.

Autoregressive model

We performed a second analysis using the internal information of AR's monthly sales. Taking the last 12 months as the historical period, we run an autoregressive model to capture the monthly tendency and the effects of the past values. After obtaining the coefficients, we project the accumulated 12 months for 2008 at ARS189,195 million, which implied a sales increase of 49% compared to 2007, similar to the growth rate predicted by the linear regression analysis. Since an autoregressive model is more suitable for short-range prediction, we use it to forecast sales for 2008. For 2009, we forecast a sales increase of 23% based on a weighted average growth: the auto-regressive model (30%) and the annual tendency (70%) observed for 2004–2007. Figure 19.3 shows the AR historical sales and the forecast from 2004 to 2008 generated by the autoregressive model.

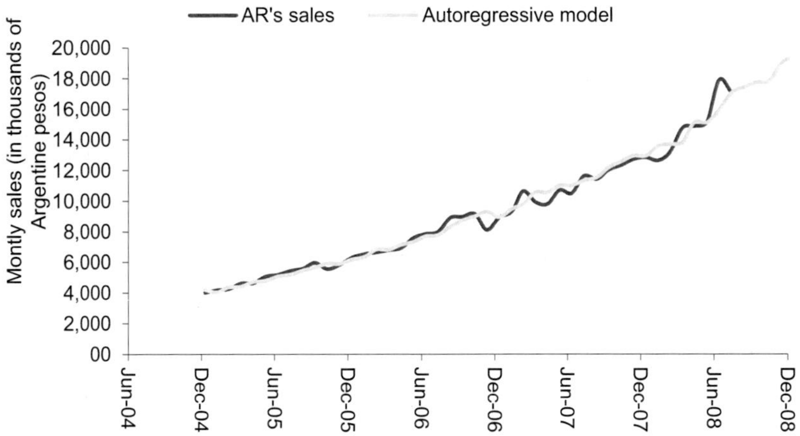

FIGURE 19.3 AR's sales and autoregressive model estimation

Assumptions

We used a "top-down approach" to develop the forecast's assumptions, starting with macroeconomic assumptions and moving on to company assumptions.

Macroeconomics assumptions

The forward exchange rate was forecasted for 2008 and 2009 using the quotes from the Rosario Future Exchange (ROFEX). For 2010, we use the yield spread differential between Argentine sovereign bonds nominated in pesos and dollars,[2] and we expect a reduction in the yield spread up to 5.5%/5% for the remainder of the projection. We assume the American inflation rate as an annual 2.5% and

TABLE 19.9 Macroeconomic assumptions

	Dec 08	Dec 09	Dec 10	Dec 11	Dec 12	Dec 13	Dec 14	Dec 15	Dec 16	Dec 17
Exchange rate	3.15	3.34	3.54	3.75	3.96	4.18	4.41	4.65	4.88	5.12
Interest rate differential			6.0%	6.0%	5.5%	5.5%	5.5%	5.5%	5.0%	5.0%
Argentina inflation rate	20.0%	12.2%	10.0%	9.0%	9.0%	8.0%	7.5%	7.0%	5%	4%
US inflation rate	3.0%	2.5%	2.5%	2.5%	2.5%	2.5%	2.5%	2.5%	2.5%	2.5%
Real exchange rate	1.41	1.37	1.35	1.35	1.34	1.34	1.35	1.36	1.39	1.44

Source: BCRA, INDEC, Buenos Aires City Consulting, and ROFEX

the domestic inflation rate was forecasted using data from Banco Central de la Republica Argentina (BCRA), (The National Institute of Statistics and Censuses (INDEC), and Buenos Aires City Consulting.[3] The real exchange rate, using as a base of comparison December 2001 = 1, was around 1.35/1.44 along the projection.

Company assumptions

After examining past ratios, revenue analysis, and macroeconomic assumptions, we create company assumptions. We meet with AR's adviser and senior management once, and they give us comprehensive inside information. Table 19.10 depicts the historical ratios where it can be seen that the company has an excellent EBITDA margin and a negative cash cycle, which are the two value drivers that we usually look at first. The assumptions are detailed below.

1. Sales growth rate: see the section revenue analysis and forecasting.
2. AR's COGS as a percentage of revenues has declined from 47.6% in 2004 to 39% in 2007. We forecast that the company will be able to achieve a COGS of 39% for 2008, declining to 37% for 2010 and beyond.
3. Administrative expenses: 17% on sales has been considered for 2008, declining to 16% in 2009 and beyond.
4. Commercial expenses: 25% on sales has been considered, declining to 24% in 2009 and beyond.
5. EBITDA/sales ratio: Operating costs should be based on sustainable margin levels; assumptions described in points 2, 3, and 4 lead to an EBITDA margin of 30% for 2008 and improving until reaching 33% in 2009 and beyond.
6. Effective tax rate: we use the marginal legal tax rate of 35% (statutory income tax rate in Argentina).
7. Fiscal liabilities: 5% on sales, reflecting the trends in the 2004–2007 periods.
8. Social liabilities: 3% on sales, reflecting the trends in the 2004–2007 periods.
9. Depreciation expense: depreciation as a percentage of gross property and equipment has remained in the 31 to 34% range over the past four years, so we have forecasted depreciation to equal 33% of the net fixed assets.

10. Capital expenses and depreciation: We assume it takes a stable amount of fixed assets to generate each dollar of sales, so capital expenditures and depreciation have been projected through the forecast period to maintain the ratio of property and equipment to sales around 20%.
11. Days sales outstanding, days sales of inventory, and days accounts payable: over the last four years, net working capital has remained a low percentage of revenues. Even though the individual components have not shown significant change, the average days on payment (159 in 2007) allow the company to finance sales and the inventory cycle. We assume for the days sales outstanding, days sales of inventory, and days payable outstanding, 35, 30, and 150 days respectively.
12. Cash and banks: we assume that the company will hold an operating cash balance around ½% of the revenues.
13. We expect non-operating income or expenses to be zero.

TABLE 19.10 Historical ratios

	Dec 04	Dec 05	Dec 06	Dec 07
Sales increase		52.2%	52.3%	38.3%
Cost of goods sold	47.6%	43.5%	40.2%	39.3%
Adm. expenses	25.7%	20.6%	19.5%	17.7%
Commercial expenses	21.8%	21.8%	23.7%	25.7%
EBITDA/sales	13%	22%	24%	26%
Effective tax rate	53%	14%	27%	35.1%
Depreciation	31%	28%	31%	34%
CAPEX	13.221	11.976	12.779	22.007
Fixed assets/sales	25%	28%	25%	26%
Other assets	5%	5%	9%	7%
Fiscal liabilities	2.9%	2.6%	5.5%	6.4%
Social liabilities	2.5%	2.3%	2.7%	3.4%
Days sale outstanding	22	24	35	36
Days sales inventory	52	29	22	39
Days accounts payable	158	194	197	159
Cash cycle	–83	–142	–140	–84

Projected cash flows and financial statements

Tables 19.11 to 19.14 show the forecasted ratios, income statements, balance sheet, and cash flow from 2008 to 2017.

TABLE 19.11 Forecasted ratios

	Dec 08	Dec 09	Dec 10	Dec 11	Dec 12	Dec 13	Dec 14	Dec 15	Dec 16	Dec 17
Sales increase	49.1%	23.0%	14.9%	14.0%	13.2%	11.6%	10.4%	9.4%	7.4%	5.0%
OPEX										
Cost of goods sold	39%	38%	37%	37%	37%	37%	37%	37%	37%	37%
Adm. Expenses	17%	16%	16%	16%	16%	16%	16%	16%	16%	16%
Commercial expenses	25%	24%	24%	24%	24%	24%	24%	24%	24%	24%
EBITDA										
EBITDA/Sales	30%	33%	33%	33%	33%	33%	33%	33%	33%	33%
CAPEX & Depreciation										
Effective tax rate	35%	35%	35%	35%	35%	35%	35%	35%	35%	35%
Depreciation	33%	33%	33%	33%	33%	33%	33%	33%	33%	33%
CAPEX (in thousands of ARS)	28,379	34,892	32,079	36,562	41,395	46,214	51,034	55,854	54,991	57,741
Fixed assets/sales	22%	22%	21%	20%	20%	20%	20%	20%	20%	20%
Other assets and liabilities										
Other assets	5%	5%	5%	5%	5%	5%	5%	5%	5%	5%
Fiscal liabilities	5%	5%	5%	5%	5%	5%	5%	5%	5%	5%
Social liabilities	3%	3%	3%	3%	3%	3%	3%	3%	3%	3%
Management ratios										
DSO	35	35	35	35	35	35	35	35	35	35
DSI	30	30	30	30	30	30	30	30	30	30
DAP	150	150	150	150	150	150	150	150	150	150

TABLE 19.12 Income statement in thousands of Argentine pesos

	Dec 08	Dec 09	Dec 10	Dec 11	Dec 12	Dec 13	Dec 14	Dec 15	Dec 16	Dec 17
Revenues (1)	189,195	232,617	267,324	304,680	344,955	385,120	425,284	465,449	499,920	524,916
Cost of goods sold	73,786	88,394	98,910	112,732	127,633	142,494	157,355	172,216	184,970	194,219
Gross margin	115,409	144,222	168,414	191,948	217,322	242,625	267,929	293,233	314,950	330,697
Adm. expenses	32,163	37,219	42,772	48,749	55,193	61,619	68,045	74,472	79,987	83,987
Commercial expenses	47,299	55,828	64,158	73,123	82,789	92,429	102,068	111,708	119,981	125,980
EBIT	35,947	51,176	61,484	70,076	79,340	88,578	97,815	107,053	114,982	120,731
Financial expenses	2,675	2,675	2,675	2,675	2,675	2,675	2,675	2,675	2,675	2,675
Income before tax	33,272	48,501	58,810	67,402	76,665	85,903	95,141	104,378	112,307	118,056
Income tax	11,645	16,975	20,583	23,591	26,833	30,066	33,299	36,532	39,307	41,320
Net income	21,627	31,526	38,226	43,811	49,832	55,837	61,841	67,846	72,999	76,736

TABLE 19.13 Forecasted balance sheet in thousands of Argentine pesos

	Dec 08	Dec 09	Dec 10	Dec 11	Dec 12	Dec 13	Dec 14	Dec 15	Dec 16	Dec 17
Cash and banks	21,413	45,348	79,980	119,883	164,670	214,606	270,005	331,044	400,411	472,907
Marketable securities	7,166	7,166	7,166	7,166	7,166	7,166	7,166	7,166	7,166	7,166
Account receivables (1)	18,142	22,306	25,634	29,216	33,078	36,929	40,781	44,632	47,938	50,334
Inventories	6,065	7,265	8,130	9,266	10,490	11,712	12,933	14,155	15,203	15,963
Other assets	143	143	143	143	143	143	143	143	143	143
Other receivables	9,460	11,631	13,366	15,234	17,248	19,256	21,264	23,272	24,996	26,246
Current assets	62,387	93,859	134,418	180,907	232,794	289,812	352,292	420,412	495,856	572,759
Net fixed assets	41,393	51,111	55,737	61,840	69,167	77,306	85,988	95,034	100,517	106,033
Intangibles	1,634	1,634	1,634	1,634	1,634	1,634	1,634	1,634	1,634	1,634
Total assets	105,414	146,604	191,790	244,381	303,596	368,752	439,913	517,080	598,007	680,425
Account payables	30,630	36,820	41,003	46,795	52,955	59,061	65,168	71,276	76,446	80,128
Social liabilities	5,676	6,978	8,020	9,140	10,349	11,554	12,759	13,963	14,998	15,747
Fiscal liabilities	9,460	11,631	13,366	15,234	17,248	19,256	21,264	23,272	24,996	26,246

(Continued)

TABLE 19.13 (Continued)

	Dec 08	Dec 09	Dec 10	Dec 11	Dec 12	Dec 13	Dec 14	Dec 15	Dec 16	Dec 17
ST financial debt	13,370	13,370	13,370	13,370	13,370	13,370	13,370	13,370	13,370	13,370
Other liabilities	306	306	306	306	306	306	306	306	306	306
Current liabilities	59,442	69,106	76,065	84,846	94,228	103,547	112,868	122,188	130,116	135,798
LT financial debt	5,736	5,736	5,736	5,736	5,736	5,736	5,736	5,736	5,736	5,736
Social and fiscal liabilities	435	435	435	435	435	435	435	435	435	435
Other liabilities	57	57	57	57	57	57	57	57	57	57
Non-current liabilities	6,227	6,227	6,227	6,227	6,227	6,227	6,227	6,227	6,227	6,227
Total liabilities	65,669	75,333	82,293	91,073	100,456	109,775	119,095	128,416	136,344	142,026
Equity	39,745	71,271	109,497	153,308	203,140	258,977	320,818	388,664	461,664	538,400
Total liabilities + equity	105,414	146,604	191,790	244,381	303,596	368,752	439,913	517,080	598,007	680,425

TABLE 19.14 Forecasted cash flow in thousands of Argentine pesos

	Dec 08	Dec 09	Dec 10	Dec 11	Dec 12	Dec 13	Dec 14	Dec 15	Dec 16	Dec 17
EBIT	35,947	51,176	61,484	70,076	79,340	88,578	97,815	107,053	114,982	120,731
Depreciation + amortization	20,387	25,174	27,453	30,459	34,067	38,076	42,352	46,808	49,508	52,225
EBITDA	56,335	76,350	88,937	100,535	113,407	126,653	140,168	153,861	164,490	172,956
Account receivables	5,644	4,164	3,328	3,582	3,862	3,851	3,851	3,851	3,305	2,397
Inventories	746	1,201	864	1,136	1,225	1,221	1,221	1,221	1,048	760
Account payables	7,516	6,190	4,183	5,792	6,160	6,106	6,107	6,107	5,170	3,682
Fiscal liabilities	1,392	2,171	1,735	1,868	2,014	2,008	2,008	2,008	1,724	1,250
Other receivables	271	2,171	1,735	1,868	2,014	2,008	2,008	2,008	1,724	1,250
Social liabilities	1,344	1,303	1,041	1,121	1,208	1,205	1,205	1,205	1,034	750
Income taxes	12,581	17,911	21,520	24,527	27,769	31,002	34,235	37,469	40,244	42,256
Cash flow from operations	47,344	60,567	68,450	78,203	87,920	97,889	108,171	118,632	126,097	131,975

(Continued)

TABLE 19.14 (Continued)

	Dec 08	Dec 09	Dec 10	Dec 11	Dec 12	Dec 13	Dec 14	Dec 15	Dec 16	Dec 17
Capex	28,379	34,892	32,079	36,562	41,395	46,214	51,034	55,854	54,991	57,741
Cash flow from investments	28,379	34,892	32,079	36,562	41,395	46,214	51,034	55,854	54,991	57,741
Free cash flow	18,965	25,674	36,371	41,641	46,526	51,675	57,137	62,778	71,106	74,234
Financial expenses	−2,675	−2,675	−2,675	−2,675	−2,675	−2,675	−2,675	−2,675	−2,675	−2,675
Tax shield	936	936	936	936	936	936	936	936	936	936
Cash flow from financing	−1,739	−1,739	−1,739	−1,739	−1,739	−1,739	−1,739	−1,739	−1,739	−1,739
Incr./decrease in cash	17,226	23,936	34,632	39,903	44,787	49,936	55,399	61,039	69,367	72,496

Cost of capital estimation

To estimate the cost of equity, we apply the capital asset pricing model (CAPM). In essence, the CAPM postulates that the opportunity cost of equity is equal to the return on risk-free securities (rf) plus a market risk premium (E(rm)-rf) multiplied by the company's systematic risk measured by beta[4], assuming the perspective of a diversified investor. In addition, as Target Company gets most of its revenues in Argentina, we consider a country risk premium (CRP) adapting the CAPM formula:

$$ke = rf + \left[E(rm) - rf\right]\beta + CRP$$

To implement the CAPM approach, we need to estimate the risk-free rate, the expected market risk premium, the systematic risk measured by the beta coefficient and the country risk premium.

Risk free rate

The risk-free rate is the return on a security that is uncorrelated with returns on a stock market index and has no default risk.

The ten-year T-Bond cash flow has a similar duration to the -cash flow of the company (T-Bond is a "bullet" bond, and the ten-year projected cash flow plus terminal value has a similar structure cash flow). The ten-year rate approximates the duration of the stock market portfolio like the S&P500, and its use is therefore consistent with the market risk premium and beta relative to these market portfolios.[5]

We used a ten-year average Treasury-bond rate of 3.8%, observed in 2007, based on the information on the Federal Reserve website.

Country risk premium discussion

Since obtaining the free cash flow in developing countries is riskier in USA and other developed countries, we include a country risk premium in the cost of capital. At the time we were valuing AR, the EMBI Argentina, as determined by JP Morgan, fluctuated around 750/800 basis points. We added a premium of 750 basis points to the cost of equity capital because it was still below 900 bps, which is the point at which the yield curve is often inverted and loses all economic significance, as we detailed in Chapter 12.

We would now like to share an anecdote with you. During the valuation process, we delivered JJ. Corp. certain draft copies of the report that included some forecasts and stated that the WACC would be approximately 18%. We once got a message from JJ Corporation in which the Chairman stated something along these lines: "Frankly, we think that your WACC is low, based on the current conditions of your country".

We answered and emphasized that they must consider the entire picture. A few days later, we had a meeting in Buenos Aires where we talked about the valuation during three hours. The primary concern of the senior management of JJ Corp. seemed to be the cost of the capital, but we only spent 15 minutes explaining howe we calculated it. The remainder of the time was spent explaining and discussing the risk of an investment in the automotive sector since they are more concerned with political risk than cost of capital. We focus our explanation on how the government could affect the business return because recovery services are directly tied to vehicle sales, which are highly correlated with GDP growth. The risk of the business is related to the GDP variation, which is too volatile in Argentina. When the economy expands, car sales increase much more than the GDP and vice-versa. To deal with this risk, they want to use a country risk premium that increase the cost of capital to near 30% to mitigate any country risks. We explained that this was nonsensical and that a haircut scenario analysis was a better way to handle this type of risk; a country risk premium about 800/900bps reflects the credit risk of the sovereign bonds, and the yield is not representative. On the other hand, the automotive industry had not suffered a unilateral government action that would generate a cash flow haircut scenario equivalent to using that country risk premium.

The meeting was very interesting not only for the discussion about the cost of capital but the fear and misgivings about the political risk and how the government could affect the revenues and earnings of the business. Been the business very related to the industry car sales (many insurance companies demand the placement of anti-theft devices for new cars), and taking into account that the industry's sales is very related to the GDP, our conversation concentrated in the effects and perspectives of a recession/expansion of the economy.

Market risk premium

The market risk premium was estimated using Shiller online data for the market return series of S&P500 from 1925 to 2007. We use a very large time frame to eliminate the effects of short-term anomalies in the measurement.

The market return series for a small cap index of S&P was observed to be between 11.9% (arithmetic mean) and 11.1% (geometric mean) from 1990 to 2007. In addition, we calculate the returns for the Latin American markets index (Brazil, Argentina, Colombia, México, and Chile), and the results show annual returns of around 11% from 1990 to 2007, measured in dollars.

We consider a market risk premium of 6.15%.

Beta coefficient

Because AR is a nonpublic company, no betas are published. Therefore, we use the bottom-up approach, looking for publicly traded competitors most similar to the company in developed capital markets. Table 19.15 shows the betas, D/E ratio, and the effective tax rate of the peer group:

TABLE 19.15 Betas in the American industry

Company	Beta	D/E	t
LoJack	1.06	29.38%	34.96%
Ituran	0.80	3.20%	28.30%
Pointer	1.94	83.66%	25.36%
Mean	1.267	0.387	29.5%

Source: Reuters, August 2008

The average levered beta of the peer group was 1,267; because the average beta of the industry reflects the effect of the capital structure, we unlever the levered beta using Hamada's formula that takes into account the levered beta, its capital structure, and its marginal tax rate:

$$\beta_U = \frac{\beta_L}{\left[1 + \frac{D}{E}(1-t)\right]}$$

$$\beta_U = \frac{1{,}267}{[1 + 0{,}388\,(1 - 0{,}295)]} = 0.995$$

Then, the unlevered beta of 0.995 is relevered for the D/E ratio of AR, obtained with the circularity approach, and the marginal tax rate of 35%:

$$\beta_L = \beta_U\left[1 + \frac{D}{E}(1-t)\right] = 0.995\left[1 + 0.68(1 - 0.35)\right] = 1.04$$

The D/E ratio was obtained using the Circularity Approach explained in Chapter 11, and we estimated the AR's cost of equity as 18.89%, as follows:

$$ke = 3.8\% + (6.15\%)1.04 + 7.5\% = 17.64\%$$

Cost of debt after taxes

For long term borrowing, we assume the domestic equivalent borrowing rate in dollars will be very close to 10%, expressed in American dollars.

Weighted average cost of capital

We use the circularity approach described in Chapter 11 to estimate the expected capital structure. It gives a D/V ratio of 5.3% and an E/V ratio of 94.7%. Finally, the weighted average cost of capital is calculated as follows:

$$WACC = 10\%(1 - 0.35) \times 0.053 + 18.89\% \times 0.947 = 17.05\%$$

Company fair value

Once all cash flows have been forecasted in domestic currency, we convert them into American dollars by dividing the expected cash flows in Argentine pesos by the expected currency rate for each year of the projection. The forward exchange rate was forecasted assuming the fulfillment of the interest rate parity, using Argentine bonds nominated in Argentine pesos and dollars. The terminal value is estimated assuming a long-term growth rate of 4%.

TABLE 19.16 AR fair value in thousands of US dollars

	Dec 08	Dec 09	Dec 10	Dec 11	Dec 12	Dec 13	Dec 14	Dec 15	Dec 16	Dec 17
Free cash flow (ARS)	18,965	25,674	36,371	41,641	46,526	51,675	57,137	62,778	71,106	74,234
Expected exchange rate	3.15	3.34	3.54	3.75	3.96	4.18	4.41	4.65	4.88	5.12
Free cash flow (US$)	6,021	7,687	10,274	11,104	11,749	12,362	12,956	13,501	14,571	14,499
Terminal value										115,560
FCF + terminal value	6,021	7,687	10,274	11,104	11,749	12,362	12,956	13,501	14,571	130,059

Terminal value was calculated as

$$TV = \frac{14{,}499(1 + 4\%)}{17.05\% - 4\%} = 115{,}589.87$$

We first estimate the present value of the forecasted free cash flow as of December 2007, which was US 71,847.72 million, but since the valuation was completed in September 2008, we capitalize the value of operations from December 2007 to September 2008 by its cost of capital to reflect the time elapsed in 2008 [$71{,}847.72(1+0.1705)^{9/12}$ = 80,851.35]. The net financial debt was estimated at

US 3,84 million in September 2008. Finally, the equity fair value was estimated at US 77.01 million.

TABLE 19.17 AR fair value in thousands of US dollars

Value of operations at December 2007	71,847.72
Value of operations adjusted to September 2008	80,851.35
– Net financial debt	3,840
Equity value at September 2008	77,012.35

Relative valuation

To contrast the fair value of operations obtained by our DCF model with enterprise value/EBITDA multiple, we search for companies involved with stolen vehicle recovery services. However, there were almost no similar businesses in this sector; we found only two companies in the Reuters database, Pointer and Ituran. While Pointer had an EV/EBITDA of 3.9, Ituran had 3.6; these ratios look too low, reflecting the effect of the crisis of the global markets in 2008. When we observe the average EV/EBITDA for the last four years, both companies exhibited an EV/EBITDA over 10. Because we did not find enough companies to constitute a peer group, and the few multiples found were biased by the global crisis, we decided to abandon the relative valuation method. Nevertheless, the estimated normalized EBITDA of AR in September 2008 was around US 14 million at an exchange rate of 3.1 ARS per dollar. Therefore, the implicit EV/EBITDA was 80,85/14 = 5.77.

Concluding thoughts

JJ Corp. was ready to make an offer for the subsidiary company, based on our analysis and considering a lack of marketability discount. However, neither the offer nor the discount could be made due to the financial crisis in the United States. It began in 2008 with a crisis in the subprime mortgage market following a full-blown international banking crisis with the collapse of the investment bank Lehman Brothers on September 15, 2008. As a result, the Senior Management of JJ Corp. declined to buy the subsidiary company.

Notes

1 It is possible to include a dummy for the intercept, slope, or both.
2 To calculate the yield spread, we use the BONAR V nominated in dollars and the BONAR V nominated in Argentine pesos.
3 The official inflation statistics in Argentina began to be questioned in 2007.
4 When the company has financial debt in its capital structure, the beta coefficient is a "levered beta".
5 The Duration of perpetuity is equal to (1+k)/k; for a cost of equity capital is around 15%, the duration is around 7,6.

References

Banco Central de la República Argentina (2008). Available at Currency rates: www.bcra.gob.ar/PublicacionesEstadisticas/Currency_rates.asp

Board of Governors of the Federal Reserve System (2006). Available at www.federalreserve.gov/releases/h15/

Shiller, R. (2008). Online Data Robert Shiller. Available at www.econ.yale.edu/~shiller/data.htm

The National Institute of Statistics and Censuses (INDEC) (2008). Available at www.indec.gob.ar/indec/web/Nivel4-Tema-3-5-31

Buenos Aires City Consulting

JPMorgan

Reuters database

CHAPTER

20

American Packages

DOI: 10.4324/9781003628491-24

Introduction

At the end of 2009, "RR", the minority party of "American Packages" (AP) hired us to estimate the equity fair value. AP was a listed Argentinean company primarily involved in the production of plastic packages for the dairy products industry, with a particular focus on the yogurt segment. It controls approximately 55% of the local market, being the major packaging manufacturer in the region, and exports to many countries across Latin America. Sixty-two percent of American Packages' shares are owned by the Brazilian corporation "Dix", with RR retaining the remaining 38%.

RR and Dix have a positive connection for many years. However, in 2009, both parties agreed to end the partnership, and RR consented to sell DIX its holding stake. Dix made an initial offer of US$10 million for the 38% stake at the start of the negotiations, but RR promptly turned it down since they thought the price was too low. DIX quickly raised its offer to US$11 million, but RR turned it down once more. A week later, DIX raised the offer once more to US$12 million, but no deal was reached. Despite RR's repeated rejection of the offer, senior management decided to travel to Brazil for a face-to-face negotiation. In the meeting, RR claimed for a price of US$14 million, which DIX rejected. The negotiations stalled and neither party knew how to proceed. We came into play a few days later when RR made the decision to hire a consultant to determine the business's fair value.

Methodology used for the valuation

The methodology used to perform the valuation was the Free Cash Flow method. Although American Packages is a public company, no betas are published since the stocks have not traded since January 2005. So, it was necessary to use the bottom-up approach to estimate the beta coefficient.

Explicit forecast period (length of forecast)

The explicit free cash flow is forecasted for ten years until the business reaches a steady state by the end of year ten, assuming the free cash flow achieves a constant growth rate during the continuing-value period, similar to the growth rate of GDP plus the internal inflation rate. The free cash flow duration matches the duration of the securities used in the cost of capital calculation.

Forecasted free cash flow and terminal value

Once we have analyzed the company's historical performance, we develop a forecasted cash flow. We estimate the terminal value using the growing perpetuity formula.

Currency for the valuation

We first made the cash flow projections in local currency since financial executives think the company operates in this currency; therefore, projections reflect a nominal growth rate compounded by an expected real growth rate and an expected inflation rate. Then, they were converted into American dollars using the expected exchange rate for each year of the projection.

Cost of capital

The weighted average cost of capital is expressed in US dollars.

Equity fair value

Once the value of operations was determined, the value of debt is subtracted to determine the equity fair value. Non-operating assets are excluded from the projections and added to the DCF value, as they do not generate EBIT or free cash flow.

Historical performance analysis

The next sections describe an analysis of the historical performance of AP from 2002 to 2009. Understanding the company's past performance provides an essential perspective for developing and evaluating forecasts of future performance.

Historical financial statements

As we explained in Chapter 2, financial statements are more useful when used in tandem with cash flow and financial ratios. Absolute numbers are less informative if you don't compare them with previous ones or to a competitor. Nonetheless, we comment on the historical cash flow since it resumes the company's operations and financing.

TABLE 20.1 Income statement in thousands of Argentine pesos

	Dec 02	Dec 03	Dec 04	Dec 05	Dec 06	Dec 07	Dec 08	Dec 09 E
Revenues	69,751	68,697	93,256	60,381	107,337	133,135	154,193	175,956
Cost of Goods sold	56,759	57,246	79,600	50,406	92,153	113,828	128,710	143,979
Gross margin	12,992	11,451	13,656	9,975	15,184	19,307	25,483	31,976
Adm. expenses	2,466	2,578	3,148	2,210	3,810	4,801	5,747	6,145
Commercial expenses	3,046	2,545	3,362	2,595	4,159	4,886	5,819	6,321
EBIT	7,480	6,328	7,146	5,170	7,215	9,620	13,917	19,510
Financial expenses	15,256	(2,878)	(1,739)	(1,921)	(2,777)	(3,323)	(3,845)	(5,800)

(*Continued*)

TABLE 20.1 (Continued)

	Dec 02	Dec 03	Dec 04	Dec 05	Dec 06	Dec 07	Dec 08	Dec 09 E
Financial income	(6,290)	49	(432)	(337)	(100)	473	790	1,094
Income before tax	17,071	3,866	5,513	3,102	4,836	7,707	11,460	14,728
Income tax	-	2,250	3,137	1,573	2,312	4,643	4,716	6,628
Net income	17,071	1,616	2,376	1,529	2,524	3,064	6,744	8,101

TABLE 20.2 Balance sheet in thousands of Argentine pesos

	Dec 02	Dec 03	Dec 04	Dec 05	Dec 06	Dec 07	Dec 08	Dec 09 E
Cash and banks	345	152	145	27	56	582	249	602
Accounts receivable	9,920	9,880	11,120	12,517	11,288	20,913	24,834	35,117
Inventories	4,098	4,563	6,524	5,769	6,759	9,843	10,646	13,412
Other assets	2,000	2,134	2,627	2,244	2,376	3,433	5,227	6,529
Current assets	16,363	16,729	20,416	20,557	20,479	34,771	40,956	55,660
Net fixed assets	36,384	31,017	38,189	43,946	34,391	34,400	32,031	43,172
LT investments	-	-	-	-	-	1,153	1,129	1,117
Other LT receivable	8,273	6,129	3,090	2,551	461	2,935	2,781	2,369
Intangibles	-	-	-	-	-	343	253	188
Non-current assets	44,657	37,146	41,279	46,497	42,504	38,831	36,194	46,846
Total assets	61,020	53,875	61,695	67,054	62,983	73,602	77,150	102,505
Accounts payable	4,248	6,297	13,329	12,797	13,875	19,205	16,828	19,298
Fiscal liabilities	588	513	1,554	1,755	725	1,171	2,382	3,385
ST provisions	470	492	587	577	516	1,310	90	345
ST financial debt	15,400	10,448	8,476	9,414	6,624	6,277	5,266	8,283
Social liabilities	1,023	1,398	362	1,341	2,081	4,050	4,988	6,582
Other ST liabilities	1,521	120	102	87	15	176	17	9,091
Current liabilities	23,250	19,268	24,410	25,971	23,836	32,189	29,572	46,985
LT financial debt	10,125	4,179	3,888	6,437	2,456	2,031	832	4,909
LT provisions	56	56	28	28	62	28	654	-
LT Social & fiscal liabilities	82	6	-	-	-	829	1,240	1,127
Non current liabilities	10,365	4,241	4,698	7,058	2,741	2,888	2,727	6,036
Equity	27,405	30,366	32,587	34,025	36,406	38,525	44,851	49,485
Total liabilities + Equity	61,020	53,875	61,695	67,054	62,983	73,602	77,150	102,505

TABLE 20.3 Shareholders' equity statement in thousands of Argentine pesos

	Dec 03	Dec 04	Dec 05	Dec 06	Dec 07	Dec 08	Dec 09 E
Equity at the beginning	27,405	30,366	32,587	34,025	36,406	38,525	44,851
Net income	1,616	2,376	1,529	2,524	3,064	6,744	8,101
Dividends	-	-	-	-	-	–361	–1,602
Partner's contribution	1,500	-	-	-	-	-	-
Others	–155	–155	–91	–143	–945	–57	–1,866
Equity at the end	30,366	32,587	34,025	36,406	38,525	44,851	49,485

The accumulated values of EBITDA, free cash flow, and other cash flow metrics for the years 2003–2009 are displayed in the final column of Tables 20.4 and 20.5, which enables us to compile historical performance.[1] The accumulated EBITDA was ARS103,05 million minus investment in working capital and income taxes, leaving ARS62.47 million in cash from operations. After investing ARS42.67 million mainly in capital expenses, the accumulated free cash flow was ARS29.42 million. Cash flow from financing was negative at ARS33.9 million, which explains an accumulated cash of ARS257 million.

TABLE 20.4 Free cash flow in thousands of Argentine pesos

	Dec 03	Dec 04	Dec 05	Dec 06	Dec 07	Dec 08	Dec 09 E	Accum 2003–2009
EBIT	6,328	7,146	5,170	7,215	9,620	13,917	19,510	
Depreciation & amortization	5,795	5,057	2,893	5,079	5,055	5,287	5,414	
EBITDA	12,123	12,203	8,063	12,294	14,675	19,204	24,924	103,486
Accounts receivable	–40	1,240	1,397	–1,229	9,625	3,921	10,283	
Inventories	465	1,961	–755	990	3,084	803	2,766	
Accounts payable	2,049	7,032	–532	1,078	5,330	–2,377	2,470	
ST provisions	22	95	–10	–61	794	–1,220	255	
Other assets	134	493	–383	132	1,057	1,794	1,302	
Fiscal liabilities	–75	1,041	201	–1,030	446	1,211	1,004	
Social liabilities	375	–1,036	979	740	1,969	938	1,593	
Working capital changes	–1,811	–3,188	1,748	–2,540	7,562	6,236	12,129	20,136

(Continued)

TABLE 20.4 (Continued)

	Dec 03	Dec 04	Dec 05	Dec 06	Dec 07	Dec 08	Dec 09 E	Accum 2003–2009
Income tax	2,250	3,137	1,573	2,312	4,643	4,716	6,628	25,259
Cash flow from operations	11,685	12,504	6,869	10,816	4,805	6,522	9,267	62,469
Capital expenses	428	12,229	8,650	−4,476	5,064	2,918	16,555	
Intangibles	0	0	0	0	343	−90	−65	
LT investments	0	0	0	0	1,153	−24	−12	
Cash flow from investments	−428	−12,229	−8,650	4,476	−6,560	−2,804	−16,477	−42,673
Other LT assets	0	0	0	7,652	−7,652	0	0	
Other ST liabilities	−1,401	−18	−15	−72	161	−159	9,074	
LT provisions	0	−28	0	34	−34	626	−654	
LT social & fiscal liab.	−76	−6	0	0	829	411	−113	
Other LT liabilities	−102	782	−189	−370	−223	0	0	
Free cash flow	11,822	4,044	−1,446	9,322	4,156	4,751	1,508	29,417

TABLE 20.5 Cash flow from financing in thousands of Argentine pesos

	Dec 03	Dec 04	Dec 05	Dec 06	Dec 07	Dec 08	Dec 09 E	Accum. 2003–2009
Free cash flow	11,822	4,044	−1,446	9,322	4,156	4,751	1,508	29,417
ST financial debt	−4,952	−1,972	938	−2,790	−347	−1,011	3,017	
LT financial debt	−5,946	−291	2,549	−3,981	−425	−1,199	4,077	
Financial expenses	−2,878	−1,739	−1,921	−2,777	−3,323	−3,845	−5,800	
Financial income	49	−432	−337	−100	473	790	1,094	
Other income	367	538	191	498	937	598	−76	
Dividends						−361	−1,602	
Others	−155	−155	−91	−143	−945	−57	−1,866	
Cash flow from financing	−12,015	−4,051	1,328	−9,293	−3,630	−5,085	−1,155	−33,900
Incr/decrease in cash	−193	−7	−118	29	526	−333	353	257

Historical revenue analysis

We first analyze the evolution of GDP expressed in current prices and AR revenues from 1993 to 2009. Table 20.6 shows the GDP and revenue growth rates from 1994 to 2009.

TABLE 20.6 GDP and company revenue growth rates 1993–2009 in thousands of Argentine pesos

Year	GDP current prices	Growth rate	Revenues	Growth rate
1993	236,505		29,089	
1994	257,440	9%	31,489	8%
1995	258,032	0.2%	39,543	26%
1996	272,150	5%	38,178	–3%
1997	292,859	8%	33,271	–13%
1998	298,948	2%	33,176	0%
1999	283,523	–5%	29,110	–12%
2000	284,204	0%	27,533	–5%
2001	268,697	–5%	27,265	–1%
2002	312,580	16%	59,513	118%
2003	375,909	20%	69,751	17%
2004	447,643	19%	68,697	–2%
2005	531,939	19%	93,256	36%
2006	654,439	23%	107,337	15%
2007	812,456	24%	133,135	24%
2008	1,032,758	27%	154,193	16%
2009	1,136,034	10%	175,585	14%

Figure 20.1 shows the evolution of a notional one unit of GDP and revenues, compounded by the respective growth rates. We often use this chart when it is possible to hypothesize that company revenues and GDP are positively related because the scatter figure provides excellent communicational power and the necessary intuition that reinforces the hypothesis behind our models. Then, we measure the relationship using some econometric models.

Notice that revenues have grown 504%, while the GDP has grown 380% from 1993 to 2009.

In a meeting with the other party, already with advanced negotiations, we presented the evidence, explaining that the company's revenue growth rate outperformed the nominal growth rate of GDP. Today, after the deal was closed

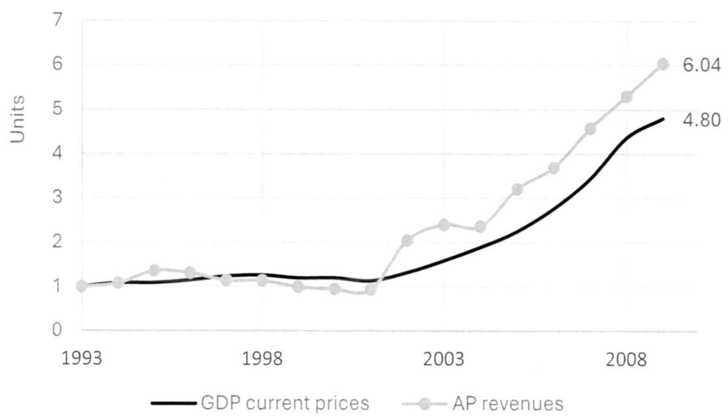

FIGURE 20.1 GDP and AP revenue growth 1993–2009

successfully, we can say without a doubt that presenting this figure unlocked the negotiations between the parties.

Projected revenues

To predict the revenues, we employ two models. We start with a basic regression model. The second was straightforward: we made the assumption that AR revenues would increase at the rate of domestic inflation plus the anticipated GDP growth rate. Lastly, we take the mean of the two outcomes.

1. Delta-log linear regression model. We perform a linear regression analysis between the AP revenues growth rate and the Argentinean GDP growth rate from 1993 to 2009. We use the GDP in current prices since revenues are also expressed in current prices. In 2002, after the devaluation in Argentina, the revenues increased by 118%; since it meant an anomalous increase, we included a dummy variable of 1 for 2002 and 0 for the rest of the projection to control the outlier. Residuals distributed normally, and there was no heteroscedasticity or autocorrelation. Notice that delta-log GDP is significant at 5%, and the dummy variable is significant at 1%.

TABLE 20.7 Delta-log regression AP revenues against GDP

	Coefficient	Std. Error	t	Prob.	Adj. R2
Interception	−0.0067	0.0411	−0.1633	0.8728	0.7357
ΔLog(GDP)	0.7882	0.3047	2.5868	0.0226	
Dummy2002	0.6681	0.1184	5.6443	0.0001	
Jarque-Bera Prob	0.5800				
White Prob. F	0.7073				

2. Domestic inflation rate plus GDP growth rate. Revenues are assumed to grow at the expected inflation rate plus an expected real growth of Argentinean GDP. We expect an inflation rate of 14% and a GDP growth of 2% for 2010. For 2011 and beyond, we expect an inflation rate decline for 2011 and until reaching 5% in 2019 and the GDP growing at 3%.

The outcomes of the two approaches and their mean are displayed in Table 20.8, which ultimately formed our revenue forecast.

TABLE 20.8 Projected revenues in thousands of Argentine pesos

Year	Delta-log model	Inflation+GDP	Mean
2010	194,517.73	204,170	199,344
2011	219,478.96	231,324	225,402
2012	242,487.92	254,942	248,715
2013	262,002.90	278,346	270,175
2014	280,961.28	301,031	290,996
2015	299,010.42	325,565	312,288
2016	318,219.05	352,099	335,159
2017	338,661.65	380,795	359,728
2018	360,417.50	411,830	386,124
2019	383,570.96	445,394	414,482

Assumptions

The next parts go over macroeconomic assumptions before moving on to company assumptions.

Macroeconomic assumptions

Table 20.9's first row displays the forecasted exchange rate for a ten-year period. For 2010 and 2011 we use the forward prices published by the Rosario Futures Exchange (ROFEX); for 2012 and beyond, we assume the fulfillment of interest rate parity, and forward prices were forecasted by multiplying the previous forward price by the ratio (1 + id)/(1 + iUS). Interest rate parity theory postulates that changes in foreign exchange rates reflect changes in the ratio of expected interest rates between two countries.

The third row shows the expected domestic interest rate, and the fourth row shows the domestic inflation rate, calculated assuming the purchasing power parity (PPP) using the model we explained in Chapter 13. The difference in inflation rates explains most of the difference in nominal interest rates of different countries.

The fifth row shows the expected inflation rate in the USA, and the last row shows the real exchange rate US/ARS in Argentina for the explicit forecast period. The real exchange rate remains constant throughout the projection since we assume the fulfillment of purchasing power parity.

TABLE 20.9 Exchange rate, interest and inflation rates projections

	Dec 10	Dec 11	Dec 12	Dec 13	Dec 14	Dec 15	Dec 16	Dec 17	Dec 18	Dec 19
Exchange rate	4.30	4.61	4.83	5.02	5.21	5.41	5.61	5.83	5.99	6.16
US interest rate (US)	3.3%	3.5%	4%	5%	5%	5%	5%	5%	5%	5%
Domestic interest rate (ARS)	13%	11.00%	9.0%	9%	9.0%	9%	9%	9%	8%	8%
Domestic inflation rate	13.0%	9.9%	7.4%	6.4%	6.4%	6.4%	6.4%	6.4%	5.4%	5.4%
International inflation rate	2.5%	2.5%	2.5%	2.5%	2.5%	2.5%	2.5%	2.5%	2.5%	2.5%
Real exchange rate	1.65	1.65	1.65	1.65	1.65	1.65	1.65	1.65	1.65	1.65

Source: ROFEX, BCRA, The National Institute of Statistics and Censuses (INDEC), and Buenos Aires City Consulting.

The interest-rate parity theory lets us forecast the exchange rate between the peso and the dollar; however, it is logical to ask if the forward exchange rate is consistent with a long-term real exchange rate or if it suggests a depreciation/appreciation.

On company valuation matters, the question would be if a mistake in the projections for the exchange rate or/and the inflation rate would lead to an appreciation/depreciation. Many questions naturally come up, such as what happens if the inflation rate is higher than expected. What happens if the exchange rate is lower than expected? Does this mean that the RER will be lower and American Packages will receive a lower cash flow expressed in dollars? Not necessarily. A mechanism known as exchange rate pass-through will eventually cause the inflation rate to rise in tandem with the exchange rate increase, increasing the cash flow in pesos. What if the rate of domestic inflation is higher than anticipated? The domestic currency might appreciate as a result, but eventually the exchange rate would rise. A less cash flow in dollars would be received by the business in the interim.

As we describe in Chapter 13, we compute the RER using the December 2001 = 1 base, taking into account the nominal exchange rate, the local inflation rate, and the US inflation rate as a stand-in for the global inflation rate. Our projections assume that the RER will remain around 1.65, above the equilibrium consensus level signaled by most Argentinian economists. Argentina's real exchange rate between December 1979 and December 2009 is depicted in Figure 20.2. Note that the Argentine peso has experienced periods of strong appreciation/depreciation; the horizontal line marks the consensus RER among economists at the time (ARS 1.40 = 1 US$). We based our valuation on a real exchange rate that was 20% higher.

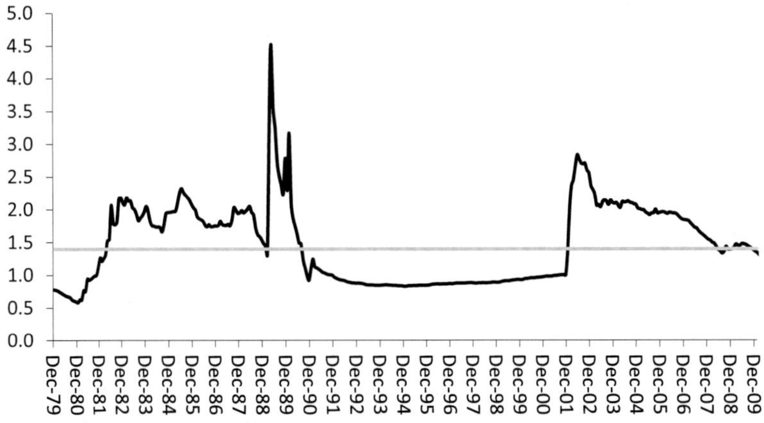

FIGURE 20.2 Real exchange rate 1979–2009

Source: INDEC and Buenos Aires City

Company assumptions

Table 20.10 shows the historical performance ratios.

TABLE 20.10 Historical ratios 2000–2008

	Dec 02	Dec 03	Dec 04	Dec 05	Dec 06	Dec 07	Dec 08	Dec 09
Operational expenses								
COGS (%)	81.4%	83.3%	85.4%	83.5%	85.9%	85.5%	83.5%	82.0%
Gross margin (5)	18.6%	16.7%	14.6%	16.5%	14.1%	14.5%	16.5%	18.2%
Administrative expenses	3.5%	3.8%	3.4%	3.7%	3.5%	3.6%	3.7%	3.5%
Commercial expenses	4.4%	3.7%	3.6%	4.3%	3.9%	3.7%	3.8%	3.6%
EBITDA								
EBITDA/revenues	20.6%	17.6%	13.1%	13.4%	11.5%	11.0%	12.5%	14.2%
EBIT/revenues	10.7%	9.2%	7.7%	5.5%	11.9%	9.0%	10.5%	12.7%
Income tax	0%	58%	57%	51%	48%	60%	41%	45%
Investments & depreciation								
Global depreciation rate	19%	19%	13%	7%	15%	15%	17%	13%
Fixed assets/Revenues	52%	45%	41%	73%	32%	26%	21%	25%
Capital expenses (million ARS)	7.8	0.4	12.2	8.7	−4.5	5.1	2.9	16.6

(*Continued*)

TABLE 20.10 (Continued)

	Dec 02	Dec 03	Dec 04	Dec 05	Dec 06	Dec 07	Dec 08	Dec 09
Management ratios								
Days sales outstanding	52	52	44	76	38	57	59	73
Days sales of inventory	26	29	30	42	27	32	30	34
Days accounts payable	29	40	60	94	54	60	47	48
Operative cycle	78	82	73	117	65	89	89	107
Cash cycle	49	42	14	23	11	29	42	59

The statement of the assumptions constitutes the summary of a much longer and perhaps tedious process than it seems (as in all our valuation processes). It was based on the analysis of historical performance, the reading of research reports, and internal discussions with senior management.

1. Cost of good sales: American Packages' COGS as a percentage of revenues has declined from 88% in 2001 to 80/82% in 2009. We assume the company will be able to achieve a COGS of 82% for 2010 and beyond.
2. Administrative expenses: a 3.3% on sales have been considered for 2010, declining until 3.2% in 2019 and beyond.
3. Commercial expenses: 3.5% of the sales were forecasted for 2010 to 2014, declining to 3.2% in 2019 and beyond.
4. EBITDA/Sales ratio: the projected ratios of operating expenses lead to an EBITDA margin of 14%.
5. Effective tax rate: we use the legal tax rate of 35% for 2010 and beyond.
6. Global depreciation: depreciation as a percentage of gross property and equipment has remained in the 12% to 21% range over the past five years, so we have forecasted depreciation to equal 13% of the net fixed assets for 2009, reflecting the last trends, and 15% for 2010 and beyond.
7. CAPEX and depreciation: we forecast a capital expense slightly above the depreciation charge.
8. Day sales outstanding, days sales of inventory, and days payable outstanding: over the last five years, net working capital has remained a low percentage of revenues. Even though the individual components have not shown significant change, the average days on payment (60 in the last five years) allow the company to finance the revenues and the inventory cycle. We assume that DSO, DSI, and DAP will move to 55, 30, and 50 days, which means a cash cycle of approximately 35 days.
9. Fiscal liabilities: 1.5% on sales, reflecting the trends in the 2003–2009 periods.
10. Social liabilities: 2.5% on sales, reflecting the trends in the 2003–2009 periods.
11. Cash and banks: we assume that the company will hold a cash balance of 0.3% of the revenues for 2010 and beyond, reflecting the trends in the 2003–2008 periods.
12. Export reimbursements: a 0.35% on sales, reflecting the trends in the 2003–2008 periods.

13. Other assets: are composed of tax credits and were forecasted as 3.5% on sales, reflecting the trends in the 2003–2008 periods.
14. Non-operative assets: Long-term receivables and long-term investments were not forecasted since they are not part of the EBIT and free cash flow. However, we then add them to the equity fair value.
15. Other assets and liabilities: Intangibles and long-term social and fiscal liabilities were considered to maintain similar values and have no effect on the forecasted cash flows.
16. We expect nonoperating income or expenses to be zero.

Table 20.11 shows the projected ratios used to forecast the financial statements (balance sheet, income statement and cash flows)

TABLE 20.11 Projected ratios 2010–2019

	Dec 10	Dec 11	Dec 12	Dec 13	Dec 14	Dec 15	Dec 16	Dec 17	Dec 18	Dec 19
Operational expenses										
COGS (%)	82.0%	82.0%	82.0%	82.0%	82.0%	82.0%	82.0%	82.0%	82.0%	82.0%
Gross margin (5)	18.4%	18.4%	18.4%	18.4%	18.4%	18.4%	18.4%	18.4%	18.4%	18.4%
Administrative expenses	3.3%	3.3%	3.2%	3.2%	3.2%	3.2%	3.2%	3.2%	3.2%	3.2%
Commercial expenses	3.5%	3.5%	3.5%	3.5%	3.5%	3.4%	3.4%	3.3%	3.3%	3.2%
EBITDA										
EBITDA/revenues	14.8%	15.0%	14.8%	14.8%	14.6%	14.5%	14.3%	14.2%	14.1%	14.0%
EBIT/revenues	11.6%	11.6%	11.7%	11.7%	11.7%	11.8%	11.8%	11.9%	11.9%	12.0%
Income tax	35.0%	35.0%	35.0%	35.0%	35.0%	35.0%	35.0%	35.0%	35.0%	35.0%
CAPEX & depreciation										
Global depreciation rate	13.0%	15.0%	15.0%	16.0%	16.0%	16.0%	16.0%	16.0%	16.0%	16.0%
Fixed assets/revenues	21.7%	19.3%	17.8%	16.4%	15.3%	14.4%	13.5%	12.6%	11.8%	10.9%
CAPEX (in thousands of ARS)	6,600	8,000	8,400	8,600	8,800	8,800	8,800	8,800	8,800	8,600
Management ratios										
Days sales outstanding	60	55	55	55	55	55	55	55	55	55
Day sales of inventory	32	30	30	30	30	30	30	30	30	30
Days payable outstanding	48	50	50	50	50	50	50	50	50	50
Operative cycle	92	85	85	85	85	85	85	85	85	85
Cash cycle	44	35	35	35	35	35	35	35	35	35

Forecasted financial statements and cash flows

Tables 20.12, 20.13, and 20.14 show the forecasted financial statements for the 2010 to 2018 periods.

TABLE 20.12 Forecasted income statement in thousands of Argentine pesos

	Dec 10	Dec 11	Dec 12	Dec 13	Dec 14	Dec 15	Dec 16	Dec 17	Dec 18	Dec 19
Revenues	200,041	226,190	249,586	271,120	292,015	313,381	336,332	360,987	387,475	415,933
Cost of goods sold	163,462	184,829	203,946	221,543	238,617	256,076	274,830	294,977	316,621	339,876
Gross margin	36,580	41,361	45,639	49,577	53,398	57,305	61,502	66,010	70,854	76,058
Administrative expenses	6,578	7,438	7,959	8,646	9,312	9,993	10,725	11,511	12,356	13,263
Commercial expenses	6,977	7,889	8,705	9,456	10,185	10,618	11,395	11,871	12,742	13,263
EBIT	23,024	26,034	28,975	31,475	33,901	36,694	39,381	42,628	45,756	49,531
Financial expenses	2,902	2,591	2,930	3,233	3,512	3,783	4,060	4,357	4,676	5,020
Income before tax	20,122	23,442	26,045	28,242	30,389	32,911	35,321	38,271	41,079	44,511
Income tax	7,043	8,205	9,116	9,885	10,636	11,519	12,363	13,395	14,378	15,579
Net income	13,079	15,238	16,929	18,357	19,753	21,392	22,959	24,876	26,701	28,932

TABLE 20.13 Forecasted balance sheet in millions of Argentine pesos

	Dec 10	Dec 11	Dec 12	Dec 13	Dec 14	Dec 15	Dec 16	Dec 17	Dec 18	Dec 19
Cash and Banks	652	702	752	802	852	902	952	1,002	1,052	1,102
Accounts receivable	32,769	33,965	37,478	40,711	43,849	47,057	50,503	54,206	58,183	62,456
Inventories	14,331	15,191	16,763	18,209	19,612	21,047	22,589	24,245	26,024	27,935
Other assets	6,977	7,889	8,705	9,456	10,185	10,930	11,731	12,590	13,514	14,507
Current assets	54,729	57,747	63,697	69,178	74,498	79,936	85,775	92,043	98,773	106,000
Net fixed assets	43,302	43,607	44,206	44,357	44,652	44,899	45,107	45,282	45,429	45,384
LT investments	1,117	1,117	1,117	1,117	1,117	1,117	1,117	1,117	1,117	1,117
Other LT receivables	2,369	2,369	2,369	2,369	2,369	2,369	2,369	2,369	2,369	2,369
Intangibles	188	188	188	188	188	188	188	188	188	188
Non current assets	46,975	47,280	47,879	48,030	48,325	48,573	48,781	48,956	49,102	49,058
Total assets	101,704	105,027	111,576	117,208	122,823	128,509	134,555	140,998	147,875	155,058

(Continued)

TABLE 20.13 (Continued)

	Dec 10	Dec 11	Dec 12	Dec 13	Dec 14	Dec 15	Dec 16	Dec 17	Dec 18	Dec 19
Accounts payable	21,617	27,400	28,271	30,762	33,078	35,468	38,056	40,846	43,843	47,064
Fiscal liabilities	2,990	3,381	3,731	4,053	4,365	4,684	5,027	5,396	5,792	6,217
ST provisions	345	345	345	345	345	345	345	345	345	345
ST financial debt	7,974	9,016	9,949	10,807	11,640	12,492	13,406	14,389	15,445	16,579
Social liabilities	4,984	5,635	6,218	6,754	7,275	7,807	8,379	8,993	9,653	10,362
Other ST liabilities	9,091	9,091	9,091	9,091	9,091	9,091	9,091	9,091	9,091	9,091
Current liabilities	47,001	54,869	57,605	61,812	65,794	69,887	74,305	79,060	84,170	89,659
LT financial debt	4,984	5,635	6,218	6,754	7,275	7,807	8,379	8,993	9,653	10,362
LT social & fiscal liabilities	1,127	1,127	1,127	1,127	1,127	1,127	1,127	1,127	1,127	1,127
Non current liabilities	6,110	6,762	7,345	7,881	8,402	8,934	9,506	10,120	10,780	11,489
Equity	48,592	43,396	46,627	47,515	48,627	49,688	50,745	51,818	52,926	53,910
Total liabilities + equity	101,704	105,027	111,576	117,208	122,823	128,509	134,555	140,998	147,875	155,058

TABLE 20.14 Forecasted cash flows in millions of Argentine pesos

	Dec 10	Dec 11	Dec 12	Dec 13	Dec 14	Dec 15	Dec 16	Dec 17	Dec 18	Dec 19
EBIT	23,024	26,034	28,975	31,475	33,901	36,694	39,381	42,628	45,756	49,531
Depreciation & amortization	6,470	7,695	7,801	8,449	8,505	8,552	8,592	8,625	8,653	8,645
EBITDA	29,495	33,729	36,776	39,924	42,406	45,246	47,973	51,253	54,409	58,175
Accounts receivable	−2,348	1,196	3,513	3,234	3,138	3,208	3,446	3,702	3,977	4,273
Inventories	919	861	1,571	1,446	1,403	1,435	1,541	1,656	1,779	1,911
Accounts payable	2,319	5,783	871	2,491	2,316	2,390	2,588	2,790	2,997	3,220
Other assets	448	912	816	751	729	745	800	860	924	993
Fiscal liabilities	−395	391	350	322	312	319	343	369	396	425
Social liabilities	−1,598	651	583	536	521	532	572	614	660	709
Working capital investment	−6,189	−3,596	4,330	2,296	2,329	2,360	2,514	2,691	2,891	3,106
Income taxes	8,058	9,112	10,141	11,016	11,865	12,843	13,783	14,920	16,014	17,336
Cash flow from operations	22,743	28,474	22,538	26,826	28,420	30,256	31,904	33,888	35,767	38,017
Capital expenses	6,600	8,000	8,400	8,600	8,800	8,800	8,800	8,800	8,800	8,600
Free cash flow	16,143	20,474	14,138	18,226	19,620	21,456	23,104	25,088	26,967	29,417

Cost of capital estimation

To estimate the cost of equity, we apply the Capital Asset Pricing Model (CAPM). In addition, since AP gets most of its revenues in South America, we consider a country risk premium (CRP) adapting the CAPM formula.

Risk-free rate

We used the US ten-year treasury returns observed in the 2005–2009 periods to estimate the risk-free rate, which was 4.15%. Source: Board of Governors of the Federal Reserve System.

Market risk premium

It is estimated using the market return series from 1925 to 2008 using Robert Shiller online data. We use a very long-time frame to eliminate the effects of short-term anomalies in the measurement. We use a market risk premium of 6.37%.

Beta coefficient

Because American Packages shares have not been traded since January 2005, we looked for the betas in the industry of Containers & Packaging as a proxy. The levered beta for the industry containers & Packaging was 0.80 (Source: Reuters 25/9/2009).

Because the industry beta is an average beta that reflects the effect of the financial debt, we unlever it using Hamada's formula that takes into account the levered beta (0.80), the industry capital structure (32%) and the industry marginal tax rate (34.65%):

$$\beta u = \frac{\beta e}{\left[1 + \frac{D}{E}(1 - t)\right]} = \frac{0,80}{[1 + 0,32\,(1 - 0,3465)]} = 0,66$$

The unlevered beta for the industry is about 0.66 and reflects only its business risk. Then, the unleveraged beta of 0.66 is leveraged for the expected capital structure, taking into account the legal tax rate in Argentina:

$$\beta e = \beta\left[1 + \frac{D}{E}(1 - t)\right] = 0,66[1 + 0,089(1 - 0,35)] = 0,72$$

Country risk premium

Since obtaining the free cash flow in developing countries is riskier in the US and other developed countries, we include a country risk premium in the cost of capital. This premium reflects factors such as GDP volatility, devaluation, institutional stability, legal security, price controls, civil disorder, and expropriations, which we explained in Chapter 12. To compute the country risk, we add a premium of 400 basis points to the cost of equity capital.

Cost of equity

We calculate the cost of equity using the circularity approach described in Chapter 11. Using the CAPM and adding a country risk premium, we estimated American Packages' cost of equity to be 13,85%, as follows:

$$ke = 4.15\% + [6.45\%]0,72 + 4.0\% = 12.79\%$$

Cost of debt

Argentinean Corporate Bonds with a BBB rating have a spread over treasuries of about 500 basis points, and their coupon rates are around 9% on average. We assume the domestic equivalent borrowing rate in dollars will be 10%.

TABLE 20.15 Argentinean corporate bonds

Company	Maturity	Coupon
Edenor	10 September, 2017	10.50%
HPDA	11 July, 2017	9.00%
IRSA	2 February, 2017	8.50%
Impsa	22 October, 2014	11.25%
Loma Negra	15 March, 2013	7.25%
Metrogas	31 December, 2014	8.00%
Pan Am Energy	9 February, 2012	7.75%
Petrobras Energia	15 July, 2010	8.13%
Petrobras Energia	30 October, 2013	9.38%
Quilmes	22 March, 2012	7.38%
Telecom	22 December, 2010	9.25%
Telefonica	7 August, 2010	9.13%
Telefonica	1 August, 2011	8.85%
Transener	15 December, 2016	8.89%
TGS	14 May, 2017	7.88%

WACC and capital structure

The capital structure weights were estimated using the Circularity Approach described in Chapter 11, resulting in a D/V ratio[2] of 8.97% and an E/V ratio of 91.03%.

$$WACC = 10\%(1 - 0.35) \times 0.089 + 12.79\% \times 0.91 = 12.28\%$$

Company fair value

Our original cash flow projections were in Argentinean pesos, which reflect a nominal growth rate compounded by an expected real growth rate and an expected inflation rate. Then, we converted them into American dollars, dividing the expected cash flows in pesos by the expected currency rate for each year of the projection.

Table 20.16 shows the free cash flow in domestic and foreign currency. We calculate the terminal value assuming a long-term growth rate of 4%, which includes an expected long-term inflation rate of 2% and an organic real growth rate of 2%.

TABLE 20.16 American Packages fair value in thousands of US dollars

	Dec 10	Dec 11	Dec 12	Dec 13	Dec 14	Dec 15	Dec 16	Dec 17	Dec 18	Dec 19
FCF (ARS)	16.1	20.5	14.1	18.2	19.6	21.5	23.1	25.1	27.0	29.4
Exchange rate	4.30	4.61	4.83	5.02	5.21	5.41	5.61	5.83	5.99	6.16
FCF (US)	3.8	4.4	2.9	3.6	3.8	4.0	4.1	4.3	4.5	4.8
Terminal value (US)										60.3
FCF + TV (US)	3.8	4.4	2.9	3.6	3.8	4.0	4.1	4.3	4.5	65.4

Terminal value was calculated as

$$TV = \frac{4,8(1+4\%)}{12.28\% - 4\%} = 60,29$$

The DCF value was estimated at US$40.78 million. Lastly, we added the value of a rental property which is a non-operating asset and subtracted the financial debt from the fair value of current operations to arrive at the equity fair value in December 2009.

TABLE 20.17 American Packages fair value in millions of US dollars

Fair value of current operations	**40.78**
+ non-operative assets	1.12
– financial debt	3.36
Equity fair value at December 2009	38.54

EBITDA multiples

Since Dix Brasil controlled AP, its senior management knew all the financial information. In 2009, Dix Brasil's EV/EBITDA multiple had fluctuated between 4 and 5. Trading started with an offer from Dix that implied an EV/EBITDA of 4, and then DIX made a new offer implying an EV/EBITDA of 5. Bemis do Brasil, another manufacturer of flexible packaging products, had an EV/EBITDA of 5.15. These were the references we had at the time.

Since the AP fair value of current operations was 40.78 million, the implied EV/EBITDA ratio was 6.43 (40.78/6.34), considering an estimated EBITDA of US$6.34 million, considering an EBITDA of 24.92 million Argentine pesos at an exchange rate of USD/ARS = 0.2545 equivalent to an exchange rate of 3.92 Argentine pesos for one US dollar.

Concluding thoughts

Finally, both parties agreed on a fair price very close to our DCF value. The process took a month, but we believe a win-win deal was closed. AP shareholders were satisfied with the final price since it was near that the number they had in mind at the time. We don´t value a control premium, although the argument of a compensation for the control was put on the table by the minority part during the negotiation.

Since we clarified and provided the majority interest partner with explanations and justifications to strengthen the final offer, we believed that our presentation undoubtedly aided the negotiation.

Notes

1 The year 2009 was estimated based on the internal information we had in November 2009.

2 For this ratio, we consider the short-term debt forming part of the capital structure due to the intention of the senior management to hold a portion of short-term debt as permanent.

References

Banco Central de la República Argentina (2008). Available at Currency rates: www.bcra.gob.ar/PublicacionesEstadisticas/Currency_rates.asp

Board of Governors of the Federal Reserve System (2009). Available at www.federalreserve.gov/releases/h15/

Shiller, R. (2009). Online Data Robert Shiller. Available at www.econ.yale.edu/~shiller/data.htm

The National Institute of Statistics and Censuses (INDEC) (2008). Available at www.indec.gob.ar/indec/web/Nivel4–Tema–3–5–31

Buenos Aires City Consulting

Reuters database

Rosario Future Exchanges (ROFEX)

INDEX

Note: **Bold** page numbers refer to tables, *italic* page numbers refer to figures.